general editor John ...

Established in the belief that imperialism as a cultural phenomenon had as significant an effect on the dominant as on the subordinate societies, Studies in Imperialism seeks to develop the new socio-cultural approach which has emerged through cross-disciplinary work on popular culture, media studies, art history, the study of education and religion, sports history and children's literature. The cultural emphasis embraces studies of migration and race, while the older political and constitutional, economic and military concerns are never far away. It incorporates comparative work on European and American empire-building, with the chronological focus primarily, though not exclusively, on the nineteenth and twentieth centuries, when these cultural exchanges were most powerfully at work.

Martial races

Published in our
centenary year
❧ **2004** ❧
MANCHESTER
UNIVERSITY
PRESS

AVAILABLE IN THE SERIES

Martial races

THE MILITARY, RACE AND MASCULINITY IN BRITISH IMPERIAL CULTURE, 1857–1914

Heather Streets

MANCHESTER
UNIVERSITY PRESS
Manchester and New York

distributed exclusively in the USA by
PALGRAVE

The right of Heather Streets to be identified as the author of this work has
been asserted by her in accordance with the Copyright, Designs and Patents
Act 1988.

Published by Manchester University Press
Oxford Road, Manchester M13 9NR, UK
and Room 400, 175 Fifth Avenue, New York, NY 10010, USA
www.manchesteruniversitypress.co.uk

Distributed exclusively in the USA by
Palgrave, 175 Fifth Avenue, New York NY 10010, USA

Distributed exclusively in Canada by
UBC Press, University of British Columbia, 2029 West Mall,
Vancouver, BC, Canada V6T 1Z2

British Library Cataloguing-in-Publication Data
A catalogue record for this book is available from the British Library

Library of Congress Cataloging-in-Publication Data
A catalog record for this book is available from the Library of Congress

ISBN 13: 978 0 7190 6963 5

First published 2004 by Manchester University Press

First digital paperback edition published 2010

Printed by Lightning Source

For my parents, Malcolm and Elizabeth Gillis

CONTENTS

[vii]

GENERAL EDITOR'S INTRODUCTION

Since its inception almost twenty years ago, the 'Studies in Imperialism' series has been centrally concerned with the interaction of ideas as well as political, military and cultural phenomena between the European empires and their metropoles. With Heather Streets's book, we have a study which fits these concerns perfectly. As she amply demonstrates, the concept of martial races was not colour-specific. Although it is a notion that has been principally applied to 'subaltern' peoples in the British Empire (and perhaps in other empires too) who were considered to be ideal, born warriors, it is apparent that it was also attached to Highland Scots. By bringing together Highlanders, Sikhs and Gurkhas, Streets reveals the fluid manner in which such an idea could be applied by leading figures concerned with the recruitment and performance of soldiers in the imperial forces.

In doing so, she unveils further complexities in the processes of 'othering' within the imperial context. It is abundantly apparent that the English categorised peoples within the British Isles as 'others'. These would include the Scots and the Irish, and also, perhaps, the Welsh. Anyone who examines the representations of 'Celts' in the cartoons in *Punch* in the nineteenth and early twentieth centuries can readily see these processes at work. Irish and Scots were invariably gendered, both with feminine and with ultra-masculine characteristics. They were also given specific and unappealing attributes, often animalistic, some of which were attached to politicians of the day. Indeed, we can disentangle further complexities. Within Scotland, people created stereotypical contrasts as between Lowlanders and Highlanders. In Ireland, those of the 'Pale' thought of the people of the West as crucially different. Contrasts were also inevitably drawn between the Protestants of the northern counties and those who inhabited the counties of the West and the South. Martial race theory fits these representations of 'others' in a curious way. Here was a theory which, instead of ascribing negative characteristics, offered supposedly positive ones. In the case of Scotland, it permitted kilted 'others' to be heroes and saviours (as in the Indian revolt of 1857), icons of the alleged moral force of empire.

Of course all of these representations, both in their negative and positive forms, were in several senses fabrications. The 'Highlanders' who were recruited to the martial kilted regiments were as likely to be the inhabitants of the urban slums or the rural Lowlands as of the Highland glens where pastoralism allegedly produced natural warriors, concerned – like the peoples of northwestern India - to protect herds and lands against the depredations of neighbours. The extolling of the kilted warrior in countless paintings and engravings of imperial actions concealed the fact that the kilt was a garb singularly unsuited to military activity, particularly in hot climates. Moreover, indigenous peoples were often intrigued by the gendered instability that the kilt seemed to convey. But just as leading imperial and military figures placed martial race theory at the forefront of their recruitment and deployment policies, so did reputations, inflated or not, often have an effect upon the self-image of the regiments and the soldiers concerned. In these ways did the theory produce a circular, self-replicating effect. It may even be that the supposed martial races became more warlike precisely because it was expected of them, not just by senior officers, but also by a public influenced by perpetual images and stories celebrating their prowess.

It is tempting to imagine that Scots, Sikhs and Gurkhas all shared these energising myths, promoting recruitment in very different home locations and military action in similar imperial ones. While economic disadvantage must always be seen as playing a key role in the motivation of individuals joining the colours, still there must equally be a complex set of social and cultural forces at play. It could well be that Highlanders, Sikhs and Gurkhas shared more in motivations and experiences than just the martial theory which lumped them together in the minds of an imperial elite and the framers of public opinion.

John M. MacKenzie

ACKNOWLEDGEMENTS

Writing a book is never an individual effort, and this one is no exception. This project had its genesis as a doctoral dissertation at Duke University, where I was fortunate to have Susan Thorne as my supervisor. Susan's intellectual energy, challenging questions and enthusiasm were crucial in sustaining me through graduate school. Cynthia Herrup was another critical force guiding my intellectual endeavours and professional development from the beginning. I owe many thanks to Claudia Koonz for her professional advice and support, and for her editorial suggestions. John Richards, Alex Roland and Jack Cell also provided intellectual guidance and assistance during my graduate career.

I have received invaluable intellectual and professional mentoring from Antoinette Burton over the past decade. I am grateful for her generous assistance – from reading drafts of chapters to providing crucial advice and encouragement – through all the stages in the production of this book. Philippa Levine, as well, has provided support, advice and intellectual exchange from the early days of my graduate career. Numerous colleagues provided helpful suggestions for parts of the book, including Patricia Lin, Tom Metcalfe, David Omissi, Doug Peers and the group of historians who gathered for the 2000 Conference on the New Imperial History in Austin, Texas – especially, in addition to those mentioned earlier, Dane Kennedy, Mrinalini Sinha and Kathleen Wilson. Many thanks go to John MacKenzie for his careful reading of the manuscript as well as his encouragement and support for the project. The anonymous reader, in addition, provided many useful suggestions for improving the manuscript. I am grateful also to the members of the Washington State University faculty writing group, especially Jose Alamillo, Matthew Guterl and Linda Heidenreich, for reading and commenting on numerous early chapter drafts. My colleagues in the History Department at Washington State University deserve special thanks, both for their tolerance in seeing me through the completion of this manuscript and for providing a supportive intellectual community in which to work. I would also like to thank my students, both graduate and undergraduate, for challenging me to bring new questions and perspectives to this project.

This book has benefited from the financial assistance of Duke University in the form of the Halstead Fellowship and the James B. Duke Research Fellowship, from the College of Liberal Arts at Washington State University for three travel grants and a completion grant, from the American Historical Association's Bernadotte Schmitt Award, and from a summer stipend from the National Endowment for the Humanities. Without such generous support, this book could never have been written. The archivists at the following public and private collections have provided generous, cheerful and helpful assistance in researching the material for this book: the India Office Library, the Public Record Office, the National Army Museum, the National Library of Scotland, the Scottish Record Office, the United Services Museum, the Black Watch Museum, the Gordon Highlanders' Museum,

ACKNOWLEDGEMENTS

the Argyll and Sutherland Highlanders' Museum, the British Library, and the Duke University Rare Book, Manuscript and Special Collections. The editorial staff at Manchester University Press have also provided patient and helpful assistance in the production of this book.

The debt I owe to my family and friends is incalculable. To Steve Streets I owe the most sincere gratitude for his continuous faith and love, for helping me to face life with good humour, and for being there through thick and thin. To my children, Jessica and Travis, I owe my greatest joy and appreciation for living. They have both lifted me up and kept my feet on the ground throughout their lives. I am grateful also for the unconditional love, friendship and guidance of my siblings and sibling-in-law – Nora Bynum, David Bynum and Stephen Gillis. Gene and Tanny Streets have treated me like a daughter throughout my marriage to their son. Sheri and Alex Colter, Alexia Grosjean, Wayne Lee, Rhonda Lee, Glenn Moseley, Steve Murdoch and our community of friends in Moscow, Idaho, have all provided wonderful friendship and support. Without the selfless help of Dr Robert Grossman and Dr Ralph Feigin in 1999, I might not have made it this far. Finally, the depth of my gratitude to my parents, to whom this book is dedicated, is beyond words. I do not exaggerate when I say that I owe everything to their active and constant love and support. They have been models of tolerance, patience, intellectual curiosity and the spirit of adventure since I was a child. They are the real inspiration for this book, and to them belongs my greatest love, appreciation and admiration.

INTRODUCTION

On an October day in 1897, British and Indian troops in a remote mountain area of India's northwest frontier were in the midst of a pitched battle against some intransigent Afridi border tribes. Twelve thousand well-armed Afridis had secured themselves at the top of a 6,000-foot ridge guarding a mountain pass and were firing down at will on British forces. Taking the position seemed impossible. Nevertheless, the British officer in command ordered it to be done. The Derbyshire and Dorsetshire regiments were moved into attack position, but two attempts failed to get more than a few soldiers across the fire-swept zone leading to the ridge. Any advance at all was reported to be 'impracticable'. An official military report told the rest of the story like this:

> The Gordon Highlanders, supported by the 3rd Sikh Infantry, were then moved up to the front, and after a brief halt, during which a heavy artillery fire was concentrated on the enemy's position, were directed to attack. Dashing across the open, the Gordons, supported by the 2nd Gurkhas and the 3rd Sikhs, went straight up the hill without check or hesitation through a murderous fire, carried the long-contested heights, and drove the enemy headlong into the Khanki Valley.[1]

When all seemed lost, Highlanders, Gurkhas and Sikhs triumphed after other soldiers had failed. As if invincible, these brave troops somehow managed to will themselves – though heavily outnumbered and moving uphill – through a battle zone that for anyone else would have been fatal.

This book examines the nineteenth-century ideology of 'martial races' – the belief that some groups of men are biologically or culturally predisposed to the arts of war – in order to explore how and why Scottish Highlanders, Punjabi Sikhs and Nepalese Gurkhas became linked in both military and popular discourse as the British Empire's fiercest, most manly soldiers. I argue that the connections contemporaries saw between these three groups demonstrate the historical instability of conceptions of 'race' as well as the political uses and contradictory purposes to which such conceptions could be put. I also argue that the savage representations of masculinity that lay at the heart of martial race ideology were a crucial imaginative site upon which Anglo-Indian military elites responded to, and attempted to manipulate, historically specific global-imperial politics after 1850 – particularly with regard to the rebellion of 1857, Russian military expansion, Indian and Irish nationalism, and recruiting problems in the British Army. Far from being a phenomenon with effects limited to the imperial 'periphery', the interventions of these military elites in the popular British media helped bring their racial and gendered constructs before a wide public. Thus, this book claims that the British Army in India was neither apolitical nor marginal to British culture; rather, its representatives exerted considerable efforts trying to shape the values of Victorian culture. Moreover, their racial and gendered constructions profoundly affected the identities of so-called 'martial race' populations in both Britain and India, who both embraced and manipulated their own representations as martial heroes.

Although a variety of scholars have noted the links between Highlanders, Sikhs and Gurkhas in the language of 'martial races', the implications of such a connection have received little attention.[2] One of the primary reasons for this is that the practical impact of martial race ideology was most obvious in India. Indeed, the idea that some 'races' were more martial than others gave rise to policies that, between 1857 and 1914, radically shifted the recruiting base of the Indian Army from Bengal and lower India to the Punjab and Nepal. From a mere 30,000 troops later identified as of the 'martial races' in 1857, by 1893 almost 44 per cent of the native Indian Army was recruited from populations thought to produce martial races.[3] In 1904 that number had risen to 57 per cent, and by 1914 a stunning three-quarters of the native infantry was composed of martial races.[4] As a result of these wide-ranging changes, scholars have focused their attention on the effects of martial race ideology almost exclusively in its Indian context.[5]

Critical work on the 'martial races', however, is relatively new. Sir George MacMunn's *The Martial Races of India* (1933), for a long time the only monograph on the subject, was written by a British officer in the Indian Army wholeheartedly invested in the truth of martial race ideology.[6] Most other twentieth-century accounts have been nostalgic and celebratory, often geared toward a popular audience.[7] These works have solidly reinforced the idea that men hailing from the Punjab and Nepal are 'naturally' martial. They continue to be written today, demonstrating that nineteenth-century conceptions of race and gender still carry some credibility with western readers – particularly when the subjects are exotically foreign.[8] Perhaps not surprisingly, television has also uncritically reproduced the assumptions undergirding martial race ideology. This was witnessed most clearly in the BBC's 1995 production of *Gurkha*, in which Gurkhas were presented as a group whose love of war and devotion to Britain are, even after the end of Empire, still perfectly matched. The 1996/97 New Year edition of the *U.S. News and World Report* also fell prey to these old stereotypes when it advocated hiring Gurkhas for a UN rapid reaction force to tackle conflict-ridden areas: 'Want peacekeepers with spine? Hire the world's fiercest mercenaries ... Let's hire the nerves-of-steel warriors who defended the Raj to do the world's dirty work in Bosnia and Rwanda.'[9] Popular sources like these are indebted to constructions of race and gender produced in the nexus between late nineteenth-century historical events and particular British-imperial responses to them.

Only in the past decade have historians begun to deconstruct the meanings and functions of martial race ideology in its late Victorian context.[10] This scholarship treats martial race ideology as a British construction, a strategic set of beliefs born out of specific recruiting needs, a uniquely colonial comprehension of Indian society, and nineteenth-century conceptions of race. The majority of studies argue that these beliefs came to their most coherent expression in the years between 1880 and 1914. In this period, proponents of martial race policies consciously and systematically sought to proliferate information about the 'martial' worthiness (and unworthiness) of different groups of Indians.[11] British officers wrote a series of handbooks on the merits of the various 'races' from which recruits might be drawn, and authored articles in both professional military journals and more popular mediums about their relative worth.[12] This period was also unique for the pretensions of martial race advocates to 'scientific' knowledge about racial proclivities, and for the widespread credence with which such theories were received in both military and civilian circles.[13] Finally, these years witnessed the proliferation of an astonishing abundance of stories, legends and anecdotes, related in both military and popular texts, about the miraculous capabilities of 'martial race' soldiers. Thus, the racial and gendered conceptions undergirding martial race ideology were sustained by more than abstract beliefs or statistical data; rather, they were backed up by these 'proverbial tales' of heroism which simultaneously conveyed the crucial elements of martial race ideology and 'proved' the truth of its claims.[14]

It is in this realm of mythic narrative that the importance of the Highland element of martial race ideology becomes clear, for the 'proverbial tales' that sustained it were replete with explicit connections between the Indian 'martial races' and Highland soldiers. However, despite the frequency with which they were paired, scholars have tended to ignore these connections, for there is an unwritten assumption that 'white' Highlanders could not possibly have been paired, in any serious way, with 'dark' Indians of the subcontinent. Yet it is increasingly clear that such conceptual binaries are inadequate to understanding the ideologies and institutions of 'imperial social formations'.[15] This book endeavours, above all, to demonstrate that the historically specific context in which martial race ideology became dominant was neither a 'metropolitan' nor an 'imperial' matter, but one that transcended both. I argue, as Antoinette Burton and Mrinalini Sinha have also suggested, that understanding martial race ideology requires an approach that goes beyond 'national' history, that seeks to complicate divisions between 'home' and 'empire' and between

European 'self' and foreign 'other'.[16] For the racial and gendered conceptions that undergirded the ideology of martial races were framed and produced in relation to conditions in Britain, India and even outside the Empire altogether. Bringing Highlanders, Sikhs and Gurkhas within the same purview allows us to explore the ways in which ideologies of race and gender were tightly bound across the boundaries of Empire, and how British-Indian military culture – so marginalised in histories of Victorian popular culture – was in fact integral to shaping and sustaining some of these bonds.

The purpose of undertaking this exercise, however, is not to demonstrate that the ideology of martial races functioned the same way in Britain as it did in India. Indeed, the power of martial race ideology stemmed from its very flexibility and ambiguity: it was adaptable to a variety of historical and geographical situations and functioned alternately to inspire, intimidate, exclude and include. Although Highlanders, Sikhs and Gurkhas were clearly linked in contemporary martial race discourse, that connection was given different – and even contradictory – significance in the distinct social-historical contexts of Britain and India. This becomes abundantly clear in my discussion of the purposes of martial race discourse for recruiting the armies in India and Britain. In India, authorities were overwhelmingly concerned to legitimate their exclusive recruiting strategies in terms of race and masculinity to keep politically suspect recruits out of the army. In Britain, however, most Britons were perfectly aware that the Highland regiments were not ethnically 'pure'. In that context, then, the superlative qualities of Highland soldiers functioned as an inspirational tool, an image of ideal masculinity and racial superiority to which all potential recruits could aspire. Thus while I argue for crossing conceptual 'national' frontiers to comprehend the ideological connections made possible by Empire, I also wish to emphasise, as Sinha has suggested, the 'incommensurability' of martial race applications in their British and Indian contexts.[17]

One of the central concerns of this book is to demonstrate the value of integrating military history more fully with the growing field of 'new imperial' history. Until recently, these fields remained isolated from one another both in terms of approach and in terms of archival focus.[18] Broadly defined, the 'new imperial' history has sought to demonstrate the vital significance of the Empire in British popular, cultural and political life in the late nineteenth century.[19] Many scholars associated with this field have been influenced in some way by post-colonial critiques of imperialism framed, but not resolved, by Edward Said's 1978 *Orientalism*.[20] As a result, much 'new imperial' history has taken a strong interest in the values and ideologies that sustained the imperial project, as well as in the language and texts that conveyed them. Moreover, 'new imperial' historians have utilised a wide variety of sources formerly ignored by historians of 'Empire' – including art, music, advertisements, popular journalism and school textbooks.

Conventional military history, on the other hand, has primarily been concerned to demonstrate the importance of military structures, tactics and strategy – particularly during wartime – for the maintenance, increase or loss of national power. In recent years, the 'new' military history has also sought to demonstrate the social and psychological impact of war, both for active combatants and for civil societies exposed to the difficulties of invasion, loss of kin and the necessities of wartime production.[21] Whether conventional or 'new', however, most military historians still rely deeply on archival sources generated by military branches, by the government, or by individual soldiers themselves – including despatches, orders, inquiries, handbooks, correspondence, memoranda, confidential and secret reports, diaries and memoirs.

Most historical work on nineteenth-century British military history has not been deeply influenced by the 'new' military history. Historians in this sub-field have, instead, tenaciously held to an age-old maxim that the army was both apolitical and marginal to Victorian culture.[22] Its officers, they argue, deliberately isolated themselves from party politics and acted only on behalf of Crown – rather than their own – interests.[23] Additionally, although Britain maintained a vast army in India and garrisoned a wide variety of colonial stations, British military historians have largely neglected the Empire. Rather, they have focused their attentions on the domestic structure of the army and on its relationship to – and competition with – European armies. As a result, they have been largely blind to the role of the Empire as 'the most consistent and most continuous influence in shaping the army as an institution'.[24] The 'new imperial' history, then, has held little appeal for British military historians who are concerned neither with Victorian popular culture nor with the influence of Empire on the British Army.

This lack of interest has been mutual. 'New imperial' historians, so often influenced by post-colonial concerns with language and ideology, have tended – like many of their colleagues in other fields – to write British military history off as a hopeless backwater, uninformed by theoretical considerations of race, gender or relations of power. Yet such disinterest fits uncomfortably with the fact that one of the most influential schools of 'new imperial' history insists that public esteem for the army and colonial warfare rose dramatically in this era. Historians of this school argue that tales of army adventures abounded in a varied and expanding media culture – which included newspapers, periodicals, music hall, advertisements and literature – and reflected an increasingly jingoistic, militaristic and imperially minded popular culture.[25] Unfortunately, because 'new imperial' historians generally hold the field of military history in disdain, they have seldom ventured into the traditional archival domains of military historians to explore possible connections between the 'real' army and its popular representations.[26]

The sources for this book straddle the archival 'territories' of both conventional military history and the 'new imperial' history. I have relied on official military documents, diaries and correspondence of army officers and men, as well as on popular journals, newspapers and fiction, in order to bring the two fields into closer dialogue. Explored in conjunction, they offer a reassessment of the relationship between the army and late Victorian culture – a reassessment based on their fundamental connectedness. Indeed, one of the central premises of this book is that the racial and gendered conceptions of officers in the British and Indian armies helped to shape the contours of Victorian 'high imperialism' in the last half of the century. British officers were not apolitical: instead, they were highly political figures, and were frequently involved in lobbying the press and other public forums for their own interests.[27] Whether in Parliament, in the Empire or in Britain, these officers were invested in political decision-making and the formation of public opinion, and used all of the tools at their disposal – with varying degrees of success – to influence both.

This book also argues that in addition to helping shape Victorian culture more generally, the army influenced the regional cultures of the Highlands, the Punjab and Nepal in remarkably enduring ways. Soldiers' letters and diaries, particularly from the Highland regiments, expose the ways in which the army's use of martial race language – with its attendant expectations of valour and loyalty – co-opted men into behaviours that ultimately served the state. Moreover, the use of martial race language came to overshadow other regional expressions of cultural identity, and thus threatened to erase other competing, and potentially subversive, expressions. This effect was even more apparent in terms of public perceptions of the so-called 'martial race' cultures, for the army's use of martial race language reduced and simplified the Highlands, the Punjab and Nepal into regions identified primarily with warrior heroes. As a result, massive transformations and difficulties brought about by poverty, modernisation and changes in land-use were largely ignored. The legacy of this phenomenon still survives, as popular fascination with the 'martial' cultures of Gurkhas, Sikhs and Highlanders testifies. Indeed, the constructed warriors of the nineteenth-century past have cast long shadows over their subsequent histories.

As its epithet suggests, ideologies of 'race' were integral to 'martial race' ideology. The meanings and functions of the 'race' in 'martial race' must be understood in two contradictory ways. First, it must be located within the larger context of shifting racial ideologies during the last half of the nineteenth century, as part of an increasingly 'scientific' understanding of race as a set of objective, biological characteristics. Second, and paradoxically, 'race' must be understood as a consciously manipulated linguistic and performative tool: in other words, as an artificial strategy of rule during a period of imperial anxiety.

Although the concept of 'race' was not new to the last half of the nineteenth century, the meanings attached to it shifted considerably after mid-century.[28] Prior to this, 'race' was commonly used more flexibly, in much the same way as 'nation' or 'stock', to denote a geographically bound group of people or a population of common genealogical descent.[29] Moreover, differences among peoples of the world were imagined based as much on relative levels of civilisation as on physical characteristics such as skin colour. In Enlightenment as well as Evangelical and Utilitarian thinking before 1850, 'races' of people were separated by their differing locations on the ladder of progress, from the bottom rung of hunter/gatherer societies to the top rung of fully industrialised and capitalised ones.[30] While a clear hierarchical relationship – as well as an implicit moral judgement of their worth – linked the 'highest' and 'lowest' civilisations, physical attributes were only one way in which that relationship was described. Religion, language and the relative advancement of technologies and government institutions also served as markers to describe racial difference.[31] Indeed, British and European Orientalists of the late eighteenth and early nineteenth centuries argued that linguistic similarities between the European languages and Sanskrit demonstrated the common ancestral background of Europeans and Indians.[32]

Whatever their intellectual base, conceptions of difference justified extensive violence and exploitation against indigenous peoples throughout the history of European imperial expansion. But in the last half of the nineteenth century (and particularly after 1875) 'race' had come to be understood in much more fixed terms, as an immutable, biological set of observable characteristics. A person's 'race' was increasingly understood to be rooted in heredity and in the body. Skin colour, head size and nose shape came to be used as markers of discrete 'races', and Britons categorised these racial 'types' with what they believed to be scientific measurements and empirical evidence. In addition to physical characteristics, 'racial types' were also believed to possess inborn characteristics such as courage and honesty or servility and deceitfulness.[33]

Martial race ideology grew, at least in part, out of this emerging racial world-view. However, like the concept of race generally, the idea of martial races was not wholly new to the last half of the nineteenth century, nor was it entirely a British invention.[34] Pre-colonial Indian societies and groups, like their European counterparts, had for centuries defined themselves and one another as either 'warlike' or 'peaceful'. In Europe, Enlightenment preoccupations with the 'stage' theory of civilisation encouraged the labelling of certain societies as 'martial', as did Romantic celebrations of the 'noble savage'.[35] Existing evidence shows various Britons advocated preferential recruitment from certain populations since at least the eighteenth century.[36] Highland, Sikh and Gurkha communities were singled out early on as prime examples of 'martial' societies. Scottish Highlanders had long been feared and detested in Britain for their violent, militaristic culture, but quickly established a reputation for fierceness and bravery during their service in the British Army in the Seven Years War (1757), when they were believed to have possessed a 'ferocity natural to savages'.[37] Indeed, British experience with Scottish Highlanders seems to have conditioned officers to look for and recognise other 'martial' societies in the Empire – particularly in India.[38] In 1819 a Briton by the name of Hamilton was already referring to Nepal's 'martial tribes', and during the Second Sikh War (1848–49) General Gall wrote that Sikhs were 'naturally brave'.[39] Yet following the explosion of social Darwinist racial theories at the end of the nineteenth century, the idea that some groups of people were more martial than others found 'scientific' justification. For the rest of the century and into the next, the martialness (or not) of particular populations was couched not in terms of opinion, experience or sensibility, but in terms of scientific 'fact'. As such, the 'race' in 'martial race' increasingly referred to the idea that the ability to make war inhered in the blood of some populations more than in others – that a 'natural' proclivity to arms denoted a 'biological' proclivity as well.[40]

While it is clear that British perceptions of race were highly influenced by 'scientific', biological explanations in the last half of the nineteenth century, the language of race also masked conscious, practical strategies of rule. In other words, Victorian Britons were not completely 'brainwashed' by biological conceptions of race – just as often, contemporaries seem to have been aware of the inconsistencies, contradictions and weaknesses they encompassed, and yet used the power and appeal of such language for their own purposes.

For example, those groups targeted for martial race recruiting in India in the last quarter of the century were, tellingly, also those groups who had remained loyal to the British during the crisis of the 1857 Rebellion. Prior to the Rebellion, high-caste Hindus of northern India were considered to be the most desirable soldiers because they were considered to be 'the largest, handsomest, and cleanest looking men'.[41] Yet because these same men played a central role in fomenting the Rebellion in the Bengal Army, British officers were quick to deride them as inherently cowardly, feminine and racially unfit for service in its aftermath. Within the next quarter-century, Gurkhas, Sikhs and other Punjabi and border groups – who had, significantly, largely fought to defend the Raj – had taken the place of the disgraced high-caste Hindus as the Indian Army's most preferred soldiers. This dramatic shift in the army's recruiting base, for the political and strategic goal of securing India from internal revolt, was increasingly justified in racial terms. Sikhs and Gurkhas were recruited into the army because, as British officers put it, they were a 'martial people' who needed outlets for their martial propensities. 'Race', in effect, became a guise in the search for unquestioned loyalty, and was marshalled to lend authority to British strategies for selective recruiting.

The use of 'race' as a tool in colonial power relations is starkly revealed by even the most cursory examination of the use of Sikhs, Gurkhas and Highlanders as representative 'martial races'. Sikhs were not a 'race' at all but a monotheistic religious group transformed by the teachings of Guru Gobind Singh, at the turn of the eighteenth century, into a militaristic and spiritual 'brotherhood of warriors', or Khalsa. Sikh men could enter the Khalsa by being baptised with a double-edged sword in a ritual called the *pahul*, and by observing the outward symbols of membership such as leaving the hair uncut.[42] British officers used this knowledge to their own advantage, and when existing Sikh recruits were few on the ground, the army sometimes found it useful to ensure 'Hindu Jats [be] encouraged to take the Pahul'.[43] Yet in recruiting handbooks and in martial race discourse, Sikhs were treated as an identifiable 'race' with common physical and mental characteristics – as men identifiably 'steady, earnest and stubborn', who are 'undoubtedly brave ... possess a strong feeling of independence, are straightforward and manly, genial in disposition and not quarrelsome'.[44]

British constructions of 'Gurkhas' were similarly suspect on racial grounds. It has now become clear that the extensive information Britons gathered about the racial proclivities of 'Gurkha' men was relatively meaningless to those men who enlisted in Gurkha units.[45] The very appellation 'Gurkha' was a British construction that elided the fact that these supposedly racially 'pure' recruits originated from a variety of culturally distinct traditions within Nepal. Once recruited, 'Gurkha' men frequently found themselves forced to adapt to British ideas about their behaviours and traditions, and in the process found themselves compelled to adopt alien rituals, customs, foods and dances as their own.[46] As a 'race', then, Gurkhas can truly be said to have been both produced and maintained in the Indian Army and nowhere else.

Highlanders, while frequently showcased for their ferocious racial proclivities for war, were also a much more diverse group than martial race discourse and ideology pretended. It was common knowledge within the British Army, and indeed among Britons generally, that the Highland soldiers of the last half of the nineteenth century were not really 'true' Highlanders at all. Instead, they were composed of poor, urban Lowland Scots, mixed in with smaller percentages of English and Irish recruits.[47] Yet the transparent nature of the racialised construction of Highlanders did nothing to discredit it. Instead, it came to be understood as shorthand for the racial capabilities of all British men. Since it was clear that any Briton could potentially 'become' a Highlander, the language of race functioned in this context as an inspirational tool – an emotive device designed to demonstrate that Britons had 'the right stuff' to take on their rivals and enemies. Though the 'lust of fighting was in their blood', as an early twentieth-century article in *Blackwood's Magazine* claimed, another clearly allowed that the continuing success of the Highland regiments demonstrated that 'prestige is a quality transmissible by other channels than blood-relationship'.[48]

The meaning of the 'race' in 'martial race', then, was both flexible and fictitious even as it used the language of fixed, immutable racial binaries that claimed so much contemporary currency. While clearly dependent upon and related to the 'science' of race, the use of race in martial race ideology cannot be explained away as merely a product of its time. 'Martial race' proponents were not, in other words, simply reading from a script of available racial ideologies, but instead were consciously using the language of race for specific political and practical ends. In so doing, they simultaneously helped to 'create' race and to influence the way it was understood in both Britain and India.

'Martial race' soldiers were not just 'raced', however: they also, significantly, came to be 'gendered' as ideally masculine. How and why this came to be so reveals a great deal about the ways in which masculinities are socially and ideologically constructed in response to changing social, economic and political circumstances.[49] The specific vision of masculinity represented by the 'martial races' also exposes the ways in which gender helped constitute both the policy and ideological outlook of the British and Indian armies – an issue to which historians have devoted scant attention.[50] This book argues that ideologies of gender played an important role in the development of the logic of imperial defence in the last half of the nineteenth century, and that those ideologies also helped to shape Victorian ideals of masculinity more generally.

Nineteenth-century militaries were, of course, highly gendered institutions both in terms of their enforced homosocial environments as well as in terms of the rigorous codes of masculinity soldiers were expected to uphold. Soldiers were expected to dissociate themselves from so-called feminine traits such as cowardliness and were encouraged to behave with reckless courage, to endure severe physical hardships and to kill when ordered. Soldiers in the British Army during the second half of the nineteenth century were actively discouraged from marrying, which meant that the presence of women within regiments in India was limited to the small number of regimental wives allowed 'on the strength' and to native prostitutes in the bazaar.[51] Indian soldiers in the Bengal Army, though frequently married, did not normally live with their wives and families in regimental barracks.[52] In both, the homosocial environment of the regiment fostered cultures of masculinity based on the particular needs of the military for discipline, loyalty and fighting efficiency.

Historians, however, have tended to view such military cultures unproblematically, as though their separation from women and 'femininity' rendered the shifting 'politics of gender' in this period irrelevant to them. Yet the emergence of the particular brand of masculinity embodied in the vision of the martial race soldier – inherent loyalty, honour and devotion in addition to racial hardiness – was a product of the re-alignment of imperial masculine values in the last half of the century. As such, martial race masculinity must be understood not as a 'natural' result of military culture, but as a construct intricately tied to global-historical events and to anxieties about femininity.

This book locates the 1857 Rebellion as a crucial moment in the articulation of martial race masculinity. The Rebellion, indeed, functioned as a crucible through which ideologies of both British and Indian masculinities were renegotiated in this period. In order to minimise criticism of the East India Company's failure to deal with the grievances of Indian soldiers and subjects, British officers and Anglo-Indians alike framed the Rebellion as a fiendish attack on innocent British women and children, for whose outrageous murders India must be brought to heel.[53] This strategy had the effect of inciting heated emotions of revenge in Britain and allowed British forces incredible license to brutally crush the revolt. It also transformed those troops defending British India into chivalric heroes, while the 'mutineers' fighting against British rule became unmanly cowards.[54] The high-caste Hindus who comprised so much of the Bengal Army in 1857 were particularly cast as treacherous, faithless, deluded and easily incited to passion – all characteristics believed to be at odds with contemporary British conceptions of manliness, and all characteristics that would help legitimise their later 'racial' exclusion from the Indian Army. Meanwhile, those groups who were highly conspicuous for their roles in quelling the Rebellion – among them Highlanders, Sikhs and Gurkhas – became strongly associated with a fierce, gallant, honourable, loyal and courageous masculinity.

These gendered constructions, forged during a moment of crisis, became invested with new legitimacy in the context of late-century global-imperial politics. British officers increasingly felt themselves challenged on all sides by the simultaneous spectres of Russian expansion into India's northwest frontier region, German militarism, British recruiting difficulties, and Indian and Irish nationalism. Their anxieties about the abilities of British and Indian armies to deal with such grave challenges were frequently expressed in terms of anxieties over the masculine calibre of the troops. In this context, the legendary performances of Highlanders, Sikhs and Gurkhas during the Rebellion were recast to fit the new political context of late century. Units from each group were brought together again during the Second Afghan War (1878–80), where their successful cooperation laid a fresh foundation for the narratives that would provide discursive 'proof', borne out in conflicts on the northwest frontier for the rest of the century, that both the British and Indian armies had troops manly enough to withstand challengers on any front. The masculine vision in martial race ideology and discourse, then, functioned as an imaginative space within which British officers could respond to the anxiety-producing historical circumstances of late Victorian Britain.

The language officers used to describe 'martial race' feats – words and phrases like 'dashing' and 'gallant', and images such as charging 'through heavy fire', 'without check or hesitation' – reflect their concern to highlight the aggressively masculine prowess of the men. The very ability of 'martial race' soldiers to make war was conflated with their masculinity, as in the well-known pronouncement that they were 'manly in [their] warlike creed'.[55] They were said to be 'strong, brave, hard-working and high-principled' and displayed 'remarkable coolness in sudden emergency, readiness to act, and complete disregard and indifference to personal danger'.[56] They would never 'turn their backs on a foe', and if angered by an enemy, their unleashed vengeance would ask 'silently for blood'.[57] Their ferocity and violence discursively erased all so-called 'feminine' qualities such as softness, weakness, vulnerability and faithlessness. So intertwined were the qualities of the 'martial races' with an idealised notion of masculinity that officers frequently referred to them simply as the 'manly' races.[58]

The idealised masculinity represented by 'martial race' soldiers increasingly became the standard by which officers compared and rated both other units and potential recruits. Officers believed soldiers in both the Indian and British armies needed – given especially the threat of war with Russian troops on the northwest frontier – the 'manly' characteristics for which 'martial race' soldiers were so noted. In this way, 'masculinity' became conflated with 'race', and the two formed an increasingly influential axis along which British imperial military power was constructed and legitimised.

Martial race masculinity, however, became more than just a military construction. This was because ambitious British officers in India frequently maintained connections with representatives of the media in Britain and British India, and used them unabashedly for their own – and the army's – purposes. As a result, the stories and anecdotes they produced about the masculine virtues and qualities of 'martial races' eventually reached a wide public in both Britain and India. In this way, they were able to shape the contours of more than just Anglo-Indian military ideology.

Indeed, the particular militaristic masculine ideal represented by 'martial race' soldiers accords suspiciously well with shifting masculine ideals in late Victorian Britain. At mid-century, hegemonic middle- and upper-class masculinity was embodied in the concept of 'muscular Christianity' – a notion that emphasised the importance of combining physical fitness with Christian morality. By the last quarter of the century, however, hegemonic masculine ideals had become decidedly more secular and were epitomised by the figure of the imperial soldier. The changed emphasis of this shift was evident in newspapers, advertisements, journals, songs and books. Everywhere the bodies and deeds of soldiers – nearly always pictured fighting on the imperial frontier – were used to convey the increasingly desirable masculine virtues of loyalty, reckless bravery, strength and willingness to fight. In the context of late Victorian popular imperial culture, images of soldier heroes took on new potency as icons of masculine distinction.[59]

This book argues that the particular masculinity envisioned by martial race ideology – as well as the anxieties that produced it – also played a role in helping to shape late Victorian masculine ideals. In other words, late Victorian hegemonic masculinity was informed by political circumstances and anxieties that ranged simultaneously from Britain to India to Europe, and was influenced by the formulations and constructions of a military establishment long believed to be marginal to Victorian culture.

A study of martial race ideology, then, provides a window into the workings of the multiple ideological connections between Britain and India. Moreover, it demonstrates that ideologies of race and gender were central to the ways in which such connections were constructed and understood. Far from being uniform or monolithic, martial race discourse exposes the instability and contextual fragility of racial and gendered ideologies, and allows us to see their evolution in relation to historical events and anxieties. These events and anxieties, I argue, were frequently matters with which the British and Indian armies were deeply concerned, and the efforts of their representatives to cope with them meant that the armies were as much producers of their times as they were products of it.

Notes

1 India Office Library and Records, London (hereafter OIOL), L/MIL/17/5/1616, General Orders India, Summary of measures considered or carried out in the military department of the Government of India (1899), 45–46.

2 Among those who have noted the connection are Cynthia Enloe, *Ethnic Soldiers: State Security in Divided Societies* (Athens: University of Georgia Press, 1980), 36; Robert Clyde, *From Rebel to Hero: The Image of the Highlander, 1745–1830* (East Linton: Tuckwell Press, 1995), 177; Stephen Wood, *The Scottish Soldier* (Manchester: Archive

Publications, 1987), 42.

3   These populations included, most notably, those from the Punjab and the North-West Frontier Province, but also included those men known as Gurkhas who lived beyond the borders of British India in Nepal.

4   David Omissi, *The Sepoy and the Raj: The Indian Army, 1860–1940* (London: Macmillan, 1994), 5, 19.

5   See Omissi, *The Sepoy and the Raj*; Pradeep Barua, 'Inventing race: the British and India's martial races', *The Historian* 58:1 (Autumn 1995); Lionel Caplan, *Warrior Gentlemen: 'Gurkhas' in the Western Imagination* (Providence: Berghahn Books, 1995); Lionel Caplan, 'Martial Gurkhas: the persistence of a British military discourse on "race"', in Peter Robb (ed.), *The Concept of Race in South Asia* (Delhi: Oxford University Press, 1995); Mary des Chene, 'Language and practice in the colonial Indian Army', paper presented at the Institute for Global Studies in Culture, Power and History, Johns Hopkins University, Autumn 1993. Richard Fox also talks about the 'invention' of Sikhs as a martial race in his *Lions of the Punjab: Culture in the Making* (Berkeley: University of California Press, 1985).

6   Sir George MacMunn, *The Martial Races of India* (London: Low, Marston & Co., 1933).

7   See especially Byron Farwell's *The Gurkhas* (New York: Norton, 1984) and *Armies of the Raj: From the Mutiny to Independence, 1858–1947* (New York: Norton, 1989).

8   For recent examples, see E. D. Smith, *Valour: A History of the Gurkhas* (Woodstock: Overlook Press, 1997); Christopher Chant, *Gurkha: The Illustrated History of an Elite Fighting Force* (Dorset: Blandford Press, 1985); E. D. Smith, *Johnny Gurkha: Friends in the Hills* (London: Arrow Books, 1987); G. M. Forteath, *Pipes, Kukris, and Nips* (Edinburgh: Pentland Press, 1991).

9   'Twenty silver bullets', *U.S. News and World Report* (30 Dec. 1996 / 6 Jan. 1997), 42, 43.

10 Much of this renewed interest may have been inspired by Cynthia Enloe's *Ethnic Soldiers*. Enloe's work is general and deals with the phenomenon of 'martial races' from a more global perspective, but she set out an important theoretical framework for historians working on specifically British imperial problems. For more focused studies, see note 5.

11 Omissi, *The Sepoy and the Raj*, 24.

12 For a good discussion of this phenomenon, see T. R. Moreman, 'The army in India and the military periodical press, 1830–1898', in David Finkelstein and Douglas Peers (eds), *Negotiating India in the Nineteenth Century Media* (Houndmills: Macmillan, 2002).

13 See especially Caplan, 'Martial Gurkhas'.

14 Des Chene, 'Language and practice in the colonial Indian Army', 4. The notion of 'proverbial tales' is Des Chene's.

15 Mrinalini Sinha uses the phrase 'imperial social formation' to emphasise 'the intersection of the imperial with the categories of nation, race, class, gender, and sexuality', as well as 'the essentially uneven and contradictory nature of that intersection'. See her *Colonial Masculinity: The 'Manly Englishman' and the 'Effeminate Bengali' in the Late Nineteenth Century* (Manchester: Manchester University Press, 1995), 2; for a recent collection of essays that directly challenges Edward Said's conception of the unilateral binaries of 'Self' and 'Other', see Julie F. Codell and Dianne Sachko Macleod (eds), *Orientalism Transposed: The Impact of the Colonies on British Culture* (Aldershot and Brookfield: Ashgate, 1998).

16 Sinha, *Colonial Masculinity*, 9–10. Antoinette Burton's works have long challenged such conceptual divisions. See, most recently, *At the Heart of the Empire: Indians and the Colonial Encounter in Late-Victorian Britain* (Berkeley: University of California Press, 1998).

17 Sinha, *Colonial Masculinity*, 10. This 'incommensurability' is in fact one of Sinha's central themes, particularly in ch. 4, 'Potent protests: the age of consent controversy, 1891'.

18 Doug Peers has recently begun to bridge the gap. See '"Those noble exemplars of the

[14]

true military tradition": constructions of the Indian Army in the mid-Victorian press', *Modern Asian Studies* 31:1 (1997).

19 The scholars who practise the 'new imperial' history are too numerous to name, but many are associated with or have been influenced by John MacKenzie and the Manchester University Press series 'Studies in Imperialism'. For starters, see John MacKenzie, *Propaganda and Empire: The Manipulation of British Public Opinion, 1880–1960* (Manchester: Manchester University Press, 1984).

20 Published in New York by Vintage Books.

21 The 'new military history' is strongly associated with John Keegan, and especially with *The Face of Battle* (Harmondsworth: Penguin, 1976). See also Paul Fussell, *The Great War and Modern Memory* (New York: Oxford University Press, 1975).

22 See, for examples, Gwyn Harries-Jenkins, *The Army in Victorian Society* (London: Routledge & Kegan Paul, 1977); more recently, David Chandler and Ian Beckett (eds), *The Oxford Illustrated History of the British Army* (Oxford: Oxford University Press, 1994), esp. xvi.

23 Hew Strachan, *The Politics of the British Army* (Oxford: Clarendon, 1997). Strachan's book is a sustained challenge to this powerful orthodoxy, which seeks to show the many ways in which the British Army was in fact a highly political institution.

24 Strachan, *The Politics of the British Army*, 74.

25 See John MacKenzie (ed.), *Imperialism and Popular Culture* (Manchester: Manchester University Press, 1986); John MacKenzie (ed.), *Popular Imperialism and the Military* (Manchester: Manchester University Press, 1992); Jeffrey Richards (ed.), *Imperialism and Juvenile Literature* (Manchester: Manchester Unversity Press, 1989); J. W. M. Hichberger, *Images of the Army: The Military in British Art, 1815–1914* (Manchester: Manchester University Press, 1988); and Robert MacDonald, *The Language of Empire: Myths and Metaphors of Popular Imperialism, 1880–1918* (Manchester: Manchester University Press, 1994).

26 This is certainly true of MacKenzie's edited volume, *Popular Imperialism and the Military*.

27 See Strachan, *The Politics of the British Army*, 8–9.

28 Thomas Holt, *The Problem of Freedom: Race, Labor, and Politics in Jamaica and Britain, 1832–1938* (Baltimore: Johns Hopkins University Press, 1992); Paul Rich, *Race and Empire in British Politics* (Cambridge: Cambridge University Press, 1986); Robb (ed.), *The Concept of Race in South Asia*; Nancy Stepan, *The Idea of Race in Science: Great Britain, 1800–1960* (Hamden, Conn.: Archon Books, 1982).

29 Thomas Trautmann, *Aryans and British India* (Berkeley: University of California Press, 1997), 191–192.

30 Ajay Skaria, 'Shades of wildness: tribe, caste, and gender in western India', *Journal of Asian Studies* 56:3 (Aug. 1997), 730.

31 For the influence of technological advancement and its relationship to European ideas of superiority, see Michael Adas, *Machines as the Measure of Men: Science, Technology, and Ideologies of Western Dominance* (Ithaca: Cornell University Press, 1989).

32 Trautmann, *Aryans and British India*, chs 3 and 5; Thomas Metcalf, *Ideologies of the Raj: The New Cambridge History of India, Volume III:4* (Cambridge: Cambridge University Press, 1994), 82. Kelli Kobor treats the complex subject of Orientalism with subtlety and nuance in her dissertation, 'Orientalism, the construction of race, and the politics of identity in British India, 1800–1930' (Ph.D. dissertation, Duke University, 1998). Her first chapter deals specifically with the idea that the early Orientalists imagined a common cultural heritage between Europeans and Indians.

33 Ann Laura Stoler, *Race and the Education of Desire: Foucault's History of Sexuality and the Colonial Order of Things* (Durham: Duke University Press, 1995), 133–134.

34 Doug Peers outlines elements of pre-Rebellion martial race ideology in India in '"Those noble exemplars of true military tradition"'.

35 Mike Hawkins, *Social Darwinism in European and American Thought, 1860–1945* (Cambridge: Cambridge University Press, 1997), 47–51.

36 Caplan, 'Martial Gurkhas', 260; Omissi, *The Sepoy and the Raj*, 23.

37 Clyde, *From Rebel to Hero*, 155.

38 Both Robert Clyde and David Omissi have noted this. See Clyde, *From Rebel to Hero*, 177; Omissi, *The Sepoy and the Raj*, 23.

39 Caplan, 'Martial Gurkhas', 263; National Army Museum, London (hereafter NAM), Number 92 GAL, Letters of the late Major-General R. H. Gall in the Sikh War and the Mutiny (1848–58), R. H. Gall, Dec. 1848.

40 Caplan, 'Martial Gurkhas', 260–261.

41 Madan Paul Singh, *Indian Army Under the East India Company* (New Delhi: Sterling Publishers, 1976), 157; see also T. A. Heathcote, *The Indian Army: The Garrison of British Imperial India, 1822–1922* (London: Hippocrene, 1974) on the cult of 'grenadierdom'.

42 W. H. McLeod, *The Sikhs: History, Religion, and Society* (New York: Columbia University Press, 1989), 4.

43 Captain A. A. Johnstone, 'Localisation of recruiting for the infantry of the Native Army', *United Services Institute of India* 25:123 (1896), 87.

44 C. H. C. P. Rice, 'Notes on the Sikhs as soldiers for our army', *United Services Institute of India* 2:57 (1871), 68.

45 Caplan, *Warrior Gentlemen*, 52; Michael Hutt, 'A hero or a traitor? The Gurkha soldier in Nepali literature', *South Asia Research* 9:1 (May 1989), 21.

46 Des Chene, 'Language and practice in the colonial Indian Army', 39.

47 For a breakdown of nationality in the British Army, see H. J. Hanham, 'Religion and nationality in the mid-Victorian army', in M. R. D. Foot (ed.), *War and Society* (London: Paul Elek, 1973), esp. 162–163. See also Diana Henderson's *Highland Soldier: A Social Study of the Highland Regiments, 1820–1920* (Edinburgh: John Donald, 1989), 15–18; and Alan Guy's *The Road to Waterloo: The British Army and the Struggle Against Revolutionary and Napoleonic France, 1793–1815* (London: National Army Museum, 1990).

48 J. M. Bulloch, 'The gay Gordons: a study in inherited prestige', *Blackwood's Magazine* 163 (Feb. 1898), 255; 'The heroes of Perthshire', *Blackwood's Magazine* 184 (Nov. 1908), 647.

49 For some recent works on masculinity, see Sinha's *Colonial Masculinity*; Michael Roper and John Tosh (eds), *Manful Assertions: Masculinities in Britain Since 1800* (London: Routledge, 1991); R. W. Connell, *Masculinities* (Berkeley: University of California Press, 1995); Michael Kimmel, *Manhood in America: A Cultural History* (New York: Free Press, 1997). Also, both the *Journal of British Studies* (38, July 1999) and the *Journal of Southern African Studies* (24:4, Dec. 1998) have published special issues devoted to masculinity.

50 See, for example, Chandler and Beckett (eds), *Oxford Illustrated History of the British Army*; Strachan, *The Politics of the British Army*; Allan Ramsay Skelley, *The Victorian Army at Home: The Recruitment and Terms of Conditions of the British Regular, 1859–1899* (London: Croom Helm, 1977); T. A. Heathcote, *The Military in British India: The Development of British Land Forces in South Asia, 1600–1947* (Manchester: Manchester University Press, 1995); Omissi, *The Sepoy and the Raj*; Edward Spiers, *The Late Victorian Army, 1868–1902* (Manchester: Manchester University Press, 1992).

51 For a discussion of the limited outlets British soldiers found in India and their frequent recourse to prostitution, see Douglas Peers, 'Privates off parade: regimenting sexuality in the nineteenth-century Indian Empire', *International History Review* 20:4 (Dec. 1998), esp. 837–839. For the wider political problems generated by the army in India's use of prostitution, see Philippa Levine, 'Rereading the 1890s: venereal disease as "constitutional crisis" in Britain and British India', *Journal of Asian Studies* 55:3 (Aug. 1996).

52 Peers, 'Privates off parade', 836.

53 For a detailed discussion of this phenomenon, see Jenny Sharpe, 'The unspeakable limits of rape: colonial violence and counter-insurgency', *Genders* 10 (Spring 1991), and Nancy Paxton, 'Mobilizing chivalry: rape in British novels about the Indian Uprising of 1857', *Victorian Studies* 36:1 (Autumn 1992).

54 Graham Dawson deals extensively with the creation of a British hero-narrative during

the Rebellion in *Soldier Heroes: British Adventure, Empire and the Imagining of Masculinities* (London: Routledge, 1994).

55 The specific reference was to Sikhs in Captain R. W. Falcon, *Handbook on Sikhs For the Use of Regimental Officers* (Allahabad: Pioneer Press, 1896), preface.

56 The first was specifically with reference to Highlanders, in *Hector MacDonald or the Private Who Became a General: A Highland Laddie's Life and Laurels*, 4th imprint edn (London: S. W. Partridge & Co., 1900), preface; the second referred to Gurkhas in 'The native army of India', *Blackwood's Magazine* 162 (Aug. 1897), 197.

57 The first is with reference to Sikhs in Alexander G. Stuart, *The Indian Empire: A Short Review and Some Hints for the Use of Soldiers Proceeding to India* (1912), British Library, London, B.S. 21/21, 59; the second referred to Highlanders, again in *Hector MacDonald or the Private Who Became a General*, 145.

58 For contemporary examples see 'Recruiting for India: deterioration in the recruiting material for the Indian Army with suggestions as to causes and remedies', *United Services Magazine* 26 (1898), 328; NAM, 7101–23–126–1, F. S. Roberts, On the occasion of a public entertainment given by the representatives of the Punjab to General Lord Roberts (1893). See also Caplan, 'Martial Gurkhas', 270.

59 See Dawson, *Soldier Heroes*; MacKenzie (ed.), *Popular Imperialism and the Military*; Cecil Eby, *The Road to Armageddon: The Martial Spirit in English Popular Literature, 1870–1914* (Durham: Duke University Press, 1987); and MacDonald, *The Language of Empire*. However, while the aggressive masculinity may have been 'hegemonic' in terms of its appeal within British imperial culture in late century, it was of course not the only masculine ideal and not, I would argue, one that was easily lived in the context of most men's day-to-day lives. For a good explanation of the function and meaning of hegemonic masculinity, see Mike Donaldson, 'What is hegemonic masculinity?', *Theory and Society* 22:5 (Oct. 1993). For alternative constructions of late Victorian masculinity, see A. James Hammerton, 'Pooterism or partnership? Marriage and masculine identity in the lower middle class, 1870–1920', *Journal of British Studies* 38 (July 1999); Andrew Davies, 'Youth gangs, masculinity and violence in late Victorian Manchester and Salford', *Journal of Social History* 32:2 (Winter 1998).

CHAPTER ONE

The transformation of the British and Indian armies in the Rebellion of 1857

In his best-selling autobiography of 1897, Field Marshal Lord Roberts waxed poetic about his personal observation of the storming of the Secunderbagh, one of the most widely celebrated events of the 1857 Indian Rebellion:

> It was a magnificent sight, a sight never to be forgotten – that glorious struggle to be the first to enter the deadly breach, the prize to the winner of the race being certain death! Highlanders and Sikhs, Punjabi Mahomedans, Dogras and Pathans, all vied with each other in a generous competition.[1]

Forty years after the fact, the image of kilted Scottish Highlanders racing loyal Indian sepoys to 'certain death' at the Secunderbagh warranted yet another re-telling to an eager British public. By that time, the story had become truly legendary, told with an almost ritualistic predictability in British accounts of the events of 1857. It was a tale that had come to represent an imperial ideal of heroism, honour and sacrifice. It was a tale that lionised certain groups of loyal Indian sepoys for their devotion to the British in the face of mass rebellion. It was also one of the first tales that powerfully linked Scottish Highland soldiers to those loyal sepoys who would one day become known as India's 'martial races'.

Although martial race ideology only came to its full fruition later in the nineteenth century, the events and stories produced by the 1857 Rebellion, and the connections forged between particular British and Indian troops during the conflict, helped to shape its future form. The memory of incidents like the storming of the Secunderbagh, and their continual re-narration in the last half of the nineteenth century, provided justification for the preferential treatment of Highland, Sikh and – later – Gurkha units as elite imperial troops.

The Rebellion is central to this story for reasons that go beyond this initial moment in the link between Highlanders and India's future 'martial races', however. For in looking to this mid-Victorian imperial crisis to understand the specific contours of late nineteenth-century martial race ideology, I point more generally to the significance of the Rebellion in the development of late-century enthusiasm for empire and the military. Moreover, although the Rebellion has received considerable attention from historians of British popular culture, British India, and – to a lesser extent – the British Army, this story bridges the concerns of all three.

The Rebellion was, in fact, a pivotal moment for the redefinition of attitudes – both public and official – about the military, empire, race and masculinity.[2] As a military crisis of truly massive proportions, it inspired the structural transformation of both the British and Indian armies, and necessitated far greater cooperation and dependence between the two establishments than had ever existed before.[3] In Britain, the crisis resulted in the amalgamation of the East India Company's European forces into the line, and the commitment of a permanent, 80,000-man garrison on the subcontinent.[4] In India, the mutiny or disbandment of sixty-nine out of the seventy-four regiments of the Bengal Army necessitated its entire reconstruction with men as different in origin as possible from those who had so recently rebelled.[5]

The Rebellion was much more than a military crisis, however, for the public interest it generated in Britain was unprecedented. Part of the reason for this was that the British media expanded markedly after 1850, thereby making possible a much larger audience for imperial events than ever before. This expansion, in conjunction with new and faster methods of transmitting news to and from India, seemed to many to bring the events occurring in India closer to home and hence to seem more immediate, more relevant and more traumatic.[6] Public interest in India, while not insignificant prior to the Rebellion, consequently increased substantially as a result of the conflict.[7]

Although the mechanics of the expanding media network were important to the scale of public interest in the Rebellion, the particular shape of the conflict was equally compelling. British renderings of the Rebellion framed it in terms of a savage attack on British women and children, who were being murdered and allegedly raped by fanatic soldiers in alarming numbers.[8] Public outrage over the violation of 'innocent' Britons fuelled an emotive response to the Rebellion that encouraged – even demanded – vengeance.

Framing the Rebellion in this way made ideologies of gender and race central to the conflict. British women, imagined and represented as saintly white angels of middle-class respectability, were positioned against representations of black, lustful, uncontrolled and deceitful Indians. That such men could transgress the 'rules' of decency by raping and murdering British women de-legitimised, in British eyes, their claims to manliness and their right to self-determination, while simultaneously 'proving' their racial inferiority.

This theme of endangered (white) womanhood also transformed military and civilian attitudes towards ordinary soldiers in both the British and Indian armies. In contrast to the 'unmanned' rebels, British and loyal native soldiers were represented as ultra-masculine saviours of British women in India. As a result, these so-called 'defenders of India' became associated with a heightened, but controlled and chivalrous, masculinity – an association that markedly improved the reputation of British soldiers. Equally, the prowess of loyal native groups like the Sikhs was used to underscore British contentions that those groups who chose to remain loyal were both racially superior and more manly than those Indians who had chosen to rebel.

The structural, cultural and discursive transformations inspired by the Rebellion thus provided the conditions under which a new set of linkages between British and Indian heroes would gain widespread fame in both popular and military circles. The power of these connections derived, in no small part, from the particular ways in which Highlanders, Sikhs and (initially to a lesser extent) Gurkhas embodied racial and masculine superiority in contrast to rebel sepoys. This chapter explores the conditions that made such connections possible; the specific context in which they developed will be the subject of Chapter 2.

The British Army before 1857

The Rebellion marked the completion of a dramatic revision in popular attitudes towards soldiers in the British Army. For the first half of the nineteenth century (indeed since Cromwell's mid-seventeenth-century military regime), the British standing army in general and soldiers in particular were widely regarded with suspicion and distaste.[9] The gendered and racial dynamics of the Rebellion, however, were to change all that, as British regulars were increasingly imagined as the heroic and chivalric saviours of British women during the conflict. Such new and intense popular appeal was foundational for the military enthusiasm of late Victorian Britain, for it provided clear evidence that imperial conflicts could mobilise and unite large sections of the reading public in patriotic support of the British Empire. Thereafter, both military and media interests sought to capture such enthusiasm for their own purposes, and these in turn helped to define the contours of a culture that increasingly turned its attention to imperial warfare and the ideal figure of the soldier-hero.

That is not to say, of course, that enthusiasm for warfare was insignificant to British culture before 1850. The Anglo-French conflicts in the eighteenth and early nineteenth centuries certainly inspired militaristic displays of patriotism and led to a wave of volunteering for home defence.[10] Similarly, British struggles against India's Tipu Sultan and the Mahrattas in 1797–98 elicited tremendous interest among the British reading public. Generals like Cornwallis and Wellington became national heroes, and institutions organised drives to commemorate their deeds in stone and canvas.[11]

What was new about British popular enthusiasm for soldiers during the Rebellion was in part a matter of scale, for the expansion of the press after 1850 allowed a far larger public to share in the news of the conflict. Also new was that the focus of popular attention during the Rebellion was as much on the heroics of British regular soldiers as it was on the officers who commanded troops. No more was it just high-ranking officers who would become popular British folk heroes – now, ordinary enlisted men were seen to be significant players in their own right, and their motives and deeds became targets of popular celebration.[12]

Prior to 1850, regular soldiers were unlikely heroes indeed. Britons of nearly every class believed that soldiers of the line were uneducated, immoral, and prone to drink and violence.[13] In contrast to their officers, who had to purchase their own commissions and hence hailed from the landed and professional classes, regular soldiers came from the lowest stratum of British society. Moreover, working-class Britons, among whom army officials hoped to find recruits, commonly despised the army as a tool of government oppression, because soldiers were routinely used to prevent or disperse organised working-class protest activities in the period before and during the defeat of the Chartist movement in 1848.[14]

The conditions of army life were widely known and did little to allay public fears about the unattractiveness of the service or about the character of its recruits. Enlisted men earned 1s a day, out of which they were expected to pay for rations (1 lb of bread and ¾ lb of meat), laundry, personal necessaries such as soap, and damages to equipment or barracks. After the deduction of these 'stoppages', as they were known, soldiers were lucky to receive more than 1d per day.[15] Such meagre pay necessitated that the army rely on only the poorest classes of society to fill its ranks – men who were either in trouble with the law or who could find few alternatives to real hunger.[16] Moreover, barracks at home and in the Empire were crowded and unsanitary, often with contaminated water supplies and primitive sewage systems. A report in 1857 confirmed that the mortality rate for British soldiers serving at home was double that of civilians.[17] In the colonies, annual mortality and hospitalisation rates could be appallingly high as well.[18] If that was not enough to make military service unattractive, the length of service repulsed many. Until 1847, service in the army was for life. In 1847, in an attempt to attract more recruits, service was shortened to twelve years with the option to re-enlist at the end of the term. However, the attempt failed as many potential recruits felt that a service of twelve years would shunt them back into civilian life at an age when it would be difficult to find gainful employment.[19]

The generally miserable conditions of army life meant that the British Army was frequently unable to fill its minimum annual quotas for recruits.[20] As a result, recruiting teams commonly resorted to deception and force to lure men into the service. Part of this resulted from the structure of the recruiting system itself, which was only loosely organised. Although recruits could enlist voluntarily at the battalion of their choice, more often necessity drove recruiting teams out into the countryside in search of new material. These teams, which could be composed of pensioned ex-soldiers, non-commissioned officers or privates, were rewarded with bounty money for each recruit brought in – a system that easily lent itself to abuses.[21] Anxious to receive as much bounty money as possible, recruiters frequented taverns and were often generous with alcohol and tall tales. Recruiters became notorious for their underhanded techniques and were frequently regarded with suspicion and mistrust by local civilians. As this confidential report on recruiting from 1859 makes plain, the War Office was well aware of the problem:

> We do not get men enough; we do not get men of the right sort; and those whom we do get are not got in a satisfactory manner. They are, generally speaking, more or less inveigled into enlisting, and almost every man would purchase his discharge within a month, if he had the means. Military service in the ranks, in short, is not looked upon as a career into which a reasonable and prudent man may be expected to enter; it is supplied, therefore, by boys, who are not old enough to judge for themselves, and, generally speaking, by an inferior description of boys, morally and physically.[22]

At mid-century, then, the image of the rank-and-file army was hardly a positive one. The means of obtaining soldiers, their living conditions and wages, and their connections with Britain's lowest classes meant that public enthusiasm for military affairs did not extend to public enthusiasm for enlisted men.

The events of the Crimean War (1854–56) provided a first, and important, step in shifting public opinion in favour of the common soldier. The first European war since the end of the Napoleonic Wars in 1815, it was begun in an atmosphere of intense patriotic fervour. The Russian Tsar was vilified as a scheming despot, and Britain entered the war on a wave of public support for rescuing Turkey from his grasp. Yet it quickly became clear that the British Army was ill-prepared for an offensive Continental war. The field command led by Lord Raglan – a 66-year-old man on his first command – was hampered by rivalry and divided responsibilities.[23] The force of 26,000 was composed of many raw recruits, and unsanitary conditions in camp as well as severe weather ravaged the force during 1854–55. At the time, British Army administration was shared by no less than six government departments – the War Office, the Colonial Office, the Home Office, the Treasury, the Horse Guards and Ordnance – and none of these had primary power over all the rest.[24] As a result, miscommunication and mismanagement between the various departments responsible for the conduct of war – especially transport and supply by the civilian-led Commissariat – took a severe toll by producing desperate shortages of clothing, food and medical supplies. Hospitals were badly managed, dirty and short of doctors, and were paralysed by uncertainties and quarrels over responsibilities within the army medical department.[25] By 1856, the disastrously conducted campaign was brought to a close at the cost of more than 17,000 British lives, most as a result of disease and sickness.[26]

The scale of such calamitous management was brought to the attention of the British public by way of a civilian, William Howard Russell, who had travelled with the expeditionary force as a reporter for *The Times*. This in itself was unprecedented and lent the Crimean War the distinction of being the first conflict in which independent press members – writing from the scene of action – played a significant role in shaping wartime public opinion. Russell's letters, published in *The Times* as they were received, quickly painted a picture of the British Army leadership under Lord Raglan as a group of incompetent bumblers completely unable to give effective orders, to organise the delivery of essential military supplies, or to provide adequate food, clothing and hospital care for their men.[27] By contrast, Russell depicted common soldiers as sympathetic victims of this monumental incompetence, and championed their plight for the nation to see. He wrote of their lack of warm clothing, their lack of medical supplies, and the pain and suffering of sick and wounded soldiers who, he declared, 'have not a bed to lie upon'.[28] At the same time, Russell's reports of acts of valiant futility, in particular his powerful account of the charge of the Light Brigade, increased public esteem for the self-sacrifice and heroism of soldiers.

The plight of the suffering, brave British regulars made so poignant by Russell's letters also had a galvanising effect on the thirty-eight women, led by Florence Nightingale, who went out to the Crimea to nurse the soldiers of the British Army.[29] In turn, Nightingale's efforts at army hospital reform highlighted still further the appalling conditions faced by British soldiers and gave them a well-connected, upper-class champion. Public opinion, once so prone to vilify the sinful nature of drunken, thieving, whoring soldiers, now perceived them as sympathetic figures with 'a soul to be saved'.[30]

The Crimean campaign, in many ways, helped to determine the British public's response to the Indian Rebellion only a year later. Concern about the army, and in particular about the situation of enlisted soldiers, was already a hot topic in Britain. Soldiers had become human by their suffering, and yet were recognised for their acts of bravery and nobility even in the face of death.[31] First-hand accounts of the war by Russell and other correspondents had honed a taste for an intimate acquaintance with campaign conditions, obstacles and worthy deeds. Additionally, the catastrophic conduct of the campaign put far greater pressure on subsequent campaigns to make up for the blunders and embarrassments of the Crimea. The British military administration had been made painfully aware of the power of the press and of the political dangers of negative reporting. No more would public opinion be an irrelevant issue to the conduct of military campaigns.

When the Bengal Army rose in Rebellion against British rule in 1857, it was against these recent developments in public perceptions of the military that the conduct of the campaign would be measured. Yet in contrast to the Crimean campaign, soldiers in the Indian campaign were also seen as saviours of British women and children whose lives were in danger. Because of this, the psychological impact of the Rebellion propelled it – and images of heroic, noble soldiers – to unprecedented heights in British popular media. Moreover, the setting in which these soldiers performed their deeds of bravery was no longer a European one: now, the backdrop against which they battled was the exotic terrain of imperial India.

The Indian Army before 1857

By 1857, the British East India Company controlled more than 1.6 million square miles of territory on the subcontinent, including the newly annexed states of Sind (1843) and Punjab (1849). This vast area was controlled and protected by an equally vast military force, composed of three distinct armies centred around the presidencies of Madras, Bombay and Bengal. In 1856 its combined native troops alone numbered 280,000 men, making it the largest all-volunteer mercenary army in the world and a powerful strategic tool for British world dominance.[32] Yet just one year later its strongest military arm – the Bengal Army – looked as though it might also prove to be the downfall of British rule in India.

Although the East India Company had begun as a trading company in the seventeenth century, its transition to a territorial empire in the eighteenth century required that it place military concerns at the heart of its policy. Foremost among these concerns was to ensure the stability of Company rule through the suppression of internal unrest and the security of its borders and alliances. The very structure of Company rule reflected these concerns. Due initially to difficulties in transport and communication and later to a strategic desire to 'forestall dangerous pan-Indian combinations', each of the three centres of Company control at Madras,

Bombay and Calcutta maintained separate military establishments, commanders-in-chief and military staffs, as well as civil governments.[33] Loosely coordinating policy between the presidencies were the Governor-General in Council and the Commander-in-Chief (CIC) of the Indian Army (also CIC of the Bengal Army), both based in Bengal. Between them they controlled policy on war, diplomacy and revenue collection for the whole of India.

The combined forces of the Indian Army were composed of a multitude of peoples and traditions. Europeans served in each of the Company's three presidency armies, and British regulars served on a rotating basis as imperial garrison troops. In 1857 the total number of European forces in India was about 40,000, though Company and Crown troops were kept quite separate and regarded one another with mutual distaste.[34] Company troops generally came from a higher social stratum than Crown troops and could expect better pay – and sometimes better prospects – than their regular counterparts once in India. In matters of command, Company troops were subject to the Commander-in-Chief in their own district, whereas Crown troops were subject only to the orders of the Commander-in-Chief of India as a whole, regardless of the presidency in which they might be serving. Further, as garrison troops Crown forces served the greater needs of the British Empire as a whole, which meant that if their services were needed elsewhere they could be withdrawn and transferred to those areas of crisis. Significantly, at the start of the Rebellion, the conflicts which had recently occurred in the Crimea, Persia and the newly conquered Punjab had reduced the number of British battalions in all of India south of the Punjab to a mere nine.[35]

Small and divided as the European forces in India were, they were nevertheless regarded as a vital security against domination and revolt by the far larger indigenous mercenary volunteers that made up the bulk of the troops in the Indian Army. Some of these forces stood outside the command structure of the presidencies as irregular troops. Units like the Frontier Scouts were commanded independently by British officers. Others, such as the Punjab Irregular Force, were commanded directly by lieutenant governors and were answerable to the Government of India in the Foreign Department rather than the Commander-in-Chief in Bengal.[36] Still others came from the standing armies of the Princely States, nominally independent areas that received British agents at court and offered friendly military alliances in return for financial and political rewards.

Most native troops, however, served in the three presidency armies of Madras, Bombay and Bengal, of which by 1857 the Bengal Army was by far the largest.[37] Native volunteers were recruited in large numbers partly because of the vast span of British territory that needed protecting, partly because of the large resources of manpower various Indian populations offered, and partly because native soldiers were less expensive, better disciplined and healthier than their European counterparts.[38] Also unlike European troops, native troops of diverse areas were relatively easy to recruit into the Indian Army. This was true for several reasons. First, the British tended to recruit from populations, like the Rajputs of northern India, who came from long traditions of pre-colonial military service and who perceived military service as both a respectable and an honourable means of employment.[39] This focus on areas of traditional military service meant that only seldom did the British have to resort to direct recruitment, relying instead on family and village connections to supply fresh recruits. Second, unlike the British regular army the salaries offered by the Company were respectable and steady, although by 1857 pay had not kept pace with the cost of living and was decreasingly attractive.[40] Third, military service in the Company offered added benefits – in the form of special pay or land grants – for those willing to serve in foreign stations and for those with long service, good conduct, or conspicuous acts of bravery in battle.[41]

Although each presidency army had its advocates, by 1857 the Bengal Army was considered by many to be the showpiece of the Indian Army. Its officers made much of the character and physique of Bengal Army recruits, who were drawn increasingly from the higher Brahmin and Rajput castes of north-central India, in particular Awadh (Oudh) and Bihar. In contrast to the Madras and Bombay armies, whose officers relied on the service of a wide variety of castes and religions, Bengal officers excluded all of the lower castes, Christians and many Muslims in their recruiting efforts.[42] British officers also established a culture of tolerance for the religious requirements of such high-caste sepoys, allowing them wide berth for observing rituals and proscriptions, and militating against the undue use of corporal punishment.[43] By mid-century, concessions to rituals of caste had become excessive and helped reinforce Bengal sepoys' sense of superiority relative to other Indian troops.[44] Nevertheless, British officers hailed Bengal Army sepoys as models of high native character and discipline, and generally believed their colonial troops held them in mutual esteem.[45]

Even while most British officers saw few signs of trouble themselves, by mid-century the Bengal Army was riven with discontent. One problem was that real sepoy wages had decreased relative to the cost of living. More serious was the increasing lack of communication and understanding between British officers and native sepoys, which resulted from a number of mutually reinforcing causes. Native officers, who might have provided an essential connection between the two, commanded little authority with their men and were not given positions of trust with British officers. This was because promotion was based on seniority rather than merit, which meant that advancement to the highest class of native officer took many years and was normally conferred only on soldiers already advanced in age.[46] Talent and leadership abilities were thus weakly rewarded, with the result that high rank bore little relationship to the respect individual officers carried among their men.[47] Additionally, native officers were positioned within the regimental structure in such a way that their rank carried almost no authority with their British officers. The highest-ranking native officer could never outrank even the lowest-ranking British officer and the opinions of native officers were rarely sought by their British superiors. This left little incentive for native officers to communicate effectively about the rank and file, and frequently resulted in low morale.

To make matters worse, British officers regularly took long absences outside their regiments to pursue other, more gainful employment in civil staff appointments or with irregular regiments.[48] Thus many officers who were on the pay lists of Company regiments were seldom in residence long enough to come to know and identify with the men nominally under their command.[49] The combination of these long absences with impaired communication between native and British officers resulted in a loss of morale among the troops and a much stronger feeling of identification among the rank and file, who already came from similar social and religious backgrounds.[50]

Several other factors specific to the decades just prior to the Rebellion added fuel to the fire of the Bengal sepoys' discontent. First, there was the rapid expansion of British power in the subcontinent, signalled by the annexation of the Punjab in 1849 and the annexation of Awadh in 1856. The final conquest of the Punjab had discontented many soldiers in the Bengal Army, who had been receiving extra pay (*batta*) for serving in an area outside of Company control. Once the Punjab officially became part of the Company's territories in 1849 the *batta* ceased – causing grumbling irritation in the ranks. The annexation of Awadh, whence as we have seen many recruits hailed, further provoked the sepoys as well as their home communities. In 1856 the King of Awadh was summarily deposed, an action many in the province perceived as a deep humiliation.[51] In his place the Company placed a British Chief Commissioner who introduced new laws concerning the ownership of land, which dispossessed many of the influential *zamindars* and *taluqdars*[52] who traditionally were at the head of society. Moreover, the transfer of Awadh to Company rule also caused extreme hardship for the bulk of the population through serious over-assessments of property for tax purposes in many districts, through unemployment and dislocations caused by the removal of the King of Awadh's court, and through a rise in prices of essential commodities.[53]

Second, sepoys in the Bengal Army increasingly feared that the British meant to convert the population of India to Christianity. Christian missionary activity had in fact increased dramatically in the 1840s and 1850s following an 1834 Act that rescinded the East India Company's right to keep British subjects (and missionaries in particular) out of India. Although many missionaries believed they held only the best intentions for Indian peoples, they were often over-zealous and almost always publicly critical of Islam and Hinduism – including not a few Bengal Army officers.[54] Indeed, Christianising India was a vital element in the Liberal project to reform and uplift Indian society, begun in earnest with the governor-generalship of Lord William Bentinck in 1828.[55]

Yet both Hindus and Muslims often felt deep horror at British Christian evangelism. Rumours of British intent to resort to forced conversions circulated widely and seemed all the more believable in light of changes in landholding, law and customary rights so recently imposed. Mistrust of British intentions with regard to religion were particularly acute in the Bengal Army, where high-caste sepoys believed the religious tolerance traditionally allowed them by British officers was rapidly being reversed.[56] Especially despised was the 1856 General Service Enlistment Act. This Act, in contrast to previous legislation which allowed most recruits to enlist on terms of service within the subcontinent only, dictated that no recruit would henceforth be accepted to any of the presidency armies unless he was prepared to undertake overseas service when required.[57] For Hindus, and especially high-caste Hindus, overseas service was abhorrent because crossing the ocean would leave individuals in a ritually impure state, requiring expensive purification ceremonies or else becoming outcasts in their home communities. At the same time, refusal to enlist entailed the loss of a highly esteemed profession, a dilemma which many potential recruits angrily faced in 1856.[58] For all these reasons, then, it appeared to many Bengal Army sepoys – and especially those from the newly conquered area of Awadh – that the British were in fact bent on seizing power, destroying their traditions, and subverting their religion in order to convert them to Christianity.

The final straw came in late 1856 when it was rumoured that the cartridges for the new Enfield muzzle-loading rifles being issued to the East India Company Army were greased with the fat of pork and beef.[59] For Hindus, eating or touching beef to the lips meant a loss of caste, and for Muslims, the ingestion of pork was repugnant to the faith. Thus, it seemed to many that the British were deliberately and openly trying to make both Hindu and Muslim soldiers lose their religion, because army drill required that the soldier bite off one end of the cartridge before loading the rifles. Upon investigation, Company administrators discovered that tallow or lard had in fact been used to lubricate the cartridges, and it was suspected that animal fat from pigs or cows had been included in the mixture.[60] The mistake was inadvertent, but was an illustration of just how out of touch were the rulers from the ruled. The British military administration moved quickly to correct the blunder by allowing the cartridge to be torn with the hands and by allowing the men to grease their own cartridges with ghee, but in Bengal it was of little use.[61] Many regiments refused the cartridges, and when eighty-five men from the 3rd Native Cavalry in Mirath (Meerut) were publicly degraded and imprisoned for refusing orders to use them, the next day – 10 May 1857 – the whole regiment mutinied in protest and killed their British commanders.[62]

The mutiny in Mirath marked the beginning of a vicious struggle for control over northern India. The struggle itself was to have profound consequences for the ideology and structure of British rule on the subcontinent, for it increased racial bitterness between rulers and the ruled and ultimately led to a fundamental reconstruction of the Indian Army. Indeed, the rebellion or disbandment of nearly all of the seventy-four regiments of the Bengal Army compelled British officers to reconsider their high opinion of the high-caste recruits who made up the bulk of the army, and to cast them instead as depraved, fiendish men intent only on rape and destruction. In turn, men who had once been marginal to the Indian Army were increasingly perceived, as a result of their loyalty during the crisis, as the most honourable, worthy and superior sepoys on the subcontinent.

The Rebellion

In spite of the serious discontent that had been building among the sepoys of the Bengal Army, the Rebellion nevertheless came as a shock to most Britons in India, and none more so than the officers who commanded the regiments that rose *en masse* against them.[63] After the first local mutiny in Mirath, other disaffected regiments in the Bengal Army quickly followed suit. Meanwhile the 3rd Cavalry, gathering strength the whole way by the constant addition of other regiments who had mutinied against their British officers, marched to Delhi, which was easily taken. At the palace, the rebel force proclaimed the 83-year-old titular Mughul Emperor Bahadur Shah the leader of their cause. Delhi became the centre for the rebel operations, and as more and more regiments in the Bengal Army mutinied, rebel soldiers came in large numbers to reinforce those who had reached the capital of the old Mughal Empire first.[64]

Over the next few months, though contemporary British sources attempted to deny it, much of north-central India became lost to British control. In Awadh, as well as in other areas nearby in Uttar Pradesh, civil rebellions accompanied the military rebellion and changed its tenor to an all-out popular revolt which enveloped all classes of the population.[65] Moreover, through the spring and summer of 1857, the rebels continued to meet with success. On 30 May they laid siege to the British garrison at

Lucknao (Lucknow), residence of the new Commissioner of Awadh and home to nearly 200 British women and children. In late June, they forced the surrender of the small British garrison in nearby Kanpur (Cawnpore). Although the terms of surrender had promised the British population free passage to Allahabad, instead the 350 men of the garrison were murdered near the Ganges river, and the 125 women and children were imprisoned in the city. A little more than a week later, the women and children were also killed, their bodies thrown into a well.[66]

Long before the 'Cawnpore Massacre', as it came to be known, surprise and embarrassment at being unable to stop the rebels from achieving initial success led many British officers to participate in vicious acts of retribution against both sepoys and Indian civilians.[67] In turn, rebels treated their British captives with little mercy, thus fanning the flames of bitter hatreds that would last on both sides for decades. After the massacre at Kanpur, however, acts of brutality on the part of British soldiers were received with willing acceptance by the British public.

Events in the autumn of 1857 began to turn to the worse for the rebel forces. In Delhi, the small British and Indian force that had been besieging the rebel stronghold for months was finally reinforced by a moveable column from the Punjab. This force, which was hastily organised by John Lawrence, then Lieutenant-General of the Punjab, has generally been credited with the successful recapture of the city on 21 September 1857.[68]

At Lucknao too British-led forces began to meet with success after a summer of disappointments. A flying column under the command of Henry Havelock had arrived in Kanpur on 17 July, only two days after the massacre of British women and children. From there, Havelock intended to march directly to Lucknao to relieve the still-besieged garrison and to save the British captives there from a similar fate. His progress was made incomparably slower, however, by an outbreak of cholera among his troops and a lack of reinforcements. As a result, Havelock's band was not able to attempt the relief of Lucknao until September. Finally, on 25 September the column succeeded in forcing its way into the besieged Residency, only to find it was not strong enough actually to break the siege and relieve the captives. Havelock's force became, in effect, as much imprisoned by the siege as the people it had come to rescue.

This state of affairs required a second relief force to be assembled. On 17 November a force under the command of Sir Colin Campbell, Commander-in-Chief in India and former hero of the Crimean War, successfully broke the siege and evacuated the Residency after much hard fighting. The end of the siege did not signify the end of the fighting, as combat continued around Lucknao, Jhansi, Gwalior and Bareilly until the middle of 1858. However, by that time most Britons were fully confident of eventual victory.[69]

Military consequences of the Rebellion

The violent disruption of the Rebellion, and the bitterness with which it was fought on both sides, had effects in both Britain and India that went far beyond the cessation of hostilities. Politically and administratively, the Rebellion brought an end to the East India Company, as its powers and territories were officially transferred to the British Crown in 1859. Militarily, the Rebellion led to wide-ranging changes in the structure, composition and outlook of both the Indian and British armies. These changes brought the two institutions into a far more direct and dependent relationship than had existed in the past.

Though the British had emerged victorious in Bengal, the Indian Army there lay in ruins. All ten regiments of the Bengal Light Cavalry had mutinied, and nearly all of the Infantry had either mutinied or had been disbanded in anticipation of mutiny.[70] The sepoys of that army, who had so recently been praised for their physique, manner and gentlemanly behaviour, were now in disgrace.

The men who stood in their place at the end of 1859 were very different. During the crisis, large numbers of new recruits had hastily been raised to fight the rebellious sepoys. Of these, many were low-caste men from various areas in Hindustan. The majority, however, were from the newly annexed province of the Punjab, which was under the leadership of John Lawrence.[71] At the outbreak of the Rebellion, Lawrence had moved quickly to quell mutiny in the regiments of the Bengal Army stationed in the Punjab, and then, on his own initiative, began immediately raising local Punjabi troops to fight the rebels. As a result of this initiative, by the end of 1858 Lawrence had increased the number of Punjabis serving in the Indian Army from a mere 30,000 to a grand total of 75,000 men.[72] It was these troops who made up the bulk of the moveable column believed to be critical in breaking the siege at Delhi in September 1857.

Historical accident and the need to construct a loyal army in the midst of an emergency had thus left the British administration with a very different army at the end of 1858 than the one that had existed at the start of 1857. Moreover, it was clear to most contemporaries that there was no going back to the old structure of the 1857 army. Less clear was the problem of how the army should be structured in the future now that the immediate crisis had passed. How could a new army be recruited and organised to prevent future discontent from igniting into mass rebellion like, as one contemporary put it, 'the seared and yellow leaves before the blast'?[73]

In the end, a mixture of pragmatism, experience and influence prevailed. Though the crisis had indeed passed, the internal defence demands of India required a combat-ready force, and the government could hardly afford to demobilise the loyal forces of the existing army in 1858 and then remobilise with hand-picked troops. As a result, the army that had been 'raised in haste' to fight the rebels, composed of the few loyal regiments of the Bengal Army and the new low-caste and Punjabi regiments, became the logical and practical base upon which the new force was built.[74]

The recommendations of the Peel Commission, a special parliamentary committee charged with reviewing the state of the Indian Army in 1858, helped determine the size of the new Indian Army.[75] After hearing testimony from a number of British officers who decried the small size of the European forces in India, the commissioners recommended a 1:2 ratio of British to Indian soldiers in Bengal.[76] To accomplish this, the British garrison in India had to be doubled to 80,000 troops, and the Bengal Army had to be reduced by 65,000 men to reach an acceptable size of 110,000 troops. Once the necessary reductions had taken place, the Bengal Army emerged as a new force. Only eighteen regiments of the old Bengal Army remained, while fourteen new regiments consisted of recruits raised in the Punjab during the Rebellion. Seven regiments of low-caste recruits were retained, as were four local regiments. A total of fifteen Gurkha, Sikh and Punjab regiments, numbered each in their own sequences, were also retained.[77]

The Peel Commission did not make many specific recommendations about how the future Indian Army should be recruited, but its report did recommend recruiting from as many different Indian nationalities as possible.[78] Officers' testimony had produced an overwhelming consensus that the old Bengal Army had relied far too heavily on high-caste Brahmins from Awadh and Bihar to fill its ranks. Many interviewees argued that British officers had pandered to every 'superstition' and ritual claimed by high-born sepoys, and that such favouritism had encouraged insolence and intransigence within the Bengal Army. As one officer put it, the Indian Army must be restructured so that 'none of the old leaven should be left to impregnate the new mass'.[79]

As a remedy to the favouritism and exclusionary recruiting practices of the old Bengal Army, the Peel Commission opined that 'the Indian Army should be composed of different nationalities mixed up in the regiments', and that all sepoys should be henceforth enlisted for general service.[80] Yet while this 'general mixture' system was implemented in about half of the Bengal Army regiments during the 1860s, it came up against a conflicting policy advocated by another report – that of the enormously influential Punjab Committee.[81] As the Adjutant-General in India was later to comment, the recommendations of the Punjab Committee – headed by Sir John Lawrence – 'became the oracle of more than one generation of Army reformers'.[82]

Because of Lawrence's recognised services for securing the Punjab, for providing new recruits for the embattled Bengal Army, and for providing the means to retake Delhi, in the aftermath of the Rebellion there was a great deal of gratitude and deference for the opinions and recommendations of his Committee's report on the future of the army. For Lawrence, the most important maxim for the British to remember in India was the concept of 'divide and rule'. Although he himself had raised thousands of troops from the Punjab during the Rebellion, he cautioned that the restructured army in India should avoid reliance on any one group of people or province for recruiting, for the dangers of such a practice had been revealed in the recent conflict.[83]

At the same time, Lawrence's Committee alleged that men from too many different areas of India had been allowed to serve together in the same regiments prior to the Rebellion. Drawn closer to one another through common religious interests, these sepoys had also discovered their similar situation as colonised subjects of the British. These bonds had, in turn, outweighed other differences resulting from background and culture, with intrigue and rebellion as the result. To prevent this situation from occurring in the future, the Committee believed that separation of the various 'races' within the army was vital. The maintenance of three separate armies in Madras, Bombay and Bengal was an important factor in keeping Indians apart (as the near absence of rebellion in Madras and Bombay had clearly demonstrated), but it was not enough.

Now, especially within the Bengal Army, the army needed to widen its recruiting base to include as many different 'races' and religions as possible in order that they might serve as checks on one another. Low castes, Muslims, Sikhs, Christians – all should be recruited into the army to replace the high-caste Brahmins who had dominated it. But rather than mix them all together as the Peel Commission had advocated, the Punjab Committee recommended they be recruited and stationed locally, each 'race' or religion kept in separate companies within regiments. That way, differences between groups could be played up to encourage 'the Muhomedan of one county [to] despise, fear, or dislike the Muhomedan of another'.[84]

These recommendations did not, clearly, advocate a policy of 'martial race' recruiting. Rather, it was intended to be the very opposite – a strategy to *widen* the recruiting base rather than narrow it. Yet the Punjab Committee's recommendations had, without intending it, provided the foundations for what would later become 'martial race' policy. Indeed, the 'divide and rule' policy so passionately laid out by the Punjab Committee powerfully articulated the idea that underscoring ethnic and local differences – and then institutionalising them in the structure of the army – could actually enhance British control over the army and hence over the subcontinent as a whole.

At the same time, even as the Punjab Committee published its report, the inclusiveness of its recruiting strategy clashed with the language and values of many military commanders who had just experienced mass rebellion in the army. The events of the Rebellion had seemed to prove that some native groups were 'naturally' more loyal to the Raj than others. As a result of emergency recruiting, as we have already seen, the post-1858 Bengal Army was already radically different from the army that existed in 1857, and its geographical base was already weighted towards the Punjab. Those Indian men who had remained loyal during the Rebellion – many of whom hailed from that region – became, in spite of official warnings, favoured populations whose loyalty was increasingly perceived as having proven both their military worth and their superiority over other native groups. The combination between this favouritism and the institutionalisation of racial difference within the army provided the foundation for a way of thinking about race and military service that would eventually stand the Punjab Committee's report on its head. Instead of widening the recruiting base, the powerful memory of the Rebellion convinced many British officers that the only men worthy to bear arms in India were those who had proven their manliness and martial ability by fighting alongside their British masters in that time of crisis.

The changes brought about by the Rebellion were no less dramatic in the British Army. To combat the rebel forces, the British government had been forced to raise twenty-five new battalions of infantry, which seriously overstretched the resources and manpower of the British Army. The strength of the army had risen from 116,434 in 1846 to a startling 217,922 by 1861, nearly the size of British forces at the close of the Napoleonic Wars in 1815.[85] Although these measures had initially been regarded as temporary, it soon became clear that a much larger force would be required on a permanent basis. The Peel Commission, as we have already seen, recommended in 1859 the size of the British forces there be doubled from 40,000 to 80,000. Combined with a reduction in strength of the Bengal Army, these numbers would achieve the 'safe' ratio of one British soldier to every two sepoys in Bengal. They agreed that henceforth the primary responsibility of the British Army would be to provide a large and effective garrison for the subcontinent, a recommendation that would require a large annual increase of recruits for the regular army.[86]

Much more fractious was the fate of the European troops of the former East India Company. When the Government of India Act abolished the East India Company and transferred its powers to the Crown in 1858, it was unclear what was to be done about that portion of the Indian Army. Some favoured their amalgamation into the line of the regular British Army; others, including such notables as Sir John Lawrence, bitterly opposed such a move.[87] The Peel Commission itself could not agree. In the end, the British government allowed former Company troops to take their discharges if they so desired: two-thirds of the 15,000 men did so and left the Indian Army without a European contingent to speak of.[88]

Now, the British Army would be solely responsible for providing the European garrison of India, and hence 'this new obligation ... became the chief feature in its life'.[89] Since the recommendations of the Peel Commission called for a permanent European force of 80,000, the British Army was forced to retain the twenty-five new battalions of infantry raised in response to the crisis.[90] This massively expanded new force, in turn, presented serious problems for an unpopular army already riddled with difficulties attracting sufficient recruits. In 1867 a contributor to *Blackwood's Magazine* was still reeling, and announced: 'we find that the overthrow of the intermediate government by the East India Company, and the amalgamation of the Indian with the English army, have thrown upon the country a burden in every respect heavier than could have been contemplated when the change of system took place'.[91]

For the first time, the British Army faced a permanent need to make military service more palatable to a wider range of recruits than ever before. No more could men be tricked into enlisting to serve the needs of a national emergency, argued a confidential memo on recruiting in 1859:

> It must be remembered that, if our army is to be kept at its present strength, we shall require, even in peace time, an annual supply of recruits amounting to 30,000 men, a supply which few believe that our existing machinery will permanently maintain. There are but two possible modes of obtaining a good and sufficient army, and of keeping it permanently on foot. One is the method of conscription, the other the method of making the army a desirable profession for rational men.[92]

Since the memorandum argued that conscription was not a feasible plan, it insisted on the necessity of offering a fair market price for recruits,[93] reducing the length of enlistment, abolishing the bounty system, and creating an organised reserve. These issues, far from being brushed aside, became some of the fundamental points of discussion for the reform of the British Army over the next decades.

The Rebellion as public spectacle

Two factors ensured that the events of the Rebellion, and the institutional changes precipitated by it, were followed with intense interest by the British reading public. First was the explosion of the British media, which coincided neatly with the timing of the Rebellion.[94] This unprecedented expansion allowed, for the first time, the events of an imperial conflict to reach a truly 'mass' audience in Britain. Second was the spectacle of the massacre of British women and children at Kanpur on 15 July 1857, and the threat of a second massacre at the still-besieged garrison at Lucknao. These events, involving as they did the fate of 'innocent' British women and children, provided 'proof' of the racial depravity of mutinous sepoys as well as justification for vengeance on a scale that might otherwise have provoked moral outrage in Britain. Moreover, rapt public attention on Kanpur and Lucknao resulted in intense focus on the role of the military in defending India and on those troops most vital in securing that defence.

What might have been a colonial side-show became an event of national importance as a result of substantial innovations within the marketing and distribution of the print media.[95] Chief among these was the rapid fall in the cost of individual newspapers due to the repeal of the 'taxes on knowledge' during the 1850s. Previously, the cost per copy of licensed newspapers had been high due to an array of taxes levied on newspaper production. In the early 1830s, rates of taxation were 3d for paper duty per pound, 3s 6d for individual advertisements, and 4d for the stamp tax per sheet of newsprint. As a result, licensed newspapers tended to have small circulations. Furthermore, the number of newspapers was small, and only in London were dailies profitably printed. *The Times*, the London newspaper with the widest circulation in Britain, sold for a very dear 7d per copy, far more than most working people could afford to pay.[96]

In 1853, however, the government repealed the advertisement tax, and followed in 1855 by repealing the stamp tax. The result was a dramatic fall in the price of individual newspapers and a sharp increase in circulations, especially in the provinces.[97] Penny daily papers were now economically viable, and weekly Sunday papers priced to fit the salaries of the working class became massively popular all over Britain.[98] Within little more than a decade the average daily readership of provincial dailies far exceeded the metropolitan dailies.[99] By the late 1850s, in addition to the growing daily and weekly metropolitan and provincial press, the three best-selling national weeklies – *News of the World*, *Reynolds's Newspaper* and *Lloyd's Weekly Newspaper* – each claimed sales of 150,000 per week.[100] And, because of the hardy composition of newsprint, actual readership of papers was far in excess of circulation figures.[101]

Technological innovations such as the telegraph and the development of rail linkages between London and the provinces further enhanced both the range of news available to the British reading public and the speed at which it could be obtained. By 1841, transportation of news from India to Britain had been reduced to a mere month in comparison to the two months required in 1836. In 1847, this system was complemented by telegraphic messages that were used to summarise the main news events before the arrival of the more detailed monthly mails.[102]

As a result of the repeal of the taxes on knowledge and such technological innovations, by the mid-1850s news of the Empire travelled faster from its sources to a greater range of British locations, and far more people than ever before were able to have access to it. Instead of radicalising the popular press, however, the upshot of such changes was that the concerns of the 'respectable' metropolitan papers were extended to classes and regions previously cut off from such concerns.[103] Indeed, until the 1870s even provincial papers geared towards the working classes looked to the metropolitan papers on many issues of foreign and public policy, and frequently echoed metropolitan views.[104] This dependence was accented by the fact that only the London papers like *The Times* could maintain British correspondents in posts all over Europe and the Empire, and could pay for their expensive telegraphic messages that brought breaking news to Britain so quickly.[105] Correspondents' reports, widely reprinted in the provincial press, lent foreign news a new authority, immediacy and decidedly British flair. Moreover, due to the novelty of such foreign reporting, news from afar was eagerly consumed by an often amazed British public and was given a truth-status far in excess of that which exists today.[106]

When the Rebellion broke out in the spring of 1857, the British reading public therefore had far greater access to recent news from India and the Empire than ever before. Yet it was the massacre of British women and children at Kanpur in July that ensured the Rebellion would become an event of intense national concern. After the murders, competing narratives about the causes or conduct of the campaign were silenced; in their place was a narrative that depicted British responses to the Rebellion as a righteous crusade of moral vengeance. The desire to vindicate British womanhood thus transformed the Rebellion – both in the press and in military accounts – into a heroic struggle for manhood. Gendered ideals of honour and dishonour, manliness and cowardliness, came to define the core of the conflict. And with the horror that accompanied tales of the massacre of 'innocents' came also a new perspective on military actions in India. Public sentiment suddenly viewed British and Indian military forces fighting the rebel sepoys as chivalric defenders of white womanhood – epic heroes whose efforts now commanded intense interest and admiration from metropolitan readers.

The Kanpur massacre was thus a critical juncture from which both army commanders and soldiers emerged as objects of improved public esteem. Without Kanpur, it is not clear whether the Rebellion would have received popular support in Britain. Indeed, were it not for Kanpur the British conduct of the war might have brought down public attacks far more damaging even than the attacks on army administration during the Crimean War. As it was, the gendered dimensions of the murders at Kanpur obscured criticisms of the causes of the campaign, and marginalised the brutal conduct of British forces in India.

Initially, neither the press nor the public was inclined to view the Rebellion through rose-coloured glasses.[107] This hardly seems surprising given the recent débâcle of the Crimean War, for British newspapers had become accustomed to using their pages as influential forums for criticising the British military high command. From this post-Crimean perspective, Indian Army commanders seemed to share remarkable similarities with their brethren in the British Army, and were widely depicted as corrupt, decadent and ineffective. The Conservative opposition party took an early lead in placing the blame for the Rebellion with the Indian government and military. In July 1857 Benjamin Disraeli openly attacked the East India Company's official position of surprised shock. To hear that version of the Rebellion, all had been well in the Bengal Army until the introduction of the greased cartridges for the new Enfield rifles had caused rumours that the lubricant was fabricated from the fat of pigs and cows. Disraeli, and others in his party, met such an explanation with scorn. In an address to the House of Commons he declared: 'The decline and fall of empires are not affairs of greased cartridges. Such results are occasioned by adequate causes, and by an accumulation of adequate causes.'[108]

British public opinion seemed to concur. Many people agreed that the East India Company had made its bed and was now lying in it. Company officers were blamed for excessive conversion efforts among their Hindu and Muslim sepoys as 'one cause of the outbreak'.[109] *Blackwood's Magazine*, a respected journal with clear connections to an imperially minded audience, suggested in addition that 'our leaders were unequal to their duty' in the crisis.[110] So great was the general contempt for the perceived blunders of the East India Company that the Anglo-Indian *Delhi Gazette Extra* was forced to concede: 'The British public remain utterly impassive and indifferent, and become impatient when the subject is broached in conversation. They have made up their mind that it was entirely owing to the insolence and incompetency of the Regimental Officers, and seem rather glad that they have suffered for their supposed dereliction of duty.'[111]

Other newspapers viewed the Rebellion as a national embarrassment, as well as a most potent threat to the British government. On 4 July 1857 the *Illustrated London News* anxiously cried: 'our house in India is on fire. We are not insured. To lose that house would be to lose power, prestige, and character – to descend in the rank of nations, and take a position more in accordance with our size on the map of Europe than with the greatness of our past glory and present ambition.'[112] Similarly, *Reynolds's Newspaper* declared: 'Strip us of our Indian Empire, and we at once sink to the level of second-rate Powers'.[113] The blame clearly lay, in their view, with the 'fierce, powerful, and terrible' oppression of the British East India Company.[114] Similar criticisms also appeared even in *The Times*, and then were widely reprinted in a variety of local and provincial papers.[115]

It is possible, if the murders at Kanpur had not focused public attention on vengeance, that these early criticisms might have spurred serious and sustained public censure about the conduct of the war being waged against Indian subjects in north-central India. For it was true that British-led forces during the Rebellion were often characterised by bumbling leadership, lack of organisation and inadequate provision. British soldiers were given to excessive drinking and frequently lacked discipline, and engaged in plunder and looting all along their marching routes.[116] Perhaps most importantly, the British response to the Rebellion was marked by vicious acts of brutality against Indian soldiers and civilians that long pre-dated the murders at Kanpur, and have even now yet to be fully measured in terms of loss of human life and property.

Once it was clear that the Rebellion might induce any number of Bengal Army regiments to mutiny, many British officers lost no time making examples of the mutineers through execution.[117] Punishment was sometimes general, involving the slaughter of whole, or nearly whole, regiments. This was the fate of the 51st and 26th regiments, who both fell victim to the 'unceasing vigilance' of John Lawrence in his proactive efforts to stem the Rebellion in the Punjab.[118] Of the 26th, Lawrence noted in August 1857 that 'we have killed and drowned 500 out of the 600 men of the ... regiment'.[119]

In addition to military executions, the British also exacted severe reprisals on civilian populations in north-central India. The notorious actions of Colonel James Neill, called to Bengal from the Madras Army to help suppress the Rebellion, bear directly on the events surrounding the Kanpur massacre. After arriving in Allahabad on 11 June 1857, Neill was responsible for thousands of murders both of sepoys and suspected rebels as well as innocent men, women and children. Describing the actions of Neill's troops around Allahabad, one officer wrote:

> Every native that appeared in sight was shot down without question, and in the morning Colonel Neill sent out parties of regiment [?] ... and burned all the villages near where the ruins of our bungalows stood, and hung every native that they could catch, on the trees that lined the road. Another party of soldiers penetrated into the native city and set fire to it, whilst volley after volley of grape and canister was poured into the fugitives as they fled from their burning houses.[120]

On 29 June 1857 Neill ordered 'the village of Mullagu and neighbourhood to be attacked and destroyed – slaughter all the men – take no prisoners'. He added, 'all insurgents that fall into good hands hang at once – and shoot all you can'.[121]

Significantly, Neill's 'bloody assizes' around Allahabad (as they came to be known) occurred before, not after, the massacre of British women and children at Kanpur on 15 July. As a result, some scholars have speculated that the Kanpur murders were ordered in retaliation for the Indian civilians whose murders Neill personally supervised.[122] Whether or not such a contention can be proven, it is nevertheless clear that Neill's brutality could not have been justified by the Kanpur massacre as was so often contended, for his own excesses preceded the event.[123]

Yet while British atrocities preceded the massacre at Kanpur, once news of the Kanpur killings spread they were used to justify retaliatory murders and punishments on an astonishing scale. Neill himself, who was with the first British force to enter the city two days after the massacre, invented macabre executions for both Hindu and Muslim sepoys that were designed to ensure both intense suffering before death and eternal damnation afterwards.[124]

British soldiers sent to India offered ample testimony to the scale of British retaliation against both military and civilian targets. Sergeant David McAusland of the 42nd Highland Regiment recalled that during his service in Bareilly during the Rebellion, 'three scaffolds and six whipping posts stood outside of the town along side of the jail and there executions to the number of six every day'. The judge in charge of trials had lost his wife during the conflict, and had told McAusland: 'if ever I get the chance of these Black rebels I will hang a man for every hair that was in my wifes head'. McAusland responded by asking him how many men he had executed already: 'he told me close on 700 well I said if you just continue you will have made good your work and turning to Sergt ... Aden I said you mind what Sir Colin [Campbell] said to us at Cawnpore that every man that had a black face was our enemy and we could not do wrong in shooting him so you know how to act here'.[125]

Private Alexander Robb, also of the 42nd, described the first summary hanging of an Indian civilian he witnessed during the Rebellion, adding, 'that was the first man I saw dancing on nothing in India, but it was not the last, for I saw some awful sights in that line'.[126] Lieutenant Robert Bruce McEwen of the 92nd Gordon Highlanders recorded, on numerous days, routinely shooting large numbers of prisoners and taking part in actions where between 500 and 700 rebels were killed.[127] And when British forces finally attacked and re-took the city of Delhi in September 1857, they were merciless in their treatment of soldiers and civilians alike.[128]

Although British forces easily matched and exceeded rebel brutalities during the campaign, such acts of violence were either glossed over or ignored completely in British narratives about the Rebellion. Military officers, especially in light of early criticisms about their role in fomenting the Rebellion, were eager to depict the enemy as barbarous fiends while praising their own forces for heroic and honourable conduct. Since the first war correspondent did not arrive in India until January 1858, military letters and despatches describing the campaign did much to obscure the savagery of British behaviour in India.[129] Still, when news of the Kanpur massacre began to filter into Britain by the late summer of 1857, the mood of the British public shifted abruptly away from its previous critical mode. In the wake of the murders, the Rebellion metamorphosed from a military conflict on the imperial periphery to a popular national struggle in which even ordinary Britons felt invested. The spectre of British women and children being murdered by colonial men provided a catalyst by which military and public interests decisively merged – and they did so in a way that made ideologies of gender and race both inseparable and central to the British 'cause' in India. Shortly after receiving news of the massacre, *The Times* claimed:

> Terrible as is the character of regular warfare, its horrors are as nothing when compared to the shocks which Englishmen in India have sustained ... It is rarely that a soldier has to contemplate the sufferings of those whose life is more precious than his own. In India these conditions of action were all reversed ... At a moment's notice they were called upon to defend, not only themselves, but their wives and children, against the ferocious attacks, not of a legitimate enemy, but of the very troops under their own command.[130]

Like the thousands of letters, editorials, news articles, poems and novels that appeared about Kanpur, *The Times* made it clear that the murder of British women and children set the Rebellion apart from other conflicts, that 'normal' conditions of war did not exist in India, and that the rebels themselves – as well as their grievances – were illegitimate. After Kanpur, when the fate of British women and children became an issue of paramount concern to Britons at home, the tremendous complexity of events in and around north-central India during the Rebellion became lost to a narrative about vengeance, (white) female purity, British masculine honour and rebel dishonour.[131]

Coverage of the event was widespread and sensational in national, provincial and local papers all over Britain. *The Times* alone carried 108 stories on the massacre between 15 August 1857 and 3 February 1860. All of the largest national newspapers, regardless of political affiliation, featured intensive coverage of the murders – including *Reynolds's*, *Lloyd's* and *News of the World*. Provincial papers such as the *Newcastle Chronicle* echoed the national papers in their outlook, as did even small, working-class, local papers.[132] The latter reprinted leading articles by the larger nationals, and added their own editorials and relevant commentary. Such coverage fostered feelings of connection among Britons even of remote provinces, as the *Aberdeen Free Press and Buchan News* noted when it claimed: 'The calamity is national. We feel the sufferers to be of ourselves. They are our brethren, our sisters, our children, who have been involved in these indescribable horrors.'[133] In addition to selling newspapers, these 'horrors' also inspired unprecedented local action, by prompting packed meetings to pledge money for the victims of the Rebellion.[134]

The depth of public reaction to the murders was due to the lurid nature of the published accounts, and the intersection of such accounts with accepted structures of mid-Victorian fiction, gender ideals and ideologies of British racial superiority. Though papers frequently argued that the 'vile tortures' practised upon British women and children should 'be remembered, not told', all of them did in fact frequently allude to rape and torture, and often in some detail.[135] Letters and telegraphs flooded the papers with accounts of women being raped in front of their children before being killed, of matted blood, of gory remains of children's limbs and of the suffocation of living children among their dead mothers when the victims were thrown into a well.[136] The tragedy of such a spectacle resonated deeply with an audience long accustomed to the narrative structures of Victorian melodrama. Stories of wronged and dishonoured women, just retribution and heroic conclusions were staples of a genre that took as its central focus the struggle between right and wrong, good and evil.[137] Within this narrative framework, the murdered women and children of Kanpur were easily recognisable as representatives of saintly virtue and their murderers as the epitome of evil.

Mid-Victorian ideals of gender, largely shaped by the increasingly dominant middle class, also influenced British responses to the massacre.[138] With the growing separation of 'home' and 'work' that characterised middle-class life-styles, virtuous womanhood came to be ever more strongly associated with the home, while respectable manhood was defined by the ability to inhabit and dominate the aggressive, competitive public sphere. Within their 'sphere' of domesticity, women were increasingly imagined as desexualised, passive, pure and innocent. Their happiness derived from their roles as wives and mothers; their satisfaction from excelling as 'keepers of the Hearth'.[139] Hence, Victorian middle-class ideals of gender and sex imagined women as the repositories of virtue – self-sacrifice, maternal instinct and morality.[140] The world of politics, war and conflict was imagined as wholly removed from these saintly, moral beings. By contrast, middle-class masculinity was ideally defined by a man's ability to provide for the material well-being of his family by working in the public sphere and by his ability to protect his family from physical harm and public shame. Although middle-class masculinity represented men as essentially sexualised, their status depended upon controlling that sexuality to protect the honour of women, and re-channelling its energy into the world of work and sport.[141] Of course, such ideological associations were always under construction and often did not reflect the complex realities of everyday life. At the same time, they offered an important structural framework within which to interpret contemporary events like the Kanpur massacre. As such, the murders were widely understood as violations – both of women's innocence and of masculine codes of honour and duty.

Thus, in the narratives of the Rebellion produced in the aftermath of Kanpur, the murdered women became tragic heroines, victims of the worst dishonour for any British woman – rape at the hands of dark, unchristian, colonial men. Imagined alone, defenceless and at the mercy of strangers unschooled in the rules of chivalry, their shrieks of pain were said to 'sound loudly in the air / Their groans – alas not heard', while their pleas for mercy were said to fall on cruelly deaf ears.[142] In the context of mid-Victorian gender ideologies, these accounts were particularly incendiary since by their very nature and sex the women at Kanpur – like the children – were perceived as being completely removed from the quarrels between British men and rebel sepoys.

Such graphic tales of rape and murder inflamed public sentiments calling for vengeance on a massive scale.[143] The *Illustrated London News* voiced its indignation in tandem with most other national, provincial and local papers when it claimed that 'every British heart, from the highest to the humblest of the land, glows with honest wrath and demands justice, prompt and unsparing, on the bloodyminded instruments of the Rebellion'.[144] Leading national and provincial papers went so far as to advocate the 'extermination' of Muslim and Hindu rebels.[145] In India, the *Delhi Gazette* also proclaimed that 'the paramount duty of the British Government is now retribution – a duty to the dead and living'.[146]

This vengeance was imagined against perpetrators who had come to represent a potent mixture of masculine, racial and religious depravity. Sepoys were represented in the press not as men, but as 'demons' and 'fiends', led by their 'passions' to 'faithlessness, rebellion, and crimes at which the heart sickens'.[147] Their apparent thirst for innocent blood – and their reported lust for forbidden women – had unmanned them and placed them outside the boundaries of masculine honour. Moreover, their decision to operate outside these rules of conduct absolved the British from addressing their grievances or from showing them mercy. A poem in the Anglo-Indian *Delhi Gazzette* put it plainly when it cried: 'No mercy's shown to men whose hands / With women's blood yet reek!'[148]

That rebel sepoys would commit such unspeakable crimes against women was attributed both to racial characteristics and to religion. In India, the conflict had hardened racial hatreds among British officers long before Kanpur. Correspondence reveals widespread use of the word 'nigger' and other racially antagonistic language when referring to Indians, and officers writing home frequently echoed the contention that '[t]he race of men in India are certainly the most abominable, degraded lot of brutes that you can imagine, they don't seem to have a single good quality'.[149] In the British and Anglo-Indian media, such racialisation received almost unqualified sanction in the wake of Kanpur. Despite the fact that a majority of high-caste Bengal Army sepoys were traditionally recruited for their tall physiques and light skin, British sources depicted 'gangs of black satyrs' raping and dismembering British women, and called rebel Indians 'that venom race', 'in heart as black as face'.[150]

These 'black' villains were also depraved because of their religion, whether Hindu or Muslim, for in both cases religion was presumed to have encouraged the rape and murder of British women. Rumours circulated that some of the women at Kanpur were raped, kidnapped and forced to convert to Islam.[151] High-caste Brahmins were said to be slaves to the requirements of caste, which supposedly included debased notions of masculine honour. Shortly after Kanpur, the *Delhi Gazette* bellowed:

> We shall never again occupy a high ground in India until we have put a yoke upon the Brahmins. We have conceded too much to the insolence of caste. Not one high caste man should henceforward be entrusted with a sword … He has been trusted with power, and how has he betrayed it? The graves of 100 English women and children – worse, the unburied bones of those poor victims – are the monuments of high bred sepoy chivalry.[152]

By their crimes at Kanpur, then, both Hindu and Muslim sepoys had given up all claims to manliness, to honour, to bravery and to chivalry. Moreover, both their 'race' and their religion were increasingly called upon to explain the loss of those claims.

British calls for retribution for the murders at Kanpur were framed in the language of masculine honour, as a struggle to punish cowardly scoundrels for violating British women, and as a mission to rescue those women still at risk in India. This language became the *a priori* legitimation for acts of vengeance, excused by the idea that the rape and murder of British women had driven British men to demonstrate the full force of their wrath. It also masked masculine anxieties provoked by the knowledge, as Graham Dawson has noted, that British men had been unable to protect their women at Kanpur from the 'perversities' and blood-lust of Indian male sexuality gone wild.[153] Finally, the language of masculine honour required masculine avengers, who would translate the desire for vengeance into palpable reality. This state of affairs virtually ensured that those who took up this mission would be intensely followed and widely celebrated in the British press. Given the nature of the conflict, it is not surprising that nearly all of them were soldiers. For their role in punishing the perpetrators of Kanpur and for fighting to protect British women still in danger, these men became popular heroes of massive proportions, and icons of the best traditions of British chivalry.[154]

As a result of the Rebellion, the armies of Britain and India were brought into new relationships both with each other and with the British reading public. The British Army had been enlarged and restructured to provide a large, permanent garrison on the Indian subcontinent. The Indian Army had been reduced and fundamentally reconstituted. But the enormous publicity of the Rebellion, due both to the timing of an expanding press network and to the resonance of the Kanpur massacre, brought both armies to the attention of a mass British audience. In so doing, the Rebellion inspired new awareness and interest in India and its peoples, and transformed British public opinion about the military in general, and ordinary soldiers in particular.

Notes

1   Field Marshal Lord Roberts, *Forty-One Years in India: From Subaltern to Commander-in-Chief* (London: Macmillian & Co., 1921 [first published 1897]), 181.

2   Edward Spiers, *The Army and Society, 1815–1914* (London: Longman, 1980), ch. 5, 'The Indian Mutiny'; Graham Dawson, *Soldier Heroes: British Adventure, Empire and the Imagining of Masculinities* (London: Routledge, 1994), ch. 4, especially 80–94; Francis Hutchins, *The Illusion of Permanence: British Imperialism in India* (Princeton: Princeton University Press, 1967), 83–86; Patrick Brantlinger, *Rule of Darkness: British Literature and Imperialism, 1830–1914* (Ithaca: Cornell University Press, 1988), 199–200.

3   For a late nineteenth-century perspective, see W. H. Goodenough and J. C. Dalton, *The Army Book for the British Empire: A Record of the Development and Present Composition of the Military Forces and Their Duties in Peace and War* (London: Harrison & Sons, 1893), 29–42. For a more recent scholarly perspective see T. A. Heathcote, *The Military in British India: The Development of British Land Forces in South Asia, 1600–1947* (Manchester: Manchester University Press, 1995), 118.

4   House of Commons, 'Reports from commissioners: organisation of Army (Indian)', *Sessional Papers* 1859, session 1, vol. V, [cd 2516], x (hereafter Peel Commission). For the process by which this came about, see Peter Stanley, *White Mutiny: British Military Culture in India* (New York: New York University Press, 1998), esp. chs 6 and 7.

5   David Omissi, *The Sepoy and the Raj: The Indian Army, 1860–1940* (London: Macmillan, 1994), 9; Heathcote, *The Military in British India*, 114–124.

6   Dawson, *Soldier Heroes*, 84–86.

7   Dawson, *Soldier Heroes*, 81; Brantlinger, *Rule of Darkness*, 202–204.

8   Jenny Sharpe, 'The unspeakable limits of rape: colonial violence and counter-insurgency', *Genders* 10 (Spring 1991); Brantlinger, *Rule of Darkness*, ch. 7; Saul David, *The Indian Mutiny* (London: Penguin, 2002), ch. 15.

9   For the long-term consequences of Cromwell's regime on British attitudes towards standing armies, see David Smith, 'The struggle for new constitutional and institutional forms', in John Morrill (ed.), *Revolution and Restoration: England in the 1650s* (London: Collins & Brown, 1992), 33.

10   Linda Colley demonstrates such enthusiasm in *Britons: Forging the Nation, 1707–1837* (New Haven: Yale University Press, 1992).

11   For commemorative imperial art in the eighteenth century, see Barbara Gloseclose, 'Death, glory, empire: art', and for representations of Tipu Sultan see Constance McPhee, 'Tipu Sultan of Mysore and British medievalism in the paintings of Mather Brown', both in Dianne Sachko MacLeod and Julie Codell (eds), *Orientalism Transposed: The Impact of the Colonies on British Culture* (Aldershot: Ashgate, 1998). On Cornwallis, see Peter Marshall, '"Cornwallis triumphant": war in India and the British public in the late eighteenth century', in Lawrence Freedman, Paul Hayes and Robert O'Neill (eds), *War, Strategy, and International Politics: Essays in Honour of Sir Michael Howard* (Oxford: Clarendon, 1992).

12   J. W. M. Hichberger, *Images of the Army: The Military in British Art, 1815–1914* (Man-

chester: Manchester University Press, 1988), ch. 4.

13   Scott Hughes Myerly, *British Military Spectacle: From the Napoleonic Wars through the Crimea* (Cambridge, Mass.: Harvard University Press, 1996), 3; Alan Ramsay Skelley, *The Victorian Army at Home: The Recruitment and Terms and Conditions of the British Regular, 1859–1899* (London: Croom Helm, 1977), 243–247.

14   Scott Hughes Myerly, '"The eye must entrap the mind": army spectacle and paradigm in nineteenth-century Britain', *Journal of Social History* 26:1 (Autumn 1992), 106; Skelley, *The Victorian Army at Home*, 244.

15   Peter Burroughs, 'An unreformed army? 1815–1868', in David Chandler and Ian Beckett (eds), *The Oxford Illustrated History of the British Army* (Oxford: Oxford University Press, 1994), 172–173; Myerly, *British Military Spectacle*, 3–4. The rate of pay was increased in the late 1860s, but only by 2d and an additional 1d per day for beer. Edward Spiers, *The Late Victorian Army, 1868–1902* (Manchester: Manchester University Press, 1992), 133.

16   House of Commons, 'Army recruiting: report of the commissioners appointed to inquire into the present system of recruiting in the army', *Sessional Papers* 1861, vol. XV, 19.

17   Skelley, *The Victorian Army at Home*, 22–23; Burroughs, 'An unreformed army', 186.

18   Take, for example, the case of the Gold Coast, which had an annual mortality rate of 668 per thousand between 1825 and 1836; Jamaica, which had a rate of 130 per thousand in the same years; and India, which had a rate of 69 per thousand. Burroughs, 'An unreformed army', 165. For more on tropical mortality at mid-century, see Philip Curtin's *Death By Migration: Europe's Encounter with the Tropical World in the Nineteenth Century* (Cambridge: Cambridge University Press, 1989), ch. 2.

19   Charles Messenger, *For Love of Regiment: A History of the British Infantry, Volume I 1660–1914* (London: Leo Cooper, 1994), 194–195.

20   This was widely acknowledged at the time. See Public Record Office, Kew (hereafter PRO), WO 33:7, #29, Memorandum on the means of recruiting the army, and on an army reserve (Confidential), John Robert Godley (1859), 1.

21   House of Commons, 'Report of the commissioners appointed to inquire into the recruiting for the army', *Sessional Papers* 1867, vol. XV, viii.

22   Godley, Memorandum on the means of recruiting the army, 1.

23   Spiers, *The Army and Society*, 97–99.

24   Horse Guards refers to the military staff headquarters of the army, which was founded in 1793 and located in Whitehall. Ordnance refers to the branch of the army in charge of military supply.

25   Spiers, *The Army and Society*, 99; Burroughs, 'An unreformed army', 182–183; Mary Poovey, *Uneven Developments: The Ideological Work of Gender in Mid-Victorian England* (Chicago: University of Chicago Press, 1988), 170.

26   The exact numbers of British to die in battle were 4,161 as opposed to 13,519 to die from disease and sickness. Messenger, *For Love of Regiment*, 181.

27   Philip Knightly, *The First Casualty. From the Crimea to Vietnam: The War Correspondent as Hero, Propagandist, and Myth Maker* (New York: Harcourt Brace Jovanovich, 1975), 4, 12, 14. See Russell's despatches in R. Hudson (ed.), *William Russell: Special Correspondent to The Times* (London: Folio Society, 1995).

28   Quoted in Spiers, *The Army and Society*, 99.

29   Poovey, *Uneven Developments*, 166.

30   Quoted in Poovey, *Uneven Developments*, 171–172.

31   See Hichberger, *Images of the Army*, ch. 3.

32   Strength quoted from Stanley, *White Mutiny*, 9.

33   Douglas Peers, *Between Mars and Mammon: Colonial Armies and the Garrison State in India, 1819–1835* (London: I. B. Tauris, 1995), 74.

34   For the strength of European forces, see T. A. Heathcote, 'The army of British India', in Chandler and Beckett (eds), *The Oxford Illustrated History of the British Army*, 381; for antagonisms between Crown and Company troops, see Stanley, *White Mutiny*, ch. 1, 'Hope of fortune and preferment'.

35 Messenger, *For the Love of Regiment*, 183.
36 T. A. Heathcote, *The Indian Army: The Garrison of British Imperial India, 1822–1922* (London: Hippocrene, 1974), 26–27.
37 Out of more than 250,000 native troops, the Bengal Army comprised more than 160,000 in 1856. Stanley, *White Mutiny*, 9.
38 Peers, *Between Mars and Mammon*, 84–85.
39 Douglas Peers, 'Sepoys, soldiers and the lash: race, caste and army discipline in India, 1820–50', *Journal of Imperial and Commonwealth History* 23:2 (1995), 218. See also Dirk Kolff, *Naukar, Rajputs, and Sepoy: The Ethnohistory of the Military Labor Market in Hindustan, 1450–1850* (Cambridge: Cambridge University Press, 1990).
40 For example, the monthly rate of pay for an ordinary private soldier in the Indian Army was Rs. 7 a month, whereas unskilled artisans made between Rs. 5 and 6 a month, and ordinary labourers around Rs. 4 a month (figures derived from 1831 statistics). Taken from Heathcote, *The Indian Army*, 111.
41 For the issue of land grants, see Seema Alavi, 'The Company Army and rural society: the invalid Thanah 1788–1830', *Modern Asian Studies* 27:1 (1993). Soldiers who committed acts of bravery received both recognition in the form of the Indian Order of Merit (est. 1837) and increased pay according to rank and the number of acts committed. Even one recognised act of bravery brought with it a one-third increase in pay and pension. See also Alavi's *The Sepoys and the Company: Tradition and Transition in Northern India, 1770–1830* (Delhi: Oxford University Press, 1995).
42 Peers, *Between Mars and Mammon*, 89.
43 Peers, 'Sepoys, soldiers and the lash', 212.
44 For example, high-caste soldiers refused to take orders from lower-caste men, and refused to do menial labour that would cause ritual pollution, such as digging trenches. Heathcote, *The Indian Army*, 83. See also Philip Mason, *A Matter of Honour: An Account of the Indian Army, Its Officers and Men* (London: Jonathan Cape, 1974), 125ff.
45 A few officers did not share this optimism. In 1849 Charles Napier had warned against complacency, arguing it was important to remember that 'All India is a conquered land'. India Office Library and Records, London (hereafter OIOL), MSS Eur C 0123, Charles Napier, Report following the conquest of the Punjab (1849), 24.
46 The ranking for Indian infantry soldiers began at sepoy, with a promotion to naik (similar to corporal in the British Army). Non-commissioned ranking began at the rank of havaldar (sergeant), and advanced to havaldar-major. Commissioned ranking began with jemadar (ensign) and advanced to subedar (lieutenant) and subedar-major. K. M. L. Saxena, *The Military System of India: 1850–1900* (New Delhi: Sterling Publishers, 1974), 205.
47 Saxena, *The Military System of India*, 204–205.
48 Peers, *Between Mars and Mammon*, 78. In contrast to regular regiments of the Indian Army which maintained between twenty and twenty-four British officers, irregular regiments (which comprised a minority in the presidency armies but a majority in the various local forces) maintained only between three and five British officers. This situation offered a much wider scope of command for individual British officers, as well as higher pay.
49 Saxena, *The Military System of India*, 201–203.
50 Peers, *Between Mars and Mammon*, 95.
51 On the threat this posed to Indian princes, see Mason, *A Matter of Honour*, 252–262.
52 Landholders, members of the landed gentry.
53 For an in-depth view of popular feeling after the annexation of Awadh, see Rudrangshu Mukherjee, *Awadh in Revolt, 1857–58: A Study of Popular Resistance* (Delhi: Oxford University Press, 1984), esp. ch. 2, 'Annexation and the summary settlement of 1856–7'.
54 Heathcote, *The Indian Army*, 85.
55 Thomas Metcalf, *Ideologies of the Raj: The New Cambridge History of India, Volume III:4* (Cambridge: Cambridge University Press, 1994), 33.
56 Madan Paul Singh, *Indian Army Under the East India Company* (New Delhi: Sterling

Publishers, 1976), 156–157; Saxena, *The Military System of India*, 88.

57 Spiers, *The Army and Society*, 123.

58 Heathcote, *The Indian Army*, 85.

59 On these rumours, see David, *The Indian Mutiny*, ch. 6.

60 Surendra Nath Sen, *Eighteen Fifty-Seven* (Delhi: Publications Division, 1957), 42.

61 Heathcote, *The Indian Army*, 86.

62 The general Rebellion discussed here refers only to the Bengal Army. The Bombay and Madras armies, with very little exception, remained quiet during the Rebellion – a fact that was widely used afterwards to support the continuance of the three-army system. The reasons they did not rise with the Bengal Army have been hotly debated, but it is generally agreed that distance between the armies discouraged communication, and that the particular conditions in the Bengal Army of mass disaffection and religious grievances did not exist in either the Madras or Bombay armies. For the events in Mirath, see J. A. B. Palmer, *The Mutiny Outbreak at Meerut in 1857* (Cambridge: Cambridge University Press, 1966).

63 Thomas Metcalf, *The Aftermath of Revolt: India, 1857–1870* (Princeton: Princeton University Press, 1964), 290.

64 Sen, *Eighteen Fifty-Seven*, 70–72.

65 An early attempt to locate the Rebellion as a large-scale peasant revolt in addition to a military mutiny was S. B. Chaudhuri's *Civil Rebellion in the Indian Mutinies, 1857–1859* (Calcutta: World Press Private, 1957). Eric Stokes later took up the subject in *The Peasant Armed: The Indian Revolt of 1857* (Oxford: Clarendon, 1986), as did Rudrangshu Mukherjee in *Awadh in Revolt*, and Ranajit Guha in *Elementary Aspects of Peasant Insurgency in Colonial India* (Delhi: Oxford University Press, 1983).

66 For further details on the events leading up to the Kanpur massacre, see Sen, *Eighteen Fifty-Seven*, ch. 4; M. P. Srivastava, *The Indian Mutiny, 1857* (Allahabad: Chugh, 1979), ch. 4; Rudrangshu Mukherjee, *Spectre of Violence: The 1857 Kanpur Massacres* (Delhi: Viking, 1998), 63–79; Pratul Chandra Gupta, *Nana Sahib and the Rising at Cawnpore* (Oxford: Clarendon, 1963).

67 For many years, historians of the Rebellion played down this aspect of the conflict. For discussions of this phenomenon, see Mukherjee, *Spectre of Violence*; S. B. Chaudhuri, *Theories of the Indian Mutiny, 1857–59* (Calcutta: World Press Private, 1965), esp. ch. 1; Snigdha Sen, *The Historiography of the Indian Revolt* (Calcutta: Punthi-Pustak, 1992); Ainslie T. Embree, *1857 in India: Mutiny or War of Independence?* (Boston: D. C. Heath, 1963).

68 See R. H. Haigh and P. W. Turner, *The Punjab Moveable Column: Its Effect on the Course of Events in the Punjab during the Indian Mutiny of 1857* (Sheffield: Sheffield Polytechnic Department of Political Studies, 1983).

69 Surendra Sen provides an in-depth narrative of the events of the Rebellion in his *Eighteen Fifty-Seven*; as does Christopher Hibbert, albeit more apologetically, in *The Great Mutiny: India 1857* (New York: Viking, 1978). P. J. O. Taylor has produced the useful *What Really Happened During the Mutiny: A Day-by-Day Account of the Major Events of 1857–59 in India* (Delhi: Oxford University Press, 1997).

70 Heathcote, 'The army of British India', 382.

71 Omissi, *The Sepoy and the Raj*, 9.

72 Omissi, *The Sepoy and the Raj*, 5, 6.

73 PRO, WO 33:6A, #101, India and her future military organisation, in a series of letters addressed to Sir Joshua Walmsley (Confidential) (1858), 1.

74 Omissi, *The Sepoy and the Raj*, 9. The quotation is by Lord Ripon in 1881. Ripon was then Viceroy of India.

75 Major-General Peel was Secretary for War in that year..

76 Peel Commission, x. In Madras and Bombay, the ratio was to be fixed at one British soldier for every three sepoys.

77 Omissi, *The Sepoy and the Raj*, 8, 9.

78 Peel Commission, xiv.

79 Peel Commission, 182.

80 Peel Commission, xiv.

81 For the numbers of 'general mixture' regiments, see Omissi, *The Sepoy and the Raj*, 87. The Punjab Committee Report was incorporated into the Peel Commission Report in an appendix.

82 OIOL, L/MIL/17/5/2152, Adjutant-General Henry Hudson, Recruiting in India before and during the war of 1914–18 (1919), 2.

83 In his private correspondence, Lawrence noted with regard to Punjabis: 'Indeed I foresee that if we are not careful, we shall raise up to ourselves a more formidable enemy than ever Pandey [the rebels] has proved'. OIOL, MSS Eur C 203/1, Correspondence of Lord Lawrence, Lawrence to A. G. Chamberlain, 8 Oct. 1857.

84 Peel Commission, 184.

85 Burroughs, 'An unreformed army', 164. The strength of the army in 1815 was 233,952.

86 Spiers, *The Army and Society*, 138.

87 The recommendation to amalgamate the Company and Crown European forces was not a new one. Lord Cornwallis had proposed it as a remedy to jealousies between the Crown and Company forces as early as 1796. Singh, *Indian Army Under the East India Company*, 35–36.

88 Spiers, *The Army and Society*, 137; for an in-depth look at the events surrounding the amalgamation of the two forces and the protests with which it met in the Company army, see Stanley's *White Mutiny*.

89 Goodenough and Dalton, *The Army Book for the British Empire*, 30.

90 Heathcote, *The Military in British India*, 118. In reality, the actual garrison normally was about 70,000 men instead of the recommended 80,000.

91 'The army', *Blackwood's Magazine* 101 (Feb. 1867), 144.

92 Godley, Memorandum on the means of recruiting the army, 1–2.

93 That is, a daily wage equal to or greater than what common labourers could command.

94 Dawson, *Soldier Heroes*, 81.

95 The terminology of colonial side-show is Dawson's. See Dawson, *Soldier Heroes*, ch. 4.

96 Lucy Brown, 'The growth of a national press', in Laurel Brake, Aled Jones and Lionel Madden (eds), *Investigating Victorian Journalism* (London: Macmillan, 1990), 134–135; Alan Lee, *The Origins of the Popular Press, 1855–1914* (London: Croom Helm, 1976), 48.

97 Lucy Brown, *Victorian News and Newspapers* (Oxford: Clarendon Press, 1985), 31.

98 Brown, *Victorian News and Newspapers*, 27.

99 Stephen Koss, *The Rise and Fall of the Political Press in Britain: The Nineteenth Century* (Chapel Hill: University of North Carolina Press, 1981), 121.

100 Dawson, *Soldier Heroes*, 84.

101 Brown, *Victorian News and Newspapers*, 27.

102 Dawson, *Soldier Heroes*, 85.

103 Koss, *The Rise and Fall of the Political Press in Britain*, 92, 93.

104 Koss, *The Rise and Fall of the Political Press in Britain*, 121.

105 Lee, *Origins of the Popular Press*, 60.

106 Dawson, *Soldier Heroes*, 85; Brown, *Victorian News and Newspapers*, 277.

107 Laura Peters has also noted the early criticisms of the East India Company administrators in '"Double-dyed traitors and infernal villains": *Illustrated London News*, *Household Words*, Charles Dickens and the Indian Rebellion', in David Finklestein and Douglas Peers (eds), *Negotiating India in the Nineteenth-Century Media* (London: Macmillan, 2000), 113.

108 Quoted in Bernard Porter, *The Lion's Share: A Short History of British Imperialism* (London: Longman, 1975), 30.

109 *Aberdeen Herald and General Advertiser* (22 Aug. 1857), 3.

110 'The Bengal Mutiny', *Blackwood's Magazine* 82 (Sept. 1857), 382.

111 'London correspondent', *Delhi Gazette Extra* (10 July 1857), 2.

112 'The Mutiny in India', *Illustrated London News* (4 July 1857), 3.

113 *Reynolds's Newspaper* (16 Aug. 1857), 8.

114   *Reynolds's Newspaper* (16 Aug. 1857), 7. Quoted in Spiers, *The Army and Society*, 126.

115   For example, the *Aberdeen Free Press and Buchan News* reprinted criticisms that appeared in *The Times* on 31 July 1857, 3.

116   Spiers, *The Army and Society*, 135.

117   Spiers, *The Army and Society*, 129.

118   The words 'unceasing vigilance' were those ascribed to Lawrence by the Governor-General in OIOL, L/MIL/17/2/306, General Orders India, General Orders for the military for 1857, 7 Oct. 1857.

119   OIOL, MSS Eur C 203/1, Correspondence of Lord Lawrence, John Lawrence, 1 Aug. 1857.

120   Quoted from Mukherjee, 'The Kanpur massacres in India', 182.

121   Duke University Rare Book, Manuscript and Special Collections (hereafter RBMSC), James George Smith Neill papers, Instructions issued by Colonel Neill on 29 June 1857 to Major Renaud commanding 400 European infantry, 3 guns, and 300 Seikhs and irregular cavalry.

122   Sen, *Eighteen Fifty-Seven*, 150; Spiers, *The Army and Society*, 131; Patrick Brantlinger, 'The well at Cawnpore: literary representations of the Indian Mutiny of 1857', in *Rule of Darkness*, 201.

123   Mukherjee, *Spectre of Violence*, 32. For the nature of the massacre, see Rudrangshu Mukherjee, '"Satan let loose upon the Earth": the Kanpur massacre in India in the revolt of 1857', *Past and Present* 128 (1990); and the later debate between Mukherjee and Barbara English in 'Debate: the Kanpur massacres in India in the Revolt of 1857', *Past and Present* 142 (1994).

124   These included the notorious punishments of requiring sepoys to lick the blood of the slain women before being hanged. See Duke University RBMSC, James George Smith Neill papers, Neill's orders for 25 July 1857 at Kanpur.

125   Black Watch Museum, Perth, accession #0214, David McAusland, Diary while in the 42nd, 84.

126   Black Watch Museum, catalog #O/NO795, accession #6161, Alexander Robb, Reminiscences of a veteran: being the experiences of a private soldier in the Crimea, and during the Indian Mutiny (1888), 98.

127   Gordon Highlanders Museum, Aberdeen, PB 157, Robert Bruce McEwen, Diary. Entries include 9, 11, 19, 25, 26 and 27 Oct. 1858.

128   Spiers, *The Army and Society*, 131–132.

129   That correspondent was none other than William Howard Russell of Crimean War fame.

130   *Aberdeen Free Press and Buchan News* (11 Sept. 1857), 5, reprinted from *The Times* (2 Sept. 1857).

131   Brantlinger, *Rule of Darkness*, 202.

132   For the *Newcastle Chronicle*, see Dawson, *Soldier Heroes*, 94. Among the local papers I sampled were the *Aberdeen Free Press and Buchan News*, the *Dundee, Perth, and Forfar People's Journal* and the *Aberdeen Herald and General Advertiser*.

133   *Aberdeen Free Press and Buchan News* (9 Oct. 1857), 3.

134   *Aberdeen Free Press and Buchan News* (11 Sept. 1857), 5.

135   'Retribution', *Delhi Gazette* (29 Dec. 1857), 4.

136   Alison Blunt, 'Embodying war: British women and domestic defilement in the Indian "Mutiny", 1857–8', *Journal of Historical Geography* 26:3 (2000), 412–414.

137   Anne Humpherys, 'Popular narrative and political discourse in *Reynolds Weekly Newspaper*', in Brake, Jones and Madden (eds), *Investigating Victorian Journalism*, 37; Brantlinger, *Rule of Darkness*, 206.

138   Poovey, *Uneven Developments*, 10. For the gender ideals of the emerging middle class in the first half of the nineteenth century, see Leonore Davidoff and Catherine Hall, *Family Fortunes: Men and Women of the English Middle Class, 1780–1850* (Chicago: University of Chicago Press, 1991).

139   Leonore Davidoff, 'Class and gender in Victorian England', in Judith Newton, Mary Ryan and Judith Walkowitz (eds), *Sex and Class in Women's History* (London:

Routledge, 1983), 19.

140 Poovey, *Uneven Developments*, 8–10.

141 Davidoff, 'Class and gender in Victorian England', 20.

142 R. Jacket, 'The Indian Mutiny', *Delhi Gazette* (11 Jan. 1858), 3.

143 Both Jenny Sharpe and Nancy Paxton call attention to the focus on rape of contemporary accounts and fictions of the Rebellion. See Sharpe, 'The unspeakable limits of rape'; Nancy Paxton, 'Mobilizing chivalry: rape in British novels about the Indian Uprising of 1857', *Victorian Studies* 36:1 (Autumn 1992).

144 'Progress of the Indian Rebellion', *Illustrated London News* (5 Sept. 1857).

145 These included *The Times*, the *Morning Post* and the *Newcastle Chronicle*. Dawson, *Soldier Heroes*, 94.

146 'Retribution', *Delhi Gazette* (29 Dec. 1857), 4.

147 OIOL, L/MIL/17/2/306, General Orders India, General Orders for the military for 1857, 7 Oct. 1857.

148 R. Jacket, 'The Indian Mutiny', *Delhi Gazette* (11 Jan. 1858), 3.

149 National Army Museum, London (hereafter NAM), 9504–22, Brevet-Major R. Poore, Letters in Indian Mutiny (1854–58), 9 March 1857.

150 Jacket, 'The Indian Mutiny', *Delhi Gazette* (11 Jan. 1858), 3; 'Retribution', *Delhi Gazette* (29 Dec. 1857), 4.

151 William Forbes-Mitchell, *The Relief of Lucknow* (London: Folio Society, 1962). Mitchell was a soldier in the 92nd Gordon Highlanders, and was in Kanpur days after the murders. His diary was unpublished until 1962.

152 'Retribution', *Delhi Gazette* (29 Dec. 1857), 4.

153 Dawson, *Soldier Heroes*, 93.

154 For the revival of chivalry, see Mark Girouard, *The Return to Camelot: Chivalry and the English Gentleman* (New Haven: Yale University Press, 1981).

CHAPTER TWO

Highlanders, Sikhs and Gurkhas
in the Rebellion

Forty years after the Rebellion, a contributor to *Blackwood's Magazine* reminisced that 'the men of that day ... had something titanic in them, something that recalled older and stronger ages than our own'.[1] That the men of the Rebellion era could still capture the imagination so many years later is testimony to the power of the British-centred narratives produced in that period. Indeed, those narratives gave rise to a profusion of 'titanic' characters, men whose stories and deeds seemed to showcase the varieties of manly heroism imperial crises could produce. Among the most captivating of these characters were military men, whose campaigns to defeat the rebels came to be imagined as part of a sacred crusade to avenge British womanhood and to restore the honour of British manhood. In such a context, these military men were catapulted into fame and they became national media heroes on an unprecedented scale.

The list of the military heroes produced by the Rebellion was long, and such men were widely celebrated in contemporary military and popular sources. But in addition to individual officers who won fame as heroes, there also emerged during the Rebellion three groups of soldiers who, by their loyalty and bravery, came to be fêted above all others as representatives of collective military heroism: Highland Scots, Punjabi Sikhs and Nepalese Gurkhas. Stories that celebrated their valour, ferocity and gallantry articulated new connections between British soldiers and the most loyal Indian soldiers, and between military service in the Empire, ideal masculinity and racial superiority.

Although stories about all three groups were made famous to a wide public by the organs of an expanding media network, it was from the letters, orders and despatches of military men in India that such tales originated. Once part of public discourse, anecdotes highlighting the sterling qualities of all three groups gathered collective velocity as they were told and retold, and as new stories added authenticity and power to old ones. In turn, the continual re-narration of astonishing deeds of daring and loyalty worked its influence on the very military commanders with whom the tales originated. Both consciously and unconsciously, these tales worked to exalt the reputation of some regiments over others, and contributed to the prestige attached to commanding 'crack corps'. More importantly, such tales demonstrated the special qualities of those Indians who had remained loyal to the British during their 'hour of crisis', and thus provided legitimation for later selective recruiting practices in the Indian Army that drew decidedly on the north and west for raw material. Finally, stories linking Highlanders with loyal sepoys inspired new conceptual links between certain British and Indian soldiers that would – though in the radically different historical-global context of European competition on India's northwest frontier – become increasingly strong in the last quarter of the century.

Making heroes: Henry Havelock and Colin Campbell

When the Rebellion broke out in May 1857, press correspondents in northern India were thin on the ground. Unlike the Crimean War three years earlier, the Rebellion was a surprise for which the papers had not been prepared. Moreover, as the revolt spread through north-central India, communications between major sites of action were often difficult, and movement around the countryside was dangerous. These factors, plus the month-long sea voyage separating Britain from India, meant that it was January 1858 – eight months after the conflict began – before the first professional war correspondent for the British metropolitan papers arrived on the scene.[2]

As a result, much of what the British public came to know of the conflict, its perils and its heroes, came directly from Britons already in India. Military officers were quickly recognised as premier authorities on all counts, for they offered eyewitness information about both rebel and British positions and strength, and were trusted to uniquely comprehend and assess the details and outcomes of battle. They were also, of course, usually closest to the areas of greatest interest to British readers. More importantly, the exigencies of command required officers to keep their superiors informed about the progress of events and to name worthy subalterns and men, for promotional purposes, who had displayed conspicuous gallantry in the field. Thus, officers produced a steady stream of telegrams, despatches and orders, and during the Rebellion these – often published verbatim – became a staple of British newspaper reporting about the progress of events. Once these military sources were published in the major metropolitan papers, regional and local papers reprinted them in their own pages – a process that expanded the 'reach' of such news to a wide spectrum of British readers.[3]

Senior commanding officers of the Rebellion were not particularly media savvy.[4] True, the Crimean War had recently demonstrated that the expanding press held a new power to influence public opinion, to create heroes and villains, and even to bring down the government. Still, these were relatively new lessons to the seasoned officers who commanded troops during the Rebellion. Yet these officers were perfectly aware of the professional importance of their telegrams and despatches, for on their construction of events could hang their own or their subalterns' prospects for recognition and advancement. Despatches in particular were the life-blood of subalterns hoping for promotion, because being mentioned signalled a soldier worthy of recognition and reward.[5] This was especially true for men who hailed from professional military families, for they often struggled to raise the funds to purchase promotions during peacetime.[6] They well knew that war offered prime opportunities to gain promotions through distinguished service, and their commanders understood how important despatches were for this purpose. Commanding officers themselves were not exempt from the power of despatches, for their reputations hung on their ability not only to accomplish successfully their military objectives, but equally to convince their superiors that success had been achieved. For these reasons, it behoved officers to construct accounts that emphasised victory and the gallantry of their own forces. During the Rebellion, this task was made infinitely easier by the fact that there were very few independent critics in attendance to publicly counterbalance reports of stunning bravery, individual heroism and collective success with tales of indiscipline, brutality and disease.

This absence of critics intersected with officers' self-serving professional interests, the power of an expanding metropolitan press, and heightened public interest in the campaign in the wake of Kanpur. The result was potent and jettisoned some officers – who were in the right place at the right time – into the national limelight.[7] These men quickly became household names and their movements in India became the focus of breathless anticipation for the next mails. Although there were many such military figures who filled the pages of despatches, newspapers and journals, two men dominated national attention to a far greater extent than any of the others – Henry Havelock and Colin Campbell.[8] Henry Havelock was a 62-year-old evangelical Christian, a hitherto unknown career soldier who was appointed in June 1857 as Brigadier-General in command of a small force with the object of relieving the besieged garrisons at Kanpur and Lucknao.[9] Colin Campbell was also a career soldier, veteran of the Napoleonic Wars, the Second Sikh War and the Crimea, who had served in the army for almost fifty years at the outbreak of the Rebellion. In August 1857 he arrived in India as Commander-in-Chief of the Indian Army and took personal command of a force to achieve the final relief of Lucknao.[10] Both men were widely praised not only for their ability to lead and inspire troops in battle, but also for their own personal morality. In a world full of corruption and selfish motives, both men were portrayed as dutiful servants of the Queen, who desired only to secure India for the glory of Britain.

Even more important than their individual characteristics was the theatre of action in which both men fought. The massacre at Kanpur had focused public attention on the urgent necessity of relieving the Lucknao garrison, where the besieged Residency housed some 200 women and children presumed to be in danger of a second massacre. Indeed, when news of the final relief of Lucknao reached Britain, *Lloyd's Weekly Newspaper* commented that 'although not first in the order of events, yet as they command a far greater amount of interest than the occurrences elsewhere, the operations at Cawnpore and Lucknow must primarily be related'.[11] Because of this public interest, the characters that drove the narratives around Kanpur and Lucknao received more attention than any others. To be sure, as Graham Dawson has pointed out with regard to Havelock's column, the small size of the force, its continual movement and its urgent mission made for much more exciting reading than the long siege of Delhi.[12] The same was true of Campbell's force; although larger than Havelock's, it was a fast-moving column charged with the desperate mission of completing the final relief of Lucknao before the garrison was either overtaken or starved. The nature of both missions, particularly in the wake of the highly gendered interpretation of the Kanpur murders, transformed both Havelock and Campbell from ordinary military commanders into chivalrous rescuers of British womanhood.[13] Thus, during the summer and autumn of 1857 the two men captivated an eager and anxious British public as the press closely followed their words and actions. This public stature – though in both cases unanticipated – gave both men influential voices in shaping British opinions about the Rebellion, the heroes it produced and the soldiers who fought on both sides.

Old heroes made new: Highlanders

One result was that those regiments serving with both Havelock and Campbell received disproportionate press coverage. As chance would have it, several Highland regiments (or contingents of those regiments) served with both men during the first and second reliefs of Lucknao.[14] Moreover, it later became plain that both men harboured a special affinity for Highlanders and considered them to be some of the finest troops in the British Army. Both Havelock and Campbell tended to favour the Highland regiments in their despatches, and this magnified the Highlanders' visibility in a popular press already disproportionately devoted to the rescue of the

Lucknao garrison.

Campbell, a Glasgow-born Scot with a Highland family background, became deeply attached to the Highland regiments while commanding the Highland Brigade during the Crimean War in 1854–55. After the battle of the Alma, Campbell wrote: 'My men behaved nobly. I never saw troops march to battle with greater sang froid and order than those ... Highland regiments.'[15] Campbell bid an emotional farewell to the Brigade after the Crimea, but soon found himself commanding some of the same Highland regiments – in particular, the 93rd – in India during the Rebellion.[16] His predilection for the kilted regiments soon became clear to all, as officers and men of other British regiments complained that the Highlanders 'get the benefit of his favours' to the exclusion of all others.[17]

To be sure, Campbell seemed to place much confidence in the Highland regiments. Before an attack near Lucknao in mid-November 1857, for example, he publicly urged the 93rd to fight well against the 'cowardly sepoys, who are eager to murder women and children', adding, to the cheers of the men, '93rd! You are my own lads. I rely on you to do the work!'[18] Such favouritism inspired not a little bitterness among officers of other regiments, including Captain Garnet Wolseley (later CIC Britain) of the 90th Regiment, who bewailed Campbell's consistent use of the Highlanders at the front. Thus, just before an attack at Lucknao Wolseley, certain that Campbell would put his beloved Highlanders first, exceeded orders and led his own men forward to the advance, determined that 'no breech-less Highlanders should get in front of them that day'.[19] Notwithstanding such efforts, the Highland regiments under Campbell's command frequently stole the show in General Orders and despatches.

Havelock had never commanded a Highland regiment before the Rebellion, but he came into contact with the 78th regiment in Egypt early in 1857, where he personally inspected it for annual British Army returns. Although unimpressed with its command, he was captivated by the 'fine spirit' of the regiment, and was sure it could easily become 'second to none in the service'.[20] Placed in command of the 78th as part of his flying column during the Rebellion, Havelock began to use it in much the same way as Campbell used the 93rd – as a 'crack' corps, placed at the front of each assault. Like Campbell, Havelock devoted much space in his despatches to praising the military abilities of the Highlanders. In this famous despatch of 20 July 1857, which appeared in newspapers all over Britain, Havelock described the Highlanders' performance in a skirmish near Kanpur:

> The opportunity had arrived, for which I have long anxiously waited, of developing the prowess of the 78th Highlanders. Three guns of the enemy were strongly posted behind a lofty hamlet, well entrenched. I directed this regiment to advance, and never have I witnessed conduct more admirable. They

were led by Colonel Hamilton, and followed him with surpassing steadiness and gallantry under a heavy fire: as they approached the village they cheered and charged with the bayonet, the pipes sounding the pibroch. Need I add that the enemy fled, the village was taken, and the guns captured?[21]

Havelock's rhetorical question only added power to the seeming invincibility of the Highlanders, who appear incapable of defeat. In a skirmish near Allahabad a few weeks later, Havelock described an action by the 78th in which they captured enemy guns and drove the enemies into retreat 'without firing a shot'.[22] In these narratives, Highlanders are a cut above ordinary soldiers and serve as the symbolic potential for the 'prowess' of British manhood in India.

As a result of narratives produced by both Havelock and Campbell, Highlanders quickly became associated with manly heroism during the suppression of the Rebellion. Yet the enthusiasm both men felt for Highland regiments – and the resonance they found with the British public – stemmed as much from an already established and growing mystique of the Highlands as from feats of bravery during the Rebellion. This mystique had a history that stretched back at least a century, to the beginning of large-scale Highland recruitment into the British Army during the Seven Years War.

Ironically, prior to 1757 Highlanders in general had been popularly despised in the rest of Britain as diseased, destitute heathens content to live by violence and cattle thieving.[23] As one observer disgustedly remarked in 1754:

> considering that they are trained up from their infancy in principles destructive to Society and are early taught by their parents a slavish dependence on their Chiefs, and that Robbery and theft are no ways criminal it's no wonder to see them making depredations on others and blindly following their Chiefs into every Rebellion.[24]

This impression seemed to be confirmed by the participation of some Highland clans in the 1745 Jacobite Rebellion, when Charles Edward Stuart attempted to gain back the British throne his grandfather had abdicated in 1688. Once the Rebellion was suppressed, the British government determined to remove the Highland thorn from its side once and for all, and mounted a sustained attack on Gaelic social structure, culture and law. Rebel Highland landlords found their estates confiscated and their traditional legal power over their tenants revoked by Acts of Parliament. Similar Acts barred Highlanders from carrying or even possessing weapons, wearing Highland dress and playing the pipes. In the wake of these Acts, Protestant missionary groups from the Lowlands also organised missions throughout the Highlands 'for instructing the children in the English language and in the principles of the Christian religion'.[25]

It was only after the military pacification of the Highlands that images of Highlanders – and in particular Highland soldiers – began to metamorphose. This transformation was no accident, coinciding as it did with the increasing use of Highland troops in the British Army. Indeed, once the Highlands had been made safe for civilisation, the state began to turn an interested eye towards its potential abundance of military manpower.[26] The first large-scale experiment with recruiting in the Highlands occurred during the Seven Years War (1756–63) and met with significant success.[27] Highland soldiers, enthusiasts reported, fought as well for the British state as they did for their own clan chiefs. Reflecting on the experiment of raising Highland men to serve in the Seven Years War, a pamphleteer writing in 1773 declared:

> They were ofte [sic] tried and proved, and were always found to be firm, and resolute, and trusty troops. Our commanders in different parts of the world, reposed the highest confidence in them, upon the most hazardous and hardy services, and never were they disappointed by them. Nay, it may be truly said, that they had no inconsiderable share in making our most important conquests.[28]

Such reports encouraged ever greater recruiting efforts, spurred by the consistent demand for fresh bodies to serve the British Army in the American and French Revolutionary wars of the late eighteenth century. Between 1777 and 1800, the Highlands had produced no fewer than twenty regiments for the British Army.[29] Although recruits were often obtained by fantastic promises of wealth as well as by force, nevertheless the distinguished performance of Highland regiments greatly improved their reputation in the rest of Britain and established a firm and lasting connection between the Highlands, martial ability and military service in the British Army.[30]

While the Highland regiments were busy fighting for the British Army, Romantic literary and artistic sensibilities were altering the ways in which both the people and the landscape of the Highlands were imagined by outsiders. James MacPherson's 'discovery' of the poems of the ancient bard Ossian in the 1760s, for example, generated fascination for the ancient virtues of Highland warriors.[31] The exploits of ancient chiefs recalled an era of glory and raw power that seemed to be lost, and aroused British (and European) Romantic sensibilities.[32] The appeal of such an Ossian-inspired past led to the creation of Highland Societies all over Britain, which were founded for the express purpose of restoring the Highland 'spirit' and promoting its past glories.[33] As a result, the already established connections between martial values and the Highlands were immeasurably strengthened by the revival of supposedly 'historic' traditions.

At roughly the same time, artistic appreciation of wild landscapes, mountains and extremes in weather simultaneously began to encourage a re-evaluation of Highland geography.[34] Whereas the Highlands had been regarded by outsiders for most of the eighteenth century as severe, untamed and ugly, new Romantic sensibilities towards the end of the century found aesthetic beauty in the same characteristics. The Highlands became, in this new aesthetic guise, an appropriate and increasingly fashionable place in which to travel.[35] And the new travellers to the Highlands saw the region through the lens of Romanticism – as a harsh, wild, primitive and captivating landscape perfectly suited to breeding generations of fearless, hardy and true-hearted warriors.

By the early nineteenth century, the novels of Sir Walter Scott blended portrayals of heroic Highland characters with poignant descriptions of the unforgiving yet awe-inspiring scenic backdrop of the Highland region. These associations became ever more firm in 1842, when Queen Victoria and her consort, Albert, purchased the lease to the Balmoral estate in the eastern Highlands. The royal patronage of the Queen and her obvious love of the Highlands – and especially the Highland regiments – capped the stunning transformation of the region and its people.[36] The result was that both outsiders and Lowlanders alike increasingly conflated all of Scotland with the signs and symbols of Highland warriors. Tartanry had risen triumphant and placed at its pinnacle the image of the kilted Highland soldier.[37]

By mid-century, then, there had developed around the Highland regiments a mystique born partly of military successes since 1757, and partly of a more general re-evaluation of Highland culture, landscape and society. Military commanders, as products of their own society, were equally susceptible to the mystique, and like other Britons frequently saw the Highland regiments through the lens of their supposedly glorious pasts. Acts of valour in battle, such as the courage displayed by the 93rd Highlanders as the 'thin red line' of Balaclava in the Crimean War, only reinforced these connections. As a result, by the time of their participation in the Rebellion of 1857, the reputation of the Highland regiments preceded them. Commanders as well as ordinary Britons were already conditioned to believe that Highland regiments would be a cut above the rest of the army.

Both military and popular sources produced during the Rebellion reflected this assumption. Some portrayed Highlanders as soldiers whose gallantry and discipline were so great that weaponry was hardly needed, as Havelock had suggested. Others intimated that the Highland reputation was a weapon in itself. On the 93rd Highlanders just before the final relief of Lucknao, the *Illustrated London News* commented: 'Strong as the regiment is, the impression which the natives have with regard to the highlanders renders them thrice armed'.[38]

The visible, distinctive and ambivalently gendered connotations of

Highland dress were a continual reminder of the Highland reputation in war, and served as a foil for the supposedly ferocious masculinity of the soldiers themselves. One officer serving alongside the Highland Brigade observed that Highland dress had a power all its own:

> They never mount guard or go on any duty except in full dress, and it makes your heart beat to see them march past, the feathers in their bonnets tossing and the graceful kilt giving easy play to their sturdy limbs. Splendid fellows they are, certainly, and I should think the sight of them advancing in line ought to make the Sepoys feel very unwell.[39]

The kilt, by covering less of the body and gracefully floating about the legs, suggested exaggerated power and violence when worn by men of such fearsome reputation. The manliness of the Highland soldiers, indeed, seemed to feed off the ambivalent nature of their dress. During the march to Lucknao at the end of 1857, *Lloyd's Weekly* noted, 'the natives gaze at the highlanders with astonishment and dread, and style them (with reference to their garb) "the ghosts of the murdered Englishwomen risen to avenge"!'[40]

Such a misreading of Highland dress, whether apocryphal or not, was only half wrong, for during the Rebellion Highland soldiers became explicitly associated with avenging and defending British women from the depredations of the rebel sepoys. One of the most widely circulated stories that cemented these connections was the tale of the discovery of the body of General Wheeler's 18-year-old daughter by the 78th Highlanders. According to legend, Miss Wheeler had been abducted by rebel soldiers at Kanpur before the massacre. However, rather than suffer the dishonour of rape she was reported to have killed her Muslim captor before taking her own life.[41] According to the *News of the World*, when the men of the 78th came upon the body:

> the sight was horrible, and aroused them to that pitch, that gathering around they removed the hair from off the poor girl's head, a portion of which was carefully selected and sent home to her surviving friends. The remainder they equally divided amongst themselves; and on each man receiving his carefully served out portion, they all quietly and very patiently applied themselves to the tedious task of counting out the number of hairs contained in each individual's lot; and when this task was accomplished, they one and all swore most solemnly by Heaven and the God that made them, that for as many hairs as they held in their fingers, so many of the cruel and treacherous mutineers should die by their hands! an oath they will no doubt most religiously keep.[42]

Here, chivalry and tender devotion to British womanhood blend convincingly with the primitive, ancient bloodlust so often implied to be in the 'nature' of Highlanders. The violent purpose of their mission – to kill innumerable rebel sepoys – is excusable by their masculine 'arousal' to vengeful passion in defence of British women.

The strength of the connection between Highland regiments and chivalric masculinity during the Rebellion was reinforced by a vast array of popular contemporary media forms. One of the earliest, a drama called *Jessie Brown*, featured a young Scottish woman in the besieged Lucknao garrison.[43] The story revolved around the last days of the siege of Lucknao, just before the garrison was relieved by Colin Campbell's force. The siege victims, believing themselves about to be vanquished by the rebels, prepare themselves to die. One wife begs her husband to kill her, to 'recollect Cawnpore', and insists that if he doesn't 'you are accessories to our dishonour and our murder'. Jessie Brown, sick and weak with fever, sleeps fitfully nearby. At the last moment, however, Jessie awakes from her fevered sleep, crying, 'Dinna ye hear it? dinna ye hear it? – Ay, I'm no dreamin', it's the slogan of the Highlanders! – We're saved! we're saved!' Her companions, all English, hear nothing and believe she is mad. She insists, 'I am not daft, my Scotch ears can hear it far awa'. And sure enough, after a moment everyone can hear the pipes playing in the distance, and Jessie cries, 'they coom! they coom! yonder is the tartan. Oh! the bonnie Highland plaid. You have not forgotten us.' Minutes later, 'the Highlanders, with their piper, charge up the breastwork and crown it in every direction, bearing down the sepoys with the bayonet'.[44]

The story of Jessie Brown proved enormously popular and inspired both song and poetry in addition to drama. A popular pianoforte piece called 'Jessie's Dream' told the tale musically. According to a letter (reprinted on the inside front cover) supposed to have inspired the story, upon hearing for certain the sound of the pipes, a survivor reverently noted, 'we seemed indeed to hear the voice of God in the distance, when the pibroch of the Highlanders brought us tidings of deliverance'.[45] Poetic interpretations like 'Jessie Brown and the Bagpipes' also appeared, and were given space in newspapers:

> The Campbell's are coming, oho, oho!
> The Campbell's are coming, oho, oho!
> The Campbell's are coming, the sepoys are running!
> The Campbell's are coming, oho, oho![46]

The connection between the Highlanders and the flight of the rebels was explicit. Indeed, in the various renderings of the story of Jessie Brown, Highlanders became shorthand for the final relief of the Lucknao garrison, the rescue of British women and children, and the destruction of sepoy power.

Another important work in reinforcing these connections was a painting by Sir Joseph Noel Paton called *In Memoriam*, submitted to the British

Royal Academy in 1858. It portrayed a British matron, four young women, a young child and two babies kneeling in a stone room, praying and readying themselves for being overtaken by rebel troops, presumably at Lucknao. But outside, through the window and open doorway, are kilted Highlanders who, unbeknownst to the women, have come to rescue them from a fate worse than death. Significantly, the original version of the painting had in fact not depicted Highlanders at all, but 'maddened sepoys, hot after blood' as the soldiers who were bursting into the room. However, this version caused such a public outcry and excited so much offence at the Royal Academy that Paton was obliged to change the mutinous sepoys into rescuing soldiers. In its modified form, the painting was 'Designed to Commemorate the Christian Heroism of the British Ladies in India During the Mutiny of 1857, and their ultimate Deliverance by *British Prowess*' (emphasis mine).[47] Paton, most likely influenced by the volume of tales celebrating the role of Highlanders in relieving Lucknao, explicitly used Highlanders to represent 'British Prowess' and, by implication, the best of British manhood.

Although the mystique of the Highland regiments long predated the Rebellion, their participation and visibility in that conflict altered the mystique. Through military descriptions of their actions and their reproduction and embellishment in the British media, Highland soldiers were reimagined; increasingly, their role in the Rebellion located them in the present rather than as the noble relics of a primitive age so captivatingly described in the Ossian legends or in the tales of Walter Scott. In the imperial setting of India, amidst exotic and ancient peoples, cities and countryside, the elaborately dressed Highland regiments shone. Their alleged primitive, fierce nature and love of fighting, when combined with their supposed chivalric notions of honour, excused them for the savage reprisals which they carried out in the service of the Empire in the name of British women; in the context of Kanpur, they simply could not control their natural urge for revenge. As such, Highlanders became not only the representatives of British military success in India; they also satisfied a wish-fulfilling fantasy on behalf of metropolitan and Anglo-Indian Britons who desired vengeance on the ungrateful and deceitful Indian rebels.[48]

New heroes: Sikhs

Although Highland soldiers may have been the darlings of both military and popular tales about the Rebellion, they did not fight in a vacuum. The Highland regiments fought alongside other British regiments (whether Queen's or East India Company troops) as well as loyal Indian sepoys. And while loyal sepoys often simply provided an exotic background for the daring exploits of the Highlanders, some groups of native soldiers began to attract more sustained attention. During the Rebellion no native group attracted as much attention or admiration – in both the military and in the media – as the Sikhs of the Punjab. In contrast to the thousands of rebellious Hindu and Muslim sepoys of the Bengal Army, Sikhs, only just conquered in two bloody wars ending in 1849, remained overwhelmingly loyal to the Raj. Their loyalty, moreover, was active, and included widespread enlistment into the Indian Army on the British side. Indeed, by 1858 23,000 Sikhs had been recruited into the new units of the Bengal Army raised by Sir John Lawrence.[49] By December 1857, *Blackwood's Magazine* was heaping praise on the Sikh religion, declaring it to be a faith 'which is by far the purest and freest from the burden of forms and ritual of any in India'. Its distance from Hindu superstition and caste restrictions, argued the author, in part explained the behaviour of the Sikhs 'during the terrible crisis of the Sepoy revolt, throughout which the Sikh regiments as a body have remained faithful amidst the universal defection of their Hindoo comrades'.[50]

Sikh loyalty during the Rebellion inspired a basic re-evaluation of their role and importance in the Indian Army. Had the Punjab – and the Sikhs with it – rebelled against the British in conjunction with the sepoys and peasants of north-central India, British rule in the north of India might well have ended in 1857.[51] As we have already seen, this was widely appreciated by many Britons in India, and helps to explain the regard in which John Lawrence's efforts to secure the Punjab were held. Faced with the traumatic disintegration of nearly the whole Bengal Army, British officers in India did not take the loyalty of Punjabi Sikhs lightly. As the General Report on the Administration of the Punjab Territories emotionally put it, '[w]hen the political horizon was darkened all round, they never doubted our present power and ultimate success, and they stood by us throughout'.[52] Circumstances seemed to have shown the British who their real 'friends' in India were, and from the Rebellion forward Sikhs were viewed with newfound interest as a source for military manpower.

That this should be so was remarkable, given that the East India Company had only annexed the Punjab in 1849 after fighting two bloody and costly wars against the massive and well-trained Sikh army.[53] Although Sikhism had originated in the fifteenth century as a monotheistic, pacifist creed under Guru Nanak, by the turn of the eighteenth century interference and persecution by the Muslim Mughal emperors at Delhi, as well as internal disunity within the faith, had transformed the religion into a martial creed. In 1699 Guru Gobind Singh – the tenth successor of Guru Nanak – announced that henceforth all true Sikhs would be his Khalsa, or 'the Pure'. Sikhs were to be initiated into the Khalsa by a ceremony of baptism by the double-edged sword (*pahul*). During the ceremony, initiates were required to drink out of the same bowl (to break caste barriers), to take the surname 'Singh' (lion), and to swear observance of the 'Five K's': wearing the hair unshorn, wearing a steel bangle on the right wrist, bearing a sword, wearing a pair of shorts and carrying a comb in the hair.[54] Under Guru Gobind Singh, then, Khalsa Sikhs identified explicitly with a warrior creed and were clearly marked by their outward appearance.[55] Persecution under the Mughals had led the Sikhs to become ever more involved in the realm of politics and war, for, as one commentator noted, 'the orchard of the Sikh faith needed the thorny hedge of armed men for its protection'.[56]

Over the course of the eighteenth century, the political and militaristic outlook of the Khalsa Sikhs coincided with the weakening of the Mughal Empire, and in that period a number of Sikhs founded territorial principalities in the Punjab. Under the skilled and charismatic leadership of Ranjit Singh, between 1799 and 1839 Sikhs created a united confederacy that controlled most of the region. Although Khalsa Sikhs dominated the ruling classes, both Hindus and Muslims were incorporated into the elite, and all sections of the population were extended state patronage.[57] Ranjit Singh had also taken care to back his rule with a large and disciplined army of more than 75,000 men, many – but not all – of whom were Sikhs.[58] Much of the army was trained by Europeans in the European style of drill and warfare, and was furnished with weaponry comparable to that of the East India Company. In 1809 the British East India Company recognised Ranjit Singh as sovereign in the Punjab, and promised not to interfere with his territorial conquests in the region provided British territory was not disturbed.[59]

When Ranjit Singh died in 1839, however, bloody fighting erupted between various claimants to the throne, and the army became an instrument of political power in its own right.[60] By 1845, the British felt compelled to quell the unrest on their sensitive northwest frontier, and in 1846, aided by treachery within the ranks of the Khalsa army, succeeded in defeating the Sikh army and establishing a protectorate over the area.[61] Rebellion flared again in 1848, and it was only after heavy fighting and near defeat that the British emerged as the victors in the campaign. Following its victory, the East India Company formally annexed the Punjab in 1849, and placed it under the tripartite leadership of John Lawrence, Henry Lawrence and Charles Mansel.[62]

In the years immediately following the annexation of the Punjab in 1849, the British were apprehensive about the danger posed by so many defeated – and now unemployed – soldiers in a heretofore proud and independent state.[63] Charles Napier, Commander-in-Chief in India in 1849, warned the government about the danger of the '100,000 fighting men' of the old Sikh army who had recently laid down their arms. The Company should not be complacent in its recent victory, he urged, for 'brave men soon find arms!'[64] To remedy the problem, some ex-Khalsa soldiers were more or less immediately absorbed into the regiments of the Bengal Army, the Punjab Frontier Force and the police force, but for security reasons these numbers were limited.[65] In fact, John Lawrence's 1849 request for permission to enlist Sikhs into Indian Army cavalry regiments was met with considerable alarm by both Napier and the Governor-General of India, James Dalhousie. In response to Lawrence's request, Dalhousie remarked that Napier 'dislikes these corps altogether, and most especially dislikes the admission of Sikhs'. Faced with such opposition from the Commander-in-Chief, Dalhousie concluded that, disappointed though Lawrence might be, 'I must act on my own judgment, fortified as it is by authoritative military opinion'.[66]

Yet only a year later, under increasing pressure from Sir John Lawrence and other regimental commanders, it had become increasingly clear to the government that increased employment of Sikhs in the Indian Army, 'in moderate numbers', might be a sensible way to occupy those men who had traditionally relied on military service. In so doing, the government might reduce crime and banditry in the Punjab even while incorporating a greater number of the defeated Sikhs into the machinery of the Raj.[67] Thus, at the outbreak of the Rebellion in 1857, Sikhs were being recruited into the Indian Army with more confidence, but they were still viewed with caution by many officers and administrators.

The primary reason why so many officers were apprehensive about the enlistment of Sikhs into the Indian Army was the recognition that the Khalsa army had very nearly beaten the British during the Sikh Wars. At the battle of Ferozeshah during the First Sikh War, over 2,000 British troops were killed, and for a time the British considered surrender.[68] According to Alexander Taylor, a participant in the battle, 'everyone knew that the army now engaged was the finest India had ever seen', and that '[i]f ever an army was thrashed our's was at Ferozepore'.[69] During the Second Sikh War, the British suffered their worst-ever defeat on the subcontinent at the battle of Chillianwallah, losing 3,000 dead and the colours of three British regiments.[70] Although the Sikhs ultimately were forced to surrender, the discipline, training and effectiveness of the Khalsa army had badly shaken British confidence.

Despite this, the very closeness of the victory inspired in many British officers respect for the Sikh army. To be sure, such professed respect may have been engineered to justify the severe losses inflicted on the British forces, for it is far less professionally costly to celebrate a worthy foe than to accept blame for inadequate performance. Nevertheless, many British officers did seem to believe they could see something decidedly 'British' in the pluck and independence with which the Sikhs fought. A proclamation sent to the British-led troops at the close of the Second Sikh War implied that the British victory had been glorious precisely because of the ferocity of their enemies. British rule, it read, 'has not been thrust upon a defenceless or unresisting people; their valour, their numbers, their means, and preparation, and the desperate energy with which, in error and deceived, the Khalsa and Sikh nation mustered and rallied for the struggle, have been conspicuously apparent'.[71] As in the best public school traditions, the two foes were well-matched and played up to the best of their abilities. Though the 'best team' won, Sikhs had been worthy opponents and had gone about the 'game' with courage, 'ardour' and 'fierceness'.[72]

These qualities seemed to demonstrate that Sikhs were, like the British, 'naturally brave'.[73] Moreover, their behaviour when laying down their arms seemed to demonstrate that these natural qualities were complemented by a masculine dignity with which British officers believed they could identify. Colin Campbell, who fought against the Sikhs in 1849 but who would, significantly, lead them in battle less than a decade later, had high words of praise for their conduct in defeat:

> There was nothing cringing in the manner of these men in laying down their arms. They acknowledged themselves beaten ... The greater number of the old men especially, when laying down their arms, made a deep reverence or salaam as they placed their swords on the heap, with the muttered words 'Runjeet Singh is dead today!' This was said with deep feeling; they are undoubtedly a fine and brave people.[74]

Their uncringing manner, controlled emotions and dignity signalled to Campbell – as to many other of his fellow officers – the manly qualities of Sikhs. The admiration these qualities inspired undoubtedly lay behind the induction of some Sikhs into the Indian Army in the early 1850s. Yet at the same time, those very 'manly' qualities seemed to caution against putting an inordinate number of Sikhs under arms.

When regiment after regiment and town after town rebelled under British rule in north-central India in 1857, however, the situation looked very different indeed. Once John Lawrence and his small group of military commanders had ruthlessly disarmed most of the Bengal Army regiments stationed in the Punjab, there was an urgent need for recruits to hold the Punjab and, even more critically, to provide support for British-led troops outside the Punjab.[75] On Lawrence's authority, new levies were raised to replace the Bengal Army regiments that had rebelled. Within a year, there were 75,000 of these new Punjabi troops, including over 20,000 Sikhs.[76]

British commanders familiar with Sikhs had few illusions about the reasons so many Sikhs, former enemies of the state and many of them former soldiers in the defeated Khalsa army, chose to side with the British. Many officers believed, as General W. R. Mansfield did, that 'it was not because they loved us' that Sikhs failed to seize 'the opportunity to strike again for their freedom'.[77] Rather, it was because they 'hated Hindostan and hated the Bengal army' for being the instruments of their defeat during the recent Sikh wars. Also, Sikhs were believed to have 'borne a grudge of centuries against Delhi' as the capital of an empire that had persecuted and murdered members of the faith.[78] On a practical level, officers felt that Sikhs – after sizing up the British and rebel forces – lent their support to the strongest of the two. In short, 'they sided with the power of the day'.[79] Most important, however, was the 'prospect of wholesale plunder' and the riches to be made from the 'spoils of that imperial city', Delhi.[80] Thus, in the eyes of many British officers, money, revenge and opportunism were the operative motives in determining Sikh loyalty during the Rebellion.

Such motives were hardly ideal, and some men, like Lieutenant Frederick Roberts (later Commander-in-Chief in India), worried that if too many Sikhs and Punjabis were enlisted into the Indian Army, 'we shall have the same work [fighting rebellion] again some day'.[81] Even John Lawrence, the man responsible for raising so many Punjabi and Sikh levies, believed that 'if we are not careful, we shall raise up to ourselves a more formidable enemy than ever Pandey[82] has proved'.[83] Still, Lawrence acknowledged the difficulty of the British situation, and in regard to an offer of the personal Sikh troops of the Maharajah Golab Singh he summed it up succinctly, arguing: 'We are not in a position to refuse them ... of course there is some risk, but the balance is far on the side of advantage'.[84]

As the Rebellion progressed, fears about the risks of employing Sikhs as soldiers grew more muted as they seemed to prove both their skill and their loyalty fighting on the British side. Sikh contingents fought well in all the major theatres of the Rebellion, where they were frequently noted for acts of conspicuous bravery. Both Colin Campbell and Henry Havelock, as we shall see, selected Sikhs for difficult and dangerous tasks. Moreover, stories of staunch Sikh loyalty, even in the face of incredible odds, increasingly endeared them to British officers. One of the most poignant of these tales was the defence of Arrah, when fifty Sikh policemen remained loyal to a handful of British civilians who had barricaded themselves in a house besieged by 2,000 rebel sepoys. Although the rebels offered clemency to the Sikhs, they defended the house until it was successfully relieved.[85]

Such examples of loyalty and bravery induced officers and men to throw some of the earlier caution aside, embrace Sikhs as kindred spirits, and praise them for their 'great gallantry and untiring zeal'.[86] As an officer of the 4th Punjab Infantry reminisced:

> It was considered doubtful at first how these [Sikhs] would behave and a few were tentatively enlisted in some of the regiments, but the Sikhs are fine fellows; after being handsomely beaten by us they bore no ill will, but were

[67]

ready to take service in our own regiments and have fought as well for us as against us. If I were to choose a man to stand by me in a tight place I would have a Sikh before any native soldier whatever.[87]

Another officer, after having just been posted as second in command in Hodson's Horse, wrote that 'the men are fine-looking fellows, all Sikhs, with a wholesome hatred of the Sepoys, and I think they will do good service'.[88] Even the men of the British regiments seemed to agree, as a private in the 42nd Black Watch remembered: 'Our friends the Sikhs would come into our tents, and they were welcome, for they are good soldiers, and were proud to fight along with us'.[89]

Confronted with the mass Rebellion of the Bengal Army, the service of Sikhs shone as a reassurance to both officers and men. Sikhs were spoken of in language that described them as hardy, warlike, moral, trusting, enduring, and above all faithful and loyal against all odds. In short, they were the perfect complement to British power in India, stalwart pillars of light in a sea of darkness. Thus, even before the affair was completely over, old cautions were being tossed aside by men like J. Craufurd, contributor to the professional military *Journal of the Royal United Services Institute*. While Craufurd acknowledged that Sikhs might have remained loyal for self-interested reasons, still he insisted that 'in recruiting for a new Native Army the first people who should be named are the Seiks, who have so well served us during the present rebellion'.[90]

Taking their cue from the military men in India, newspapers and journals in both India and Britain seized on the loyal example of the Sikhs. 'The Bengal Army has committed suicide', declared the *Delhi Gazette* in 1857:

> It remains to reconstruct a Bengal army … Sir John Lawrence, to begin with, has settled at least half the question. There would be neither honour nor policy in dismissing his new levies, or any of the Sikhs who remained faithful. We must have a large mass of one race, and the Sikhs have shewn an attachment to our rule, a readiness to aid in our defence, which gives them a claim as well as a qualification.[91]

Papers in Britain, ranging from the local to the national, seemed to agree. In November 1857 the *Illustrated London News* featured a front-page engraving of the Sikh Akali (chief), declaring that '[t]he important services which the Sikh regiments have rendered our army in India up to the present time invests with peculiar interest the above portrait of their Akali'. According to the *Illustrated London News*, Sikhs deserved re-evaluation in Britain, for their loyalty had proven that they, 'from all accounts, are not by any means the barbarous fanatics of former days'.[92]

By the end of 1857, Sikhs – like Highlanders – had been singled out for their exemplary roles in helping to crush the Rebellion, and for their supposedly premier soldierly qualities. Both groups had once been enemies of the British, and both had come from 'martial' historical traditions. Both stood out in a physical way: the Highlanders kilted, wearing feathered bonnets and marching to the sound of the pipes; Sikhs in high turbans, flowing robes, long beards and wielding *tulwars*. Stories about both groups stood out in contrast to the inept bungling of British military and civilian officials. Rather than focus on the many mistakes, miscalculations and problems caused by British officers during the Rebellion, stories about heroes such as Sikhs and Highlanders focused attention on fantasies about how real fighting and real campaigning should be done. They became, in effect, ideal representatives of soldiers serving the Empire.

The link forged: Highlanders and Sikhs together

The story, however, does not stop there – indeed, it is only the beginning. Far more significant, especially for the future, was that Sikhs and Highlanders were increasingly linked in some of the most famous and compelling heroic stories of the Rebellion. Through these tales, Highlanders and Sikhs came to be seen as two sides of the same coin. Although from far corners of the earth, the two groups represented military manliness in a form that quickly came to be described as 'natural'.

The most significant stories linking Sikhs and Highlanders were those that centred around the first and second reliefs of Lucknao. As we have already seen, both operations were followed with intense interest and anxiety in the British press. The fate of the 200 British women and children at the beleaguered Residency seemed to hang in the balance, and if relief was unsuccessful a repeat of the Kanpur murders was widely feared. British hopes for a positive outcome focused on the actions first of Henry Havelock and then, after his column pushed its way into the Residency only to find itself trapped, of Colin Campbell. Based on Havelock's gloomy despatches in September 1857 and Campbell's difficult progress in November, however, officers, East India Company officials and civilians alike believed it would take a miracle to save the garrison in time.[93]

In spite of such dim hopes, the Residency was finally relieved on 17 November, and the surviving women and children were evacuated to safety. The difficulties attached to the operations and the gendered significance with which they were invested meant that both the first and second reliefs of Lucknao were hailed as stunning feats of heroism and as major victories of chivalry and honour over the forces of depravity, lust and murder.[94] Details of events surrounding those victories were publicised in national, regional and local papers all over Britain – all of which hung off the narrative constructions of military men on the spot.

By chance, both Havelock and Campbell had serving with them contingents of Sikhs as well as Highlanders.[95] And during both reliefs of Lucknao, Highlanders and Sikhs fought alongside one another in what were touted as feats of unmatched daring and courage. The publicity surrounding the actions of both Havelock and Campbell, moreover, ensured that when tales of such feats were told, they reached a wide audience.

By far the most widely circulated story linking Highlanders and Sikhs was the storming of the Secunderbagh just prior to the successful, and final, relief of the Lucknao Residency. On the outskirts of the Residency's defences on 16 November 1857, a small force under Colin Campbell came upon the Secunderbagh, a large building with an inner courtyard, heavily defended by rebel sepoys. Finding the building impenetrable, Campbell determined to use his artillery to make a breach in the walls. Campbell told the rest of the story in his official despatch as follows:

> The attack on the Secunderbagh had now been proceeding for about an hour and a half, when it was determined to take the place by storm through a small opening which had been made. This was done in the most brilliant manner by the remainder of the Highlanders, and the 53rd and the 4th Punjaub Infantry, supported by a Battalion of Detachments under Major Barnston. There never was a bolder feat of arms, and the loss inflicted on the Enemy, after the entrance of the Secunderbagh was effected, was immense: — more than 2,000 of the enemy were afterwards carried out.[96]

By January, British newspapers all over the country had obtained and printed Campbell's despatches, as well as copies of his General Orders proclaiming that 'the storming of the Secunderbagh ... has never been surpassed in daring'.[97]

Over the next few months, the details of this act of unsurpassed 'daring' became clear from witnesses and participants. Soldiers' journals and letters describing the attack became part of the public domain, lending drama and colour to the attack. These accounts emphasised the seemingly impregnable defences of the Secunderbagh, and told of the willingness – even eagerness – of Highland and Sikh troops to enter the small breach in the wall made by the guns, knowing full well they would most likely die trying. Nearly every contemporary account depicted the storming of the breach as a grand game, a 'race' to be first, as this soldier of the 4th Punjab Infantry recorded:

> the place [Secunderbagh] was taken by storm by the 93rd Highlanders, and the Regt. I have come to, they had a race in and the Seiks having a little the start got in first. On the word to advance, a plucky native Officer jumped to the front, waved his sword and led the men in, in superb style.[98]

There is, in this account, no hesitation whatever among either the Highlanders or the Sikhs – instead, they treat the attack as a friendly competition, a chance to show their 'pluck'. Another account, recorded by an officer in the 93rd for regimental historical purposes, emphasised similarly dramatic themes:

> It was a glorious and exciting rush, for on went side by side in generous rivalry the Sikh and the Highlander. Our men strained every nerve in the race ... The building formed one mighty charnel house, for upwards of 2000 dead sepoys dressed in their old uniforms lay piled in heaps upon each other, and on almost all were apparent either the small but deadly bayonet wound or the deep gash of the Sikh tulwar.[99]

One of the regular features of the accounts that emerged from the Secunderbagh, indeed, was that the 'generous rivalry' between the Sikhs and Highlanders turned into deadly competition once they entered the breach. Lieutenant Fred Roberts wrote to his mother in a similar vein. When the British guns could not stop the rebels from shooting from the Secunderbagh, Roberts enthused, 'the Highlanders and Sikhs were ordered to storm. It was beautiful to see them going at it, regularly racing to see who should be first in. They went, and before half an hour was over, nearly 2000 Pandies were on the ground dead or dying.'[100] Contemporaries recorded grim satisfaction over the sickening scene, justified by revenge for the murdered women at Kanpur. Indeed, Highland soldiers were rumoured to have screamed 'Cawnpore!' as they made their charge into the building.[101]

Over time, as the story of the Secunderbagh was told and retold, the outlines of the story took on a formulaic shape. By October 1858, when the popular *Blackwood's Magazine* ran an article about Colin Campbell's campaign in India, that shape was well established in a form that would persist, nearly verbatim, for the rest of the century. According to the author, once the command was given to breach the wall of the Secunderbagh:

> The assault was then given by the 4th Punjaub Rifles and 93rd, supported by the 53rd and a battalion of detachments. It was a glorious rush. On went, in generous rivalry, the turban of the Sikh and the dark plume of the Highlander. A native officer of the Sikhs, waving his tulwar above his head, dashed on full five yards in front of his men. The Highlanders, determined not to be left behind, strained nerve and limb in the race. Their officers led like gallant gentlemen, shaking their broad swords in the air.[102]

The gory realities of death remain in the background of this scene, where we instead are presented with an image of war that is at once exotic, chivalrous, glorious and *fun*. Highlanders and Sikhs, moreover, are equals in battle and recognise their parity as a 'friendly competition'. In the game of war, these two teams were playing on the same side – and invariably winning the day for the British Empire. As a result of the storming of the Secunderbagh, the leadership under whom it was commanded, and the theatre in which it occurred, the unlikely combination of 'Sikh and Highlander' entered the lexicon of imperial lore. As such, the story continued to be retold and revisited through to the end of the century and beyond.[103]

The storming of the Secunderbagh was not the first or the only story connecting Highlanders and Sikhs during the Rebellion – it was only the most celebrated. Strikingly similar tales of cooperation between the 78th Highlanders and the Ferozepore Sikhs also worked their way from military sources in Henry Havelock's camp into Britain. Havelock's aide-de-camp and volunteer with the 78th Highlanders, Major North, wrote of one such notable event in his journal, which was published in Britain even before the end of hostilities. On that particular day, Havelock's column was fast advancing on Lucknao. The 78th and the Ferozepore Sikhs were guarding the rear and the front of the column, respectively. When rebel forces began to harass Havelock's force:

> The sturdy 78th Highlanders ... busily engaged with the enemy, who closed upon the route we had taken. A part of our adversaries now made their appearance on the opposite side of the ravine, but were so overawed by the Sikh regiment, that they remained concealed in the thick sugar-cane, while we steadily pushed onwards through narrow and intricate lanes and byeways.[104]

In North's story, Highlanders and Sikhs are the perfect complement to one another and to the fighting force as a whole – they are sturdy, overawing and get their jobs done. Other commentators drew on the mutual affinities of the 78th and the Ferozepore Sikhs as well. J. Craufurd, writing for the *Journal of the Royal United Services Institute*, sought to bolster his claim that the Indian Army should be recruited mainly from Sikhs by recalling an event during the storming of the Residency walls during the first relief: 'At length the 78th Highlanders and the Seik regiment of Ferozepore, with desperate valour, overcoming every obstacle, forced their way to the Residency; while one of the besieged has related, that he saw the Seiks and Highlanders advancing with a rush, and striving who should be foremost'.[105] Craufurd's intention was clearly to demonstrate the fine fighting nature of Sikhs by comparing them to elite Highland regiments. In doing so, he deliberately used language that called to mind the famous storming of the Secunderbagh, where Sikhs and Highlanders competed for the honour of being first to fight (and die) in the British cause.[106]

Over time, this image too took on formulaic qualities. James Blackwood's account in *The Military Heroes of England*, written a year after the end of the Rebellion, depicts Highlanders and Sikhs as specially chosen troops, and portrays a scene of drama and glory as the two groups successfully fight their way through the rebel defences to the Residency:

> Leaving the remainder of his men to rest there [in camp] for the night, Havelock, with Outram and Neill,[107] made the daring endeavour to cut their way through to the Residency with only the Highlanders and Sikhs. They

lighted a way for themselves with the fire of their muskets, advanced from street to street, from trench to trench, and at last, with an English and most welcome cheer, rushed into the Residency.[108]

From the context of the book, it should be clear to readers why Havelock chose only Sikhs and Highlanders to accompany him on such a dangerous mission. Readers understand that these troops are unlike others: they are nearly invincible, and with such forces, the impossible becomes reality. Additionally, it is no mistake that Blackwood describes the cheer of a Scottish and Punjabi regiment as 'English' – for 'England' has clearly embraced these men as vehicles for the nation's goals in India.

Other stories, too, continued to filter into Britain about the 'gallant way in which with a cheer' Highlanders and Sikhs 'dashed at a strong position held by the enemy'.[109] In such tales, the outcome was invariably the same – the flight of the enemy, and victory for the British side. Their power derived, at least in part, from what many people already thought they knew about both Sikhs and Highlanders. The cult of Highlandism predisposed Britons – both civilian and military – to focus attention on the actions of Highland soldiers, while new stories of heroic deeds fit neatly into the pantheon of their stunning legacy of military prowess in the service of the Empire. Sikhs, while perhaps less visible to ordinary Britons before the Rebellion, were still widely known in military circles for their abilities as warriors. That they should fight well under British direction rather than under their own leadership, then, fitted well with already established beliefs about their capabilities. This 'believability' was enhanced immeasurably, moreover, by imaginatively pairing the 'martial' Sikhs with the Highland regiments, for troops able to match Highlanders in daring, skill and courage were troops to reckon with indeed. On the Highland side, the mystique of wild Highland traditions and the unforgiving topography of the region itself lent authenticity to an imagined partnership between the Highland regiments and the semi-wild Sikh warriors.

What is more, the distinctive dress of both Highlanders and Sikhs harkened back to their respective military traditions, and invited comparisons between the two. Both groups were more physically striking in uniform than many of their British or Indian comrades, and hence attracted more attention than plain old 'Tommy Atkins' in regulation uniform. Indeed, visual descriptions of Highlanders and Sikhs continually reinforced their differences from other soldiers, and served as a constant reminder of their fierce reputations. At the same time, Sikhs and Highlanders together could provide heady images of the symbolic unity of the British Empire – for only a grand and glorious cause could incorporate such cultural diversity under the same banner. On the evening just after the storming of the Secunderbagh, an officer of the 4th Punjab Infantry (the regiment that had

[73]

competed with the Highlanders for entry into the breach at the Secunderbagh) reflected in his journal on the visual impact of such diversity:

> The Garden is now occupied by them [the 4th Punjab regt], the 93rd Highlanders and 23rd Fusiliers, and while I was sitting smoking my pipe ruminating, the men of all these regiments were collected in knots round their different fires lit among the orange trees, of which the Garden is composed, and the effect was very extraordinary and picturesque.[110]

Another officer, in a letter home, wrote: 'I don't suppose a more curious sight was ever witnessed than the camp at Futteghur – Highlanders, Sikhs, Riflemen and Fusiliers all mixed up together'.[111] Popular sources also reflected the same fascination with the exotic visual qualities of the Highland/Sikh partnership. A *Blackwood's* article depicting a cavalry charge under the command of Colin Campbell was particularly poignant, developing as it did connections between the wild, the exotic and the masculine that transcend the boundaries of Indian and Briton. First, the Sikhs and 9th Lancers (British Army) make the attack:

> Out of the clouds of dust, forth from the bending cultivation, burst suddenly the bright lances of the 9th, and the gleaming sabres of the Sikhs: their horses came striding over the plain – the charging cry of the riders smote dismally on the ear. Then despair seized upon the rebel mass; breaking their ranks, throwing aside their arms, they fled in wild confusion; but the horsemen were upon them and amongst them, and the slaughter was terrible.

The return of these troops to Colin Campbell, the author informs us, 'was a stirring sight of war':

> In front came the 9th Lancers, with three captured standards at their head; the wild-looking Sikh horsemen rode in the rear. As they passed the Commander-in-Chief, he took off his hat to them, with some words of praise and thanks. The lancers shook their lances in the air, and cheered; the Sikhs took up the cry, waving their sabres above their heads. The men carrying the standards gave them to the wind; the Highland brigade, who were encamping close by, ran down and cheered both the victorious cavalry and the veteran Chief, waving their bonnets in the air. It was a fair sight, and reminded one of the old days of chivalry.[112]

In this account, readers are presented not only with captivating and exotic visual imagery, but with the connection of such 'wild-looking' Sikhs with the British cause in general, and the Highland Brigade in particular. Indeed, the men of the Highland Brigade here go out of their way to acknowledge and hail the military exploits of their comrades under arms.

The connection between Highlanders and Sikhs represented so powerfully in this and other stories during the Rebellion was appealing for reasons that went to the heart of British anxieties about Empire and masculinity during the conflict. That Sikhs could equal Highlanders in battle prowess and unfailingly defeat rebel forces implied that perhaps the 'best and bravest' native groups had not rebelled after all, and inspired hope that the British would be able to rely on new and stronger groups to hold India by the sword. In like manner, the friendly cooperation between Sikhs and Highlanders seemed to prove that Indians and Britons could work together for a common cause – albeit a cause always defined by British needs.

Because the theme of avenging and protecting British women was so central to British narratives about the Rebellion, tales about Highlanders and Sikhs imparted to them the characteristics of an extreme form of masculinity. Sikhs, by aligning themselves with the British, were increasingly imagined, in contrast to 'dishonourable' rebels, as possessing the ideal masculine qualities rebels so clearly lacked. Highlanders, in turn, seemed even more fearless, ruthless and savage fighting alongside Sikhs – qualities that were believed necessary for punishing Indians properly for their outrages against 'innocents'. As such, tales of Highlanders and Sikhs together fulfilled fantasies about masculine revenge while providing reassurance that some Indians still held fast to the values of the British Empire.

New heroes: Gurkhas

The final part of this story concerns the Gurkhas of Nepal. In some ways, the role of Gurkhas during the Rebellion was quite different from those of both Highlanders and Sikhs. The Gurkhas earned their fame at the siege of Delhi, a campaign far different from the fast-moving, offensive operations that characterised the first and second reliefs of Lucknao. Consequently, Gurkhas did not form a celebrated contingent of Havelock's flying column or Campbell's relief force, as Sikh and Highland regiments did. Moreover, Gurkha regiments did not become imaginatively linked with Highland regiments during the conflict. Nevertheless, the story of the Gurkhas during the Rebellion is connected to the story of both the Sikh and the Highland regiments in several less obvious, but no less significant, ways. The importance of these connections, however, lies not so much in their immediate use by contemporaries, but in the ways Gurkha service would be remembered later and retroactively linked to the discourse of loyalty, hyper-masculinity and *sang froid* that came to surround Highlanders and Sikhs during the struggle.

'Gurkhas' came into the service of the British military establishment via a pattern strikingly similar to that of Sikhs and Highlanders.[113] Like both of the latter, Gurkhas had once been enemies of the state, had come into armed conflict with the British, were beaten, and were then recruited to fight on the British side. Tension between the East India Company and the Kingdom of Gorkha (now modern Nepal) stretched back to 1767, when the Company tried – for economic reasons – to prevent the Gorkha king from assuming control of Kathmandu. Its efforts to interfere failed.[114] Thereafter, the Gorkha kings were understandably suspicious of the Company and cut off trade with its representatives. Though the trade situation improved somewhat at the turn of the nineteenth century, the Gorkhas' aggressive policy of expansion to the south and west of Kathmandu ran into conflict with the territorial claims of the Company.[115] In 1814 the Company went to war in order to 'contain' the Gorkha kingdom, to establish firm boundaries for the state and to place the region under British influence.[116]

The war proved to be a difficult one for the British forces. Part of the Nepalese Army had been modelled on the European drill, dress and training used in the Bengal Army, and these forces were relatively well-organised and well-armed. Even so, the Nepalese troops involved in the war never numbered more than twelve to fourteen thousand, and many of these were irregular corps raised via forced labour. Company forces, by contrast, numbered between thirty and forty thousand men.[117] Yet in spite of their numerical advantage, still it took British forces three successive campaigns – fought between 1814 and 1816 – to achieve a solid victory.

As they would do during the Anglo-Sikh Wars, British officers during the Anglo-Nepal War attributed their difficulties to the skill and courage of Nepalese soldiers. Other Company officials, admittedly further from the scene of action, wondered aloud if such approbation might not have been designed to cover up the poor initial performance of the Indian Army.[118] Whether such motivations played a part in the accolades officers offered to enemy soldiers, it was nevertheless certain that during the war Gurkhas were increasingly represented, as Ensign John Shipp of the 87th testified, as men of 'unparalleled steadiness and bravery, who had no fear of death, though [their] comrades were falling thick around'.[119] General Ochterlony, who led the only successful wing of the first campaign in 1814, similarly commented on the 'impetuous courage of the enemy'.[120] Indeed, esteem for Nepalese soldiers was high enough during the war to prompt recruiting for the East India Company forces even before hostilities ended in 1816. By that year, British officers had already recruited three battalions of Nepalese soldiers to serve on the Company's side.[121]

Following the war, Company officers feared renewed rebellion in Nepal and worried that the existence of large numbers of unemployed ex-soldiers from the defeated Nepalese Army would help foment it. As a solution, some officers proposed (as they had done in the Highlands and would do in the Punjab) the widespread enlistment of Nepalese soldiers into the Indian Army. But Nepalese state officials, fearing a haemorrhage of skilled soldiers and a weakening of the state, opposed the plan and obstructed all such efforts to increase recruiting until the end of the century.[122] Therefore, British officers were forced to recruit from Nepal on the sly – a state of affairs that imposed obvious limitations on the quantity of new Gurkha soldiers available.

These difficulties were only of marginal importance to the Company's army before 1857. Admiration for the 'fighting qualities' of the Gurkhas, though well-established during the war, were not particularly widespread in the Indian Army as a whole, and some influential Britons – Henry Lawrence, Resident at Kathmandu in 1843–45, for example – were indifferent to them as soldiers.[123] At a time when the high-caste recruits of Awadh and Bihar were admired for their height and light skin colour, Nepalese Gurkhas – of the lower castes and small in stature – presented a less imposing physical portrait. Moreover, there were few difficulties obtaining ample numbers of recruits outside Nepal to fill the ranks of the Bengal Army.

All this changed in the Rebellion, when the Bengal Army lay in pieces and the British sought desperately for loyalty wherever they could find it. They found it in the Gurkha regiments, which remained entirely loyal to the British.[124] This fidelity endeared the Gurkhas to both British military men and – through their letters and despatches – to Britons at home. Tales abounded about the various bribes rebel sepoys used to entice Gurkhas onto their own side, and all seemed to agree on one thing: Gurkhas could not be made to turn away from the British. Major Charles Reid, commander of the Sirmur Battalion of Gurkhas who served at the siege of Delhi, recorded one such story that quickly became legendary. The setting was the march to Delhi, where the Gurkha battalion had met up with some native sepoys who had 'insolent looks' about them. They sepoys spoke to the Gurkhas, then moved off. Later, Reid recalled:

> I called up a couple of my men and asked what the [sepoys] had said to them. One little fellow said, 'They wanted to know if we were going over to Meerut to eat the otta which was sent up specially for the Gurkhas by the Governor-General and was nothing but ground bullocks' bones!' 'And what was your reply?' 'I said the regiment was going wherever it was ordered. We obey the bugle call.'[125]

In contrast to rebel sepoys, Gurkhas in such accounts seemed to embody an ideal native fidelity – they accepted without question the authority of their officers and were ready to go anywhere and do anything in their service. One of the reasons for this, in addition to their presumed attachment to the British, was that Gurkhas – like Sikhs – were believed to despise Bengal Army sepoys. Gurkhas, officers said, believed they were superior to regular sepoys on racial grounds and because they were unencumbered by the elaborate caste observances that characterised the high-caste soldiers of Bihar and Awadh. In the context of the bitter war the British were waging against many former Bengal Army soldiers, this belief may have helped displace the blame for British brutalities. A contemporary picture book about the Rebellion put it this way: 'The Goorkhas have always had a predilection for the British troops, whom they highly respect, but have a signal contempt for the Sepoys, whom they despise, looking upon them as much their inferiors, and reckoning that one Goorkha is at any time a match for three of them'.[126] Clearly, if other native groups – and particularly those with established reputations as skilled soldiers – despised rebel sepoys and loved the British, the British could hardly be wrong in their attempts to crush the Rebellion. Gurkhas, then, were a perfect complement to British goals and objectives during the campaign.

Gurkhas became famous for the critical role they played in the siege of Delhi, where they were among the first – and for a time the only – native troops to serve with the British.[127] Britons spoke with amazement about the Gurkhas' steadfast determination to defend Hindu Rao's house – a building outside the walls of Delhi that served as a garrison for the besieging force. In a letter home, then-Lieutenant Fred Roberts commented with amazement that the Gurkhas had been holding the house 'from the commencement! Nothing will induce them to leave.'[128] Others were most impressed with their steadiness under fire. Lieutenant MacDowell wrote home about an engagement he personally witnessed:

> The Ghoorkas behaved nobly. Being extended in skirmishing order, Major Reid ... made his men lie down behind a ridge, with orders to be as still as death. He then sent out about twenty men to the front with orders to retire firing. On came the Sepoys, fancying they were beating them back; so near did they come that they could be heard saying that they had broken our line. Silent lay the Ghoorkas, when the enemy being within fifty yards, Reid gave the order ... Up they sprang and poured in such a volley that the Sepoys literally staggered under it.[129]

Over time, accounts like these increased immeasurably the prestige attached to Gurkha corps. Their loyalty inspired the creation of two new battalions during the Rebellion itself, and in the long term prompted British officers to re-evaluate the Gurkhas' previously marginal role in the Indian Army.[130] Moreover, and significantly for this story, although Sikhs and Gurkhas were not depicted fighting alongside one another in battle, both military and civilian sources frequently mentioned the loyalty of the two groups in the same breath. They were linked, in other words, not in a physical sense, but by their extreme fidelity. 'Sikhs and Goorkhas', then, became a natural turn of the tongue during the Rebellion.[131] In later years, the memory of that shared loyalty would serve as the basis for a powerful perceived connection between the two groups as 'natural' fighting races.

The imaginative connection between Gurkhas and Sikhs was not the only link forged between Gurkhas and other soldiers during the Rebellion. Like their loyal comrades in arms the Sikhs, Gurkhas too developed close connections with elite British troops during the fighting. During the siege of Delhi, the Sirmur Battalion of Gurkhas became indelibly associated with the 60th Rifles, said to be the 'most distinguished' British regiment in camp.[132] Both corps were believed to have recognised in the other special soldierly qualities. According to Major Reid of the Sirmur Gurkhas, the men of the 60th and of his own battalion

> called one another 'brothers'. They shared their grog with each other and smoked their pipes together. Often were the Rifles seen carrying a wounded Gurkha off the field and vice versa ... My men used to speak of them as 'Our Rifles', and the men of the 60th, when mentioning the Gurkhas, said 'Them Gurkhees of ours'.[133]

The symbolic function of this relationship, like the similar relationship forged between Highlanders and Sikhs, worked simultaneously to reassure and inspire both military and civilian audiences. The special affinity between Gurkhas and the 60th demonstrated that Britons and Indians could maintain mutual respect and affection, and that those Indians who remained loyal were – as proven by their association with Britain's finest regiments – in fact better soldiers than those who had so recently rebelled.

For the purposes of this story, the Gurkha/British connection established at Delhi was also important in that it established a precedent for Gurkha regiments to be associated – in the field and in British imaginations – with particular, elite regiments in the British Army. Although such a connection was not initially established with a Highland regiment, in the later context of northwest frontier campaigns it was the Highlanders of Britain who were increasingly imagined as sharing a special bond with the 'highlanders' from Nepal. In that theatre, while tales about the Highland/Sikh connection continued to be constructed, the Highland/Gurkha combination increasingly came to command ever more authority and attention.

Thus, although Highlanders, Sikhs and Gurkhas were not yet all explicitly linked at the close of the Rebellion, still the seeds of what would become a much more elaborate network of connections had been sown. All three groups had been identified and singled out for their critical roles in 'saving' India for the British. All three, as well, were admired for their collective 'martial' pasts, their stellar fighting abilities, and their undying loyalty to the Empire. And, imagined in the highly gendered context of the conflict as the vanguard of efforts to avenge dishonoured and murdered British women, all three groups – but particularly Highlanders and Sikhs – were imagined as possessing a fierce masculinity, at once savage and chivalrous. In short, they embodied the warrior qualities that would increasingly come to define ideal imperial soldiers.

The connection between Sikhs and Highlanders had effects, also, that would continue to wield influence on both the public and military imaginary long after the Rebellion was finally crushed. It laid the foundations for a much stronger association between the British and the Indian armies, between British soldiers and Indian soldiers, and between the lives and duties of British soldiers and warfare in the Empire. And in time, the association first imagined between Sikhs and Highlanders would come to incorporate Gurkhas as well.

Further, the celebrated loyalty of Sikhs and Gurkhas became linked as the symbolic antithesis of rebel sepoys. Both groups became, in effect, all the rebels were not, and all the British wanted them to be. This set in motion a way of thinking about these groups that would identify their loyalty as 'natural', and would set them apart, biologically, from those sepoys who had rebelled. In turn, this way of thinking provided the modern building blocks of what was later to become formalised as 'martial race' ideology – or the idea that some groups of men possess the innate characteristics which perfectly suit them to waging war.

Finally, these phenomena were the sole province neither of the military nor of the British media. Rather, they were products of both. While many of the tales had originated with military officers and men, the enormous interest accorded to the Rebellion on account of its gendered constructions meant that tales celebrating the warrior virtues of Highlanders, Sikhs and Gurkhas entered into a much wider public discourse. This discourse magnified tales of prowess which, in turn, influenced the opinions of military men themselves. It also provided proof of the ways media attention could serve military needs and enhance both individual and collective military reputations. And although the lesson might have come too late for the older generation of officers commanding troops during the Rebellion, it was not lost on the younger generation.

Notes

1 'The Indian Mutiny in fiction', *Blackwood's Magazine* 161 (Feb. 1897), 218, 219.
2 Edward Spiers, *The Army and Society, 1815–1914* (London: Longman, 1980), 138.
3 The national papers consulted for this study include the *Lloyd's Weekly Paper* and *Reynolds's Weekly*, which in the 1850s were both mass-circulated Sunday papers with liberal and radical outlooks, respectively (Lucy Brown, *Victorian News and Newspapers* (Oxford: Clarendon Press, 1985), 27); *News of the World*, one of the most popular weeklies in the provinces, which had a liberal slant (see Cyril Bainbridge and Roy Stockdill, *The News of the World Story: 150 Years of the World's Best-Selling Newspaper* (London: Harper Collins, 1993)); the *Illustrated London News*, a relatively expensive metropolitan weekly geared toward the middle classes; and several local Scottish papers including the *Aberdeen Herald and General Advertiser*, the *Dundee, Perth, and Forfar People's Journal* and the *Aberdeen Free Press and Buchan News*, the latter of

which was to became the most important paper in northern Scotland later in the century (see William Donaldson, *Popular Literature in Victorian Scotland* (Aberdeen: Aberdeen University Press), 3). My choice of liberal and radical papers geared towards provincial or remote local areas was meant to counterbalance the inordinate attention scholars have given the metropolitan, conservative *The Times,* and to demonstrate that press coverage of the Rebellion was truly a national phenomenon.

4   That is not to say that some officers, and particularly those serving in India, were not already relatively experienced contributors to the various mediums of the British media in the first half of the nineteenth century. Indeed, some of these officers had already helped increase general interest in India among ordinary Britons in that period. For the earlier period, see Douglas Peers, "'Those noble exemplars of the true military tradition": constructions of the Indian Army in the mid-Victorian press', *Modern Asian Studies* 31:1 (1997).

5   Lieutenant (later Field Marshal) Roberts frequently wrote about his relief at being mentioned, which he believed 'may be of use hereafter'. *Letters Written During the Indian Mutiny* (New Delhi: Lal Publishers, reprinted 1979), 114.

6   Graham Dawson, *Soldier Heroes: British Adventure, Empire and the Imagining of Masculinities* (London: Routledge, 1994), 137.

7   John MacKenzie, 'Heroic myths of empire', in John MacKenzie (ed.), *Popular Imperialism and the Military* (Manchester: Manchester University Press, 1992), 117.

8   Of these two, Havelock was the more celebrated, though this was partly because he died during the campaign. For heroic constructions of Havelock, see especially Dawson's *Soldier Heroes,* and also MacKenzie's 'Heroic myths of empire'. Yet if Campbell did not quite reach the stature of heroic martyr (he survived the Rebellion), he too was widely honoured as a hero during and after the campaign. Furthermore, as a Scot Campbell was far more popular in Scotland than Havelock, and thus performed dual roles as both a national 'British' hero and as a symbol of Scottish pride in its contribution to Empire.

9   Dawson, *Soldier Heroes,* 94.

10   For more information on Campbell, see Archibald Forbes, *Colin Campbell, Lord Clyde* (London: Macmillan & Co., 1895).

11   *Lloyd's Weekly Newspaper* (17 Jan. 1858), 1.

12   Dawson, *Soldier Heroes,* 96.

13   For example, General Orders in India hailed Campbell's final relief of Lucknao as 'the completely successful rescue of the Women and Children ... from the long-beleaguered Residency'. India Office Library and Records, London (hereafter OIOL), L/MIL/ 17/2/306 General Orders India, General Orders for the military for 1857, 12 Dec.

14   The 78th (Ross-Shire Buffs) Highlanders served with Havelock, and the 93rd (Sutherland Highlanders) and part of the 42nd (Black Watch) served with Campbell.

15   Forbes, *Colin Campbell,* 87.

16   See Argyll and Sutherland Highlander Museum, Stirling (hereafter ASHM), N-C93.CAM.C-3, Colin Campbell's farewell address to the Highland Brigade, 1855.

17   Christopher Hibbert, *The Great Mutiny: India, 1857* (Middlesex: Penguin Books, 1980), 338.

18   Hibbert, *The Great Mutiny,* 338.

19   Hibbert, *The Great Mutiny,* 344.

20   Public Record Office, Kew (hereafter PRO), WO 27:468, British Army, half-yearly inspection returns, April 1857.

21   House of Commons, 'Brigadier-General Havelock to the Deputy Adjutant-General of the Army 20 July 1857', *Sessional Papers,* vol. XXXIV, session 1 (1857), 7.

22   OIOL, MSS Eur C 124/19, Telegrams to Lord Clyde during Mutiny, Henry Havelock to Lord Clyde, 12 Aug. 1857.

23   Charles Withers, 'The historical creation of the Highlands', in Ian Donnachie and Christopher Whatley (eds), *The Manufacture of Scottish History* (Edinburgh: Polygon, 1992), 145–146; see also Linda Colley, *Britons: Forging the Nation, 1707–1837* (New Haven: Yale University Press, 1992), ch. 2; Peter Womack, *Improvement and Romance: Constructing the Myth of the Highlands* (London: Macmillan, 1989), 5–6.

24 National Library of Scotland, Edinburgh (hereafter NLS), MSS 17504, Observation about the improvements and reformation of the West Highlands made in the Year 1754: remarks on the improvement of the land &C (1754), fos 57–58.

25 Observations about the improvements, fos 56–74. For the measures taken to pacify the Highlands, see Alexander Murdoch, *The People Above: Politics and Administration in Mid-Eighteenth Century Scotland* (Edinburgh: John Donald, 1980), 35–38; John Stuart Shaw, *The Management of Scottish Society, 1707–1764* (Edinburgh: John Donald, 1983), 169–179; Rosalind Mitchison, 'The government and the Highlands, 1707–1745', in N. T. Phillipson and Rosalind Mitchison (eds), *Scotland in the Age of Improvement* (Edinburgh: Edinburgh University Press, 1970), 44–45.

26 Womack, *Improvement and Romance*, 29.

27 Robert Clyde, *From Rebel to Hero: The Image of the Highlander, 1745–1830* (East Linton: Tuckwell Press, 1995), 152.

28 Quoted in Clyde, *From Rebel to Hero*, 157.

29 Diana Henderson, *Highland Soldier: A Social Study of the Highland Regiments, 1820–1920* (Edinburgh: John Donald, 1989), 5.

30 On the use of force in 'encouraging' eighteenth-century enlistment, see Clyde, *From Rebel to Hero*, 176; also Alexander Murdoch 'More "reluctant heroes": new light on military recruiting in north east Scotland, 1759–1760', in John Dwyer, Roger Mason and Alexander Murdoch (eds), *New Perspectives on the Politics and Culture of Early Modern Scotland* (Edinburgh: John Donald, 1982). For primary sources, see Scottish Record Office, Edinburgh (hereafter SRO), GD 427/302 and 427/304/3–4, Seaforth Muniments Military Papers. On fantastic promises, a recruiting poster for the 78th Fraser Highlanders during the American Revolutionary War guaranteed that 'no price will be grudged for good men', and that 'the lands of the REBELS will be divided amongst you, and every one of you become LAIRDS'. United Services Museum, Edinburgh (hereafter USM), M1982.97, 'Volunteers Wanted', recruiting poser for the 78th Fraser Highlanders, 1776.

31 John Gold and Margaret Gold, *Imagining Scotland: Tradition, Representation and Promotion in Scottish Tourism Since 1750* (Aldershot: Scolar Press, 1995), 53–57; Withers, 'The historical creation of the Highlands', 151. The Ossian poems were later discovered to be fakes manufactured by MacPherson.

32 See Howard Gaskill (ed.), *The Poems of Ossian and Related Works* (Edinburgh: Edinburgh University Press, 1996), 56.

33 J. E. Cookson, 'The Napoleonic Wars, military Scotland and Tory Highlandism', *Scottish Historical Review* 78:205 (April 1999), 60, 65.

34 T. M. Devine, 'The making of Highlandism', in *Clanship to Crofter's War: The Social Transformation of the Scottish Highlands* (Manchester: Manchester University Press, 1994), 96.

35 Gold and Gold, *Imagining Scotland*, 62–63.

36 See especially Gold and Gold, *Imagining Scotland*, ch. 4, 'Sir Walter Scott and the propagation of the Highland myth'; also Trevor Pringle, 'The privation of history: Landseer, Victoria and the Highland myth', in Denis Cosgrove and Stephen Daniels (eds), *The Iconography of Landscape: Essays on the Symbolic Representation, Design, and Use of Past Environments* (Cambridge: Cambridge University Press, 1988); Withers, 'The historical creation of the Highlands', 152–154.

37 Devine, 'The making of Highlandism', 84, 87.

38 *Illustrated London News* (28 Nov. 1857).

39 Lieutenant Macdowell, 19 Jan. 1858, in Captain Coghill, Lieutenant Macdowell and 'Shiny' Williams, *Letters from the Field During the Indian Mutiny* (London: Waterlow & Sons, 1907).

40 *Lloyd's Weekly Newspaper* (3 Jan. 1858), 2.

41 This story was later determined to be untrue, but early historians of the Rebellion declined to leave it out even so. Rudrangshu Mukherjee, *Spectre of Violence: The 1857 Kanpur Massacres* (Delhi: Viking, 1998), 134. For Wheeler's real fate, see Saul David, *The Indian Mutiny* (London: Viking, 2002), 220–222.

42 'The oath of the 78th Highlanders over Miss Wheeler's body', *News of the World* (22

Nov. 1857).

43 'The Indian Mutiny in fiction', *Blackwood's Magazine* 161 (Feb. 1897), 219.

44 Dion Bourcicault, *Jessie Brown, or, the Relief of Lucknow: A Drama in Three Acts* (London: Samuel French, 1857), 30, 31.

45 NAM, sheet music, 8310-74, John Blockley, 'Jessie's dream: or the relief of Lucknow. A descriptive fantasia'.

46 'Jessie Brown and the bagpipes', *Dundee, Perth and Forfar People's Journal* (2 Jan. 1858).

47 The photo of the painting as well as the caption are reproduced in C. A. Bayly (ed.), *The Raj: India and the British, 1600–1947* (London: National Portrait Gallery Publications, 1990), 241.

48 For wish-fulfillment, I found Graham Dawson's articulation of this idea with relation to Henry Havelock very useful. See *Soldier Heroes*, 94–104.

49 David Omissi, *The Sepoy and the Raj: The Indian Army, 1860–1940* (London: Macmillan, 1994), 6. There were also a further 52,000 non-Sikh Punjabis who enlisted in these new units, thus making up a significant portion of the 80,000 regular troops and 50,000 parliamentary police under the Bengal Army in 1858.

50 'The religions of India', *Blackwood's Magazine* 82 (Dec. 1857), 765.

51 David, *The Indian Mutiny*, 134.

52 House of Commons, 'A copy of the general report on the administration of the Punjab territories, for the years 1856–57 and 1857–58', *Sessional Papers*, vol. 28, session 1 (1859), 36.

53 Khushwant Singh, *History of the Sikhs: Volume 2, 1839–1964* (Princeton: Princeton University Press, 1966), 66 passim.

54 Ethne K. Marenco, *The Transformation of Sikh Society* (Portland: HaPi Press, 1974), 26; J. S. Grewal, *The Sikhs of the Punjab: The New Cambridge History of India, Volume II.3*, rev. edn (Cambridge: Cambridge University Press, 1999), 77; W. H. McLeod, *The Sikhs: History, Religion, and Society* (New York: Columbia University Press, 1989), 4.

55 Not all Sikhs were Singhs, but by the nineteenth century they were dominant in the faith. Grewal, *The Sikhs of the Punjab*, 95.

56 Quoted in Grewal, *The Sikhs of the Punjab*, 80.

57 Grewal, *The Sikhs of the Punjab*, 99.

58 T. A. Heathcote, *The Military in British India: The Development of British Land Forces in South Asia, 1600–1947* (Manchester: Manchester University Press, 1995), 84. David Omissi gives a more conservative estimate at 53,000. Omissi, *The Sepoy and the Raj*, 5.

59 Grewal, *The Sikhs of the Punjab*, 101.

60 Amandeep Singh and Parmjit Singh, *Warrior Saints: Three Centuries of the Sikh Military Tradition* (London: I. B. Tauris, 1999), 56.

61 Singh and Singh, *Warrior Saints*, 57.

62 Singh and Singh, *Warrior Saints*, 59.

63 For a fuller exposition of this attitude, see Kripal Chandra Yadav, 'British policy towards Sikhs, 1849–1857', in Gerald Barrier (ed.), *Punjab Past and Present: Essays in Honour of Dr Ganda Singh* (Patiala: Punjabi University, 1976).

64 OIOL, MSS Eur C 0123, Charles Napier, Report following the conquest of the Punjab (1849), 7.

65 Omissi, *The Sepoy and the Raj*, 5.

66 OIOL, MSS Eur F 90/15, Earl Dalhousie, Letter to Sir John Lawrence, 1849.

67 Military letter from the Governor-General of India to the Court of Directors, London, 4 July 1850, and Reply from India Office. House of Commons, 'Orders issued regarding the castes of Hindoos from which the native army is to be recruited', *Sessional Papers*, vol. 43 (1857–58), 14, 15.

68 Singh and Singh, *Warrior Saints*, 57, 58.

69 National Army Museum, London (hereafter NAM), 7605-21, MS letters of Sir Alexander Taylor in the Sikh War and Indian Mutiny, Sir Alexander Taylor, 28 April 1846.

70 Grewal, *The Sikhs of the Punjab*, 127.

71   NAM, 92 GAL, Letters of the late Major-General R. H. Gall in the Sikh War and the Mutiny (1848–58), R. H. Gall, March 1849.
72   R. H. Gall, March 1849. For more on the respect with which some British officers regarded Sikhs, see Charles Allen, *Soldier Sahibs: The Daring Adventurers Who Tamed India's Northwest Frontier* (New York: Carroll & Graf, 2000), 199.
73   R. H. Gall, Dec. 1848.
74   Quoted in Forbes, *Colin Campbell*, 72.
75   The Punjab Irregular Force did not rebel, but its services were used to monitor the northwest frontier, as it was feared British India's difficulties might prove to be their neighbours' opportunity to wreak havoc on the border.
76   Omissi, *The Sepoy and the Raj*, 6
77   House of Commons, 'Reports from commissioners: organisation of army (Indian)', *Sessional Papers* 1859, session 1, vol. V, [cd 2516], x (hereafter Peel Commission), 97.
78   'General report on the administration of the Punjab territories', 43.
79   'General report on the administration of the Punjab territories', 43.
80   Peel Commission, 97; 'General report on the administration of the Punjab territories', 43.
81   Roberts, *Letters Written During the Indian Mutiny*, 56.
82   The generic name given to rebel sepoys, after the name of the first executed mutineer.
83   OIOL, MSS Eur C 203/1, Correspondence of Lord Lawrence, Lawrence to Chamberlain, 8 Oct. 1857.
84   Lawrence to Chamberlain, 15 July 1857.
85   See P. J. O. Taylor, *What Really Happened During the Mutiny: A Day-by-Day Account of the Major Events of 1857–59 in India* (Delhi: Oxford University Press, 1997), 105–106.
86   Rev. C. Morrison, *Siege of Lucknow: Brigade Orders Issued between Ocober 2nd and November 18th, 1857* (London: Richard Clay & Sons, 1897), 9 Oct. 1857.
87   NAM, 7305-9, J. Fairweather, Through the Mutiny with the 4th Punjab Infantry, Punjab Irregular Force (memoir, date unknown), 152.
88   Lieutenant MacDowell to Hay, Oct. 1857, in Coghill, Macdowell and Williams, *Letters from the Field During the Indian Mutiny*, 72.
89   Alexander Robb, *Reminiscences of a Veteran: Being the Experiences of a Private Soldier in the Crimea, and During the Indian Mutiny* (Dundee: Dundee Courier, 1888), 105.
90   J. Craufurd, 'India, as connected with a native army', *Journal of the Royal United Services Institute* 2:177 (1858), 184.
91   'The reorganisation of the army', *Delhi Gazette* (11 Dec. 1857), 2.
92   *Illustrated London News* (28 Nov. 1857).
93   See, for example, Havelock's telegrams to Campbell in Aug. 1857. One dated 7 Aug. begins: 'I must prepare your Excellency for my abandonment, with great grief and reluctance, of the hope of relieving Lucknow'. OIOL, MSS Eur C 124/19, Henry Havelock, Telegrams to Lord Clyde during Mutiny (1857).
94   These interpretations were in contrast to some privately held opinions of British officers. Havelock's march from Kanpur to Lucknao, according to Lieutenant Fred Roberts, 'was simply disgraceful … Those that reached the Residency were in a state of disorderly flight, and as they brought no provisions but were an encumbrance to the garrison.' Roberts, *Letters Written During the Indian Mutiny*, 107. Campbell, likewise, was privately criticised for moving too slowly and for refusing to put his men at risk.
95   Havelock had the 78th Highlanders and the Ferozepore Sikhs, while Campbell had the 93rd Highlanders and the 4th Punjab Infantry, many of whom were Sikhs.
96   OIOL, L/MIL/17/2/306, General Orders India, General Orders for the military for 1857, Colin Campbell, 18 Nov.
97   *Aberdeen Free Press and Buchan News* (22 Jan. 1858), 3. Most of the national papers, like the *Illustrated London News* and *Lloyd's*, had printed the despatches and orders by 16 and 17 Jan.
98   OIOL, MSS Eur C 718, L. O. Smith, Journal during the Mutiny (1857), 144.
99   SRO, GD 225, Box 42, History of the 93rd Sutherland Highlanders from 16th June

1857 date of embarkation to 13th April 1859 date of arrival at Subatthoo (1859).

100 Roberts, *Letters Written During the Indian Mutiny*, 103.

101 Hibbert, *The Great Mutiny*, 340.

102 'Lord Clyde's campaign in India', *Blackwood's Magazine* 84 (Oct. 1858), 492.

103 A small sampling includes Fred Roberts's best-selling *Forty-One Years in India: From Subaltern to Commander-in-Chief*, vol. I (London: Richard Bentley & Son, 1897), 325–327; James Cromb's popular *The Highland Brigade: Its Battles and Its Heroes*, 3rd edn (London: Simkin, Marshall & Co., 1886), 160; Rai Sahib Boydo Nath Dey, *A Brief Account of the Punjab Frontier Force* (Calcutta: W. Newman & Co., 1905), 138; and recent histories such as Hibbert's *The Great Mutiny*, 340–341.

104 Deputy Judge Advocate General Major North, aide-de-camp to General Havelock, *Journal of an English Officer in India* (London: Hurst & Blackett, 1858), 25 Sept. 1857.

105 Craufurd, 'India, as connected with a native army', 184.

106 Although chronologically this assault occurred before the attack on the Secunderbagh, it was published afterwards and thus may well have borrowed from the language used about the famous offensive.

107 James Outram and James Neill, the latter the same Neill who committed so many atrocities around Allahabad.

108 James Blackwood, *The Military Heroes of England: From the Invasion of Julius Ceasar to the Suppression of the Indian Mutiny* (London: James Blackwood, 1860), 313.

109 OIOL, L/MIL/17/2/307, General Orders by the Commander in Chief (1858), Sir James Outram from Alum Bagh on 23 Dec. 1857.

110 L. O. Smith, Journal during the Mutiny, 144.

111 Lieutenant Macdowell, 19 Jan. 1858, in Coghill, Macdowell and Williams, *Letters from the Field During the Indian Mutiny*, 79.

112 'Lord Clyde's campaign in India', 508–509.

113 Chapters 5 and 6 will discuss the many problems associated with the British construction of 'Gurkha' identities – in particular, the gaps between nineteenth-century British perceptions and the social composition of Nepali society. In this chapter, however, the word 'Gurkha' is used in the British sense, as an ambiguous term denoting alternately the entire population of Nepal, or simply the lower-caste soldiers who enlisted in the Nepalese or East India Company armies.

114 Lionel Caplan, *Warrior Gentlemen: Gurkhas in the Western Imagination* (Providence: Berghahn Books, 1995), 13.

115 Purushottam Banskota, *The Gurkha Connection: A History of the Gurkha Recruitment in the British Army* (Jaipur: Nirala, 1994), 22–23; Philip Mason, *A Matter of Honour: An Account of the Indian Army, Its Officers and Men* (London: Jonathan Cape, 1974), 137.

116 Caplan, *Warrior Gentlemen*, 14.

117 Chandra Khanduri, *A Re-discovered History of Gorkhas* (Delhi: Gyan Sagar, 1997), 88–89; Caplan, *Warrior Gentlemen*, 16.

118 Caplan, *Warrior Gentlemen*, 17–18.

119 Quoted in Khanduri, *A Re-discovered History of Gorkhas*, 219.

120 Quoted in Khanduri, *A Re-discovered History of Gorkhas*, 219.

121 Michael Hutt, 'A hero or a traitor? The Gurkha soldier in Nepali literature', *South Asia Research* 9:1 (May 1989), 21; Caplan, *Warrior Gentlemen*, 18.

122 Mary des Chene, 'Relics of empire: a cultural history of the Gurkhas, 1815–1987' (Ph.D. Dissertation, Stanford University, 1991), 142.

123 Mason, *A Matter of Honour*, 308.

124 Moreover, the Nepalese Prime Minister Jang Bahadur personally led an army of 10,000 men to aid the British, although his reasons were not altruistic. Des Chene, 'Relics of empire', 123, 145.

125 Quoted in Hibbert, *The Great Mutiny*, 284.

126 George Franklin Atkinson, *The Campaign in India, 1857–58: From Drawings Made During the Eventful Period of the Great Mutiny* (London: Day & Son, Lithographers to the Queen, 1859), caption to picture 12.

127 Des Chene, 'Relics of empire', 123.

128 Roberts, *Letters Written During the Indian Mutiny*, 42.
129 Coghill, Macdowell and Williams, *Letters from the Field During the Indian Mutiny*, 26–27.
130 Des Chene, 'Relics of empire', 123.
131 For example, *Reynolds's Newspaper* declared that the most effective force Colin Campbell could gather for the relief of Lucknao should allow him '3,000 Sikhs and Gurkhas' (20 Dec. 1857), 11. The *Aberdeen Herald and General Advertiser*, enumerating the loyal Indians during the Rebellion, counted the Madras and Bombay sepoys, Sikhs and Gurkhas (12 Sept. 1857), 2.
132 This was according to Fred (later Field Marshal) Roberts, in a letter to his father on 12 and 13 Aug. 1857. Roberts, *Letters Written During the Indian Mutiny*, 35.
133 Hibbert, *The Great Indian Mutiny*, 285.

CHAPTER THREE

The European threat, recruiting, and the development of martial race ideology after 1870

[T]he war now being carried on between the great powers of Prussia and France, must make even the most careless reflect on the military position of England, and on the urgent necessity of training the people to the service of arms. It is not possible to say how soon we may be called upon to defend our own shores from the invader, but it is possible to say that after war has been declared but a very few days will elapse before the invaders endeavour to effect a landing.[1]

We must recognise the necessity for only employing on service, across the North-West frontier, troops of the hardiest and most warlike races, if we are ever engaged in a campaign against a European enemy ...[2]

So wrote Frederick Roberts of his twin obsessions: the protection of British soil from a European invasion across the Channel, and the safeguarding of India's northwest frontier from Russian invasion. Between 1870 and his death in 1914, Roberts – as one of the leading generals of the day – tirelessly advocated schemes for ensuring both, for by his estimation the rise of European power fundamentally altered the functions of the British and Indian armies. Now, the focus shifted from internal colonial unrest to the defence of the Empire from external European aggression.

Roberts was not alone in his convictions. Between 1870 and 1914, many officers, government administrators and civilians alike came to see European power as a most potent threat to the security of the British Empire. The need for military reform became an oft-heard mantra in this period, for few believed imperial military forces – whether British or Indian – were up to the challenge. A culture of anxiety grew quickly as Britons realised they would have to defend their global dominance against other well-armed, ambitious European states whose military and financial capabilities increasingly began to exceed their own.[3]

This chapter argues that the rise of Continental European powers after 1870 transformed the ways in which military administrators imagined the functions of the British and Indian armies. The conscript armies of

Russia, France and Germany became the main measures against which the composition and efficiency of British imperial forces were evaluated. British officers and administrators suggested reforms in both armies designed, ultimately, to ready British and Indian troops for a war against Europeans. In effect, the European, and especially Russian, bogey became the primary driving force behind policy and ideological changes in the British imperial forces.

Concern about the 'European threat' also coincided with the heyday of scientific racism – a wildly varied group of theories and 'sciences' that sought to prove the biological origins of human difference.[4] In particular, late Victorian racial 'science' sought to explain why some groups of people were dominant and why others were dominated, as well as how the social Darwinist theorem of 'survival of the fittest' manifested itself in modern global relationships. Such theories, of course, were eminently applicable to militaries, since they represented states' ultimate ability to fight in the struggle for survival. As a result, the British Army's response to the European threat in both India and Britain was deeply influenced by Victorian racial concepts.

In particular, British military leaders were exercised by near-obsessive anxieties over the quality and quantity of recruits to the British and Indian armies, especially whether each had what it took to stand up to well-trained European conscripts. In India, these anxieties provided the conditions under which a new cadre of reform-minded officers came to dominate the Indian Army. Their policies dramatically altered the recruiting base of the army to include only sepoys believed to hail from those 'martial races' deemed capable of successfully fighting against a European enemy. In Britain, these same anxieties increased officers' awareness about the abysmal state of recruiting, the 'inferior' quality of most British soldiers, and the need to create a positive image of the army if reforms were to be effected. Together, the reactions of the British and Indian armies to the European threat created the preconditions for the rise of martial race ideology and discourse. As such, martial race ideology must be viewed not only as a construct brought about by the interconnections between 'home' and 'empire', but also between 'home', 'empire' and the global system within which they were enmeshed. In this case, Europe – whether Russia, France, Germany, or all three in various combinations – functioned as the 'third wheel' to the making of British imperial military policy at the end of the nineteenth century.

The new global situation – Britain and Europe

To be sure, the world Britain inhabited after 1870 seemed very different from that of mid-century. While the 1857 Rebellion had seriously threatened the internal stability of the British Empire, external threats now had far more potential for long-term destruction of British interests, because for the first time European nations were in a position to challenge British industrial, financial, imperial and even naval world dominance.[5]

British mastery at mid-century had owed much to the fact that, during the 1850s and 1860s, many European states were occupied with coming to terms – politically, constitutionally and economically – with the revolutions of 1848. While Conservatives in France, Austria, the Italian peninsula and the German states struggled to regroup after the turmoil of the revolutions, Britain remained generally aloof and pursued its own interests in the world relatively undisturbed. However, this ideal situation (as far as Britain was concerned) began to change by 1870. Nationalist movements culminated in a unified Italy (completed in 1870) and, much more significantly for Britain, Germany (completed in 1871). In 1870–71, as well, the humiliating defeat of the French in the Franco-Prussian War altered the balance of power on the Continent as the newly unified Germany assumed the dominant position in European politics.[6]

This transformation of European power politics coincided with an economic downturn in Britain in the early 1870s. Profits faltered and trade slowed, resulting in an economic depression.[7] At the same time, other European states were expanding their industrial capabilities, foreign trade and colonial ambitions. Germany, Russia and France especially experienced tremendous growth in this period. By 1880 Germany's construction of railway mileage outstripped that of Great Britain, with France only slightly behind. Britain's former status as the dominant world power was now being challenged by relative newcomers to the scene of global empire-building and foreign trade, who threatened to push Britain to the sidelines through the sheer power of size and resources.

The most potent and immediate threat to British imperial security in this period was widely believed to come from Russia.[8] France had traditionally occupied this position, and in fact relations between France and Britain remained strained throughout the nineteenth century.[9] However, in the aftermath of the Franco-Prussian War and the rise of Germany as an effective counterpoint to French power, Britons became far more worried about the potential impact of Russian ambitions in both the Near East and Central Asia.[10]

By the 1870s, Russia was in the midst of a series of reform efforts designed to improve the efficiency of its armed forces. Beginning in 1875, all males over the age of 21 – regardless of social class – were required to register for service each year, out of which about one-quarter were chosen randomly. These recruits were required to serve for fifteen years, which included seven years of active service and eight in the reserves.[11] As a result of this system, more than 100,000 Russian recruits were brought into service annually – numbers beyond even the wildest dreams of Britain's military leaders.[12]

These efforts at modernisation and reform led the Tsar, Alexander II, to turn his attention to areas outside Russia's borders.[13] In 1877, in a bid to gain control of strategic Ottoman territory, Alexander declared war on Turkey. This step immediately put Russia at odds with Britain. British financial and political interests in Turkey were deep, for Britain had long been propping up the decrepit Ottoman Empire in order to protect those areas that bordered the Mediterranean. The Mediterranean, of course, was vital to British interests, especially after the opening of the Suez Canal in 1869. Without access to the Mediterranean, the quickest and most efficient route to India would have been lost, compromising in turn Britain's ability to defend its most prized colony. As a result, British alarmists in the government interpreted Russia's aggression against Turkey as a grave threat to British global security. By 1878, the conflict brought Britain and Russia to the brink of war.[14]

The situation was complicated by the fact that the British felt the 'Russian threat' simultaneously on another front that also had direct bearing on Indian security – Central Asia. This was because Russian expansion in Central Asia became more focused and deliberate after mid-century.[15] While uneasiness about Russian designs on Central Asia was by no means new to British administrators,[16] fears of encroachment or invasion had been mediated by the fact that the buffer between Russian territories and British India was 1,000 miles wide even as late as 1858. By 1876, however, that buffer zone had shrunk to a mere 400 miles, and only Afghanistan stood between them.

Due to its strategic location as a buffer to British territories in north India, Afghanistan played a central role in the tense rivalry between Britain and Russia. Both parties believed control of Afghanistan opened the door either south to British India or north to Russian-controlled Central Asia, and both feared the other would gain that control. Since 1839, the British had been striving to shape Afghanistan into a sphere of influence that would preclude Russia from becoming a dominant influence there, but with little success. In the early 1870s, the British redoubled their efforts to exert control over Afghanistan. In 1878, however, the Viceroy of India was dismayed to learn that the Afghan Amir had received a Russian diplomatic mission to the capital at Kabul after having recently refused British diplomatic overtures. The British decided to force the issue by sending an envoy of their own, and when it was turned back by an Afghan commander at the Khyber Pass on 21 September 1878, war quickly followed.[17]

The result of the war was stalemate. Between 1878 and 1880, British forces twice defeated Afghan armies, and twice signed treaties favourable to British interests. Yet in the end the British evacuated Afghanistan, leaving not even the British Resident they had demanded at the start of the conflict. What this meant, of course, was that the problem of Afghanistan as a buffer between British and Russian territories was far from resolved. Thus the years following the war were marked by espionage, military preparations and intrigue as both Britain and Russia struggled for greater power, security and influence along the 400-mile barrier that separated their respective frontiers in Central Asia.[18]

The situation became dire in 1885. In March of that year, the government in India learned that Russian and Afghan troops had clashed at Pendjeh, a border town just outside of Afghanistan and a strategic position for controlling a critical pass to Herat in western Afghanistan. News of Russian troops so close to Afghanistan sent the British government into a panic, and brought the two countries once more to the brink of war.[19]

While the Pendjeh crisis did not ultimately result in war, it did heighten already hostile relations between Moscow and London. Concern over the security of India's northwest frontier became more acute than ever, encouraged by the continual extension of Russian railways, which by 1899 reached the Afghan border.[20] British authorities were alarmed by the presence of a number of tribes hostile to British rule on the border between India and Afghanistan, who (it was believed) might spark a general uprising in India in concert with potential invading Russian forces. As a result, between 1888 and 1902 the British engaged in a costly series of campaigns designed to bring the border tribes under control.[21] While such campaigns were seldom definitive, they continually highlighted the precarious vulnerability of the northwest frontier, and helped focus attention on the ever-present danger of Russian invasion from that quarter.

Although Russia was central to British anxieties over diplomatic and military security, in the last two decades of the century tensions with other European nations increased British feelings of isolation and alarm on a global level. Chief among these others was Britain's historic enemy, France. In the 126 years between 1689 and 1815, the two countries had been at war for a total of 57 years.[22] After 1815, Anglo-French relations improved and the two allied against Russia during the Crimean War in 1854–55, but a naval arms race in the 1860s increased suspicions between them.[23] In 1882 the British occupation of Egypt on a temporary but indefinite basis angered the French, who had imperial interests in North Africa and had collaborated with the British to keep Egypt from suffering financial ruin.[24] Ten years later, British and French imperial interests clashed again over French incursions in Siam (Thailand), and in 1898 the installation of a French military commander at Fashoda in the Sudan brought the two countries to a diplomatic crisis in which the possibility of war seemed all too real.[25]

Such incidents merely punctuated a period of near-constant Anglo-French hostility in the last quarter of the century, and increased British isolation in European politics. Making matters much worse was the potential for a combination between Britain's European enemies that would force Britain to wage a war on both a European and an imperial front. These fears seemed to be approaching reality from the late 1880s, when the British Admiralty became concerned that France and Russia were co-operating to out-build and overpower the capabilities of the Royal Navy.[26] To counter such a threat to British security, Parliament passed the Naval Defence Act in 1889, which provided £21.5 million for strengthening the navy. Henceforth, the Admiralty resolved that British naval strength should always equal or exceed the strength of any two powers combined.[27] In 1892, during the Anglo-French crisis over French encroachments into Siam, Britons widely believed that France and Russia were working together to strike at India from its two weakest points – the northwest frontier and Burma.[28] Two years later, France and Russia reached an *entente* protecting one another from German aggression, which gave a new solidity to Franco-Russian cooperation and united Britain's two greatest rivals. As a result of the *entente*, a simultaneous attack on India's northwest frontier and invasion across the English Channel now seemed a distinct possibility.[29]

Also worrisome was the rise of German power after unification in 1871. Since that time, the new state had built the most powerful and disciplined conscript army on the Continent. By the mid-1880s Germany joined the ranks of the other European powers as an imperial contender, grabbing territory in the Pacific and in Africa. Although Anglo-German relations were on a better footing in the 1890s than either Anglo-French or Anglo-Russian relations, still many officers and civilians were keenly aware – and suspicious – of Germany's growing military might.[30] By the 1890s, with the fall of Bismarck and the accession of Wilhelm II, continued German expansion in Africa and its growing industrial power caused Anglo-German relations to take a turn for the worse. By 1900, one British peer asserted that Britain had become so diplomatically isolated in the world as to be surrounded on all sides 'with an atmosphere of hatred'.[31]

To military alarmists in both Britain and India, then, the problem of military preparedness was nothing less than urgent. The possibility of war on a global imperial scale seemed all too real, as crisis after crisis appeared to prove. Threats to the security of the Empire seemed to emerge simultaneously at key strategic locations in the Empire just at a time when Britons could no longer feel confident of their naval, industrial and technological superiority relative to their European neighbours. While we have the benefit of hindsight in the knowledge that war did not break out before 1914, contemporaries saw the possibilities everywhere – and deeply feared their armed forces were not up to the challenge.

The shift to martial race recruiting in the Indian Army

In India, these fears prompted a complete re-evaluation of the nature and purpose of the Indian Army. As we know, the Rebellion had prompted India's military leadership to focus almost exclusively on protecting against the possibility of future internal revolts. And even while post-1857 recruiting practices leaned far more heavily toward the Punjab and other areas that had remained loyal to the Raj, still the recommendations of the Punjab Committee had at least ensured that recruits would be enlisted (more or less) evenly from Bengal, Madras and Bombay. *Divide et impera* – by a judicious mixture of Indians representing different castes, classes and regions – was a motto that guided a majority of Indian Army officers anxious to prevent future revolts. Yet in the face of the threat from Russia on India's northwest frontier, that all changed. The Government of India put it this way in 1887:

> By the recent advance of Russia, the military problem with which the Government of India has to deal has been profoundly modified. We have now in close proximity to our frontier a great European power with which we may at any time be brought into hostile contact; and consequently our existing military establishments are no longer adequate for the duties they may have to fulfil.[32]

As a result of these altered military circumstances, the period between 1880 and 1914 was marked by a transformation in the way the Indian Army was recruited and organised. During those thirty-four years, the policies recommended by the Punjab Committee were completely overturned in favour of a new policy that disparaged the soldiers from Bombay, Madras and large parts of Bengal and sought to recruit only from areas in the north and northwest increasingly believed to produce the subcontinent's most 'martial races'. This new policy went from a minority to a hegemonic position within the Indian military administration in direct relation to the perceived Russian threat. With each crisis on the northwest frontier, the ideology of martial races gained greater credibility and influence.

The particular shape and authority of martial race policies, however, can only be fully explained by their relationship to late Victorian ideologies of race. By the last thirty years of the century, these ideologies were expressed in terms of incontrovertible scientific knowledge and biological laws. 'Race' was increasingly understood as a fixed set of inherited physical and moral qualities, and drew heavily from a combination of Lamarckian,

Darwinian and Spencerian theory. Practitioners of the racial 'sciences' insisted that physical characteristics like skin, eye and hair colour, nose shape, body type and head size were outward markers of less observable 'internal traits, psychological dispositions, and moral essence[s]'.[33]

At the same time, late Victorian racial theorists also posited that supposedly inherent racial qualities could degenerate as a result of environmental factors, or as a result of racial mixing.[34] For example, many British theorists believed that human constitutions were negatively affected by hot, humid, tropical areas. The hotter and more tropical the area, the more lazy, lascivious, passive, effeminate and degenerate the population was assumed to be. Even the 'superior' races, according to this theory, could degenerate after too much exposure to tropical climates.[35] Conversely, colder, more northerly climates were believed to produce and sustain hard-working, aggressive and masculine people. Moreover, British (and European) theorists widely held that miscegenation also inevitably led to racial corruption.[36] Crosses between individuals of 'inferior' and 'superior' races, especially, were believed to pollute the racial stock of the 'superior' race, which in turn could spell biological disaster for all.[37]

In India, such racial beliefs had long-term consequences for the development of martial race theory. Early in the nineteenth century, British scholars of India (called Orientalists) had hypothesised a fundamental link between ancient Indian and European civilisation. According to these Orientalists, an original 'Aryan' race had peopled both the Indian subcontinent and Europe, leaving behind a tell-tale trail of basic linguistic roots. Because of the similar 'Aryan' origins of Indian and European civilisation, early Orientalists often insisted that Indian Hindu civilisation – at least in its ancient form – should be admired and respected.[38] Between 1860 and 1880, however, British Orientalists shifted markedly away from the early linguistic approach towards an approach more commensurate with developing ideologies of racial science. Ancient India was not originally inhabited by people of Aryan stock, they argued. Instead, the aboriginal, Dravidian 'race' of Indians had been invaded by the 'pure' Aryan race from the north.[39] In this 'racial theory of Indian civilisation', the many different castes and tribes of India were believed to have been formed by a racial mixing of these two groups, the purest of which were racially closest to Europeans.[40] The deleterious effects of this mixture between the two races were most pronounced in the hottest regions of southern India, where the effects of such a climate were also believed to have contributed to the general racial degeneration of the population.[41] In the southwest and southeast, which included Madras, Bombay and Bengal, this degeneration resulted chiefly in the feminisation and enervation of the men. In the north and northwest of India, however, where the Aryan blood of the Indian conquerors was believed to have been most pure, and where the effects of climate were believed to have been most advantageous, men were tall and light-skinned, and were perceived as physically attractive and ultra-masculine.[42]

Military commanders who feared war with Russia latched on to these theories and increasingly used them to justify their preferred recruiting practices from India's northern 'races'. Even though many military officials had once praised the sepoys of Madras and Bombay for their loyalty during the Rebellion, these officers now argued that science had now proven that southern Indians were inherently unfit for warfare.[43] Men in the south, because of environmental and biological factors, were dark, slight and cowardly. Their upbringing in the heat made them unsuited to warfare on the northwest frontier, where they would never be able to stand up to a European enemy in the field. What the Indian Army needed, it was argued, was more northern men – men who were racially or environmentally closer to Europeans. Sikhs, with their light skins, 'European' features and homeland in northwest India were widely touted as some of the most genetically pure descendants of the once-great Aryan race that had conquered ancient India. Gurkhas, although acknowledged as physically small, nevertheless hailed from the cold, character-building regions of the Himalayas, untroubled by the degenerating effects of tropical heat and urban squalor. Only men such as these, argued their proponents, could hope to defeat Europeans in war. As Lord Roberts put it just after he became Commander-in-Chief in India in 1886: 'We cannot afford to keep up a single surplus man of whose martial spirit there can be any doubt'.[44] Whereas once upon a time soldiers of the southern 'races' had been adequate because 'they had only to fight against an enemy of much the same calibre as themselves', Roberts argued that once 'they came into collision with the hardier races of northern India and Afghanistan, it was evident that they were overmatched'. Indeed, Roberts insisted that 'these [northern] races are unmistakably superior as soldiers to those of southern India'.[45] Arguments based on the racial deficiencies of southern Indians, then, became the pat, 'scientific' explanation for their rapid decline in popularity with British officers in late century.

On closer inspection, however, it is clear that this lack of popularity had little to do with the quality of recruits, and much to do with the structure of the presidency armies themselves. The heart of the Indian civil and military administration lay in Bengal, and many officers believed service in the other two presidential armies took them far away from the centres of power and positions of real influence. Equally important, the Madras and Bombay armies hardly ever saw active duty, as nearly all military conflicts shifted to the north and northwest frontiers after mid-century. Hence, the most competent and ambitious officers sought service in Bengal or in the Punjab Frontier Force, where the possibility for active service (and the opportunity for field promotions, fame and increased income) was greater. As a result, regiments in Madras and Bombay increasingly had difficulty attracting any but the youngest or least capable officers, who in turn often failed to provide adequate leadership for their troops. This failure quite often reflected badly on the troops themselves, and consequently officers outside the system, particularly those with background and training in the Bengal Army, tended to view the soldiers of Madras and Bombay as less efficient and less capable than those of the Bengal or Punjab Frontier forces.[46]

These perceptions appeared to be confirmed by the poor performance of several regiments of the Madras Army during the Third Burma War (1885–89). During that conflict – the first time the Madras Army had seen active service in more than thirty years – a number of soldiers were reported to have disgraced themselves by being 'very ready to lie down and extremely difficult to get up' and becoming 'utterly done up and demoralised' after a hasty retreat.[47] What went unreported was that Madrasi soldiers were almost bound to fail in the circumstances under which they had been led. British officers held service in the Madras Army in such low regard that few senior officers could be found to lead the troops into battle. To remedy the problem, the Indian government offered a commanding post to any officer under the age of twenty-five, regardless of experience.[48] As a result, Madrasi sepoys were led by 'green' officers, totally unfamiliar with the men under their command. Yet the failure of the Madrasis was interpreted as yet another example of these native soldiers' racially based ineptitude in the arts of war. It appeared as though they had been given a chance to prove themselves on the battlefield, and their performance seemed to confirm what many British officers believed they already knew: southern Indians just could not fight, because it was not in their racial makeup.

During the Second Afghan War, these beliefs – and the threat of conflict with Russian forces on the northwest frontier – inspired a vocal minority who hoped to effect sweeping reforms in the Indian Army. For these men, the reality of the Russian threat was proof that external dangers to the stability of British rule in India now outweighed the dangers of internal rebellion. They believed that the function of the Indian Army should now be geared primarily toward the defence of India from foes beyond its borders, and that the structure of the army – and its recruiting base – should reflect that priority.

The first formal document advocating reform was the 1879 Eden Commission report. The purpose of the Commission, according to the India Office in London, had ostensibly been to devise a way of cutting military costs in India. This agenda was embraced by Governor-General Lytton as an opportunity for securing badly needed reform in the Indian Army. As a result, he did his best to stack the Commission with military and government men open to change and favourable to reform.[49] Among these men was then Lieutenant-General Roberts, who would later become the most important advocate of martial race policies in the Indian Army.

The report of the Commission, published just after the start of the second phase of the Afghan War, advocated a distinct shift away from the Punjab Committee's recommendations of 1859. Structurally, it proposed the abolition of the presidential armies in favour of the creation of four army corps. By these new principles, the Punjab Frontier Force, hitherto under the command of the Lieutenant-Governor of the province, would be brought into the regular establishment of the Indian Army under the Commander-in-Chief in India. The army corps would be drawn from the old Punjab Force plus the old presidential armies of Bengal, Madras and Bombay. Furthermore, all would now fall under the direct command of a single commander-in-chief, thus obviating the need for commanders-in-chief (with their large, expensive staffs) in either Madras or Bombay. The armies, with the exception of already existing Sikh, Gurkha and Muzbi (low-caste Sikh) regiments in the Punjab and Bengal forces, would be locally recruited and locally stationed. The Commission also recommended that the army establishment in Madras be considerably reduced. Significantly, it asserted that more soldiers should be drawn from the northwest, for '[t]he Punjab is the home of the most martial races of India and is the nursery of our best soldiers'.[50]

At the time of their release, however, the recommendations of the Eden Commission were bitterly opposed by the Duke of Cambridge, the India Office, and the Commander-in-Chief of India himself, Sir Frederick Haines. Their hostility to reforming the principles of the Punjab Committee was bitter. Haines in particular was unmoved by calls for greater efficiency, steadily maintaining that any attempt at reform might spell the collapse of British rule in India. He was not at all willing to rule out the possibility of another rebellion within India, and firmly believed that the Commission's recommendations ignored 'every safeguard' instituted after 1857. Moreover, he firmly opposed reducing the establishment of the Madras Army, arguing that both 'Madras and Bombay on their present footing have well stood the test of time and trial'.[51] Haines's firm opposition, along with objections from London, effectively killed the recommendations of the Commission.

Despite its temporary failure, the report had long-term consequences. A large and growing body of reformist military opinion had found an official voice in the Commission, and promised future changes. The sacrosanct dictums of the Punjab Committee had been questioned in a moment of crisis for the Indian Army. Those advocating reform had now become not only audible, but increasingly credible, and men serving on the Commission became part of a new generation guiding military policy in India.

In any case, increasing tensions with Russia over the northwest frontier in the mid-1880s helped to chip away at the credibility of those stalwart believers in the dictums of the Punjab Committee. In March 1885, the Pendjeh incident provided critical ammunition for the reformers. With Russian troops on the northern border of Afghanistan, the British and Indian governments nearly panicked. In Britain, the Army Reserve was called out and put on the ready. In India, British civilians rushed to serve in the Volunteers, and Indian princes offered their own troops for use by the British government.[52] Sir Donald Stewart, then Commander-in-Chief and previous member of the Eden Commission, took the opportunity to press for an increase in the Indian Army. The proposal was accepted. It entailed increasing the strength of all Indian battalions by 150 men and raising five new battalions – an overall increase of 16,450 men.[53] Of these new battalions, four were to be recruited from the 'martial races': three of Sikhs and one of Gurkhas.[54] At the same time, Stewart also pushed for and won the amalgamation of the Punjab Frontier Force into the Bengal Army, a move that now placed the command of the highly regarded Punjabi units directly in the control of the Commander-in-Chief in India.[55]

When General Roberts took over the job of Commander-in-Chief in November 1885, then, the cards were already stacked in favour of reform. Yet during his eight-year tenure he was to carry Stewart's initial reforms much further. Roberts was convinced that the threat to India's northwest frontier was real, and was tireless in his efforts to persuade both the British and Indian governments of its urgency. Just prior to his appointment to the Eden Commission, Roberts had penned an internal military paper 'To Consider the Measures Which Should be Adopted in India in the Event of England Joining Turkey in the War Against Russia'. He followed this in 1883 with another called 'Is an Invasion of India by Russia Possible?'. Two years later, he published yet another entitled 'What are Russia's Vulnerable Points, and How Have Recent Events Affected our Frontier Policy?'.[56] In addition to these efforts, as we shall see in the next chapter, Roberts also bombarded the British press with his warnings about the Russian threat.

In tandem with his views about the dangers of Russia, Roberts was certain that only select groups of Indians had the right qualities to stand up to a European enemy in the field. 'I have no hesitation', he asserted in 1890, 'in stating that except Goorkhas, Dogras, Sikhs, the pick of Panjabi Muhammadans, Hindustanis of the Jat and Ranghur castes … and certain classes of Pathans, there are no Native soldiers in our service whom we could venture with safety to place in the field against the Russians.'[57] Roberts had come to his opinions through a variety of routes. As a young man in the Rebellion of 1857, he had served with both Gurkhas and Sikhs, and – like many other officers – had been deeply affected by their loyalty to the Raj. Later, during the Second Afghan War, Roberts (already predisposed to think highly of both groups) was impressed by what he saw as the endurance and fighting abilities of Sikhs, Gurkhas and northwest hill tribes like the Pathans. Finally, as Commander-in-Chief in Madras from 1881 to 1885 Roberts became convinced that Madrasi men lacked 'the innate love of fighting' so necessary to all good soldiers.[58]

Although Roberts did seem to believe in both the reality of the Russian threat and the racial superiority of the 'martial races', his motivations to shift attention to India's northwest frontier were not altogether altruistic. Roberts was an ambitious man. He was known to advocate those policies that were in line with his professional interests, and few were unaware that when he ended his career in India he aimed for the position of Adjutant-General, and then Commander-in-Chief, in the British Army. These objectives were complicated, however, by an intense rivalry with the other great general of the day, Sir Garnet Wolseley. Wolseley, for his part, frequently forwarded the interests of the British Army at the expense of the Indian Army on matters of imperial defence, and made a point of marginalising Indian Army officers under his command. At the end of the century, he admitted confidentially that he took the position of Commander-in-Chief in Britain in large part 'to keep Roberts out of it'.[59] Roberts's attempts to place India at the 'centre of strategic gravity' in questions of imperial defence, then, must be viewed in the context of this rivalry.[60] Both men knew that the resources available for defence were limited, and each sought to advocate policies that would enhance their relative opportunities for recognition, advancement and patronage. From this perspective, Roberts's urgent warnings about the safety of the northwest frontier, and his elaborate efforts to secure the area, were part of a strategy designed to focus resources and attention in India.

In any case, Roberts was determined to institute reforms that would promote the efficient defence of the northwest frontier when he took the reins of military command in India in 1885. The creation of new Sikh and Gurkha units under Stewart had been an important step, he believed, but only the first of many. There was still much to be done, and in 1886 he clearly set his agenda for his tenure as Commander-in-Chief. Foremost among his recommendations was to 'get rid of every sepoy, not required for local purposes, from [the Madras] Army, also from that of Bombay and from the Hindustani regiments of Bengal, replacing them by soldiers of the most warlike races'. Roberts was aware of the riskiness of his proposals, but was willing to take them:

> Should it be urged that these measures would have the effect of increasing to a dangerous extent the more warlike races in our armies, and that there would no longer exist the same counterpoise to this element which is now

afforded by having in our ranks a certain proportion of the races of Hindustani and Southern India, I would reply that whatever weight this argument may have, it sinks into insignificance when compared with the peril of confronting a European enemy on our frontier, without an army fit in all respects to cope with him.[61]

What had been the unofficial drift of enlistment policy since the end of the Rebellion thus became official policy under Roberts.

The results were dramatic. By 1893, soldiers from the 'martial races' comprised almost 44 per cent of the Indian Army, including 21,966 Sikhs, 21,837 Punjabi Muslims and 12,334 Gurkhas.[62] By 1904, that number had risen to 57 per cent, and by 1914, 75 per cent.[63] Between 1862 and 1914, the number of infantry units maintained by each major recruiting area also underwent profound changes, reflecting the overwhelmingly northern bias of the military by the end of the period. Whereas in 1862 only 33 out of the 121 infantry units were composed of the northern 'martial races', by 1892 that number had risen to 49 out of 115 units, and by 1914 it had reached a stunning 77 out of 121.[64] Additionally, even those units maintained by the so-called 'non-martial' areas increasingly drew their recruits from the 'martial races'. By 1897, 24,000 men hailing from the Punjab and Nepal were serving in Madras, Bombay and Bengal.[65]

The move towards recruiting from the Punjab and Nepal was also accompanied by efforts to organise the Indian Army systematically by 'race' or 'class' (as they were often interchangeably called). Before the late 1880s, the general trend in the Indian Army was to organise a number of different 'classes' of sepoys into the same regiment, but to separate them into homogeneous companies. These became known as 'class company' regiments. By the 1890s, however, that system was increasingly discarded in favour of the 'class regiment', where regiments consisted exclusively of a single 'race' or caste.[66] In the fifteen years between 1887 and 1902, the number of class regiments in the Bengal Army rose from 22 to 42, while the number of class company regiments shrank from 42 to 22. Of the former, more than half hailed from the Punjab or Nepal. In the remaining class company regiments, all but two were composed of men from the Punjab, Nepal or the northwest frontier in 1887; in 1899 that number had shrunk to one.[67]

Under Roberts's leadership, the idea of martial races evolved to become the dominant model on which the Indian Army was organised and recruited. Martial race ideology was based on a combination of circumstantial evidence and Victorian racial 'science', and was immeasurably strengthened with each new crisis that threatened war with Russia on the northwest frontier. Increasingly, the only populations from which the Indian military sought to obtain recruits were those of the extreme north and northwest of India – those men who were believed to 'love fighting for fighting's sake', in contrast to the sepoys of lower India.[68] By the time of Roberts's departure from India in 1893, this strategy had become natural-ised into dogma. It was continued by his protégé and successor as Com-mander-in-Chief, Sir George White (1893–97), and continued to shape Indian military policy through the 1930s.[69] In 1892 a popular book on the organisation of British imperial forces unselfconsciously remarked that 'the northern races of India [are] incontestably those among which the best fighting material is to be found'.[70] In 1894 Sir Edwin Collen noted that 'if the commanding officers of the Indian Army were polled and their views accepted, the whole army would be composed of Sikhs, Pathans and Gurkhas'.[71] In the next chapter, we will see that the hegemony of martial race policy rested on a narrative discourse – articulated by key military figures – that featured the 'martial races' as the only possible Indian sol-diers able to fight as equals with Britons and against Europeans in battle.

The 'recruiting question' in the British Army

The 'European threat' also prompted a re-evaluation of the adequacy of the British Army for imperial and home defence. Faced with the possibility that British troops might be called upon to fight European soldiers in ei-ther Europe or Central Asia, officers and administrators in Britain and India grew increasingly concerned that the British Army was not up to the tasks that might be set before it. These concerns centred around two re-lated issues. The first was the fact that, despite a series of military reforms between 1870 and 1881, the British Army continued to experience serious difficulties attracting even the minimum number of recruits to man impe-rial and home garrisons. The second was that because of low pay and poor conditions, the only men the army was consistently able to attract were those of Britain's lowest classes. Moreover, by late century it became clear that even the often malnourished and under-educated men who enlisted were the cream of the crop – thousands of other potential enlistees had to be turned away every year because of poor health, small stature or bad teeth.

This last was certainly not a new problem. However, given the strong conscript armies of the Continent and Britain's diplomatic isolation, it took on new meaning. In the past, British Army strategists had accepted the dictums of the 'Blue Water' school, which held that a large standing army was unnecessary because Britain's vast and unequalled navy was adequate for home and imperial defence. Yet naval arms races with France and Germany in the last quarter of the century led a vocal contingent of army men to call the 'Blue Water' theory into question. If Britain's naval superiority could not be assured, they argued, then the British Army must be strong enough and large enough to defend itself on land. Thus the 'recruiting question', they insisted, must be resolved before it proved to be the undoing of the whole Empire. In 1890 an officer voiced the concerns of many when he despaired over the problem:

> The unpopularity, and consequent inefficiency, of the Army has reached to such a pitch and has become so notorious that it appears absolutely necessary that the matter should be taken up without further loss of time, and dealt with by our legislators as a non-political question of very serious national importance. It is essentially an Imperial question, on which it is not too much to say the safety of the Empire depends ... [improvements are needed] to render that Army more efficient in every respect, more characteristic of our great nation, and therefore, better adapted to represent the national will and power than it is at present.[72]

As in India, these concerns over the efficiency of the army must be understood in the context of late Victorian ideologies of race. The spectre of racial degeneration, in particular, haunted army commanders and social commentators alike. Did the state of British soldiery, they wondered, indicate that Britain was in the midst of racial decline just as nations like Germany appeared to be at their prime? These concerns, made urgent by what seemed to be impending conflict, led many army men to believe that if Britain were to protect itself and its Empire, the army would have to be made more efficient, more inclusive of all classes, and – above all – more popular. It was this last objective, as we shall see in the next two chapters, for which the Highland element of martial race discourse came to be utilised.

In 1877, at the height of the Near East crisis with Russia, General Roberts published a paper about the defects of the British Army's new recruiting system. It had not, in his view, improved the quality or quantity of recruits, and it did not adequately address the issue of popularity. '[I]f we are to have a voluntary Army', he argued, 'we must have a content one. To get recruits in the first place, we must make military service popular.'[73] The irony was that Roberts wrote after nearly a decade of reform, when army administrators had enacted a series of practical improvements designed to do just that. Such changes, their proponents had hoped, would transform the army into a respectable institution many men would choose, of their own accord, to enter.

Under the leadership of Edward Cardwell (Secretary for War, 1868–74), the complicated army structure of the past was radically simplified. Six military departments were reduced to two: one civilian-based under the Secretary for War and one military-based under the Commander-in-Chief.[74] Army administration was divided into only three departments: one headed by the Commander-in-Chief, who was to be the chief advisor to the Secretary and who was in charge of the men of the regular army and auxiliary forces; one headed by the Surveyor-General, in charge of supply;

and one headed by the Financial Secretary.[75] All were made firmly subordinate to the civilian Secretary for War and all were physically moved to the War Office.

With the new army leadership clearly established, reforms during the 1870s set out to increase the appeal of army service to a wider class of men. Foremost among these reforms was shortening the length of service for which recruits were expected to enlist. Thus, the Army Enlistment Act of 1870 reduced active service in the army to a period of six years, which was to be followed by a period of six years in the reserve.[76] Reformers hoped this Act would kill two birds with one stone: first, that it would stimulate increased enlistment, and second, that it would create a permanent reserve for use in wartime.

Cardwell also legislated reforms aimed at reducing the numbers of British soldiers serving long terms in colonial areas outside of India, a condition of service believed greatly to reduce the appeal of the army. Accordingly, he reduced troop strength in garrisons such as Australia, New Zealand and Canada. This, Cardwell hoped, would also create a more equal balance between the number of regiments serving overseas and the number of regiments stationed at home.[77] As a means of encouraging middle-class men to enlist as officers, in 1871 Cardwell abolished the purchase system by Royal Warrant (amidst loud protest in the House of Lords). In so doing, he and like-minded military reformers hoped to eliminate financial wealth as a prerequisite for holding high rank, and encourage instead promotion by merit and long service.

To improve the respectability of army service, the War Office tried to disavow the old recruiting methods of tricks, bribes and alcohol. In 1871 the Commander-in-Chief sent out a circular to all recruiting districts warning them to deal more honestly and fairly with potential recruits, and eliciting suggestions for 'the best means of removing all recruiting for the Regular Army from public-houses, any spersion [?] of intoxication, doing away with all bringers, agencies, and pecuniary rewards upon recruiting'.[78] The idea was that recruits should no longer be inveigled into the army, as they had been before. Now, they were supposed to be brought in through honest means when they were sober. However, as Edward Spiers has noted, this policy was easier advocated than enforced.[79]

In any case, the impact of these reforms was manifestly disappointing. In 1875 an army-based Committee on Recruiting reported that recruiting had not improved enough even to maintain the desired levels for that year, much less for the future. Furthermore, because the short service system allowed men to complete their tours of duty every six years, the report announced that 'after 1876 [when the first round of short service recruits passed out of the army] the present inducements will be insufficient to obtain the number of recruits required to keep up the establishment of the

Army'.[80] The report continued by pointing out that the reforms had not managed to bring the 'moral status' of the army up to its hoped-for heights.

The situation did not improve markedly with time. Indeed, recruiting remained a central problem in the British Army until 1914. Although recruiting did expand by 45 per cent during the period 1859–1901, the population of men between the ages of fifteen to twenty-four also expanded by 57 per cent.[81] Thus while the actual numbers annually recruited were much higher at the end of this period than at the beginning, the figures did not represent an increase of recruits relative to the population. And, as the 1875 report for the Committee on Recruiting had feared, the yearly wastage of troops transferring to the reserves under the short service system only added to the problem, for despite increased annual figures for enlistment, recruiting barely kept pace with the need to replace discharged soldiers.[82] Seldom did the army recruit enough men even to meet the annual targets voted by Parliament.[83]

The real problem, as reformers well knew, was money. True, the Cardwell reforms had ameliorated many of the most onerous problems of army service. Yet the one thing they were unable to do was markedly to improve soldiers' rates of pay. The simple fact remained that until 1906 even common labourers earned more than soldiers in the army.[84] This was glumly noted by the Parliamentary Commission on Recruiting in 1874, which grumbled that:

> The Soldier has his market value just like all other commodities; and it is highly unreasonable to expect, when land, houses, horses, beef and mutton, domestic servants, etc. etc- command a far higher price than formerly, that the price of the soldier can remain the same. This is the proper reply to the economists who oppose any increase in the military estimates; for if those estimates are to remain arbitrarily fixed, while prices continue to rise, the English Army must soon dwindle to a very low figure.[85]

In short, if Britons wanted an adequate army, then the government had to put up the money to pay it. Without that money, military officials feared that not only would the lowest classes continue to be the only ones attracted into service, but even *they* might begin to find employment elsewhere.

Parliament did not vote the necessary funds to increase soldiers' pay to an attractive level, and thus the situation remained relatively unchanged for the rest of the century. In 1892 yet another commission was charged with inquiring into army recruiting difficulties. The Wantage Committee, as it was called, came up with the same conclusions as earlier commissions. To no one's surprise, its final report determined that 'the pay of the soldiers is inadequate, and under the ordinary market rate for unskilled labour. Improvement in their pay and position is essential.'[86]

Given the tense international situation in the last decades of the century, army advocates argued that denying necessary funds to the army was dangerous at best. Because of the existence of potentially hostile, conscript armies on the Continent, new technologies in transport and weaponry, and the development of steam navigation, they insisted that Britain was now more vulnerable than ever to a land invasion.[87] In fact, invasion scares continually punctuated the period between 1880 to 1914, and were fed by a genre of popular invasion novels and rumours about espionage.[88] Poor relations with France and Russia, as well as deteriorating relations with Germany in the 1890s, led some army advocates to believe that both the means and the motivation for invasion already existed. In this context, they argued, soldiers' meagre pay – and the recruiting crisis that had developed out of it – could prove to be the Achilles' heel of Britain and its Empire. To remedy the situation, the army needed more resources so that it could attract not only more men, but better men.

Yet efforts to increase army expenditure had always to face the opposition and rivalry of the British Navy. Indeed, the problem of army pay was mired in a deep inter-service rivalry. Both services competed for scarce resources, and thus advocates for each fought hard to make a case for their own branch.[89] In opposition to army advocates, naval advocates insisted that the key to the defence of an island nation and its maritime Empire was a strong, powerful navy, whose ships would ensure the destruction of any invasion fleet and protect the sea-lanes of imperial territories.[90] Thus, they argued, increased expenditures on the army were unnecessary. Instead, military spending should give primacy to naval building to keep the British Navy competitive and superior to other European navies.

Despite loud army warnings about the dangers of a land invasion, the government seemed to agree. Accordingly, in 1889 Parliament passed a Naval Defence Act that gave extra money to the navy for shipbuilding, which essentially relegated the army to a secondary division of imperial defence.[91] Army advocates continued to press their case and did manage to prompt an official investigation into the likelihood of invasion. In 1903, however, the government officially sanctioned the navy's 'Blue Water' theory, arguing that a mass foreign invasion was impossible.[92]

Throughout this period, then, the army was forced to make do with what it had: too little money and too few men. Not only that, but the men it did have appeared ever more unsatisfactory in contrast, especially, to the German conscript army. To a number of officers and administrators, the state of British soldiery reflected no less than the overall racial degeneration of the British people.

As in India, theories of race lent a 'scientific' veneer to explanations of the recruiting crisis that went deeper than economic or practical explanations. Although Britons presumed themselves to be members of the 'superior' race, still many believed in the theory of environmental degeneration, whereby even superior races could be rendered racially unfit. As we know, theories of degeneration as a result of long exposure to tropical climates were already well established. Yet after 1870, the theory of urban degeneration – in any climate – gained credibility in British scientific and popular circles.[93] Contemporaries cited the deleterious environmental effects of infant mortality, disease and overcrowding in urban areas, the combination of which were perceived to have stunted racial development to an appalling degree.[94] The urban slums of East London, especially, came to symbolise the potential racial degeneracy of Britain as a whole, 'the quintessence of inner London poverty, the "boldest blotch on the face" of the capital of the civilised world'.[95] The contrast between the physical characteristics of the London poor, the 'white dull skin that looked degenerate and ominous to a West-end eye',[96] and the health and hardiness of country folk seemed as stark as the contrast between East and West. Fresh, bracing air, physical labour – Britons regretfully viewed these conditions of rural life as part of the British past that had made its people great and strong, conditions which many believed were rapidly being lost in Britain's increasingly urban population.

It was certainly true that Britain's large urban centres were the main suppliers of recruits to the army. By 1891, the Inspector-General reported that despite special efforts to recruit in the counties, 'the increase in numbers taken in 1890 proceeds, with hardly an exception, from a few of the largest towns'.[97] The consequences, in terms of the physical condition of the army, seemed all too apparent. For adequate numbers to be maintained in the army, the War Office found it necessary continually to lower the height and weight standards for recruits. From a minimum of 5 feet 6 inches in 1878, the requirements were reduced in 1880–82 to 5 feet 4 inches and in 1883 to 5 feet 3 inches. In 1889 it was raised again to 5 feet 4 inches, but during the South African War the standard was lowered again to eventually reach 5 feet 3 inches. The minimum weight throughout the period from 1884 to the end of the century was 115 lb. Even these minimal and, in Roberts's opinion, 'almost dwarfish' standards proved to be too difficult to maintain, and throughout the 1890s between 18 and 36 per cent of all recruits were accepted below the minimum as 'special enlistments'.[98] To many officers, these statistics proved that the army represented the very worst 'blood' of the nation. This, they argued, would not do in a period of such tension and instability. As one officer warned, '[t]he necessity of making a Voluntary Army like ours thoroughly representative of the nation and of drawing it from the best blood of the nation is too apparent to need pressing home'.[99]

Fears about the military consequences of the racial degeneration of the British people reached a crescendo during the South African War of 1899–

1902. During that conflict, the world's largest empire was crippled by a relatively small population of Boer farmers. What should have been a short, decisive war instead lasted three years, required the deployment of nearly half a million British troops, and cost an estimated £222 million.[100] Moreover, the concentration of forces necessary to defeat the Boers had, in turn, only been accomplished by 'virtually denuding the defences of the Empire', which left the British home and imperial territories vulnerable to attack by hostile powers.[101] This situation became incomparably more grave towards the end of the war, when Anglo-German relations rapidly deteriorated from their already precarious state. By 1902, it seemed apparent that Britain was faced with an enemy who possessed both the Continent's most powerful army as well as its most threatening navy.[102]

It also seemed apparent – as many had feared in the two decades preceding the war – that the British Army was in no way ready to meet such an enemy.[103] A letter to Lord Roberts from a fellow officer in 1907 summed up decades of frustration in one line. The officer had been observing the manoeuvres of the German Army, and concluded that unlike the Germans, 'we are quite unprepared, and the contrast between their splendid, well-organised, army, composed of the manhood of a virile nation, and our Home army composed of anything but our manhood is enough to make us shudder'.[104]

Such sentiments, as we know, were hardly new. For the past quarter-century the army had been faced with the unenviable dilemma of what seemed an urgent problem of obtaining enough good men to fight a European enemy while simultaneously being unable to offer market value for them. In response to the situation, even the conservative and traditionally un-savvy army found itself – in an era of intense media expansion – faced with the necessity of systematically promoting itself to the wider public. Arguably, the results of the South African War demonstrated that these efforts were at best only partially successful in terms of recruiting. But in terms of popular sentiment, army attempts to devote ever more attention to advertising, appearance, emotion, morale and patriotism may have been a good deal more effective.

One of the more controversial reforms designed to these ends was the reorganisations of 1881, which introduced the multi-battalion territorial regiment as the primary unit of the British Army.[105] The 1881 reforms were, in fact, extensions of an earlier 1872 Localisation Act which had linked British Army regiments in pairs and given each new unit specific territorial recruiting areas. The idea had been to increase local identification with the particular regiments attached to it in order to foster local pride in individual regiments. As one writer for the military journal *Colburn's* in 1875 put it, localisation would (hopefully) induce country people to be 'attracted to the service, companions at the plough, or loom, well fed, well dressed, with ample leisure and few cares, and admired by the village lasses, would be objects of envy; the display of the parade and its martial music would inflame them with military ardour, and there would be no difficulty in filling the ranks with good material'.[106]

In 1881 this initial plan was extended by formally joining each linked pair of battalions and by adding to them two militia battalions – thereby forming one large, territorial regiment with a clearly delineated home region and recruiting territory. As with the original Localisation Bill, the intention was to increase public interest in and affection for individual home regiments and hence increase the attraction and prestige of serving in them. By adding the militia battalions, it was hoped that association with regular battalions would give the militia a morale boost as a 'real' and important military unit. At the same time, the close association between the militia and the regular army was meant to foster a great deal of recruiting from the former to the latter.[107]

Another tactic was an unprecedented advertising campaign designed by the War Office. The idea, of course, was to sell itself and the virtues of military service to young British men. Given the influence of newspapers, journals and other media, the War Office hoped that 'the printer will get three times the number of men for one-third of the money' than any recruiting officer could supply.[108] In 1881 the War Office determined to advertise directly for recruits in 8 London papers, 75 provincial English papers, 25 Scottish papers, 27 Irish papers and 10 Welsh papers on a weekly or bi-weekly basis. Each paper was chosen for its high circulation rates.[109] Furthermore, posters detailing the 'Advantages of the Army' were to be strategically placed around the country, directing potential recruits to their nearest post office for further information and applications. Paid recruiters, who would be assigned to particular areas within their regimental district, were to ensure that posters were posted, and that applicants to the post offices were pursued. In 1886 the War Office supplemented these methods of advertisement by an illustrated poster to be displayed at railway stations. In the same year, it extended the number of newspapers to carry the recruiting advertisement to 256 metropolitan and provincial dailies and weeklies.[110] As one inspector-general noted in 1890, 'for an Army maintained by voluntary enlistment, the importance of a wide advertisement of the terms and condition of military service can hardly be overrated'.[111]

Increasingly, this advertising campaign was extended to regular, promotional lectures to be given by local recruiting officers, aided by the use of magic lanterns (whenever possible) to provide appropriate visual stimulation. District recruiting officers were instructed to schedule recruiting marches and drills in order to bring local people face to face with the sights and sounds of regiments in full dress, accompanied by military music.[112]

The War Office also began to publish official regimental histories of the territorial regiments, which were directed to 'be judiciously distributed as an aid to recruiting, and in order to stimulate local interest in the regiments'.[113] These histories were to be kept up to date by regimental commanding officers, who were directed to furnish the War Office with the names and ranks of all officers and men who received the Victoria Cross or Distinguished Conduct Medal (as well as descriptions of what occurred) for inclusion in later editions.[114] By 1907, the motivation for requiring such details were clearly articulated in Recruiting Regulations, as was the desired connection between the military and the press:

> Officers [in charge of] recruiting should give as much publicity as possible to any honours or successes gained by any soldier of the territorial regiment. With this object they should invoke the assistance of the local press, and endeavour to induce the editors to insert such items of information in the papers circulating in the district from which the soldier comes.[115]

Clearly, the army had become alive to the power of advertisement. Like so many other Victorian institutions, political parties and pressure groups, the military had discovered that using the media was an effective way to gain public attention. As Recruiting Regulations suggested, recruiting efforts were to focus on the pomp and glory of soldiering. Music, medals, marches, imagery and stories of heroism were all to be used to encourage enlistment. In what seemed a desperate recruiting shortage in the face of an imminent European war, the military sought to focus on transforming the image of the British soldier from a drunken lout to a hero, from an urban street rat to an ideal citizen. This desire, then, created the preconditions for which the language of Highland Scots as a modern 'martial race' grew into a national phenomenon, with full army approval.

Yet these institutional interventions were only – as we shall see in the next chapter – the tip of the iceberg. Indeed, many individual officers concerned with the threat from Europe in both Central Asia and in Britain believed the efforts of the War Office were too slow and too slight. Given the seriousness of the international situation, they took matters into their own hands. This was a generation of men, let us remember, who were far more alert to the power of the media than their predecessors – and in late century, they sought to use it to manipulate public opinion about the military. It was in their hands that martial race discourse rose to its fullest expression in Britain at the end of the century – as a seductive language of masculinity, courage and honour embodied by the most popular British soldier of all, the Highland Scot.

Britain's changing – and worsening – relationship with other European nations had thus transformed the ways in which military administrators imagined the nature and purposes of the British and Indian armies. The shape of responses to the 'European threat', naturally, differed as a result of particular circumstances within each army. In India, where the military leadership had much greater freedom to implement policy and where the population was vastly larger than in Britain, fears of a European invasion completed a fundamental shift in the recruiting base of the Indian Army towards those 'races' who had remained loyal during the Rebellion. In Britain, the failure of reforms designed to improve the condition of military service led to an increasing reliance on advertising and propaganda to enhance recruiting efforts.

Different as these responses may seem, they shared important connections. As a result of the European (Russian) threat to India, military administrators increasingly viewed the British and Indian armies in tandem, as different but complementary forces who might very possibly be called upon, together, to fight against a European enemy in the foreseeable future. The increased links between the two military forces which had resulted as a consequence of the Rebellion now grew stronger, and military voices advocating preparation for a European conflict hailed from both armies. Moreover, the response in both the Indian and British armies to European competition was shaped by the legacy of the Rebellion. In India, the memory surrounding those populations who remained loyal during the conflict was a critical factor in determining British perceptions about which men would make the best soldiers against European enemies. In Britain, as we shall see, the imagery surrounding Highlanders fighting alongside their Indian counterparts during the Rebellion provided inspiration for a discourse that popularised soldiers, the army and imperial service. This, of course, was the language of 'martial races' – a language that illustrates the active involvement of military men in the development of British popular imperialism.

Notes

1   Public Record Office, Kew (hereafter PRO), WO 105/41, Lieutenant-Colonel Frederick Roberts, Memorandum on the employment of soldiers in the several government offices, state railways, &c, &c, with a view to the formation of an efficient reserve (Reprinted from the *Pioneer*, 26 Sept. 1870).

2   India Office Library and Records, London (hereafter OIOL), L/MIL/7/7056, Lord Roberts, On the desirability of clearly defining the principles on which the administration of the army in India should be based, and of persevering in the policy which has guided the Government of India in its efforts to strengthen the military position in this country (1893).

3   For this culture of anxiety, see I. F. Clarke, *Voices Prophesying War: Future Wars, 1763–3749* (Oxford: Oxford University Press, 1992); A. J. A. Morris, *The Scaremongers: The Advocacy of War and Rearmament, 1896–1914* (London: Routledge & Kegan Paul, 1984).

4   See Mike Hawkins, *Social Darwinism in European and American Thought, 1860–1945* (Cambridge: Cambridge University Press, 1997), 30–31; Ann Laura Stoler, 'Making the Empire respectable: the politics of race and sexual morality', *American*

Ethnologist 16:4 (Nov. 1989), 635; Paul Rich, *Race and Empire in British Politics* (Cambridge: Cambridge University Press, 1986), 13; Douglas Lorimer, *Colour, Class and the Victorians* (Leicester: Leicester University Press, 1978), 14.

5 Muriel Chamberlain, *Pax Britannica? British Foreign Policy, 1789–1914* (London: Longman, 1988), 126; Bernard Porter, 'Mid-Victorian heyday, 1848–70' and 'Doubts and fears, 1870–95', in *Britain, Europe and the World, 1850–1982* (London: Allen & Unwin, 1983), 1–55.

6 For selected documents regarding German unification and the Franco-Prussian War in the context of European diplomatic relations, see Herman Weill, *European Diplomatic History, 1815–1914: Documents and Interpretations* (New York: Exposition, 1972), ch. 4.

7 Porter, *Britain, Europe and the World, 1850–1982*, 34.

8 There is a substantial literature on the subject of Anglo-Russian rivalry during the nineteenth century. For the antecedents to the late Victorian rivalry, see the works of Edward Ingram, especially *The Beginning of the Great Game in Asia, 1828–1834* (Oxford: Clarendon, 1979), *Commitment to Empire: Prophecies of the Great Game in Asia, 1797–1800* (Oxford: Clarendon, 1981) and *In Defence of British India: Great Britain and the Middle East, 1775–1842* (London: Frank Cass, 1984). For the later period, see David Gillard, *The Struggle for Asia, 1828–1914: A Study in British and Russian Imperialism* (London: Methuen, 1977).

9 C. J. Bartlett, *Defence and Diplomacy: Britain and the Great Powers, 1815–1914* (Manchester: Manchester University Press, 1993), 72.

10 Peter Waldron, *The End of Imperial Russia, 1855–1917* (New York: St Martin's Press, 1997), 107–108.

11 J. N. Westwood, *Endurance and Endeavor: Russian History 1812–1980* (Oxford: Oxford University Press, 1981), 95. These terms were quite different from those that had existed under Alexander II's predecessor, Nicholas I. Under Nicholas, recruits were drawn only from the peasant class, and were required to serve for twenty-five years, which meant that most soldiers never saw their families again (62–63).

12 Westwood, *Endurance and Endeavor*, 95, 190.

13 The impetus for Russian expansion was partly due to the lack of natural barriers between Russia and Europe or Central Asia, which made it both relatively easy to expand and dangerous not to consolidate border areas. Waldron, *The End of Imperial Russia*, 106–107.

14 For a more nuanced account of the Eastern Crisis of 1877–78, see Malcolm Yapp, *The Making of the Modern Near East, 1792–1923* (London: Longman, 1987), 77–83.

15 Yapp, *The Making of the Modern Near East*, 76; Gillard, *The Struggle for Asia*, 115–133.

16 See House of Commons, 'Papers relating to European and native troops', *Sessional Papers*, vol. 52 (1867). Although the report itself dates from 1867, most of the contents are memoranda and military letters dating from the 1830s regarding the Russian threat in Central Asia. The warnings of then Governor-General William Bentinck (1828–35) feature prominently in these papers. See also works by Edward Ingram cited in note 8 above.

17 The Viceroy was Lord Lytton. For a detailed analysis of the lead-up to the war, see Brian Robson, *The Road to Kabul: The Second Afghan War, 1878–1881* (London: Arms and Armour Press, 1986), 39–52.

18 Gillard, *The Struggle for Asia*, ch. 7.

19 Kenneth Bourne, *The Foreign Policy of Victorian England, 1830–1902* (Oxford: Clarendon, 1970), 143–145.

20 Bourne, *The Foreign Policy of Victorian England*, 163.

21 Tim Moreman has dealt with these campaigns in *The Army in India and the Development of Frontier Warfare, 1849–1947* (London: Macmillan, 1998).

22 Linda Colley, *Britons: Forging the Nation, 1707–1837* (New Haven: Yale University Press, 1992), 1.

23 Bartlett, *Defence and Diplomacy*, 64.

24 Keith Robbins, *The Eclipse of a Great Power: Modern Britain, 1870–1992* (London:

Longman, 1983), 29.

25 On Siam, see William Langer, *The Diplomacy of Imperialism, 1890–1902* (New York: Alfred Knopf, 1956), 43–46; For Fashoda, see Robbins, *The Eclipse of a Great Power*, 29–30; Chamberlain, *Pax Britannica?*, 158; Bourne, *The Foreign Policy of Victorian England*, 160–161.

26 Bartlett, *Defence and Diplomacy*, 76; Robbins, *The Eclipse of a Great Power*, 38.

27 Bartlett, *Defence and Diplomacy*, 86–87.

28 Indeed, Lord Curzon published an article in *Nineteenth Century* entitled 'India between two fires' (Aug. 1893) about the situation. See Langer, *The Diplomacy of Imperialism*, 43–46.

29 This becomes strikingly clear in Roberts's papers concerning the likelihood of invasion, gathered together in WO 105/44 at the PRO.

30 For detailed analysis of Anglo-German relations in the last decade of the nineteenth century, see Paul Kennedy, *The Rise of the Anglo-German Antagonism, 1860–1914* (London: George Allen & Unwin, 1980), chs 11–13.

31 Quoted in Michael Allison, 'The national service issue, 1900–1914' (Ph.D. thesis, University of London, 1975), 7. This was, of course, during the South African War.

32 House of Commons, 'Correspondence relating to the increase of the army in India', *Sessional Papers*, vol. 62 (1887), 26.

33 Ann Laura Stoler, *Race and the Education of Desire: Foucault's History of Sexuality and the Colonial Order of Things* (Durham: Duke University Press, 1995), 133–134.

34 Emphasis on the importance of environmental factors was not unique to Darwin's thought, and was a vital aspect of Lamarckianism as well. The roots of environmental thinking were deep, but were expressed in the late nineteenth century in scientific terms, whether by followers of Lamarck or of Darwin. Hawkins, *Social Darwinism in European and American Thought*, 26–27.

35 Dane Kennedy, *The Magic Mountains: Hill Stations and the British Raj* (Berkeley: University of California Press, 1996), 32–35.

36 Nancy Stepan, 'Biological degeneration: races and proper places', in J. Edward Chamberlin and Sander Gilman (eds), *Degeneration: The Darker Side of Progress* (New York: Columbia University Press, 1985), 105.

37 Hawkins, *Social Darwinism in European and American Thought*, 187.

38 For a complex account of late nineteenth-century Orientalism, see Kelli Kobor, 'Orientalism, the construction of rce, and the politics of identity in British India, 1800–1930' (Ph.D. dissertation, Duke University, 1998), esp. ch. 3.

39 Thomas Trautmann, *Aryans and British India* (Berkeley: University of California Press, 1997), esp. ch. 7.

40 Ajay Skaria, 'Shades of wildness: tribe, caste, and gender in western India', *Journal of Asian Studies* 56:3 (Aug. 1997), 728. See also Crispin Bates, 'Race, caste and tribe in central India: the early origins of Indian anthromopetry', in Peter Robb (ed.), *The Concept of Race in South Asia* (New Delhi: Oxford University Press, 1995).

41 Thomas Metcalf, *Ideologies of the Raj: The New Cambridge History of India, Volume III:4* (Cambridge: Cambridge University Press, 1994), 84.

42 David Omissi, *The Sepoy and the Raj: The Indian Army, 1860–1940* (London: Macmillan, 1994), 32; Metcalf, *Ideologies of the Raj*, 82–85.

43 For the high opinion in which many military officials held the armies of Madras and Bombay, see the letters in OIOL, L/MIL/5/525, Despatches re-organisation of army and strength of forces for India (1861).

44 OIOL, L/MIL/17/5/1615/ 6, F. S. Roberts, Correspondence and minutes while in India (1877–93), Note on the necessity for increasing the efficiency of the Indian Army (1886).

45 Roberts to Lieutenant-General Sir James Dormer, CIC Madras, Sept. 1891, in Correspondence and minutes while in India (1877–93).

46 Omissi, *The Sepoy and the Raj*, 13.

47 Quoted from official reports in Omissi, *The Sepoy and the Raj*, 14.

48 T. A. Heathcote, *The Military in British India: The Development of British Land Forces in South Asia, 1600–1947* (Manchester: Manchester University Press, 1995), 173.

49 Heathcote, *The Military in British India*, 136–148.
50 OIOL, L/MIL/17/5/1687, Eden Commission, Report of the special commission appointed by His Excellency the Governor-General in Council to enquire into the organisation and expenditure of the army in India (1879), 16.
51 OIOL, L/MIL/17/5/1698 Frederick Haines, Memorandum by His Excellency General Sir Frederick P. Haines, Commander-in-Chief in India, on the report of the special army commission (1880), 15.
52 Gillard, *The Struggle for Asia*, 144; Heathcote, *The Military in British India*, 151. Mrinalini Sinha also has demonstrated that thousands of educated, middle-class Indians petitioned to join the Volunteers in India, although the offers were rejected. Sinha, *Colonial Masculinity: The 'Manly Englishman' and the 'Effeminate Bengali' in the Late Nineteenth Century* (Manchester: Manchester University Press, 1995), 69–97.
53 House of Commons, 'Correspondence relating to the increase of the army in India', 173.
54 The fifth was to be a battalion of pioneers. 'Correspondence relating to the increase of the army in India', 173.
55 Heathcote, *The Military in British India*, 153. The transfer did not officially occur until 1886, when Roberts had already stepped in as Commander-in-Chief.
56 Brian Robson (ed.), *Roberts in India: The Military Papers of Field Marshal Lord Roberts, 1876–1893* (Phoenix Mill: Alan Sutton, 1993), 10–17, 231.
57 OIOL, MSS Eur D734, Lord Roberts's printed papers, Lord Roberts, 'On the necessity for improving the fighting qualities of the Indian Army' (c. 1890).
58 Roberts to Sir Philip Hutchins, K.C.S.I., July 1892. In Correspondence and minutes ehile in India (1877–93).
59 Adrian Preston, 'Wolseley, the Khartoum relief expedition and the defence of India', *Journal of Imperial and Commonwealth History* 6:3 (May 1978), 261, 262.
60 Preston, 'Wolseley, the Khartoum relief expedition and the defence of India', 258.
61 F. S. Roberts, Note on the necessity for increasing the efficiency of the Indian Army (1886), in Correspondence and minutes while in India (1877–93).
62 Omissi, *The Sepoy and the Raj*, 16. The total strength of the Indian Army in 1893 was 144,020.
63 Omissi, *The Sepoy and the Raj*, 9.
64 OIOL, L/MIL/17/5/2152, H. Hudson (Adjutant-General in India), Recruiting in India before and during the war of 1914–18 (1919), 6–7.
65 'The native army of India', *Blackwood's Magazine* 162 (Aug. 1897), 204. The same article gives the breakdown of Punjabi and Nepalese soldiers serving outside of the Punjab. In Bengal there were '8 battalions of Gurkhas, 5½ squadrons of Sikhs and ½ squadron each of Dogras and Punjabi Muhammadans'. In Madras there was '1 battalion of Gurkhas, 22 companies of Sikhs, 16 companies of Punjabi Muhammadans, 3 companies of Pathans, 2 companies of Dogras' and in Bombay there were 'three regiments of cavalry and five battalions of infantry, localised in Sindh, and composed entirely of Punjabi and frontier classes' as well as '4 squadrons of Sikhs, 1 squadron and four companies of Pathans, [and] 1 squadron and 17 companies of Punjabi Muhammedans' (203).
66 A. J. Johnstone, 'Localisation of recruiting for the infantry of the Indian Army', *United Services Institute of India* 25:123 (1896), 87.
67 House of Commons, 'Memorandum showing recent changes in the mode of recruiting and organising the native army in India', *Sessional Papers*, vol. 70 (1902).
68 Roberts to W. Benett, Secretary to the Governmentt of India, Revenue and Agriculture Department, July 1890, in Correspondence and minutes while in India (1877–93).
69 Roberts promoted White over the heads of several more senior officers who were Wolseley men. See Preston, 'Wolseley, the Khartoum relief expedition and the defence of India', 261.
70 J. C. Dalton and William H. Goodenough, *The Army Book for the British Empire: A Record of the Development and Present Composition of the Military Forces and their Duties in Peace and War* (London: Harrison & Sons, 1893), 467.
71 H. Hudson, Recruiting in India before and during the war of 1914–18, 9.

72 Colonel M. J. King-Harman, 'How to make the army popular', *United Services Magazine* 2 (1890–91), 391.

73 F. S. Roberts, 'Free trade in the army', in Correspondence and minutes while in India (1877–93).

74 For a full explanation of the structural reforms Cardwell implemented, see Edward Spiers, *The Late Victorian Army, 1868–1902* (Manchester: Manchester University Press, 1992), esp. ch. 1.

75 Edward Spiers, 'The late Victorian army, 1868–1914', in David Chandler and Ian Beckett (eds), *The Oxford Illustrated History of the British Army* (Oxford: Oxford University Press, 1994), 189.

76 Allan Ramsay Skelley, *The Victorian Army at Home: The Recruitment and Terms and Conditions of the British Regular, 1859–1899* (London: Croom Helm, 1977), 253.

77 Spiers, 'The late Victorian army', 189–190. In fact, the principle of balance was upset almost immediately by the Ashanti War in 1873 and the Zulu and Afghan Wars in 1879, resulting in a far larger number of battalions abroad than at home – creating home battalions that resembled, according to Lord Wolseley, 'squeezed lemons' (191).

78 PRO, WO 33/22, Reports from the inspecting officers of recruiting districts (1871).

79 Spiers, *The Late Victorian Army*, 126.

80 PRO, WO 33/27 #585, Report of the committee on recruiting (1875), 19.

81 Skelley, *The Victorian Army at Home*, 237.

82 Skelley, *The Victorian Army at Home*, 237. Because of the short service system, annual discharges were nearly double what they had been before the effects of the system were felt in full force by 1876.

83 Spiers, *The Late Victorian Army*, 121.

84 House of Commons, 'Annual report on recruiting', *Sessional Papers*, vol. 14 (1906) [cd. 2693].

85 PRO, WO 33/26 #569, On recruiting (1874).

86 PRO, WO 33/52 #226, number 20, Lord Wantage, Terms and conditions of service in the army (recruiting) (1892).

87 Howard Moon, 'The invasion of the United Kingdom' (Ph.D. thesis, University of London, 1968), 5.

88 Christopher Andrew, *Secret Service: The Making of the British Intelligence Community* (London: Guild Publishers, 1985), 44 passim; Clarke, *Voices Prophesying War*, 124–25; Morris, *The Scaremongers*, 156.

89 On the competition for financial resources, see Morris, *The Scaremongers*, 107.

90 Andrew S. Thompson, *Imperial Britain: The Empire in British Politics, c. 1880–1932* (Harlow: Pearson Education, 2000), 111; R. J. Q. Adams and Philip Poirier, *The Conscription Controversy in Great Britain, 1900–18* (London: Macmillan, 1987), 24–25.

91 Thompson, *Imperial Britain*, 111.

92 Rhodri Williams, *Defending the Empire: The Conservative Party and British Defence Policy, 1899–1915* (New Haven: Yale University Press, 1991), 25.

93 Robert Nye, 'Sociology: the irony of progress', in J. Edward Chamberlain and Sander Gilman (eds), *Degeneration: The Dark Side of Progress* (New York: Columbia University Press, 1985), 64–65.

94 See Anna Davin's pathbreaking article, 'Imperialism and motherhood', reprinted in Frederick Cooper and Ann Stoler (eds), *Tensions of Empire: Colonial Cultures in a Bourgeois World* (Berkeley: University of California Press, 1997).

95 Judith Walkowitz, *City of Dreadful Delight: Narratives of Sexual Danger in Late-Victorian London* (Chicago: University of Chicago Press, 1992), 30.

96 Raymond Williams quoting H. G. Wells, in Williams, *The Country and the City* (New York: Oxford University Press, 1973), 229.

97 House of Commons, 'Annual report of the inspector general of recruiting', *Sessional Papers*, vol. 19, session 1 (1890–91), 6.

98 PRO, WO 33/52 #244, General Lord Roberts, Four papers recently prepared or referred to by General Lord Roberts with reference to subjects connected with the report on terms and conditions of service in the army (1892), 1; Spiers, *The Late Victorian Army*, 123.

99   J. A., 'Population and recruiting', *United Services Magazine* 9 (1894), 249. For more on the question of national efficiency, see Geoffrey Searle, *The Quest for National Efficiency: A Study in British Politics and Political Thought, 1899–1914* (Berkeley: University of California Press, 1971).

100   Anne Summers, 'Militarism in Britain before the Great War', *History Workshop Journal* 2 (1976), 111.

101   Summers, 'Militarism in Britain Before the Great War', 111; Williams, *Defending the Empire*, 9.

102   Kennedy, *The Rise of the Anglo-German Antagonism*, 251.

103   For some of the social arguments for reform, see Hendley, '"Help us to secure a strong, healthy, prosperous and peaceful Britain"', *Canadian Journal of History* 30 (Aug. 1995), 268–270.

104   PRO, WO 105/45, Beauvoir de Lisle to Lord Roberts, 1907.

105   Hew Strachan, *The Politics of the British Army* (Oxford: Clarendon, 1997), 202.

106   Quoted in Skelley, *The Victorian Army at Home*, 255.

107   House of Commons, 'Annual report of the inspector general of recruiting', *Sessional Papers*, vol. 20 (1881), 2. For the extremely controversial nature of the 1881 reorganisations see Strachan, *The Politics of the British Army*, 202–204.

108   Skelley, *The Victorian Army at Home*, 241.

109   See PRO, WO 32/6886, Methods, advertising in press and post office and rewards (1881–82).

110   House of Commons, 'Annual report of the inspector general of recruiting', *Sessional Papers*, vol. 13 (1886), 8.

111   House of Commons, 'Annual report of the inspector general of recruiting', *Sessional Papers*, vol. 19 (1890–91), 10.

112   Skelley, *The Victorian Army at Home*, 243. Robert Giddings talks about the seductive effect of military music in 'Delusive seduction: pride, pomp, circumstance and military music', in John MacKenzie (ed.), *Popular Imperialism and the Military* (Manchester: Manchester University Press, 1992), 25–49.

113   British Library, London (BL), War Office, Regulations for recruiting the regular army (1900), 11.

114   Regulations for recruiting the regular army, 11.

115   BL, War Office, Regulations for recruiting the regular army (1907), 3.

CHAPTER FOUR

Military influence and martial race discourse in British popular culture

> The press has become a power which a man should try to manage for himself; ... it is an influence which one cannot deny, and therefore should try to make one's own.[1]

In June 1889 General Frederick Roberts sent a letter to William Blackwood, editor of the popular and successful periodical *Blackwood's Magazine*. This was not their first communication: the two men had been friendly for at least a decade, when Roberts had risen to fame for his military exploits during the Second Afghan War (1878–80). Yet this particular letter had an unusually stilted tone, as though Roberts was self-conscious of the transparent game he was about to play. He began by reminding Blackwood of what was apparently an earlier pledge: 'It is very kind of you to say you would be glad to publish any paper of mine in which I might wish to bring a particular policy under the notice of the public. I will not fail to avail myself of your offer.'[2] Unfortunately, Roberts continued, it would be inappropriate to speak publicly about political matters while he was Commander-in-Chief in India. However, in three pages of single-spaced, articulate type Roberts proceeded to detail his opinions on the controversial – and deeply political – issue of defending India's northwest frontier against a potential Russian invasion. In closing, Roberts feigned surprise at his long-windedness, and ended with an obvious suggestion that would allow his opinion to be published without violating his obligation to keep political matters to himself:

> I had no intention of inflicting this long letter upon you when I began to write, but it is a subject which interests me intensely, and which I fear is but little understood even by the best informed at home. You may, perhaps, be able to make use of what I have written without using my words or expressions, and without letting me be pointed to as your correspondent.[3]

The letter, buried in Blackwood's correspondence, speaks volumes about the relationship between the army and the media in late Victorian culture.

It demonstrates Roberts's belief that he could use his personal connection with Blackwood to influence the magazine's readership in support of his own political agenda. Its very existence hints at the wider implications of the connection between Roberts and Blackwood, for it suggests that similar arrangements between other officers and media agents also existed. At the same time, the fact that the letter insists on confidentiality and anonymity reminds us that the networks linking army interests and the media were often hidden from the public eye.

Whether by covert or overt means, by the last quarter of the nineteenth century ambitious officers like Roberts increasingly tried to manipulate public opinion through recourse to the Victorian media. They were motivated by a variety of concerns, including the hope of professional advancement, personal and professional rivalry with fellow officers, and the desire to sway the public on matters of military security and organisation. Their involvement with both the media and agents of the media was extensive. Officers wrote books, articles and memoirs both in their own names and anonymously. They cultivated friendships with press editors, war correspondents and media artists. While on campaign, they frequently sought to manipulate, censor or supersede agents of the press. They used their connections to advance their own interests and also to ensure their junior protégés' media access. They were, in short, active participants in Britain's rapidly expanding media culture and sought no less than to mould public opinion in their own favour.

This chapter argues that the Victorian army, so frequently depicted by historians as peripheral to 'mainstream' culture, was in fact instrumental in shaping late Victorian British popular culture. Recent scholarship has already demonstrated that public esteem for the army and colonial warfare rose dramatically in this era. Tales of army adventures abounded, reflecting an increasingly jingoistic, militaristic and imperially minded popular culture.[4] Yet in spite of the centrality of soldiers and warfare to this media culture, such scholarship has focused largely on the agency of the media in inspiring and sustaining military enthusiasm. Here, I argue that the timing of British popular militarism was no accident, and that it corresponded with officers' influence in the media. In other words, late-century popular militarism reflected the role that self-interested and media-savvy military figures played in helping to shape the values and ideologies of a more aggressively imperial state.

There were many such military men in the late Victorian period, but one in particular – General Frederick Roberts – stands out. Few officers, indeed, expended more energy or met with more success in their efforts to manipulate the media. As such, Roberts's story serves as a case study that highlights the range of media interventions available to ambitious officers, and demonstrates the cultural impact such interventions could have.

Equally important, through his extensive use of the Victorian media, Roberts inevitably brought his preoccupation with martial race ideology before a very wide public. From despatches written during the Second Afghan War to interviews, speeches and his own best-selling book, Roberts's characterisations of Highlanders, Sikhs and Gurkhas as inherently martial men revived connections initially made during the Rebellion of 1857. As a result, the discourse of martial races re-entered the public lexicon and inspired others – both military and civilian – to use its seductive imagery of masculinity, courage and honour with increasing frequency. By the end of the nineteenth century, the connections between 'martial' Sikhs, Gurkhas and Highlanders had become naturalised as part of a public discourse that sought to convey the values of the ultimate male imperial subject.

In order to understand how the ideology of martial races could be transformed from a military policy in India to a popular sentiment that included Scottish Highlanders, this chapter begins with a reassessment of the role played by army officers in Victorian culture. Through the multiple cultural interventions of officers generally – and Roberts in particular – I argue that Victorian officers frequently gained privileged access to the Victorian media, and that they used this access to forward their own interests. In Roberts's case, this access allowed his fascination with 'martial' Highlanders, Sikhs and Gurkhas to enter public discourse on a mass scale. In turn, Roberts's own fascination led others to focus ever greater attention on these three groups, until their connections as superior fighting men came to seem irrefutable.

The military and late Victorian society

Historians of popular imperialism have frequently assumed a division between the 'real' Victorian army and its popular representations.[5] This perception has been aided by British military historians themselves, who have insisted that, at least since the days of Cromwell, the army has intentionally held itself apart from British political and cultural concerns.[6] However, some scholars have challenged this assumption by pointing to the myriad ways in which 'real' military figures were not only involved in British social and political life, but actively tried to shape political outcomes in Britain and its Empire.[7]

Socially, British officers in the army maintained firm connections with those at the centres of political and cultural power. Indeed, in the late nineteenth century approximately half of the army's officer corps hailed from Britain's elite classes of aristocrats and landed gentry. As a result, these men shared family connections and social ties with their class peers who dominated British political and social life.[8] Not surprisingly, then, officers frequently moved in the same social circles as political elites, and also used their connections to gain access to others.

Those remaining officers who were not of Britain's landed classes came instead from Britain's professional middle classes, whose values and norms increasingly dominated British culture after 1850.[9] Here again social and family connections between officers and representatives of the law, clergy, publishing industry and medicine were the norm. Links to the press were particularly strong. Leading journalists and publishers had regular and virtually unrestricted contact with military officials, and, as Lucy Brown has pointed out, this professional and personal affinity reduced resistance and criticism by the news-makers to the influence of special-interest lobbyists in the military.[10]

If the divide between officers and those at the centres of power were indistinct, officers' separation from British political life was equally blurred. Perhaps most visibly, army officers were heavily represented in Parliament throughout the Victorian period.[11] In 1885 and 1898, for example, officers made up 27 and 35 per cent of the membership of the House of Lords, respectively.[12] Moreover, by the 1870s and 1880s a significant number of MPs also had strong ties to the Volunteers (Britain's voluntary auxiliary force for home defence) just at a time when the volunteer force was gaining real connections with the regular army.[13] At any given time, then, Parliament contained a strong minority of men with interests in either the regular or home armies. In the colonies, army officers frequently served in civil appointments as governors and administrators, and thus combined their military service with distinctly political duties. In fact, many officers used their experience in these venues to penetrate political circles once home in Britain.[14]

In addition to their societal and parliamentary roles, military men often became celebrities in their own right. This celebrity status was firmly linked to the expansion of the British media in the last half of the century, which brought increasing numbers of Britons into contact with news from the Empire. We have already seen that the 1857 Rebellion was one of the first imperial campaigns to coincide with a massive boom in the production of news from afar. Yet the Rebellion was only the first in a long series of imperial campaigns that attracted widespread interest and press coverage in Britain. Due to the increased reach of the press in the last three decades of the nineteenth century, later campaigns were publicised before an ever wider audience. Newspaper circulations increased beyond the imaginations of mid-century Britons, largely because prices for individual papers fell markedly in this period. The chief causes of this drop in price included innovations in production, technological advances in obtaining news (especially the increased use of the telegram after 1870), and the availability of cheap news to the provinces via the Press Association (formed in 1868). The results were nothing short of spectacular. Whereas in 1860 there were 31 daily newspapers in the whole of Britain, by the early 1890s there were 150.[15] Moreover, by 1880 the cost of many newspapers had dropped from a penny to a halfpenny, which meant that even relatively poor people could afford to buy more than just a weekly paper.[16] Popular papers such as the *Daily Telegraph* and the *Morning and Evening Standard* more than doubled their circulations between 1860 and 1890, and the *Liverpool Echo* (the most successful provincial daily) circulated more than 800,000 copies by 1892.[17] In addition to newspapers, print culture of all varieties expanded along similar lines during the same period, including magazines, inexpensive books, sheet music and advertisements.[18]

It was in this context that military men such as Fred Roberts, Garnet Wolseley, Herbert Kitchener and a host of now-forgotten officers rose to fame as a result of imperial campaigns. While the phenomenon was not new to this period, still in the last three decades of the century the celebration of military heroes became something of an industry in itself, where countless officers from imperial campaigns appeared in newspapers, illustrated papers and boys' serials.[19] Their stories became a stock in trade: individual men campaigned in faraway, exotic areas of the Empire, each successfully performing extraordinary feats of military 'prowess' against all odds and under intense pressure, all the while campaigning for Britannia's good and moral causes. The pantheon of these personalities proved to be the fuel that fired many a British heart with enthusiasm for the opportunities the Empire had to offer – adventure, glory and Christian militarism.[20]

Scholars of this phenomenon have tended to view the production of these military heroes as media events – inspired by the initial actions of individuals, but made legendary through the increasingly powerful and influential organs of the media.[21] This approach, however, obscures the active role officers played in their own creation as military heroes. Indeed, officers frequently influenced the way they were depicted in the press by attempting to control access to news at the front, by assuming the role of war correspondents themselves, by their own (frequently anonymous) contributions to the media, and by exerting pressure on contacts within the press. Moreover, once officers entered the public limelight, their fame allowed them ever greater access to media networks through contacts with eminent journalists and publishers. While this was certainly true of Fred Roberts, as we shall see, it was equally true of other military celebrities. Sir Garnet Wolseley was well known for attempting to use the media to his own – and to the army's – advantage once he gained fame from his imperial campaigns. From the early 1870s, Wolseley used the press as a forum for advocating reform of the army, and also for ambitiously advancing his own military career – a habit that sometimes provoked bitter criticism from fellow officers.[22] When on active service, he actively cultivated the good graces of war correspondents in the hopes of getting good press. Between 1870 and 1900, he also contributed directly, though sometimes anonymously, to influential journals such as *Blackwood's, MacMillan's,* the *Fortnightly Review* and the *Nineteenth Century.*[23]

Many other officers also sought to use the popular media for their own purposes. General Sir Horatio Herbert Kitchener, in addition to contributing directly to Victorian serials, used covert contacts with the editor of the *Standard* and the military correspondent of *The Times* to pressure the British government to accept his views of reform while he was Commander-in-Chief in India (1902–5).[24] George White and Winston Churchill are only the most conspicuous examples of officers who served double duty as war correspondents for metropolitan papers.[25] Evelyn Wood was one of many officers who left direct evidence of his attempts to control the access of war correspondents to military news in imperial campaigns.[26] Evelyn Wood, George Chesney and William Lockhart were among the numerous military men who published both fiction and non-fiction in the Victorian media, and who sought to introduce the work of their protégés to influential editors.[27] Taken together, the activities of such men present a picture of British media culture in which officers, as well as military interests, played an active and formative part. As such, they were no less separate from British culture than they were from British society and politics.

Roberts and the media

Few officers better demonstrate the networks that bridged military interests and British media culture than Frederick Roberts. To be sure, his career was exceptional. He was, along with Sir Garnet Wolseley, one of the most famous and successful military men of his era. After gaining widespread fame for his role as commander of the Kabul-Kandahar Field Force during the Second Afghan War (1878–80), he rose to the position of Commander-in-Chief of the armies in Madras (1881–85), India (1885–93), Ireland (1895–99), South Africa (1899–1900), and finally Britain (1901–4). In 1911 an article in *Strand Magazine* named Roberts as one of the ten greatest living men.[28] At his death in November 1914, Roberts was mourned by every leading metropolitan and provincial newspaper, as well as newspapers from India, South Africa, Australia and Canada. The *Times of India* called him a 'veteran who has for so many years personified the finest traditions of Great Britain', and his state funeral was attended by the highest civil and military dignitaries of the day.[29]

Yet Roberts's exceptional story should not obscure the fact that he was only one of many officers who attempted to use the media to his own – and to the army's – advantage. Indeed, the outlines of his story bear striking similarity to the stories of other late Victorian war heroes, including Garnet Wolseley, George White, William Lockhart and Herbert Kitchener. Like a number of his contemporary officers, Roberts's own influence with the metropolitan media was cemented by his participation in a colonial war and the massive fame he achieved while in command. Yet the seamless, authoritative and often anonymous representations contemporary Britons encountered of 'Roberts the hero' were in large part engineered and manipulated by Roberts himself. Moreover, once Roberts became a popular hero, he used his fame both covertly and openly to intervene on behalf of the army in a variety of public media, including newspapers, journals and literature. In the process, Roberts made his own indelible mark on British popular culture.

Roberts's story merits special attention because few historians of popular imperialism have devoted more than cursory attention to his significance in Victorian culture and society. In contrast to Henry Havelock, Robert Baden-Powell or T. E. Lawrence, Roberts has yet to receive sustained attention as a popular hero.[30] Nor indeed has Roberts received extended attention for his role in the development and articulation of martial race ideology. Instead, recent historical scholarship on Roberts has been the domain of military and political historians, who, while not ignoring Roberts's relationship to British media culture, have considered it in relation to much broader historical questions, or in the context of specific historical issues.[31] Here, Roberts's rise to fame and his subsequent involvement in the media serve as just one illustration of how blurred the line between the 'real' military and British popular culture could be, as well as the cultural consequences that might result.

Roberts became a household name during the Second Afghan War when in August 1880 he successfully commanded a 320-mile march from Kabul to Kandahar. The march, whose purpose was to rescue the beleaguered British garrison at Kandahar, was considered remarkable because of the rough terrain over which the troops had to travel, the speed with which the column had to move, and the isolation of the force from British lines of supply. As such, the march captured the attention of the British media, and its progress – as well as its resolution – was followed with intense interest by the reading public. Roberts's success in reaching Kandahar quickly and in soundly defeating the Afghan Army he found there seemed to seal his fortune, for via the widespread publication of his exploits in the press he became a darling of society and a national hero.

Contemporary media accounts during and after the march from Kabul to Kandahar were certainly, in that sense, responsible for 'making' Roberts the hero. Without them, Roberts's march would have been significant only in a military sense, and even then only questionably so.[32] Yet if we were to focus only on Roberts as a popular media icon, his own hand in creating that image – as well as his motivations for doing so – would be rendered invisible. By shifting the focus from the media to Roberts himself, we are able to see beyond the unified narratives of 'Roberts of Kandahar' to the historical fragility and contingency of such narratives, and the complex means by which 'heroes' – as actors – were able to shape them.

That Roberts emerged from the conflict a hero was remarkable in itself, for it was unpopular from the start. The war had erupted over the controversial and politically charged Conservative 'forward' policy, which advocated an interventionist approach to ensuring the friendly disposition of the Afghan Amir. Such 'friendliness' was considered important to British strategic interests in Central Asia because – as we know – Afghanistan was a critical buffer zone between British territory in South Asia and the expanding Russian Empire. Moreover, the fact that Britain and Russia had nearly come to blows in the Near East over the fate of Turkey in 1876–77 lent an air of added anxiety to the situation, for the northwest frontier seemed to be at greater risk from a Russian advance through Afghanistan. Thus when the 'forward'-leaning Viceroy discovered, in 1878, that the Afghan Amir had received a Russian envoy after having recently refused British diplomatic overtures, he decided to force the issue by sending an envoy of his own. The envoy was turned back by an Afghan commander at the Khyber Pass on 21 September 1878, and the result was war.[33]

Immediate reaction to the war – in both public and political circles – was decidedly cool. Many Britons shared the idea that the war was based on 'hysterical cries of Russian intrigue' and was conducted by 'masterful and arrogant' men who were bent only on 'plunder and promotion'.[34] Even a quick victory in the spring of 1879, which resulted in a treaty with a new Amir, could not generate positive enthusiasm for the war. Moreover, these attitudes were in no small measure due to the reported actions of Roberts himself. Although Roberts had distinguished himself as commander of one of the three victorious invasion forces into Afghanistan, he had also been plagued by allegations of incompetence and ruthlessness towards the Afghan people in the winter of 1879. These allegations, in turn, fuelled the fires of anti-war interests in Britain by seeming to confirm the war's unjust and immoral nature. As we shall see, then, the fact that Roberts emerged from the war as a popular hero demonstrates that such an outcome was neither natural nor inevitable, but instead represented a self-conscious attempt to restore his damaged reputation via skilful manipulation of the press.

Roberts's problems with the press began at the start of 1879, when the war correspondent from the *Standard*, Maurice MacPherson, sent a series of telegrams and letters accusing Roberts of military bungling, ineptness and cruelty in the treatment of both Afghan prisoners and his own troops. On 2 January 1879 MacPherson told the *Standard* that Roberts had already deleted and refused to countersign portions of MacPherson's telegram concerning a reconnaissance around the Peiwar Kotal. MacPherson thus followed the telegram with an uncensored letter, so that he could show 'how near the Peiwar Kotal action approached the condition of being a disaster'. Specifically, he criticised Roberts's abilities as a general, arguing that 'the Khurum field force has been cruelly treated in order that forced and objectless marches might be made, and that positions of danger might be run into from which escape from disaster was possible only through the indiscreet impatience of the enemy'.[35] These criticisms inspired considerable editorial condemnation in the *Standard*, and to make matters worse both the despatches and the editorials were widely reprinted in newspapers around Britain.[36]

MacPherson was also one of the first to level charges of brutality against Roberts. In particular, MacPherson decried an incident in which several Afghan prisoners, bound together in a group, had been shot for attempting escape. According to the report, British forces did not then unbind the dead and wounded prisoners from the rest, but instead allowed them to writhe in agony and die as an example to the survivors to whom they were still attached.[37] These reports were serious enough to instigate discussion in the House of Commons, where Roberts's tactics were scrutinised and criticised by Members of Parliament.[38]

Roberts, horrified at such negative and potentially damaging publicity, determined to take action against MacPherson. First, he sent a telegram to the Viceroy's private secretary asking for help in getting 'rid' of MacPherson. Second, on receiving word that he had the authority to dismiss any 'correspondents who misbehave' Roberts arranged for MacPherson's dismissal from camp the very next day. Third, Roberts immediately took matters into his own hands by writing a letter of defence to Major-General Martin Dillon, Assistant Military Secretary to the Commander-in-Chief in London. When the controversy continued to dog him, Roberts wrote a further letter of defence to the private secretary to the Under-Secretary of India with the thinly veiled suggestion that it be published. He followed this with a letter to the Quartermaster-General in India, which was printed and presented to the House of Commons in his defence on 16 June 1879.[39] Finally, he appointed a military aide-de-camp as official correspondent to the *Standard*. MacPherson's bitter response was also printed in the papers, alleging that Roberts was not only brutal in the field but undemocratic as well, for his actions had stifled free criticism and left 'the whole correspondence of the London and Indian press ... in the hands of General Roberts's personal staff'.[40] MacPherson had a point, for Roberts's damage-control campaign had eliminated criticism and left him with a temporary monopoly of control over the stories and information leaving camp. Moreover, when Roberts did allow another civilian war correspondent to accompany him in the field, it was someone – Howard Hensman of the *Daily Mail* – who would paint him in a most favourable light.

Roberts's conflict with MacPherson reminds us that military commanders could hold significant influence over what civilian correspondents could say, where they could go, whether they would be allowed to remain in the field, or indeed whether they would be welcomed in future campaigns. Those critical of individual commanders or campaigns might find themselves, as MacPherson did, banished from the front altogether. The MacPherson incident also highlights the ambiguity in determining the source of information printed in the Victorian press. As we know, after MacPherson was banished it was Roberts's own military aide-de-camp who served as war correspondent, not a civilian agent of the press. And this was hardly an isolated case. George White, future Commander-in-Chief in India, was a prominent example in his capacity as special correspondent to *The Times* during his service in Afghanistan.[41] In fact, so many actively serving officers played the dual role of paid war correspondent during the Second Afghan War that a discussion of its propriety ensued in the House of Commons during the summer of 1879. When confronted with questions about officers serving as 'special correspondents for *The Times*, the *Daily Telegraph*, the *Standard* and other papers', the Under-Secretary of State for India insisted that the matter was private and best settled between individual officers and newspapers.[42]

What this means is that we can hardly be sure of the interests 'war correspondents' represented. In cases where officers served in the dual role of press correspondent, surely their capacity to criticise was minimal at best. Further, if war correspondents could be hand-picked by commanding officers, as Roberts did for the *Standard* after MacPherson's dismissal, or in the case of Hensman for the *Daily Mail*, they would be almost certain to represent the campaign – and its command – in a most satisfactory manner.

Roberts's conflict with MacPherson demonstrates his active engagement with, and attention to, his own representation in the press. But this was just the beginning. When the war erupted again in earnest during the autumn and winter of 1879–80, Roberts was forced again to manage his public image. This second phase of the war was inaugurated by the murder, on 3 September, of the British Resident (Sir Louis Cavagnari) and his retinue at Kabul. Roberts was chosen to lead a new invasion force into Kabul, where he was instructed by the Viceroy to punish those who had been involved in Cavagnari's murder. Once again, however, Roberts's alleged brutality in that city during the winter of 1879–80 turned the public against him specifically and against the war in general.

Although Roberts had eliminated unfavourable war correspondents from his force, still his actions were extreme enough to raise the ire of both the British press and the Liberal opposition, much to the embarrassment of the Indian government.[43] Roberts's own officers had cause to feel uncomfortable with the scale of 'justice' he saw fit to mete out – by all accounts, the military court established to try suspects at Kabul seldom gave its verdicts on reliable or substantial evidence. Sir Charles MacGregor, Chief of Staff under Roberts at Kabul, wrote with disgust about the sham trials and executions being conducted in the name of justice, adding: 'I think Bobs [Roberts] is the most blood thirsty little beast I know'.[44] Indeed, a serious uprising around Kabul in December 1879 was blamed, at least in part, on Roberts's excessive executions in the two preceding months. By January, so strong were the criticisms coming from the press and the opposition that Roberts found himself once again having to defend his actions in print. On the 10th and 27th of that month he sent a letter and official report, respectively, to the House of Commons, arguing that the executions he had authorised were necessary.[45] He also enlisted the help of officers in his camp, including the reluctant MacGregor, to exonerate him in the press.[46] Yet the war had already become so unpopular in Britain – in large part due to allegations of Roberts's brutality in Kabul – that the Liberals were able to capitalise on anti-war sentiment to sweep the Conservatives out of power in April.[47]

Suddenly, Roberts was faced with the rule of a party that strongly opposed the war. Moreover, he found himself in the unwelcome position of second-in-command in Kabul by the arrival in May of Sir Donald Stewart. In consequence, when Stewart (at the urging of a newly elected Liberal ministry under Gladstone) set about transferring power to the friendly Afghan leader, Roberts's chances for glory seemed spent. Suffering from a seriously damaged reputation and discredited as a political liability, it seemed unlikely that he would be given the chance to redeem himself.

It was under these circumstances that Stewart and Roberts received news of the disastrous defeat of British forces attached to the Kandahar garrison at Maiwand – more than 300 miles away – late in the summer of 1880. The Afghan Army that had inflicted the defeat subsequently laid siege to the city of Kandahar, where it was threatening the imminent demise of the remaining British garrison. Sensing his opportunity, Roberts vigorously pressed both Stewart and the Government of India to send him in command of a relief force.[48] Stewart, needed in Kabul, assented. Roberts's reasons for wanting the command so desperately were clear, for the mission must have seemed the perfect vehicle to salvage his damaged reputation. Instead of Roberts the Brutal, he could – if successful – become Roberts the Rescuer. In so doing, he could increase his chances for military advancement, and even aim for royal honours as well.

Thus, with picked troops and much fanfare, Roberts set out on 8

August 1880. His hand-picked and highly favourable war correspondent, Howard Hensman of the *Daily News*, did his best to play up the romance and danger of the mission. In his despatch of 10 August, Hensman penned a dramatic and emotional farewell to civilisation:

> To-day we look upon as the last we shall be in communication with Cabul, and consequently with India ... We have cut ourselves off completely from any supports; we are self-supporting in every sense of the word; and we have as our objective point a town nominally held by our own troops, but which may, before our arrival, be surrounded by an army far surpassing our own in numbers and guns.[49]

That such words had the desired effect can be garnered from press accounts that fretted '[t]here is great eagerness, if not anxiety ... with regard to General Roberts's position. No news has been received from him for the last ten days.'[50] When, therefore, Roberts emerged at Kandahar twenty-four days later only to defeat the Afghan forces in battle less than a day after arriving, the reaction in the press was euphoric. On 1 September 1880 *The Times* marvelled at Roberts's 'remarkable march': 'General Roberts has conclusively proved that under proper leadership a British Army can still go anywhere and do anything, and, considering the circumstances, we doubt whether his feat has ever been surpassed'.[51]

Even staunchly anti-war papers like *Reynolds's*, which had previously called the war 'the most unjustifiable and useless ever waged by a civilised country', still called Roberts's march 'bold and rapid', crowned by a 'brilliant victory'.[52] The *Penny Illustrated News and Illustrated Times*, which had similarly castigated the war, nevertheless featured Roberts's 'Great March' on the front page of its 11 September edition. Inside, an editorial proclaimed:

> If we have during previous episodes of the unrighteous war ... felt constrained to join in the fault found with the seemingly rash haste General Sir F.S. Roberts, V.C., showed in advancing into Afghanistan, we hasten to bear tribute to the good Generalship he displayed in the rapid march from Cabul to Candahar, and in his effectual defeat of Ayoub Khan in one decisive battle.[53]

Fittingly, and no doubt satisfactorily for Roberts, the professional military *United Service Gazette* also joined in the accolades. Although the same journal had recently sharply criticised Roberts for his incompetence as a general and for his heavy-handedness in dealing with Afghans, following the march to Kandahar it complimented Roberts on 'the good work which he has done, and in the brilliant manner in which he has confirmed Lord Lytton's good judgement in selecting him for command'.[54]

In the wake of his 'brilliant march', Roberts's early reputation as a brutal warmonger was superseded by a new one that emphasised ability, endurance and courage. And though the media played a critical role in both 'breaking' and 'making' him, Roberts was hardly a passive image to be created or rejected at will. The march to Kandahar had been a carefully stage-managed affair designed to redeem a damaged reputation. That Roberts was successful in using the press to transform this reputation is testament to the powerful lessons he had learned earlier in the war.

Once Roberts had entered the limelight as a popular hero he quickly discovered that celebrity status brought with it much more than immediate fame. He found that such status also opened a number of doors – to society, to improved finances, and to the networks of the Victorian media. Indeed, Roberts's new-found popularity led him into relationships with prominent journalists, editors, artists and officials, whose attention provided the means by which his voice – as well as his like-minded protégés – could be heard in ever wider circles.

We have already seen that Roberts's rise to fame in Afghanistan brought him into contact with William Blackwood, editor of the Conservative, popular, middle-class and imperially minded *Blackwood's Magazine*. Their correspondence reveals that the two men developed a relationship which included personal visits between their respective families, and which lasted at least through the 1890s. The relationship was not unusual, as a significant number of *Blackwood's* regular contributors were officers in the British Army.[55] Moreover, *Blackwood's* carried a special appeal for military men hoping to contribute their own writing, for they were free to remain anonymous by using pseudonyms. As a result, William Blackwood's correspondence abounds with letters from army officers – including Roberts, Wolseley, Evelyn Wood and William Lockhart – desiring to publish articles or seeking to introduce the work of their hopeful young protégés.[56] Roberts's relationship with Blackwood, then, was part of a much wider association between military men and the magazine's editor.

The primary factor motivating Roberts's contributions to *Blackwood's* was the desire to win support for his opinions on India's northwest frontier policy. From surviving fragments of the correspondence between the two men, it is clear that Roberts clandestinely contributed items of interest to Blackwood – as we have already seen – with the intention that they would be used to awaken public concern over Russian expansion and, hence, the defence of India's northwest frontier. In the following case, Roberts had sent Blackwood an official (and confidential) military memorandum regarding Russia's potential for invading India: 'I was very glad to receive your letter of 26th March last, and to hear that you had been able to make use of my memorandum on the "Invasion of India" – I read the article "Russia in Search of a Frontier" in the April no. of your magazine with great interest – your contributor put the case very well'.[57] Clearly, by previous arrangement Blackwood did not publish the memorandum directly, but instead circulated it to a secondary writer, who based an article on it. Roberts had every reason to be pleased with the result, for his goal of reaching the public had been covertly achieved. That such an arrangement was likely to continue was made clear by Roberts's next lines: 'I now send you a second paper, a sort of sequel to the first, which you may, perhaps, like to read. It is "confidential", as must [be] anything I write while holding an appointment, and of course not for publication, but you are most welcome to make use of it.'[58] These fragments of correspondence suggest that the stories and information collected in newspapers and journals, while designed to present a seamless flow of objective information, in fact originated from a conglomeration of connections and interests that was hidden both to contemporary readers and, later, to us. Moreover, in the period under examination here, the correspondence between Blackwood and Roberts serves as a timely reminder that some of these 'interests' originated with army officers who were more than willing to covertly manipulate the popular media for their own ends.

While Roberts clearly resorted to such covert methods, he also grew adept at openly advocating his interests through popular forms. Upon his retirement from Indian service in 1893, Roberts composed his memoirs. *Forty-One Years in India* was published in two volumes in 1897, and proved to be a perfect device for bringing his long-standing military concerns about the northwest frontier before the public. Ostensibly, Roberts claimed the book was about nothing more than his own personal reminiscences of 'Indian life and adventure' spanning the period between the Indian Rebellion of 1857 and the end of his tenure as Commander-in-Chief in 1893. His self-effacing assurance that he 'would never have ventured to intrude upon the public' with his story except to 'contribute towards a more intimate knowledge of the glorious heritage our forefathers have bequeathed to us' seemed to confirm this non-political objective.[59] Yet just a few pages into the preface, Roberts is clear about the political agenda behind his personal recollections:

> I have endeavoured to bring before my readers the change of our position in India that has been the inevitable consequence of the propinquity upon our North-West Frontier of a first-class European power [Russia] ... The object I have at heart is to make my fellow-subjects recognise that, under these altered conditions, Great Britain now occupies in Asia the position of a Continental Power, and that her interests in that part of the globe must be protected by Continental means of defence.

His self-avowed goal in writing the book was 'not to sound an alarm, but to give a warning and to show the danger of shutting our eyes to plain facts and their probable consequences'.[60] Brilliantly, however, the narrative that follows Roberts through his personal and professional life incorporates political issues into the daily life and experiences of its protagonist, which makes them seem at once less obviously political and more clearly visible. Since the reader sees India only through Roberts's eyes, competing visions of the subcontinent or the military policies that guide it are either subtly discredited or rendered invisible. His authority for writing the book was difficult to challenge; he was, after all, the hero of Kandahar and former Commander-in-Chief in both Madras and India. Besides, as he pointed out in the preface, he and his father spent between them 'nearly ninety years in India'.[61] His capacity to 'know' both India and the army, then, extended even beyond his own career and experience.

The story itself is, of course, brimming with colonial warfare on the northwest frontier, soldier-heroes, strange and exotic Indians, and the personalities of India's brightest lights, both military and civilian. We are told in intimate detail of Roberts's views on the Indian Army and its fitness to face the 'Russian threat', particularly his belief that only certain Indian 'races' could 'confidently be trusted to take their share of fighting against a European foe'.[62] We see how glorious soldiering can be through the tale of the Highland private MacMahon in battle, to whose 'coolness and daring was in a great measure due the capture' of the enemy's post, and whose intrepidity was rewarded by the coveted Victoria Cross.[63] The British soldiers in this story are not the seedy striplings who inspired despair in Roberts's confidential papers and letters, but soldiers as he wished them to be: brave, temperate and honourable men determined to do their duty for Queen and country. Such a formula could hardly have appealed more to a British reading public enthralled with colonial adventure narratives of all kinds and for all ages. Just four years later Kipling himself would use India's northwest frontier – and the rivalry between Britain and Russia for power there – as the setting for intense and exotic adventure in his enormously popular *Kim*.

That *Forty-One Years in India* helped to shape public conceptions about India, Anglo-Russian relations, the British Army and imperial defence can hardly be doubted. At least eighty-seven national, international, provincial and local papers prominently reviewed the book on or close to its release date (4 January), including papers in Australia, the United States, Germany and India.[64] The conclusions of each were nearly everywhere the same: Roberts had written a valuable *tour de force* that all Britons – and perhaps all people of European descent – should read. So much did the public agree that *Forty-One Years in India* became a national best-seller. Within one year it had gone through twenty-seven editions, and by 1901 it reached its thirty-fourth. Roberts's views on imperial defence, already well-established through other, more covert channels in Britain, were now brought before the public in his own name and on a vast scale.

During the South African War, Roberts continued to hone his skills at media manipulation. Following his experience in the Second Afghan War, as Commander-in-Chief in South Africa (1900–1) Roberts took extra care to manage the war correspondents who accompanied him, and to make sure the British public heard his own version of the campaign's affairs.[65] By all accounts, these efforts had the desired effect, for Roberts's prestige rose to its pinnacle when he returned from South Africa in early 1901.[66]

Roberts's celebrity in the South African War brought him into contact with an ever-widening circle of media agents, with whom he was eager to cultivate mutually beneficial relationships. One of these men was Charles Frederic Moberly Bell, managing director of *The Times*. Their association appears to have begun during the South African War and continued through the early years of the century. For Roberts, Moberly Bell's inside line to one of the most influential papers in Britain was a pipeline to the public through which Roberts could direct information about himself, the army and its interests.

Surviving evidence indicates that Roberts also used *The Times* as a bill-board for enhancing the visibility and appeal of the army by reporting parades, manoeuvres and speeches that were sure to include smart-looking, uniformed units and marching music – just the sort of event to inspire pride in the army.[67] In addition, Roberts used his connection with Moberly Bell to forward the plans and interests of his allies in the military. Indeed, Roberts functioned, like many senior officers, as a conduit through which junior officers could make use of established networks with representatives of the press, thus expanding the influence of army interests beyond a few well-known heroes. For example, Roberts informed Moberly Bell that one of his friends, a captain in the army, 'has come to me with a scheme which he has [arranged] to be considered by you, in the chance of its being written up in "The Times". It certainly has the possibilities of attracting interest.'[68] The captain clearly was not previously acquainted with Moberly Bell, yet through Roberts's patronage his ideas reached the attention of the managing director of this prestigious metropolitan newspaper. Moreover, this type of mediation does not seem to be an isolated case, for Roberts's correspondence with a fellow-officer refers to his connection with the press as 'your correspondent'.[69]

In return for his numerous interventions in *The Times*, Roberts made every effort to compensate Moberly Bell. Although Moberly Bell was a well-respected and influential member of society in his own right, Roberts still sought to provide favours to benefit his friend, which ranged from invitations to star-studded dinners at the Roberts home to sending tickets to elite society functions such as Guildhall dinners.[70] Roberts also secured much more complicated – and potentially compromising – favours, including an army commission for Moberly Bell's underage son in 1902.[71]

For the rest of his life, Roberts continued to develop close relationships with editors, media magnates and journalists, including Charles à Court

Repington (military writer for *The Times*), Leopold Maxse (editor of the *National Review*) and Alfred Harmsworth (later Lord Northcliffe, and one of the most influential press barons of his time). Through such men, Roberts covertly 'leaked military secrets with abandon'.[72] Roberts also continued to contribute to British media culture openly, authoring several articles and another book in the early years of the twentieth century. In addition, he aided and publicly supported the fictional work of William Le Queux, author of a series of highly popular invasion novels.

Roberts's story, then, provides exceptionally rich evidence of a world in which military figures were self-consciously connected to editors, journalists, publishers and novelists through a network of relationships and common interests. Moreover, it provides insight into the myriad ways in which men like Roberts used these networks for their own personal and political ends – ends that included damage control, the desire for recognition and the promotion of controversial policies. If Roberts was exceptional in the range of his connections, it can also be argued that his story demonstrates the variety of shapes these connections could assume. And while it is clear that although Roberts commanded far greater influence in the media than most officers, he also used that influence to help forward the schemes of his subaltern protégés. As such, Roberts's story hints at a much more extensive, albeit hierarchical, network of connections between subalterns, superiors and the press.

Roberts and martial race discourse

Roberts's interventions in the Victorian media are also important for understanding the growing popular enthusiasm for martial race ideology in late century. During the Second Afghan War, Roberts's developing views about the threat from Russia began to take concrete shape. In Afghanistan, he became convinced that neither the British nor the Indian armies were prepared to meet a Russian challenge along the northwest frontier. Instead, Roberts believed that only certain parts of both armies were up to such a contest. In the British Army, these included 'ethnic' regiments that could draw upon a strong tradition of *esprit de corps*. In the Indian Army, Roberts believed that only particular 'races' possessed the biological fortitude to stand up to a European enemy.

Roberts, like so many officers of his age, had been deeply conditioned by his past experience during the Rebellion, and this conditioning told in his choice of 'model' British and Indian soldiers. For him, no soldiers were more exemplary of the 'right' kind of fighting men for the Afghan situation than those who had proven their worth so dramatically in the Rebellion of 1857 – in particular Scottish Highlanders, Sikhs and Gurkhas. Highlanders and Sikhs not only fought well in that conflict, but they had fought well together, and in 1878 Roberts believed this was surely a time for concerted action between Indian and Briton. Although Gurkhas had not had the opportunity to fight alongside Highlanders and Sikhs during the Rebellion, Roberts was a strong believer in their capabilities, and was largely responsible for pairing them with – and discursively connecting them to – the latter two groups in Afghanistan.

All this might have had limited impact on British media culture except for the fact that during the Afghan War Roberts grew increasingly adept at using the press to forward his own interests. One of these interests, as we have just seen, was to control damage to his reputation spurred by critical reporting of, among other things, his own actions. Another was his desire – which grew to an obsession – to convince both the government and the public of the strategic importance of the northwest frontier, and of the grave importance of preparing the British and Indian armies for conflict with Russia in that quarter. For this reason, Roberts was keen to emphasise the difficulty of northwest frontier battle conditions and the nearly superhuman qualities required of soldiers who were called upon to fight in the area.

In particular, he had a habit of playing up the feats of Highlanders, Sikhs and Gurkhas, who for him embodied the physical and masculine qualities of ideal soldiers. As Roberts's reputation during the Afghan War shifted from infamy to renown, so too did his constructions of ideal soldiers – and the connections between them – begin to carry more weight. By the end of the war, when Roberts emerged a national hero, his favoured Highlanders, Sikhs and Gurkhas emerged with him, as did the symbolic qualities of hyper-masculinity and loyalty they were meant to represent. In Roberts's deft hands, India's 'martial races' were joined to Britain's own 'martial' soldiers by physical prowess, unrestrained bravery and solidarity of spirit to defend the Empire.

That Roberts would come to favour Highlanders, Sikhs and Gurkhas above all others was due to both the popular legacy of the Rebellion and his own personal experience during the conflict. As we saw in Chapter 2, each of these groups gained renown in military and popular circles for their dramatic roles in saving the Raj. Roberts, like his contemporaries, would therefore have been exposed to multiple stories singing the praises of their loyalty and bravery in battle. But Roberts was not merely influenced by hearsay and the spirit of the times. He also had direct experience with all three groups, for he served first under John Nicholson's command of the Punjab Moveable Column, and then under Colin Campbell at the final relief of Lucknao. With Nicholson, Roberts had witnessed (with a slight chill of foreboding lest such formidable soldiers were to turn on their new masters) the determination of Sikh volunteers to bring ruin to the rebel forces.[73] At the siege of Delhi, he had also been struck by the steadfastness of Gurkha recruits who refused to give up their positions, regardless of the danger to themselves.[74] When his duties took him to Colin Campbell's flying column later in the conflict, Roberts was equally impressed by the performance of the 93rd Highlanders, who seemed to strike awe into their enemies simply by their reputation and appearance.[75] Even more importantly for his later conceptualisation of the connections between Highlanders and Indian 'martial races', Roberts had personally witnessed the storming of the Secunderbagh, where Sikhs and Highlanders gained their greatest fame together. 'It was beautiful to see them going at it', he claimed at the time, 'regularly racing to see who should be first in. They went, and before half an hour was over, nearly 2000 Pandies were on the ground dead or dying.'[76] Even at this early date, Roberts was already according near-legendary capabilities to the men he believed responsible for saving the Raj from the rebels.

When Roberts formed these opinions of Sikhs, Highlanders and Gurkhas in the Rebellion, he was quite a young man (twenty-five) and had only been in India for five years. He was, in short, still quite 'impressionable' as an Anglo-Indian officer, for his convictions had not been tempered by long experience among a variety of Indian and British groups. As a result, Roberts's own experiences during the trauma and upheavals of the Rebellion were formative: those men who had remained loyal during the conflict remained his favourites throughout his career, and those who had rebelled he systematically tried to root out of the Indian military altogether.

Roberts himself self-consciously looked back to the Rebellion as the inspirational beginning of a new kind of partnership between Indian and British soldiers. In his view, no event was more symbolic of this new partnership than the storming of the Secunderbagh, where he had seen Highlanders and Sikhs demonstrate to the world their equally matched bravery, endurance and fidelity. In 1897, Roberts again recounted this episode in his best-selling *Forty-One Years in India*, arguing that the 'generous competition' between Highlanders and 'martial' Indians was 'a magnificent sight, a sight never to be forgotten'.[77] For Roberts, the storming of the Secunderbagh distilled in one short story the beginning of a long and fruitful relationship between the Empire's best, most manly soldiers. As the Russian threat seemed to take greater shape over the next two decades, the masculine qualities Roberts had come to admire during the Rebellion took on ever greater significance. Only now, 'real' men were needed not to avenge and protect British women (as in the Rebellion), but to avenge and protect the borders of the Raj from Russian attack.

When the Second Afghan War broke out two decades after the Rebellion, Roberts turned once again to Highlanders, Sikhs and Gurkhas – and the masculine ideal they had come to represent – to make the northwest frontier safe for British strategic interests. To be sure, Roberts had had little reason to change his mind in the intervening period between the Rebellion and 1878. For one thing, he had been posted to the northern provinces of Bengal and the Punjab for the duration of that period, where prejudice in favour of Sikhs and Gurkhas was strongest among military men. The Bengal Army was in the midst of reconstruction, and a number of British officers who had fought during the Rebellion came forward to offer their opinions about the superiority of the 'loyal' men from Punjab and Nepal. As a result, Roberts's own opinions about the capabilities of Sikhs and Gurkhas would have been continually buttressed by many of his peers. Roberts had also fought briefly in the Ambeyla expedition of 1863, where his preconceptions about the exceptional abilities of Sikhs, Highlanders and Gurkhas were reconfirmed all over again when each group performed well in the campaign.[78]

Thus, when Roberts found himself in command of the Kurram Field Force at the start of the Afghan War in 1878, it seemed only natural that he turn again to those soldiers he had come to trust so many years earlier. Immediately after his appointment, he specifically requested the 72nd and 92nd Highlanders, the 5th Punjab Infantry, the 3rd or 4th Sikhs (with all Muslim corps replaced by Sikhs) and the 5th Gurkhas.[79] For Roberts, the need for only the best soldiers was critical, for as he put it, 'the possibility of meeting Russian troops' made it 'necessary that every regiment should be efficient in all respects'.[80] In his opinion, the most 'efficient' soldiers were those who had proven themselves on the field two decades ago. Now more than ever, the Raj needed a display of strength and unity akin to that provided by Highlanders, Sikhs and Gurkhas in 1857.

Roberts's special affinity for Highlanders, Sikhs and Gurkhas had several concrete results during the Afghan campaign. Like Havelock and Campbell during the Rebellion, Roberts tended to highlight the actions of his favoured troops in despatches, which heightened their visibility in the Victorian media. When this practice joined with Roberts's own attempts to garner fame out of events like the capture of the Peiwar Kotal or the march from Kabul to Kandahar, the result was that Highlanders, Sikhs and Gurkhas all became indelibly associated with the heroism of such feats. Roberts's widely published despatches about these events also served to renew the discursive connection between the British and Indian 'martial races' that gained so much popularity during the Rebellion. Yet Roberts's despatches highlighted not just the Rebellion-era connections between Highlanders and Sikhs: now, he devoted equal attention to a similar connection between Highlanders and Gurkhas. Both sets of connections, however, served similar purposes – to call attention to a masculine soldierly ideal, to enhance the masculine prestige of Roberts himself, and to deflect attention away from the ugly side of war.

Almost immediately after the campaign began, Roberts's despatches began to detail the outstanding fighting abilities of his favourite troops. No engagement seemed too small to emphasise their skills and valour, as this telegram to the Viceroy demonstrates:

> We marched yesterday to Kariah on the Kuram; enroute the baggage was attacked by a band of marauders belonging to the Monguls ... Owing to the great steadiness of the 5th Goorkhas who were on rear guard, the baggage was all saved, and the Mongols suffered severely ... Some of the 72nd Highlanders did admirable service with the Henry-Martini Rifle. The conduct of the 5th Goorkhas is beyond all praise.[81]

Even in this rather trifling episode, Roberts painted a scene of heroism against wild 'marauders': in contrast, his own Gurkhas and Highlanders had displayed 'steadiness' and 'admirable service', causing the enemy to suffer and thereby saving the day.

Unlike Havelock or Campbell, Roberts was attuned – and would grow ever more so – to the fact that his words would reach a national press. By the late 1870s, it was standard practice for metropolitan and provincial papers to include both the stories of war correspondents and excerpts from original despatches, telegrams and official letters sent by commanders in the field. Roberts, who had a flair for the dramatic, was well suited to his era. In contrast to the reticent and sometimes downright spare prose of Campbell, Roberts took the time to tell a good story – to play on the emotions of his intended audiences and to construct narratives of personal struggle, heroism and courage that brought out the qualities he believed so necessary for military success on the northwest frontier. Here, the enemy is nearly invisible, noted only as a 'warm engagement', while the actions of Sikhs and Highlanders seem like a dangerous version of a team sport:

> a warm engagement had for some hours been carried on in the direction of Karatiga, and presently large numbers of the enemy were seen retreating before a small detachment of the 92nd Highlanders and 3rd Sikhs, which had been sent out from Karatiga, and which were with excellent judgment and boldness led up a steep spur commanding the defile.[82]

In Roberts's hands the engagement was a military spectacle, populated by exotic visions of kilted Highlanders and bearded Sikhs bursting onto the scene, chasing faceless enemies in their mountain fastnesses. Their physical and martial abilities here appear natural and effortless as they rid the area, with perfect discipline and obedience, of Britain's foes.

Roberts emphasised similar abilities in his much more famous despatches regarding the battle for the Peiwar Kotal (2 December 1878). The goal of the battle itself had been to take a seemingly impregnable, Afghan-occupied ridge (the Peiwar Kotal). The attack was carried out under cover of night and was meant to be a surprise, but disaster nearly struck when two Pathans in Roberts's force fired shots of warning to alert the enemy's piquet of the impending assault.[83] According to Roberts's account, the 5th Gurkhas at once took measures to salvage the situation, and 'immediately formed up' into a company line and 'rushed straight at a barricade which now became apparent about 50 yards in their front'. After this, the 72nd Highlanders joined their comrades, and they and the Gurkhas 'continued to advance rapidly up the steep side of the Kotal, and captured three stockades in quick succession'. Roberts then reported:

> I brought up the remainder of the 72nd Highlanders as soon as the firing commenced, and I cannot praise too highly the gallant conduct of this splendid regiment ... Of the admirable conduct of the 5th Gorkhas, I have already spoken. They were not one whit behind their brethren of the 72nd in their eager desire to close with the enemy.[84]

In this account, Gurkhas and Highlanders demonstrate (again) their superlative fighting capabilities and (again) save the day. But there is more to the story than that, for Roberts's story hints that the 5th Gurkhas did not even need to be told to 'form up', that instead they reacted instinctively to the danger. Similarly, the participation of the 72nd Highlanders seems to have originated entirely with the men, who quickly judged that their 'comrades' needed help. Roberts encouraged his readers to see the Highlanders and Gurkhas here as comrades-in-arms, equal on the battlefield, *brethren*. The setting itself invited such a perception, for the storming of a heavily guarded set of stockades recalled Highland/Sikh cooperation at the storming of the Secunderbagh in 1857. And, as in the Rebellion, the Gurkhas and Highlanders at the Peiwar Kotal served as both inspiration and as symbols of strength – illustrating the qualities of bravery, endurance and grit necessary for maintaining the integrity of the army and, writ large, the Empire. Roberts might as well have added as a post-script to his despatch, '*This* is what it takes to win battles out here'.

The theme of cooperation and 'brotherhood' between Highlanders and Indian 'martial races' also dominated Roberts's accounts of the march from Kabul to Kandahar. Roberts began by indulging his favouritism by requesting – on the claim that only the best soldiers would be able to withstand such a march – a force composed almost exclusively of Highlanders, Sikhs and Gurkhas.[85] Indeed, Roberts made quite a show of the forces he had chosen for what was supposedly such an arduous and dangerous venture, and ever after maintained that his success was in large part due to the exceptional soldiers under his command. He claimed that 'with men such as these' in the ranks, 'failure was an impossibility'. It was the troops who served him with such a 'high state of discipline' and 'grand esprit de corps' that allowed him to complete his mission for Queen and country. In a speech after the march, Roberts was explicit about the soldierly qualities that had made such a feat possible:

> British and Native soldiers vied with each other; throughout the most perfect camaraderie existed, and when the time for separation arrived, it was with mutual feelings of regard and respect that the Highlanders and Goorkhas, the Riflemen and Sikhs said good bye to each other ... So strong was the tie between the 72nd Highlanders and the 5th Goorkhas that the men of the latter regiment collected a considerable sum of money, upwards of £100, to make a present to the Highlanders, who returned the compliment by presenting the Goorkhas with some token of their friendly feeling.[86]

Once again, Roberts emphasised the importance of camaraderie and friendly competition between Briton and Indian, of the mutual awareness between these groups of their common abilities on the battlefield. These were the kind of men, he implied, who would be able to fight any of the Empire's battles – including what he believed was an impending conflict with Russian troops on the northwest frontier. The march, he believed, had demonstrated to the world 'of what material my Highlanders and Goorkhas are made'. In the process, he argued, they had convincingly shown 'that the very last troops the Afghans ever want to meet in the field are Scottish Highlanders and Goorkhas'.[87] Alone, Roberts suggested, Highlanders and Gurkhas were fearsome enough, but together they were invincible.

Central to Roberts's constructions of 'martial' Highlanders, Gurkhas and Sikhs, then, was his use of language that implied a specific conception of masculine characteristics. These men were 'made' of the right 'material', they maintained a 'high state of discipline', they were 'gallant' and 'admirable', they conducted their attacks with 'boldness', and they were all, under even the most difficult circumstances, 'eager to close with the enemy'.[88] They were physically strong, they were not afraid to act even when their lives were in danger, and although they showed initiative when it was necessary, they always acted in the interests of the Empire. There was nothing of the so-called 'feminine' qualities of softness, weakness or vulnerability about these men. Instead, so intertwined were the qualities of these 'martial races' with Roberts's idealised notions of hyper-masculinity that, in later years, he sometimes called them simply the 'manly' races.[89] His fascination with them – and his resulting attention to them in despatches – reflected his belief that they embodied the masculine qualities that would allow the Empire to withstand a Russian attack on India's vulnerable northwest frontier.

Roberts's attention to 'martial race' soldiers in his accounts of the Second Afghan War may also have carried the potential for increasing his own masculine prestige. In Roberts's narratives, Highlanders, Sikhs and Gurkhas are represented as ultra-masculine warriors who are a 'cut above' most other men in terms of their physical powers and ferocity. If, however, Roberts was so able to command such men – as his reports clearly suggest – then those reports also implicitly suggest Roberts's own ultra-masculine prowess. Put simply, Roberts's tales implied that it took a manly man to know, command, and command respect from other manly men. Roberts's British and Indian 'martial' soldiers, then, may also have functioned as an exotic and appealing foil to enhance his own masculine prestige as an able commander in a dangerous environment.

Some commentaries on Roberts's successes suggested as much. In the wake of the march from Kabul to Kandahar, when Highlanders, Sikhs and Gurkhas had featured so prominently as Roberts's selected troops, the *London Gazette* claimed that the march 'will remain an enduring record, no less of the courage and devotion of the troops than of the skill of the officers on whose services the Queen-Empress can rely for the security and honour of Her Indian Empire'. In fact, the *Gazette* argued, the march 'could not have been prudently entrusted to a leader less able or to troops less efficient than Sir Frederick Roberts and the soldiers so worthy of his leading'.[90] Roberts could hardly have said it better himself. At the beginning of the war, military and civilian sources alike suggested that he was incompetent to lead any soldiers in battle. By the end of the war, the most ultra-masculine soldiers in the Empire were worthy of his leadership.

Roberts's focus on the 'martial races' during the Second Afghan War may also have carried the potential for other personal rewards. We must remember that, at several points during the conflict, Roberts was locked in battle with the forces of the popular press, and used every means at his disposal to reverse widespread allegations of his own brutality and unfitness for command. With that in mind, Roberts's narrative accounts depicting Highlanders, Sikhs and Gurkhas as heroes during the war may have served as 'a distraction from the harsh facts; presenting a different and more dramatic reality'.[91] Roberts's 'martial' men appeared to the public as brave, bold and loyal, not viciously murderous. Their actions tell of honour, glory, self-sacrifice and adventure, luring attention away from the death and destruction wreaked by British-led forces and by Roberts himself. In place of brutality, Roberts depicted a campaign of difficult obstacles and skilled fighting for honourable and legitimate goals. Seen this way, Roberts's attention to Highlanders, Sikhs and Gurkhas in the campaign could have been part of a strategy to deflect attention away from the ugly side of the war and towards its heroic moments.

Although Roberts's accounts of the feats of Highlanders, Sikhs and Gurkhas may have served a variety of purposes, one thing was certainly clear by the end of the war: Roberts had renewed the popular imaginative connection between Highlanders and Indian 'martial races' originally made during the Rebellion. Now, however, that connection included Gurkhas as well as Punjabi Sikhs – a connection that would grow ever stronger in the last years of the century.

Moreover, Roberts's fascination with the feats of Highlanders, Sikhs and Gurkhas proved to be infectious. His own protégés quickly caught on to the idea, and their stories connecting the three groups also made it to a variety of media venues. In this official despatch which reached the pages of the *London Gazette*, Brigadier-General Thomas Baker – who served under Roberts in Afghanistan – wrote about the behaviour of his troops near Kabul in glowing terms:

> the general advance was then immediately sounded, and the enemy's first position was carried in the most dashing and gallant manner by the 72nd Highlanders and the men of the 5th Goorkhas and the 5th Punjab Infantry … I must not omit to bring to notice here the extremely gallant behaviour of a young man of the 72nd Highlanders, by name McMahon, who by his cour-age and coolness and forward position he held in the advance, followed as he was by a few Goorkhas, was to a great extent instrumental in expediting the taking of the extremely strong position referred to on the left flank, and which offered so great a resistance to our advance.[92]

Baker's despatch bore remarkable similarities, in both theme and tone, to Roberts's despatches. Here, we have 'dashing' and 'gallant' troops, who display 'courage and coolness' in taking an 'extremely strong' enemy posi-tion. At an individual level, the figure of McMahon illustrates the *sang froid* of the Highlanders, while the depiction of the Gurkhas' willingness to follow him is a recognition of their similar qualities as soldiers.

Minor episodes of personal heroism such as the one described by Baker often appeared in the pages of the popular press, and – like stories from the Rebellion – were told and retold for public consumption. The following story, which appeared in the *Pioneer*, unmistakably tells the same story:

> I have already mentioned in my telegram the gallantry of a private soldier of the 72nd in facing almost alone a sungar-topped hill where the enemy was in great force. Taking advantage of every bit of cover, he loaded and fired with a coolness that the General and his staff watched with unqualified admiration and delight. Soon four or five staunch little Goorkhas broke from the line of skirmishers and 'followed their leader' sturdily upwards, and as the little party breasted the hill top the defenders of the sungar took to their heels …[93]

The coolness of the private (presumably McMahon) summoned both the admiration of his commanders and the inspiration of his fellow (Gurkha) soldiers. His prowess as a soldier was so great that he faced, and then took, a well-defended position 'almost alone'. Even though McMahon's party was small, the enemy fled as soon as it reached the top of the hill. It is not difficult to imagine – from this rendering of the scene – the generals wish-ing they had more privates like McMahon and the 'staunch' Gurkhas who followed him. Indeed, their actions, especially in combination, symbolised the ideal qualities required for soldiers fighting in that theatre.

In another example, the *Penny Pictorial News and Family Story Paper* took up the events that resulted in George White (later Commander-in-Chief in India, 1893–98) receiving the Victoria Cross. The setting was just outside of Kabul:

> Major White's party, aided by the three guns, stormed the hill on the right in gallant style, with two companies of the 92nd [Highlanders], against, it is reported, two thousand of the enemy, who waited until the Highlanders were within 20 yards and fled precipitately … The 72nd and the Goorkhas took height after height in grand style, capturing two standards then, bringing all the available artillery to bear, inflicted heavy loss on the enemy, finally capturing the main peak of their position.[94]

In this setting, Highlanders and Gurkhas appear superhuman as several small companies attack *two thousand* of the enemy without hesitation. Fear of death does not feature here. Instead, Highlanders and Gurkhas perform with style and enthusiasm their duty to the Empire. This was not a war of ugliness and death – this was a war of romance, of capturing heights, of glory, and of masculine potential for strength and controlled violence carried to an extreme.

The *Army and Navy Magazine*, a professional military journal with a largely military audience in Britain, praised the actions of Highlanders, Sikhs and Gurkhas in yet another context. This time the setting was Kandahar, during the famous battle after the conclusion of the march from Kabul:

> The first to come under fire were the gallant 92nd Highlanders and tough little 2nd Goorkhas … Meantime, the 2nd Brigade, headed by the 72nd Highlanders and 2nd Sikhs, had been working its way through gardens and narrow paths bordered by high loop-holed walls from which the enemy kept up a heavy fire, inflicting severe loss on the column … the Gordon Highlanders, after hardly a perceptible pause to gather breath, supported by some of the 23rd Pioneers and 2nd Goorkhas, and covered by the fire of one of our batteries, made one splendid rush at the enemy's entrenchments, and drove them from their guns and camp.[95]

Here, all the glorious elements of the Rebellion lived again. From the narrow paths and loop-holed walls to the 'one splendid rush', the setting of the Second Afghan War had resurrected, once again, the glorious partnership between Britons and Indians that had so characterised the Rebellion.

Out of the Second Afghan War, Highlanders, Sikhs and Gurkhas emerged – via the tales first of Roberts and then of his subordinates – as the ultimate symbols of soldierly masculinity, strength and heroism. Their exoticism helped draw attention to the strategically sensitive northwest frontier, while their formidable feats in rugged country enhanced a romantic imagery of warfare. More specifically, a focus on the 'martial races' both enhanced the masculine prestige of their commanders and helped hide the ugly realities of late Victorian colonial wars. By the end of the Second Afghan War, these connections had become so regular and so widely publicised that imagined links between Sikhs, Gurkhas and Highlanders became an apparently 'natural' part of imperial military lore.

The naturalisation of martial race discourse

For the rest of the nineteenth century and well into the twentieth, the theme of a 'special connection' between Highlanders, Sikhs and Gurkhas was revisited time and again. In late century, Roberts himself cemented the link by taking a Highland and a Gurkha soldier as the supporters for his coat of arms.[96] The connection also became so strongly rooted in regimental cultures that Indian 'martial race' regiments were encouraged to adopt the music and regalia of their Highland 'brethren'. In addition, even in the periods when regiments of Highlanders, Sikhs and Gurkhas could not be found in the field together, military and popular sources repeatedly referred back to – and retold the stories of – battles from the past. Because of this, when these groups did fight together on the northwest frontier in the last two decades of the nineteenth century, news about their apparently miraculous feats in that quarter continually fed the legendary image that surrounded them.

One of the more remarkable aspects of the imagined connection between 'martial' Highlanders, Sikhs and Gurkhas was that, over time, the physical and material differences between them were intentionally blurred. For example, both Sikh and Gurkha regiments developed pipe bands in imitation of the highly distinctive Highland military music – frequently with such success that the strength of the Indian pipe bands rivalled those in actual Highland regiments. Moreover, Highland dress was adopted on more than one occasion by Indian 'martial race' regiments. In one noted example, guest nights in the officers' mess of the 2nd Gurkha regiment featured Gurkhas dressed in kilts, who entered the mess and 'circumambulat[ed] the diners while serenading them with the familiar strains of bagpipes'.[97] This display of Highland regimental culture was not meant to be funny, but rather to demonstrate the strong connections between the Gurkhas and Britain's most famous – and reputedly finest – soldiers.

The same blurring was also evinced in a speech given by Sir George White – a prominent supporter of martial race policy – in 1894 while he was Commander-in-Chief of the Indian Army. Here, he was speaking at a St Andrew's dinner[98] held by the Gordon Highlanders, and the connections he made leave little doubt about his awareness of firm links between Sikhs and Highlanders:

> There is something not only in the anniversary which we are celebrating to-night, but also in the locality that recalls Scotland. We have met to-night in the northern capital of our Eastern Empire [Delhi] ... We find this northern capital and her great sister, Amritsar, the Paisley of the Punjab, peopled by a race brave by descent and soldiers by instinct, who within the last fifty years fought us as bravely as Gael ever fought Sassenach [English], and now serve us as loyally (cheers). Another point of resemblance is that the Sikh is now nearly as ubiquitous as the Scotsman himself (hear, hear), we find him fighting under British officers in most adverse climates; to-day on the snowy slopes of the mountains of Afghanistan, to-morrow on the sun steeped sands of Central Africa (cheers). Another point of kindred tastes is in the common cultivation of that art which is said to have charms to soothe the savage breast, till the [bag]pipe makers in Auld Reekie [Edinburgh] must be reaping a rich harvest from the Punjab (hear, hear). So far is this resemblance carried out that we had evidence yesterday, both ocular and oral, of battalions made up of the Sikhs of the plains marching past to the appropriate tune of 'Hielan' Laddie' (cheers).[99]

Here, White painted a picture of Highland/Sikh connections based on their similarities as 'soldiers by instinct', as once-rebellious warriors who now serve the Empire 'loyally', in great numbers and all over the world. Their kindred spirit, he argued, could be demonstrated by the fact that Sikhs had taken up piping in the ranks, a musical form that supposedly 'soothe[s] the savage breast'. Indeed, so close were the connections between the two groups that White did not seem to regard the spectacle of Sikh pipers playing 'Hielan' Laddie' as out of place.

In part, this was because both military and popular sources continued to revisit the old battle stories that seemed to document the connection between Highlanders, Sikhs and Gurkhas so clearly. Thus, even as regiments of these groups continued to 'perform' together on the northwest frontier in late century, new stories were regularly buttressed by stories from a more distant past. It may not come as a surprise that the story of the Secunderbagh dominated these re-narrations. Britons remained captivated by the drama and trauma of the Rebellion of 1857 until after the turn of the century, and both fiction and non-fiction about the event found a brisk popular market in that period. [100] The Secunderbagh had been one of the more dramatic military episodes of the conflict, and the performance of Highlanders and Sikhs had come to symbolise the virtues of loyalty, cooperation and military manliness that became so important during and after the campaign.

Late-century narratives of the Secunderbagh appeared in a wide variety of texts and genres. Military commanders in India frequently used the battle as a pointed way of reminding their troops about the glories – and rewards – of loyalty. When the Punjab Frontier Force was transferred to the control of the Commander-in-Chief in India in 1886, for example, the Lieutenant-Governor of the Punjab (Sir Charles Aitchison) eulogised the event in his speech to be read in Military Orders:

> It would be impossible fully to relate the services to the State rendered at this critical period by the Punjab Frontier Force. But special attention may be made of one or two of the more memorable incidents of the Mutiny days: ... the capture of the Sikhandra Bagh, that brilliant feat of arms, in which the 4th Punjab Infantry vied with the 93rd Highlanders for the place of honour, and in which the conspicuous gallantry of Subedar Gokal Singh, 4th Punjab Infantry, was specially mentioned by Sir Colin Campbell and eulogised by the Governor-General in Council.[101]

That Aitchison chose to recall the Secunderbagh in orders he knew would be read to the officers and men of the Frontier Force was no accident. His closing remarks, in fact, betrayed his purpose, for he expressed the hope that 'whenever and wherever called upon to render service to the State, [the Punjab Frontier Force] will prove true to the noble traditions which have accumulated round its name during the years of its connection with the Government of the Punjab'.[102] In short, Aitchison exhorted the men to live up to the reputation that Sikhs had established during the Rebellion as loyal soldiers capable of fighting alongside Britain's most martial troops.

Sources intended for a popular audience in both Britain and India also made frequent recourse to the trope of the Secunderbagh. Authors like James Cromb, who wrote numerous books on Highlanders and imperial campaigns, featured the story of the Secunderbagh in his *Highland Brigade: Its Battles and Heroes*. As in nearly all narratives about the event, Cromb described Highlanders and Sikhs in a glorious rush, vying with one another to be the first to gain access over the wall.[103] Others found a ready audience for their memoirs, where the story of the Secunderbagh made a frequent appearance. Surgeon General Munro, who served as a medical officer in the Rebellion, gave the following account, which is distinctive only for its repetition of the event's standard themes: 'It was a grand and exciting rush, for there were Highlander and Sikh together side by side striving for the first place, but the 93rd got the lead and kept it, and, arriving at the foot of the high wall, were first to enter at the breach'.[104] The theme, as indeed the very words, was nearly the same in all the various accounts of the event. The advance to the walls of the Secunderbagh was 'grand', 'glorious' or 'exciting'. Highlanders and Sikhs displayed their friendly competition – and their manly bravery – by 'vying' 'side by side' to be the first inside the walls. Through this one episode, Sikhs demonstrated their qualifications as loyal and brave soldiers at the same time as a firm relationship was established between that 'martial race' and Britain's finest 'martial' soldiers.

The power of this imagery proved to be long-lasting. As late as 1912, the story of the Secunderbagh continued to live on actively in legend, and to function as a symbolic narrative of British–Indian cooperation and Indian loyalty to the Raj. By that time, of course, officers and men had no personal memories of the Rebellion; instead, stories had to suffice. In this military handbook for soldiers on their way to serve in India, the author alluded to the events at the Secunderbagh when describing the qualities of Sikh soldiers:

> To relate in detail their [the Sikhs] services during the Mutiny would be to recount the history of the whole of that great episode, for there were few occasions when fighting took place in which they did not bear their share, vying with British soldiers for the honour of being the first to cross bayonets with the rebels. Here we can only state in general terms that they remained faithful to us during the whole of that trying time, and that theirs was no impassive loyalty, for they were eager to be in the thick of the battle and when there acquitted themselves like men.[105]

Here, Sikhs had unequivocally demonstrated their loyalty, their manliness, and their comparability to Britain's best soldiers through their willingness to 'vie' for the 'honour' of being first to engage the enemy more than fifty years earlier.

Thanks to the continual re-telling of these old stories, newer stories about the Second Afghan War and subsequent northwest frontier campaigns seemed to fit within an established framework of well-documented links between Highland and Indian 'martial race' regiments. Frequent reference to heroic acts in the past sustained and nurtured the discourse of martial races, and helped keep the imagined links between its targeted soldiers current, strong and relevant. In short, the past was used to explain the present, and the present helped to naturalise the past.

But the discourse of martial races did not rely solely on stories from the past. Instead, it was continually replenished by fresh stories from the northwest frontier, where regiments of Highlanders, Sikhs and Gurkhas were likely to receive more than their fair share of attention. As one private from the Derbyshire regiment put it after a battle: 'They will praise the kilt regiment. It's no use an English regiment trying to get on when there's a regiment with the kilts.'[106] Although the private referred to a Highland regiment, had he been a native soldier he might have expressed similar sentiments about Gurkha or Sikh regiments, for it was true that all three groups were more visible than most on the northwest frontier. When they fought together and seemed to be renewing their old ties of friendly competition, they were doubly so.

The battle of Dargai, which took place on 20 October 1897, was a compelling example of this phenomenon. The battle was one of the last in the

Tirah campaign of September–October 1897, which itself was only one of several punitive expeditions undertaken by British forces between the summer of 1897 and the winter of 1898 to crush what has become known as the Great Frontier Rising.[107] Although campaigns along the northwest frontier were frequent in the last two decades of the nineteenth century, the Great Frontier Rising represented the most concentrated threat to British dominance in the subcontinent since the Rebellion of 1857. More than 59,000 regular troops in the Indian Army were deployed to fight in the various campaigns organised to quell the Rising, and casualties exceeded those of the Second Afghan War.[108] The 34,506 troops assembled to take part in the Tirah campaign alone represented, as Tim Moreman has commented, 'the largest concentration of imperial troops ever deployed on the North-West Frontier'.[109]

If only for that reason, the Tirah campaign might have attracted considerable attention from the British media. But there was more at stake here than a large-scale campaign against 'Indians'. Although the British-led campaigns were all conducted against discontented trans-border tribespeople along the frontier, it was always fear of Russian infiltration and influence in the area that dominated concern over the region. British officers in India made no secret of the fact that struggles on the northwest frontier – including the Great Frontier Rising – were an integral part of the 'Great Game' between Britain and Russia, and that the stake in the game might be the Empire itself.

Moreover, from a media perspective the rugged terrain and harsh weather conditions of the northwest frontier enhanced the drama of each conflict in that quarter, and underscored the need for the most physically hardy troops available. High elevations, deep snow and fierce (as well as increasingly well-armed) enemies necessitated individual hardiness and strength in addition to group discipline. General Roberts had long tried to argue that only the most fit, most devoted, and most manly men should be recruited to fight on the northwest frontier, and the scale and risks of the Great Frontier Rising only underlined the importance of such precautions.[110] During the Tirah campaign especially, all eyes were on those men who had already proven themselves on the northwest frontier. When Highlanders, Sikhs and Gurkhas not only fought in the campaign but also renewed their past glories together, they gave both commanders and the media excellent fodder for pressing home the virtues of these ultimate soldiers.

Like the Secunderbagh four decades earlier, the battle of Dargai focused the connections between Highlanders and India's 'martial races' in a single event. However, while the Secunderbagh linked only Highlanders and Sikhs, Dargai linked all three groups. Moreover, Dargai solidified the more recent connection between Highlanders and Gurkhas, and seemed to prove irrefutably the 'truth' of old stories by demonstrating that these groups really did possess astonishing military capabilities.

The conditions of the battle were in fact not unlike the Secunderbagh, in that outnumbered British-led troops sought to gain control of a heavily defended enemy position. At Dargai, however, this position was a mountainous ridge guarded by an enemy armed with modern rifles.[111] British forces had attacked and cleared the position on 18 October 1897, only to find it strongly occupied two days later. A series of attacks on the position on the 20th resulted in serious losses for British forces, who were unable to make gains on the ground below the ridge because of heavy enemy rifle-fire. But just when all seemed lost, the Gordon Highlanders, 3rd Sikhs and 2nd Gurkhas made a rush for the position and won the day for the British-led forces. The official report told the story like this:

> Under cover of a concentrated artillery fire from twenty-four guns the 3rd Brigade advanced to the attack ... In doing this they were compelled to cross an open space which was swept from end to end by the musketry of the enemy on the heights ... the Dorsetshire and Derbyshire Regiments were directed to attack, but only a few men succeeded in getting across 'the fire-swept zone', and it was then reported that owing to the large number of the enemy lining the edge of the Dargai plateau and the steepness of the ascent, any advance beyond the line held by the 2nd Gurkhas was impracticable. The Gordon Highlanders, supported by the 3rd Sikh Infantry, were then moved up to the front, and after a brief halt ... were directed to attack. Dashing across the open, the Gordons, supported by the 2nd Gurkhas and the 3rd Sikhs, went straight up the hill without check or hesitation through a murderous fire, carried the long-contested heights, and drove the enemy headlong into the Khanki Valley.[112]

This image of Highlanders, supported by their Sikh and Gurkha allies, charging up through the death zone to reach the top of the ridge, embodied the very essence of heroic adventure narratives: fearful odds, difficult terrain, a fierce enemy and death-defying bravery. It displayed, moreover, the qualities of British/Indian camaraderie and cooperation necessary for achieving victory in such difficult conditions, and thus captured the imagination – and attention – of officers and media agents alike. In taking the Dargai Heights, these men had done what other soldiers could not do. Moreover, after learning they were to attack, they had charged 'straight up the hill without check or hesitation', apparently giving no thought for their own lives. Not only had they done their duty as soldiers, but they had done their duty with enthusiasm, *élan* and extraordinary physical prowess.

Once news of the battle was out, British newspapers and journals of every description told and retold the story as a narrative of superhuman heroism, while painters, composers and public entertainers drew inspiration from the example of the 'martial races'. Popular illustrated and conventional papers, for example, were quick to capitalise on the drama of Dargai. As early as 21 October, British newspapers were already printing despatches from India with news of the battle. On that date, Aberdeen's provincial *Daily Free Press* reported that 'the Gurkhas, reinforced by the Gordon Highlanders, made a magnificent rush ... in face of a destructive fire'.[113] Several days later, a more detailed story – provided by an unknown war correspondent – appeared in the papers. This story, with its emphasis on drama, bravery and cooperation, was rapidly reproduced in nearly all metropolitan and provincial newspapers by the end of October. The outlines of the story started out just as the *Daily Free Press* had reported. On 24 October *Reynolds's Newspaper* confirmed that 'the Ghoorkhas, reinforced by the Gordon Highlanders', had indeed 'made a magnificent rush across the open space in face of a destructive fire'. But what followed, the report insisted, was truly remarkable. It had become clear, according to the account, that the other (English) regiments who had been charged with storming the Heights had been unable to do so. As a result, the Gordon Highlanders were assembled:

> and Colonel Mathias, who commanded, addressed them. 'Men of the Gordon Highlanders', he said, 'the General says that position must be taken at all costs. The Gordon Highlanders will take it.' This announcement the men received with a ringing cheer, and at the word of command to advance they bounded after their leader. Dashing across the open ground, their officers at their head, they scaled the height and drove the enemy from their position, the 3rd Sikhs and other troops following close behind them. As the Highlanders were led down the slopes back to camp, after their splendid and successful charge, they were spontaneously cheered by all the other regiments. They then fell out, and helped in the work of carrying down the Goorkhas who were killed in the action. The Goorkhas also behaved magnificently throughout the engagement.[114]

London's *Penny Illustrated* and the *United Service Gazette and Military and Naval Chronicle* reported a nearly verbatim account on 30 October.[115]

In this standard version of the event, then, we see the fantastic abilities of Highland soldiers as evidenced by their readiness to go into battle in spite of poor odds, by their physical prowess during the charge, and by their leadership abilities on the field. We see Highlanders being acknowledged by the whole British-led force for their critical role in taking the position. Most importantly, we can envision the special relationship between Highlanders, Sikhs and Gurkhas by the fact that they were paired together to fight such a difficult battle, as well as by the Highlanders' efforts to clear the field of the dead Gurkhas in the wake of the battle. This narrative account was at pains to demonstrate that these were no ordinary feats, and that it took a particular calibre of soldier to perform them – or, in the words of the Dundee *People's Journal*, that it took the 'cream of the

British and Indian infantry'.[116]

In the wake of the battle, military and civilian sources alike made much of the camaraderie that had developed between the British and the Indian 'martial races' – in particular, the more recent relationship between Highlanders and Gurkhas. Subscribers to the *Englishman*, for example, began a charity called the 'Gordon and Gurkha Fund' to benefit the children and widows of those soldiers who had died during the Great Frontier Rising.[117] The Gordons' regimental magazine, *The Tiger and Sphinx*, recorded that the 2nd Prince of Wales' Own Gurkhas sent their British counterparts a present of two *kukris* upon their return to Edinburgh after the Rising. Even soldiers themselves recorded sentimental attachments to Gurkhas, evidenced through poems like 'The Gordons' Own Gurkhas'.[118]

The battle – and the relationship of Highlanders to both Sikhs and Gurkhas – also stirred popular interest in media other than prose. Shortly after the event, a song depicting the Gordons' role in the battle – called 'The Gallant Gordons' – featured at the Albert Hall in London.[119] Richard Caton Woodville, one of the most famous military illustrators of the period, found that his depiction of the battle, *Cock o' the North*, was received with great acclaim by fellow Britons.[120] Citizens penned poems inspired by the battle and contributed them to the national press.[121] Dargai was even featured in one of eight panoramic scenes displayed at Madame Tussaud's wax museum between 1885 and 1901. The Dargai panorama was created in 1899, and pictured the Gordon Highlanders storming the heights of what seemed an impossibly fortified cliff. The sign accompanying the display highlighted the Sikhs and Gurkhas cheering their friends on, crying, 'Well done, petticoat regiment', in appreciation.[122]

Madame Tussaud's display simply confirmed the extent to which the idea of a connection between 'martial' Highlanders, Sikhs and Gurkhas had become accepted in popular (not to mention military) culture. Initial credit must go in large part to Frederick Roberts, who – along with his subordinates – used the initial link forged between Highlanders and Sikhs during the Rebellion to build a discourse, bolstered by an anthology of heroic events, linking Highlanders to India's 'martial races'. Although the discourse itself originally served a variety of Roberts's self-interested purposes, at its centre was an insistence on the cultivation of a specific type of warrior masculinity in the soldiers who might be called upon to face Russian troops in the field. Roberts himself became nearly obsessed with the need to build a strong army – filled with strong soldiers – for this very objective, and he held up Highlanders, Sikhs and Gurkhas as the kind of men who could do the job.

When Roberts became famous as a soldier hero during the Second Afghan War, his opinions about soldiers who were the 'right stamp of men' gained a very wide press. His language describing the feats of Highlanders,

Sikhs and Gurkhas resonated with his fellow officers in the field, who themselves focused on the superior abilities of the 'martial races'. But the influence of this language did not end with Roberts and his military cadre. Instead, the virtues of the 'martial' Britons and Indians also resonated deeply in the British press, as story after story detailing the miraculous abilities of Highlanders, Sikhs and Gurkhas seem to attest. Moreover, Roberts – who had learned the hard way about the power of the press – seemed determined to use the popular example of the 'martial races' to forward his own interests in reforming the army and focusing attention on India's northwest frontier.

In so doing, the discourse of 'martial races' became part of the public domain, where it was appropriated and utilised in a variety of ways. Officers in India sought to use it much as Roberts did – to strengthen both the image and the recruiting base of the Indian and British armies, and to strengthen the ties between the two. The Adjutant-General in India put it succinctly when he said in 1880 that this 'bond of union between the British and Native soldiers … cannot fail to be a source of strength to the Government'.[123] As part of the language and imagery of British media culture, the discourse of 'martial races' was utilised in a variety of forms and venues in the last decades of the century, from standard newspapers to poems, from journal articles to music, and from books to paintings. As such, it became part of the lexicon on which an increasingly aggressive, soldier-centred imperial culture was built.

What emerges here is a late Victorian world in which the media and the army were not starkly separate but deeply connected, and where self-interested and media-savvy military figures played a role in helping to shape the values and ideologies of a more aggressively imperial state. Thus while it is certainly true, as Graham Dawson has argued, that 'heroes are made not by their deeds but by the stories that are told about them',[124] I would argue that we must also know who is telling the stories. Once we do, it may be necessary to rethink the relationship between the army, the late Victorian media and the values of popular imperialism.

Notes

1 Sir Garnet Wolseley, quoted in Hew Strachan, *The Politics of the British Army* (Oxford: Clarendon, 1997), 96.

2 National Library of Scotland, Edinburgh (hereafter NLS), MS 30687 C, William Blackwood papers, F. S. Roberts to William Blackwood, 14 June 1889.

3 Roberts to Blackwood, 14 June 1889. It does not appear that Blackwood made use of this particular letter in either 1889 or 1890 – though he did make use of others.

4 See John MacKenzie (ed.), *Imperialism and Popular Culture* (Manchester: Manchester University Press, 1986); John MacKenzie (ed.), *Popular Imperialism and the Military* (Manchester: Manchester University Press, 1992); Jeffrey Richards (ed.), *Imperialism and Juvenile Literature* (Manchester: Manchester University Press, 1989); J. W. M.

Hichberger, *Images of the Army: The Military in British Art, 1815–1914* (Manchester: Manchester University Press, 1988); and Robert MacDonald, *The Language of Empire: Myths and Metaphors of Popular Imperialism, 1880–1918* (Manchester: Manchester University Press, 1994).

5   Take, for example, MacKenzie's edited volume, *Popular Imperialism and the Military*. While the essays in the volume all explore military themes, none deal explicitly with the institutional interests of the army.

6   A recent example of this trend, as noted by Hew Strachan, is David Chandler and Ian Beckett (eds), *The Oxford Illustrated History of the British Army* (Oxford: Oxford University Press, 1994), where the editors claim that 'compared with other armies, the British Army has been largely apolitical' (xvi).

7   See especially Edward Spiers, *The Army and Society, 1815–1914* (London: Longman, 1980) and his more recent 'Civil–military relations', in *The Late Victorian Army, 1868–1902* (Manchester: Manchester University Press, 1992), and Strachan, *The Politics of the British Army*. For military–media relationships, though for an earlier period, see Douglas Peers, '"Those noble exemplars of the true military tradition": constructions of the Indian Army in the mid-Victorian press', *Modern Asian Studies* 31:1 (1997).

8   Gwyn Harries-Jenkins, *The Army in Victorian Society* (London: Routledge & Kegan Paul, 1977), 218.

9   Strachan, *The Politics of the British Army*, 25.

10   Lucy Brown, *Victorian News and Newspapers* (Oxford: Clarendon, 1985), 137, 276.

11   Strachan, *The Politics of the British Army*, 26.

12   Harries-Jenkins, *The Army in Victorian Society*, 218.

13   Glenn Steppler, *Britons, to Arms! The Story of the British Volunteer Soldier* (Pheonix Mill: Alan Sutton, 1992), 41. Steppler gives the figure of 130 MPs with Volunteer connections in the 1870s. In the 1872 and 1881 army localisation acts, Volunteer regiments were first linked with territorial battalions and then became part of the territorial regiments along with the regular and militia battalions. For these connections, see Ian Beckett, *The Amateur Military Tradition, 1558–1945* (Manchester: Manchester University Press, 1991), 184–185.

14   Harries-Jenkins, *The Army in Victorian Society*, 218.

15   Brown, *Victorian News and Newspapers*, 4.

16   Brown, *Victorian News and Newspapers*, 30.

17   Circulation figures for the *Daily Telegraph* rose from 141,700 in 1861 to 300,000 in 1888; and those for for the *Standard* rose from 46,000 in 1860 to 255,000 in 1889. Taken from Brown, *Victorian News and Newspapers*, 52–53.

18   MacKenzie (ed.), *Popular Imperialism and the Military*, 12.

19   MacKenzie, 'Introduction', 1; Jeffrey Richards, 'Popular imperialism and the image of the army in juvenile literature', 81, R. T. Stearn, 'War correspondents and colonial war, c. 1870–1900', 151, all in MacKenzie (ed.), *Popular Imperialism in the Military*.

20   Martin Green, *Dreams of Adventure, Deeds of Empire* (London: Routledge & Kegan Paul, 1980), 3.

21   See especially Graham Dawson, *Soldier Heroes: British Adventure, Empire, and the Imagining of Masculinities* (London: Routledge, 1994), ch. 4, 'The imagining of a hero: Sir Henry Havelock, the Indian Rebellion and the news'. Roger Stearn's focus on war correspondents and war artists also gives a similar impression, even while he acknowledges other influences. See his 'War and the media in the 19th century: Victorian military artists and the image of war, 1870–1914', *Journal of the Royal United Services Institute for Defence* 131:3 (1986).

22   Adrian Preston, 'Wolseley, the Khartoum relief expedition and the defence of India, 1885–1900', *Journal of Imperial and Commonwealth History* 6:3 (May 1978), 262. Also see Spiers, *The Late Victorian Army*, 154–155; Strachan, *The Politics of the British Army*, 96.

23   Wolseley anonymously contributed to *Blackwood's* in Dec. 1870, Jan. 1871 and Feb. 1871 ('The Red River expedition'); and publicly to *MacMillan's* in April 1871 ('Our military requirements') and Feb. 1878 ('Military staff systems abroad and in Eng-

land'); to the *Fortnightly Review* in Aug. 1888 ('Courage'), Sept. 1888 ('Military genius'), Dec. 1888 ('The negro as soldier') and May 1889 ('Is a soldier's life worth living?'); and to the *Nineteenth Century* in Jan. 1878 ('France as a military power'), March 1878 ('England as a military power') and March 1881 ('Long and short service').

24 Kitchener contributed to *Blackwood's* in Feb. 1878 ('Visit to Sophia and Kamerleh') and Aug. 1879 ('Notes from Cyprus'), as well as to the *Fortnightly Review* in Nov. 1885 ('The future of the Fellah'). For his contacts with the *Standard* and *The Times*, see Strachan, *The Politics of the British Army*, 105.

25 For White as war correspondent, see India Office Library and Records, London (hereafter OIOL), MSS Eur F 108/47, Sir George White papers. For Churchill, see Stephen Badsey, 'War correspondents in the Boer War', in John Gooch (ed.), *The Boer War: Direction, Experience, and Image* (London: Frank Cass, 2000), 195. For Churchill's own works, see for a start *The Story of the Malakand Field Force* (New York: W. W. Norton & Co., 1989; originally published in 1898 by Longmans, Green & Co).

26 See a Zulu War (c. 1878) note in Wood's papers regarding giving a preferential tip to *The Times* journalist. Duke University Rare Book, Manuscript and Special Collections (hereafter RBMSC), Evelyn Wood papers.

27 Both Wood and Lockhart maintained a correspondence with William Blackwood of *Blackwood's*, regarding their own and their protégés' contributions. See NLS, MSS 4352, 4340, 4618, 4519, 4575, William Blackwood papers. Wood also published in the *Fortnightly Review* in Oct. 1894 and Feb. 1895 ('The Crimea in 1854 and 1894'). For the contributions of Chesney and others, see Spiers, *The Late Victorian Army*, 198.

28 'Who are the ten greatest men now alive? A symposium of representative opinions', *The Strand Magazine* (Dec. 1911), 42.

29 *Times of India* (16 Nov. 1914). Perhaps fittingly, Roberts died while visiting Indian troops at the front in France during the Second World War.

30 For Havelock and Lawrence, see Dawson, *Soldier Heroes*; John MacKenzie also looks at Havelock and Lawrence in 'Heroic myths of empire', in MacKenzie (ed.), *Popular Imperialism and the Military*. Much has been written on Baden-Powell and popular imperialism: one example is Allen Warren's 'Citizens of the Empire: Baden-Powell, Scouts and Guides, and an imperial ideal', in MacKenzie (ed.), *Imperialism and Popular Culture*.

31 Brian Robson has dealt at length with Roberts in the context of the Second Afghan War in *The Road to Kabul: The Second Afghan War, 1878–1881* (London: Arms and Armour Press, 1986) and in editing Roberts's letters in *Roberts in India: The Military Papers of Field Marshal Lord Roberts, 1876–1893* (Phoenix Mill: Alan Sutton, 1993); Hew Strachan devotes half of ch. 5 to Roberts in *The Politics of the British Army*; while Spiers refers to Roberts on a variety of issues in *The Late Victorian Army*. Historians concerned with the early twentieth-century movement for conscription in Britain have also devoted attention to Roberts, including R. J. Q. Adams and Philip Poirier, *The Conscription Controversy in Great Britain, 1900–1918* (London: Macmillan, 1987); and R. J. Q. Adams, 'Field Marshal Earl Roberts: army and Empire', in J. A. Thompson and Arthur Mejia (eds), *Edwardian Conservatism: Five Studies in Adaptation* (London: Croom Helm, 1988). André Wessels has edited Roberts's papers during the Boer War in *Lord Roberts and the War in South Africa, 1899–1902* (Stroud: Sutton, 2000); and S. B. Spies has written about Roberts in the context of his actions against civilians in South Africa in *Methods of Barbarism? Roberts and Kitchener and Civilians in the Boer Republics, January 1900–May 1902* (Capetown: Human and Rousseau, 1977).

32 Brian Robson notes that Roberts's march was hardly as spectacular as it was made out to be, as Sir Donald Stewart had recently done the march in reverse order from Kandahar to Kabul. Robson, *The Road to Kabul*, 189.

33 Robson, *The Road to Kabul*, 50.

34 NLS, AB.2.82.11.(18), Henry Richard, MP, The Afghan Question (1878), 1, 2–3.

35 *Standard* (2 Jan. 1879), 4.

36 The 3 and 9 Jan. editions of the *Standard* were particularly harsh towards Roberts. For reprints in other papers, see, for example, the anti-war *Reynolds's Newspaper* on 5 Jan. 1879.

37 The truth of this charge is very likely. See Robson (ed.), *Roberts in India*, 81–82, 85–87.

38 Robson (ed.), *Roberts in India*, 85.

39 Robson (ed.), *Roberts in India*, 62, 64–66, 81–83, 85–87.

40 'The troubles of press correspondents', *Homeward Mail* (10 March 1879).

41 See OIOL, MSS Eur F 108/47, Sir George White papers.

42 *Hansard's Parliamentary Debates, 3rd Series*, 10 July 1879–2 Aug. 1879, Volume VI (London: Cornelius Buck, 1879), c. 1174.

43 Robson, *The Road to Kabul*, 122, 176.

44 William Trousdale (ed.), *War in Afghanistan, 1879–80* (Detroit: Wayne State University Press, 1985), 111.

45 Robson, *The Road to Kabul*, 161, 176–77.

46 Trousdale, *War in Afghanistan*, 60.

47 Robson, *The Road to Kabul*, 203.

48 Roberts to the Adjutant-General India, 30 July 1880, in Robson (ed.), *Roberts in India*, 205.

49 Howard Hensman, *The Afghan War of 1879–80* (London: H. Allen & Co.), 470.

50 *Daily Free Press (Aberdeen)* (21 Aug. 1880), 5. The *Daily Free Press* had reprinted these concerns from *The Times* the day before.

51 *The Times* (1 Sept. 1880).

52 *Reynolds's Newspaper* (12 Sept. 1880), 3.

53 *Penny Illustrated News and Illustrated Times* (11 Sept. 1880), 164.

54 *United Service Gazette* (9 Oct. 1880), 4. The earlier critical edition had been that of 4 Jan. 1879, 10.

55 See David Finkelstein, 'Imperial self-representation: constructions of Empire in *Blackwood's* Magazine, 1880–1900', in Julie Codell (ed.), *Imperial Co-histories: National Identities and the British and Colonial Press* (Madison: Farleigh Dickinson University Press, 2003).

56 See NLS, William Blackwood papers.

57 NLS, MS 4477, William Blackwood papers, Frederick Roberts to William Blackwood, 4 July 1885. The paper he sent was probably his 1883 'Is an invasion of India by Russia possible?'. The article that appeared was written by Alexander Allardyce, a regular writer for *Blackwood's*, and appeared in the April 1885 (137) issue, 549–537.

58 Frederick Roberts to William Blackwood, 4 July 1885. The second paper was probably his May 1885 'What are Russia's vulnerable points?'. Blackwood does not appear to have used this second paper.

59 Frederick Roberts, *Forty-One Years In India* (London: Macmillan, 1897), x, vii.

60 Roberts, *Forty-One Years*, ix, x.

61 Roberts, *Forty-One Years*, viii.

62 Roberts, *Forty-One Years*, 532.

63 Roberts, *Forty-One Years*, 405.

64 One of the twenty scrapbooks of press cuttings in the Roberts collection at the National Army Museum, London (hereafter NAM), is entirely devoted to reviews of the book. NAM, Frederick Roberts papers, 7101-23-139-10.

65 Badsey, 'War correspondents in the Boer War', 196; Wessels, *Lord Roberts and the War in South Africa*, 33.

66 Adams, 'Field Marshal Earl Roberts: army and empire', 56.

67 See, for example, the letter from Roberts to Moberly-Bell, 13 Aug. 1902. Duke University RBMSC, Frederick Roberts papers.

68 Duke University RBMSC, Frederick Roberts papers, Roberts to Moberly-Bell, 27 March 1906.

69 Duke University RBMSC, Sir Reginald Pole-Carew papers, Roberts to Sir Reginald Pole-Carew, n.d. but probably 1897.

70 Duke University RBMSC, Frederick Roberts papers, Roberts to Moberly-Bell, 6 Aug.

1902.

71 Duke University RBMSC, Frederick Roberts papers, Roberts to Moberly-Bell, 18 Sept. 1902. Roberts had done the same for Rudyard Kipling's son.

72 Adams and Poirier, *The Conscription Controversy*, 26. The quote here concerns Roberts's relationship with Repington, but works in general as well.

73 Roberts to his mother, *Letters Written During the Indian Mutiny* (New Delhi: Lal Publishers, 1979), 56.

74 Roberts, *Letters Written During the Indian Mutiny*, 42.

75 Roberts, *Letters Written During the Indian Mutiny*, 91.

76 Roberts, *Letters Written During the Indian Mutiny*, 103.

77 Roberts, *Forty-One Years in India*, 327.

78 Roberts, *Forty-One Years in India*, 285–289. Private George Greig of the 93rd Highlanders recorded an event, also recorded by Roberts (289), where 'the determined valour of the Ghoorkhas, sturdy little fellows, who unmindful that they carried such a thing as a rifle dashed with their sharp knives upon their tall antagonists bringing them quickly to Mother Earth either killed or mostly wounded. The Sikhs too were not a whit less brave but they did their work more scientific with bullet or bayonet.' Argyll and Sutherland Highlander Museum, Stirling (hereafter ASHM), N-C93 GRE, 51–52, Private George Greig's diary.

79 The only other regiments Roberts requested were the 23rd Pioneers and the 44th from Assam. NAM, 7101-23-101-1, Frederick Roberts letters while commanding in Afghanistan (1878–81), Roberts to Colonel G. Colley (private secretary to the Viceroy), 10 Dec. 1878.

80 Roberts letters while commanding in Afghanistan (1878–81), Roberts to Colley, 10 Dec. 1878.

81 Roberts letters while commanding in Afghanistan (1878–81), Telegram from F. S. Roberts to Viceroy, 14 Dec. 1878,

82 'Despatch from Afghan War', *London Gazette* (16 Jan. 1880).

83 Roberts's despatch recorded the shots as enemy fire, but his letter to the Adjutant-General India on 16 Dec. 1878 revealed that the shots were fired by men of Roberts's own force. See Robson (ed.), *Roberts in India*, 41.

84 'Afghan War', *London Gazette* (4 Feb. 1879).

85 Alan Harfield, *The Indian Army of the Empress, 1861–1903* (Tunbridge Wells: Spellmount, 1990), 71.

86 NAM, 7101-23-126-1, F. S. Roberts, Speech at a banquet at the United Service Club, 1880.

87 Quoted in James Cromb, *The Highland Brigade: Its Battles and Its Heroes*, 3rd edn (London: Simkin, Marshall & Co., 1886), 285.

88 All of these terms were taken from Roberts's own words in previously cited sources.

89 See, for example, NAM, 7101-23-126-1, F. S. Roberts, On the occasion of a public entertainment given by the representatives of the Punjab to General Lord Roberts, 1893.

90 *London Gazette* (3 Dec. 1880). The specific troops were noted in the article, but throughout the knowledge was taken as a given. For weeks, everyone already knew exactly who had accompanied Roberts to Kandahar.

91 MacDonald, *The Language of Empire*, 81. This is MacDonald's formulation of the function of hero myths.

92 *London Gazette* (16 Jan. 1880).

93 *The Pioneer* (22 Oct. 1879). The date for this article is earlier than when the despatch appeared in the *London Gazette*, but it is entirely possible that the *Gazette* was simply late in publishing the official word, and that the *Pioneer* was using information received by telegram.

94 *Penny Pictorial News and Family Story Paper* (18 Oct. 1879).

95 Free Lance, 'Act 3 of the Afghan War', *Army and Navy Magazine* 1 (1881), 249–50.

96 NAM, 7101-23-126-5, F. S. Roberts, Speech at a dinner given by the Highland Society to the officers of the Highland regiments which served in South Africa (1903), 46.

97 Mary des Chene, 'Language and practice in the colonial Indian Army', paper given at

the Institute for Global Studies in Culture, Power and History, Johns Hopkins University, Autumn 1993, 32.

98 St Andrew is the patron saint of Scotland.

99 Sir George White, 'St. Andrew's dinner', *Tiger and Sphinx* 19 (15 Dec. 1894), 294.

100 For a contemporary comment on this, see 'The Indian Mutiny in fiction', *Blackwood's Magazine* 161 (Feb. 1897).

101 Punjab Government Military Department Orders, no. 138 (1886), quoted in Rai Sahib Boydo Nath Dey, *A Brief Account of the Punjab Frontier Force* (Calcutta: W. Newman & Co., 1905), 45.

102 Punjab Government Military Department Orders, no. 138 (1886), quoted in Dey, *A Brief Account of the Punjab Frontier Force*, 45.

103 Cromb, *The Highland Brigade*, 160.

104 Surgeon-General Munro, *Records of Service and Campaigning in Many Lands, Volume II* (London: Hurst and Blackett, 1887), 191.

105 British Library, London, B.S. 21/21, Alexander G. Stuart, *The Indian Empire: A Short Review and Some Hints for the Use of Soldiers Proceeding to India* (1912), 59.

106 Quoted in Stearn, 'War correspondents and colonial war', 148.

107 For a detailed appraisal of the military importance of these campaigns, see Tim Moreman's *The Army in India and the Development of Frontier Warfare, 1849–1947* (London: Macmillan, 1998), esp. ch. 2.

108 Moreman, *The Army in India*, 68.

109 Moreman, *The Army in India*, 57.

110 That the military believed only certain kinds of men could fight adequately in the region was evidenced by the 1881 inquiry 'Classes of men of the native army who have best withstood the hardships of the Afghan campaign'. The report concluded that Pathans, Punjabi Muslims, Sikhs and Gurkhas were the troops best fitted to fighting in such a climate and terrain. The worst troops were considered to be 'Dogras and Hindus'. OIOL, L/MIL/7/7018.

111 These included Enfield, Martini-Henry and Snider rifles. Moreman, *The Army in India*, 58.

112 OIOL, L/MIL/17/5/1616, General Orders India, Summary of measures considered or carried out in the military department of the Government of India (1899).

113 'The Indian frontier campaign', *Daily Free Press* (21 Oct. 1897), 5.

114 *Reynolds's Newspaper* (24 Oct. 1897), 1.

115 'The plucky capture of the Dargai Ridge by the Gordon Highlanders', *Penny Illustrated Paper* (30 Oct. 1897), 280. The *Penny Illustrated* also carried a fresh story about the charge in the 20 Nov. edition.

116 'Crossing the passage of death', *People's Journal* (20 Nov. 1897), 3.

117 Reported in the *Tiger and Sphinx* (15 May 1898), 19.

118 *Tiger and Sphinx* (15 May 1898), 85–86; also 31 Dec. 1898.

119 NAM, 7601-66, press #112-s-1897, The Gallant Gordons, Albert Hall (1897).

120 John Canning, 'The military art of Richard Caton Woodville', *Military Illustrated* 11 (Feb./March 1988), 37.

121 For example, a poem called 'At Dargai', contributed by Sir Edwin Arnold to the *Daily Telegraph* and reprinted by the *Daily Free Press* (Aberdeen) (28 Oct. 1897), 5.

122 MacDonald, *The Language of Empire*, 98.

123 'Despatch from Major-General Greaves dated Oct. 7, 1880', *London Gazette* (3 Dec. 1880).

124 Graham Dawson, 'The blond bedouin: Lawrence of Arabia, imperial adventure and the imagining of English-British masculinity', in Michael Roper and John Tosh (eds), *Manful Assertions: Masculinities in Britain Since 1800* (London: Routledge, 1991), 138.

CHAPTER FIVE

Martial races: the inter-imperial uses of a racially gendered language

By the start of the 1880s, native-owned Indian newspapers were making it clear that Indian nationalists saw common cause with the Irish nationalist struggles then rocking the United Kingdom. The *Bengalee* put it plainly when it announced that '[b]etween Ireland and India there ought to exist the closest relations of sympathy and mutual regard'.[1] In 1887, just a year after the Irish Home Rule crisis split the Liberal Party, British feminist Josephine Butler orchestrated a national campaign that attacked the Indian Army policy of licensing native prostitutes to service British soldiers. Butler and her allies publicly castigated army authorities as worse even than native 'degraded sinners' for allowing such a system to exist, questioned the morality of British rule in India, and raised doubts about the military efficiency of British soldiers.[2]

While late nineteenth-century Indian nationalism, Irish nationalism and British feminism may at first glance seem unconnected both to one another and to the ideology of martial races, each was in fact part of a deeply interconnected web of events and ideologies that informed the subjectivities of Anglo-Indian officers and the shape of martial race discourse. We have already seen the ways in which intensified threats of war with Russia, France and Germany formed a crucial inspiration for the development of martial race policies and ideologies in late century. Yet the identities, consciousness and politics of the Anglo-Indian officers who so clearly and consistently articulated the language of martial races were shaped by other historical and ideological contexts as well. In the last two decades of the nineteenth century, these included the (roughly simultaneous) threats of Indian and Irish nationalism and the British feminist campaign to eliminate licensed prostitution in India. Indeed, Anglo-Indian officers did not experience global security issues as separate from nationalist or feminist challenges; rather, most perceived such issues as part of a complex imperial whole, where 'domestic' political challenges were clearly relevant to larger issues of global imperial security.[3] The articulation of martial race discourse, then, must be read as a strategic set of images whose components could be deployed not only to answer the European military challenge from without, but also to do battle with nationalists and feminists who, it was feared, might destroy the Empire from within. In short, Highlanders, Sikhs and Gurkhas were imagined as ideological counterpoints to nationalists and feminist critics: they were obedient, loyal, strong, masculine, hardy, healthy and moral.

Central to my argument is that martial race discourse must not be viewed simply as a *reflection* of a time in which scientific theories of race and gender held sway. While such theories were clearly important to the development of the discourse, the language of martial races was also a discursive *tool* – a strategy of domination and rule that used the power and appeal of racial and gendered language for political purposes.[4] In other words, officers who made use of martial race discourse were not simply 'brainwashed' by biological conceptions of race and gender. Instead, as we shall see, the architects of martial race discourse were frequently aware of inconsistencies and contradictions internal to the language itself, and yet attempted to achieve political outcomes or to manipulate public opinion through an idealised discourse of racial hierarchies and masculine prowess.

Once part of the public domain, however, this discourse and its component images became one of the languages by which 'race' and 'masculinity' were described and understood by contemporaries. In other words, although martial race discourse was constructed in response to specific historical events and challenges, it also exceeded the political intentions of its originators as it became widely available for public interpretation and appropriation. As such, the discourse of martial races functioned simultaneously as a political tool and as an agent in the material world in its own right.

This chapter explores the intentional and unintentional ways that martial race discourse was deployed against nationalist claims in both Britain and India. In addition, it documents the concrete ways that the 'martial races' themselves were, in a very real sense, self-conscious constructs of the British imagination in spite of the naturalised racial and gendered language that surrounded them. Finally, this chapter charts the uneven impact of martial race discourse across the metropolitan and colonial contexts.[5] In India, for example, martial race discourse was used to gloss exclusionary recruiting strategies by insisting that only certain races were suited to bearing arms. In Britain, however, the same discourse was used as a means of widening the appeal of the army by providing an idealised image of loyalty and service to the Empire, and by countering rival claims of dissipation, drunkenness and poor health within the ranks – especially those made by feminist reformers opposed to regulated prostitution in

India. The meanings of 'race' and 'manliness' in martial race discourse, then, were imprecise and flexible, ready to be applied to widely divergent circumstances as a discursive means to control or to liberate, to include or to exclude, to inspire, to distract, or to produce fear. This flexibility reminds us of the historical instability of notions of both race and gender even as it explains the enormous utility and popular appeal of martial race discourse after 1880.

Martial races, the imperial antidote to nationalism

One of the neglected sub-plots in the growing appeal of martial race discourse between 1880 and 1914 was its relationship to colonial nationalist movements in Ireland and India. Yet the emergence of the ultra-loyal images embodied by martial race soldiers in this period can hardly be isolated from the threats of imperial ruin that nationalists were believed to represent. Irish and Indian nationalists were believed to imperil the very integrity of the Empire: and in a period of already precarious global security, British administrators and officers alike were alarmed at the potential disorder and divisiveness their concerns represented. In response, the architects of martial race discourse framed their constructions of ideal soldiers in radical opposition to such images. The discourse of martial races expressed the military's ideal males in a language that framed them as the mirror image of supposedly irrational, effeminate, child-like and ungrateful nationalists. Sikhs and Gurkhas became the 'good' Indians, loyal to their British masters at whatever cost. Highlanders became the 'good' Celtic heroes, serving the Empire in all corners of the globe. And, as loyal servants of the Crown, the martial races were imagined as lethal weapons who could, should the need arise, be used to keep their 'disloyal' counterparts in line.

As nationalist criticisms in both Ireland and India became more strident towards the end of the century, constructions of nationalists became ever more cowardly, weak, racially degenerate and effeminate. Not coincidentally, this was the same period in which the 'martial races' were constructed with increasing frequency as invincible, loyal, racially pure and manly figures. The two constructions cannot be separated, for each was formed and articulated in dialogic relationship to the other.[6] Any attempt to understand the particular racial and gendered shape of martial race discourse, then, must also take into account the effects of Irish and Indian nationalism on its development.

Certainly, the principal architects of martial race discourse were highly attuned to the dangers that Indian and Irish nationalism posed to imperial military security in general and to British military forces in particular. To Anglo-Indian officers, nationalists seemed to represent an internal military threat precisely at a time when the Empire was beset by external enemies in Europe. This perception was enhanced by the fact that nationalists frequently framed their challenges in terms of opposition to British military policy in both India and Ireland. Even more alarming, in the last quarter of the century it seemed increasingly clear that Irish and Indian nationalists had recognised the significance of inter-imperial struggles for autonomy, and looked to one another for precedents, inspiration and even collaboration.[7]

Anglo-Indian officers and administrators were uniquely positioned to apprehend the connections between the Irish and Indian nationalist movements in a negative light. To begin with, men who had experience in both areas were disproportionately represented in high-level imperial positions. Most frequently, this dual experience was attained through the export of Anglican Anglo-Irish or Ulster Protestant men for military and administrative service in India.[8] Indeed, some of the most influential Anglo-Indian officers of the late nineteenth century were Irishmen. Of these, two in particular were instrumental in the development of martial race policy and discourse: Frederick Roberts and George White, who between them held the post of Commander-in-Chief India from 1885 to 1898.[9] In Indian civil administration, two Viceroys of the 1880s, Lords Dufferin and Landsdowne, had 'strong personal and proprietary ties' to Ireland's Anglo-Irish elite. Further, as Scott Cook has pointed out, in 1886 two Irishmen sat on the Viceregal Council, Irishmen headed the Legislative and Finance and Commerce Departments in the Indian government, and in the 1890s 'seven out of the eight Indian provinces (including Burma) were run by Irishmen'.[10] With the exception of a few prominent individuals, nearly all of these men hailed from the Irish Protestant population, and thus were predisposed to view Irish Catholic nationalism with alarm.[11]

Other individuals gained experience in both Ireland and India through inter-imperial service. On occasion, commanders-in-chief of the Indian Army went on to take command of imperial forces in Ireland.[12] Or civil administrators might consecutively hold key positions in the Irish and Indian governments.[13] The disproportionate representation of high-level imperial personnel with both Irish and Indian experience was an important factor in the ways these men responded to problems and issues in both colonial areas. Significantly, officers and administrators alike noted broad similarities between Indian and Irish society, and regularly cited parallels in rural poverty, sectarian strife, conflicts over land use and difficulties in enforcing law and order. In turn, this perception of similarity resulted in frequent 'borrowing' in matters of imperial policy, and on several occasions officials formulated policy in India based on previous experience in Ireland. In 1881 the publicist William Digby voiced an already well-established conception when he argued that '[i]n India, Great Britain possesses a larger Ireland'.[14] And, as practised as they were in noting similarities between Ireland and India, officers and administrators also had little difficulty imagining the consequences of combined nationalist agitation between the two.

Neither, it seems, did some nationalists. As early as the 1840s, certain Irish nationalists like Daniel O'Connell and Thomas Davis hoped to encourage anti-British sentiment in Ireland by suggesting connections between their own cause and British conduct in India.[15] Between 1870 and 1886, especially, the Irish Home Rule movement led by Charles Stewart Parnell sought to establish direct links with Indian nationalists. Frank Hugh O'Donnell, a prominent member of Parnell's Home Rule Party, publicly advocated the idea that the Irish should form a 'coalition with the oppressed natives of India' in order to achieve mutual independence.[16] O'Donnell also organised several rather unsuccessful organisations meant to lobby British MPs for Indian reform, and suggested that the Home Rule Party give an Irish parliamentary seat to an Indian nationalist.[17] More generally, Home Rulers were some of the primary advocates of Indian interests in Parliament between 1877 and 1886.[18] At the end of the nineteenth century, Irish nationalist meetings were voicing common cause with those who had taken up arms against the Raj. In the midst of the Tirah campaign, for example, a spokesman for a 'Parnellite Convention' in Dublin claimed that '[t]he Irish people ... sympathised with the natives of India fighting against England, and he called for cheers for them'.[19]

The western-educated Indians who would later lead India's nationalist movement were equally interested in Ireland in this period. The Irish Home Rule movement captured the sustained interest of Indians hoping for greater participation in the government of India, and Indian nationalists were quick to recognise and extemporise on the relevance of the Irish struggle for their own cause. The Indian press in particular made much of these connections, and consistently publicised the victories and defeats of the Home Rule Party to Indian audiences. And although Indian nationalist demands in the 1880s were moderate and non-violent, still the press flirted with the threat of violence through the Irish example: warning, for example, that '"Irish" treatment' by the Government of India 'must inevitably result in "Irish" retaliation'.[20]

The spectre of Indian agitation on the Irish model was deeply alarming to British officers and administrators, whose experience had taught them only too well that nationalists in both areas shared many similar grievances with British rule. In 1877 Secretary of State for India Lord Salisbury worried that certain Indians were beginning to adopt a 'Home Rule tone'.[21] When the Indian National Congress was formed in 1885, then-Viceroy Lord Dufferin – Irish landlord and Ulster Protestant – wrote that Indian members of Congress were very like the Irish in their 'Celtic perverseness, vivacity, and cunning', and were in fact intent upon organising along Irish Home Rule lines. By 1886, as the Home Rule crisis reached a peak in Britain, Dufferin began referring to the Congress as the 'Indian Home Rule Movement'.[22] Writing to the Secretary of State for India that same year, Dufferin fretted:

> I cannot help having a strong suspicion that the course of events at home in regard to Ireland has produced a very considerable effect upon the minds of the intelligent and educated section of our own native community. Associations and sub-associations are being formed all over the country which are also being furnished with a network of caucuses ... I cannot help asking myself how long an autocratic government like that of India – and a government which every one will admit for many a long year to come must remain autocratic – will be able to stand the strain implied by the importation en bloc from England or rather from Ireland, of the perfected machinery of modern democratic agitation.[23]

Worries of this sort did not abate with the decline of the Irish Home Rule movement in the early 1890s. In 1897 the Bombay government viewed the strategies of Bal Ganghadar Tilak – who would become one of the most important militant Indian nationalist leaders – as 'a steady endeavour to imitate Irish Nationalist methods as closely as possible'.[24]

Widespread perceptions that Indian nationalists were bent on Irish-style agitation were, in fact, a primary weapon of the anti-Home Rule opposition in both Britain and India. Conservatives and Unionists pointed to the all-too-believable spectre of an Irish 'monster' developing in India as reason enough to refuse to concede to Irish demands. Home Rule in Ireland, they argued, would only open Pandora's box, for if Ireland were allowed its own parliament separatist movements bent on similar goals would follow throughout the Empire. As an English contributor to the *Indian Spectator* put it, 'if a Parliament in Ireland be given to it with the absolute power of granting the supplies or of raising taxes, a dismemberment of the Empire is a necessary and inevitable consequence sooner or later'.[25] This 'domino theory' exerted tremendous power in the anti-Home Rule debate, and was mobilised time and again in response to crises over Home Rule in the late nineteenth and early twentieth centuries.[26]

In this context, martial race discourse must be understood as part of a wider political terrain in which colonial authorities battled with nationalists over the ideal characteristics of imperial subjects. In India, the fierce language of martial races was deployed with ever more frequency in late century, just as criticisms levelled by India's educated elite rose sharply. Moreover, at the same time that martial races appeared increasingly masculine and loyal, British officers and administrators sought to discredit nationalist claims through recourse to the language of effeminacy. The result was two radically different constructions of Indian subjecthood that were nevertheless fundamentally connected.

Though expressed in terms of race and masculinity, the key to the differences behind effeminate and martial native constructions was loyalty. The more nationalists criticised and questioned government policy, the more effeminate they seemed to become, until by the end of the nineteenth century the stereotype of the effeminate nationalist was a stock in trade. That is not to say, however, that this perception of effeminacy was invented out of whole cloth. Bengali men in particular – a region from whence many nationalists originated – had long been believed to be 'of weaker frame and more enervated character' than other Indians.[27] Yet what was new in the late nineteenth century, as Mrinalini Sinha has noted, was that British stereotypes of effeminacy shifted from the entire male Bengali population to focus instead on a specific group of middle-class, professional, western-educated men believed to be at the root of nationalist discontent – men known derogatorily as Bengali *babus*. Moreover, as similar groups emerged in other Indian provinces in late century, the concept of the 'effeminate Bengali *babu*' simply became shorthand for 'politically discontented middle-class "Indians" from all over India'.[28] Effeminacy, in other words, was no longer associated simply with regional characteristics, but with a particular class and its political orientation towards the British Raj.

The vehemence with which British officers and administrators pursued images of *babu* effeminacy closely paralleled the perceived threat behind nationalist organisation and agitation. Frequently, concern over military security lay at the heart of the alarm caused even by mild nationalist demands. Recourse to the language of *babu* effeminacy, then, functioned as a tool to discredit nationalists as fraudulent men, incapable of commenting on or understanding issues such as citizenship, war or chivalry. This tactic grew widespread in the 1870s, when Indian elites began to use their most powerful weapon to advocate change and to criticise government military policy: the native-owned, vernacular press. Most alarmingly from the British perspective, native newspapers openly questioned the financial cost and the morality of British intervention in Afghanistan during the Second Afghan War (1878–80). Viceroy Lord Lytton was so concerned about the potential effects of such criticism in 1878 that he pushed an Act through the Legislative Council designed to muzzle the press. The Vernacular Press Act, as it was called, would have charged offending papers with sedition and subjected them to heavy fines.[29] Despite his apparent concern with the potential effects of military criticism by the elite, however, Lytton denied the legitimacy of elite concerns through the language of effeminacy: in 1879 he assured a correspondent that the Bengali middle class 'though disloyal is fortunately cowardly and its only revolver is its ink bottle; which though dirty, is not dangerous'.[30] Like women, elites' only weapons were words – weapons that could be ignored, as Lytton implied, by 'real' men backed by the force of arms.

The use of the effeminate *babu* stereotype reached new heights in the 1880s, as a series of crises rocked the subcontinent in that decade. The first began in 1883 over the proposed introduction of what came to be known as the 'Ilbert Bill' in the Indian Legislative Council. The Bill, which would have allowed a limited number of Indian magistrates to preside over Britons in some rural courts, was greeted by a storm of protest from Anglo-Indians who feared loosening their racially exclusive stranglehold on positions of power within the Raj. To combat the legislation, Anglo-Indians mobilised as never before, and in the process made extensive recourse to the imagery of the 'effeminate *babu*' as a means of discrediting native authority. In particular, Anglo-Indians argued that *babus* lacked even a basic understanding of manly chivalry, and thus might intentionally compromise the virtue of British women who came under their jurisdiction.[31] So loud and so many were such protests that the Government of India was forced to modify the Bill.[32]

Only two years after the Ilbert Bill crisis, a new battle between Britons and Indian elites yielded fresh articulations of the 'effeminate *babu*' stereotype in ways that were directly related to military security. As we have seen in previous chapters, 1885 was a critical moment in the Anglo-Russian 'Great Game', for in that year clashes between Russian and Afghan forces at Pendjeh brought Britain and Russia to the brink of war. In response to the threat of imminent war, and with the initial encouragement of then-Viceroy Lord Dufferin, hundreds of educated Indians offered their services as native Volunteers to help defend India's internal security. Yet the initial encouragement by the Government of India for such units was quickly reversed on the advice of the Military Department, and thereafter Indians were systematically excluded from joining Volunteer units. The reversal was a clear rebuff to Indian elites and stimulated a flurry of meetings and petitions highlighting the injustice of not being allowed to demonstrate loyalty to the Raj.[33]

As in 1883, colonial authorities responded to the demands of colonial elites by deprecating the masculine pretensions of supposedly effeminate Indian elites. This time, however, the contrast with the loyal martial races was explicit. In the midst of the crisis, the Lahore *Civil and Military Gazette* claimed that 'none but the fighting classes should be enrolled [in the Volunteer corps]. The clerkly element should be as conspicuous by its absence, as it is in the regular army ... the *babu* although a valiant wielder of the pen, is not so handy with the sword.'[34] Yet such strident assertions of *babu* effeminacy disguised deeper reasons for rejecting native Volunteers, for the spectre of elite native Volunteers also brought with it visions of armed insurrection, of verbal criticism and growing nationalism converging with the force of firepower. This memorandum by Lieutenant-General Robert Phayre in 1885 stated it baldly:

> The educated Hindoo classes throughout India (Brahmins particularly) – men whose violent advocacy in the Native press of national freedom, self-government, native advancement to the highest offices of the State as a matter of right ... exercises an incessantly unsettling effect upon ... native society generally. These are the men who are loudest in advocating the extension of the Volunteer movement ... in order that when the time comes they may have an armed, drilled, and organised force to back them up in advancing their insolent demands.[35]

Clearly, despite public ridicule of the martial capabilities of educated Indians, the prospect of native Volunteers was perceived, at least by some, as a potential threat to internal Indian military stability. After more than a year of intense public debate, the Indian government decided to err on the side of caution and announced its official rejection of native Volunteer units.[36] The domination of India's military forces by the 'martial races' remained unaltered.

In the midst of the controversy over native volunteering, educated Indian elites convened the first all-India organisation to advocate reform. The Indian National Congress, which met for the first time in December 1885, was by any standards a moderate institution engineered to work within the British imperial system. Yet many colonial authorities perceived its founding by educated, middle-class 'babus' – not to mention its appearance at a time of both internal and international tension – as yet another challenge to British hegemony in India.[37] In particular, British officers and administrators feared the disruptive and destabilising effects of Congress interests in the Indian press. The results, authorities argued, could have disastrous consequences for military security across the subcontinent, and could even begin to effect the loyalties of the martial races. By 1894 the Commander-in-Chief in India, Sir George White, contended that '[t]his invidious teaching [of the native press] must, I believe, sap the loyalty of our native soldiers in the near future'. Specifically, White drew attention to the sharply increasing number of soldiers who were reading native newspapers regularly, adding with alarm that the practice 'has even spread to the Goorkha regiments'. The native press, White concluded, could only damage the Indian Army – that foundation upon which British rule ultimately rested:

> Our native soldiers of the future will learn dislike and distrust of our intentions, from their earliest years. The village schoolmaster will complete their political education in the principles and in the beliefs which he himself has imbibed from the native press. The recruit, thus educated, will join the

regiment no longer prepared to accept the simple faith of the old subadar in the power and integrity of the Sirkar ...[38]

The incendiary indictments of British rule supposedly inspired by the native, nationalist press were frequently traced to the official newspaper of the Congress British Committee: the London-published *India*. Dubbed a 'poisonous little rag' by one Secretary of State for India, *India* was blamed for 'attacking the Government and insulting British rule', and thus for stirring the waters of Indian public opinion against the Raj.[39] One of the reasons the journal appeared so threatening was because it frequently contested British military policy in India. In particular, contributors to *India* sought to challenge the idea that massive intervention along India's northwest frontier region (an intervention which, let us remember, legitimised the policy of martial race recruiting) was necessary to British Indian defence. Instead, essays in *India* hoped to expose that such a policy was promulgated at the expense of – rather than in defence of – Indian interests. As one contributor put it, the policy was a 'fatuous pursuit ... originated by a purely military clique for the usual reasons, [which] has cost India much more than the accounts indicate'.[40]

Colonial authorities responded to the challenge posed by nationalist criticisms, as before, by ridiculing the pretensions of *'babus'* to speak on military matters. Moreover, as in the Volunteer crisis, this ridicule was explicitly counter-balanced by the oppositional figure of the 'martial' Indian soldier. In 1897 an anonymous contributor to the *United Services Magazine* put the case plainly:

> Anyone who has lived in India any time and has used his faculties of observation must have noticed that the only manly men are now to be found in the ranks of our native soldiery. All natives of other professions are of, or approach to, the emasculated type. One has only to look at the Bengalees, a race of many millions who do not provide a single soldier, to see this proved, or to compare the whole bearing and character of a native in civil employ with that of a native subedar, jemadar, or even common soldier. [In India we have] ... deprived the people of their natural leaders, i.e. the more manly and dependable men. Our educational system raises up in his place the flabby charactered emasculated specimens of manhood such as are now becoming the leaders of the people – the blatant orator, the unscrupulous pleader, the contributor to the 'reptile' press, etc.[41]

Here, Indians who dare to criticise British rule are caricatured as 'flabby', 'emasculated' and 'unscrupulous'. British education has made monsters of them, unmanning them even while contributing to their insolence. Bengali men are held up as the prime example of effeminacy: a contention 'proved' by the fact that 'not one' of them was man enough to serve in the Indian Army. In direct contrast, soldiers in the Indian Army were held up as icons of manliness, dependability and 'natural' leadership ability.

[165]

In spite of official worries that nationalist sentiment might be infiltrating the ranks of the army, officers emphasised the supposedly vast differences between the 'semi-Europeanised Bengali and other races who are perpetually declaiming about their imaginary rights' and the 'warrior races' found in the military.[42] The martial races were Indian men who knew their place, who were willing and able to fight alongside Britons, who were strong and manly. They were the ones who would help keep India for the British – the ones who could be counted on, in the words of one author writing for the *United Services Magazine* in 1890, to 'make very short work of a representative assembly of Baboos and such crew, however great their number'.[43]

As nationalist agitation grew stronger over the last twenty-five years of the nineteenth century, then, so too did the conscious juxtaposition of effeminate elites with manly martial races become more frequent. The two constructions were in fact inseparable, for each served to define the contours of the other. While the figure of the *babu* served to denigrate and discredit those who were critical of the Raj, the figure of the martial race soldier embodied the qualities loyal Indian subjects should possess. Only loyal men, moreover, could claim access to manliness: those who chose to criticise were condemned, at least rhetorically, to effeminacy.

So powerful was this dichotomy that elite nationalist groups felt compelled to respond to colonial claims about *babu* effeminacy. Newspapers such as the English-language *National Paper* and *India* published articles and editorials countering allegations of effeminacy and recommending a programme for reform. In 1868 the *National Paper* argued that Bengali men must be allowed to take up arms 'if we wish to be a nation, if we wish to live in terms of equality and friendship with Europeans, if we wish to be one with Rajpoots, Sikhs and Marathas'.[44] In 1890, under the heading 'A Plea for the Hindus as a Warlike People', an anonymous Hindu Punjabi argued that Hindus were not physically weak as Anglo-Indians contended, and claimed among their number such 'warlike' peoples as Sikhs, Gurkhas and Mahrattas.[45] Other nationalist organisations sought to institutionalise body building and gymnasiums as a way to access the masculinity of the martial races.[46]

Even when the opposing figures of the *babu* and the martial race soldier were not summoned together, by the end of the century the image of one clearly called up the other as a silent but powerful referent. Thus when we read that the Sikhs who defended the northwest frontier outpost at Siraghiri in 1897 were 'true to the martial instincts of their faith' and 'died to a man at their posts, covering themselves with glory, and giving imperishable renown to the grand regiment to which it was their privilege to belong',[47] we must also consider that the story was told in a climate of increasingly militant Hindu nationalism, epitomised by Bal Gangadhar

Tilak in the 1890s. As men like Tilak struggled to define a positive Indian identity based on traditional Hinduism, the language of martial races struggled ever harder to discredit any but its own version of ideal Indian identity. Hence, we read that Gurkhas have never 'failed in their duty against any enemy', and that they possess a remarkable and inherent 'pugnacity and love of fighting for fighting's sake'.[48] The 'martial races', indeed, are imagined as the perfect colonial subjects, as in the portrayal of Sikhs in a military handbook written for the benefit of recruiters. Sikhs, we are told, represent 'that splendid pattern of a native soldier, simple in his religion, worshipping the one God; broad in his views; free in not observing the prejudices of caste; manly in his warlike creed, in his love of sports and in being a true son of the soil; a buffalo, not quick of understanding, but brave, strong and true'.[49] The contrast with educated, nationalist Hindus is implicit. Nationalists, depicted as feminine, deceitful, clerkish cowards, pale beside these rather slow but doggedly loyal, ferociously masculine soldiers.

This phenomenon of discursively pitting supposedly 'martial' races against threatening nationalists was not unique to India. Indeed, a similar oppositional relationship existed between representations of ultra-masculine, ultra-loyal Highland Scots and Irish nationalists. Significantly, the reputation of Highland soldiers grew most popularised and unassailable in the same period that Irish Catholic nationalism came to be regarded as increasingly threatening to British internal and imperial security. From Daniel O'Connell's movement for the Repeal of the Union in the 1840s until 1914, Irish nationalism was a regular and reviled feature on the political map of Great Britain. Between the Land Wars of the late 1870s and the debate over the Second Home Rule Bill in 1892, it is fair to say that Irish nationalism was *the* dominant political issue in the British Isles, prompting response and reaction from official, popular and individual sources.[50] The issue of Home Rule, especially, was so divisive that it split the Liberal Party when Gladstone lent his support to the cause in 1886, and, as we know, caused a national uproar in Britain over its potential for inspiring Indian nationalists and for destroying the Empire.[51] In that period, it would have been difficult indeed for Britons to isolate themselves from images and descriptions of Irish Catholic nationalists as savage, cunning and uncontrollable.[52] In this extraordinarily turbulent political context, Highland soldiers increasingly served as the positive Celtic alter ego to Ireland's reputedly degenerate – and disloyal – Celts. Although terms like 'Highland soldier' and 'Irish nationalist' were far from simple and frequently were fraught with inconsistencies, discursively contemporaries portrayed the two groups in clear, unambiguous, oppositional terms: Highlanders were 'good', Irish nationalists were 'bad'. The function of these characterisations were twofold. First, like the dichotomous relationship between Indian 'martial races' and *babus*, they helped articulate the contours of ideal versus unacceptable imperial citizenship. Second, they served as a reassurance to Britons that not all Celts were disloyal: against the disloyalty of the Irish Celts, Highlanders – the very best and most manly Celts – remained unshakably loyal and continually 'proved' that loyalty in countless imperial venues.

As in India, issues of loyalty lay at the heart of differing constructions between Highland and Irish Celts. Also as in India, the problem of political and social loyalty was frequently cloaked in the language of gender and race. However, in Britain the shape of such language was dependent upon different historical circumstances. Whereas in India Britons were able to embellish and exaggerate old stereotypes of effeminacy among Bengali males to feed the construction of the *babu*, in Ireland Catholic men were reputed to be physically strong. Moreover, unlike Bengali men, Irish men had a long tradition of service in the British military. Until 1850 Irish men dominated the ranks of the British infantry, at times even outnumbering the English.[53] Of these, the great majority were Irish Catholics from the poorer classes of Irish society (also frequently called Celts or Gaels): the same group associated most strongly with nineteenth-century Irish nationalism. Finally, Irish Catholic men, despite being reviled for their 'popish' religion, had a reputation of being quick to the fight and of being good soldiers, especially in the attack.[54] As Lord Roberts put it during a speech in 1893: 'I suppose that no one who has lived in Ireland has any doubt as to Irishmen not being altogether averse to an occasional fight. Well, gentlemen, depend upon it, it is this very quality which makes them such admirable soldiers on service.'[55] Because of this reputation, the strategy of discrediting nationalist claims through attacks on their masculine physical prowess (used to such successful effect in India) was unavailable to Britons in Ireland.

Both Britons and Protestant Anglo-Irish did, however, attack the masculinity of Irish Catholic nationalists in other ways. Most significantly, Irish Catholic men were associated with certain qualities normally ascribed to those with 'womanly temperaments'. These included especially unreliability, unpredictability, child-like behaviour and extreme displays of emotion. As a writer for the *National Review* put it in 1889, it was impossible to treat the Irish as equals because of 'a rare identity of temperament in the Celtic race in all ages and under the most diverse conditions'. Celts, he continued, were '[w]arm-hearted, but fickle; brave, but wanting in endurance; brilliant, but ineffective; religious, but unprincipled; fascinating, but infinitely provoking; with the fierce passions of men, the lack of sober calculation which often limits the power of the cleverest woman, and the unreasonableness of children'.[56] In short, while the Irish Celts had good qualities, they were inconstant – closer in fact to women and children than to adult men. They could not be expected to know how to govern themselves, but only to follow the lead of stronger, more mature men. Thus, even when the Celtic Irish were acknowledged as good and brave fighters, they could also be construed as dangerously unreliable, with the 'passions' of men but only the intellect of women. In contrast, the figure of the Highland soldier stood as a readily available example of men who were both fierce fighters and disciplined (like 'real' men) to control their emotions and to complete their commitments.

The language of race was also a central player in the battle to discredit the claims of Irish nationalist groups. Indeed, as Irish nationalist movements grew in scale and power in the last sixty years of the century, so too did Britons and Anglo-Irish increasingly seek to attack the legitimacy of Irish nationalist demands via racialised imagery. Although we have become accustomed to thinking about race in terms of skin colour, the Irish case (as indeed the Scottish) helps us to remember the multiple uses of racial typologies in nineteenth-century Britain, as well as the political motivations behind those uses. Certainly, Britons and Anglo-Irish recognised that the Celtic Irish differed from themselves in religion and, frequently, in social class. These differences, in fact, had encouraged the belief that Irish Celts were somehow a 'breed apart' from other Britons for several centuries.[57] Yet in the nineteenth century, the development of human 'sciences' such as philology, phrenology, craniometry, anthropometry, and Darwinian evolution theory led Britons and Anglo-Irish to articulate Celtic Irish differences in terms of inherent racial inadequacy. Poor Catholics in particular, who were increasingly involved in Irish politics through Daniel O'Connell's Repeal movement, Fenianism, the Land Wars and Home Rule, were singled out as 'morally, intellectually, and racially inferior', and were frequently referred to as 'wild' or 'savage' by charity workers and missionaries.[58] In popular sources, descriptions of Irish Catholic nationalists as Negroid, ape-like and monstrous grew both more insistent and more vehement with each Irish crisis.[59] Well-known and influential Anglo-Irish and Britons likened Irish Catholics to 'aborigines', 'human chimpanzees' and 'carved ivory negro mask[s]'.[60] When the revolutionary Fenians sought to achieve Irish independence through physical force in the 1860s, British popular media reviled the instigators as the semi-evolved 'missing link' between apes and Africans. In 1862 *Punch Magazine* declared that a 'creature manifestly between the gorilla and the negro is to be met with in some of the lowest districts of London and Liverpool by adventurous explorers. It comes from Ireland, whence it has contrived to migrate.'[61] Cartoons, especially in the English *Punch Magazine* and *The Tomahawk*, depicted Fenians for all to see as grotesque, simian-like creatures bent only on violent destruction.[62]

Racialised depictions of the Irish continued into the 1880s and 1890s, when cartoons and editorials in popular sources sought to incite the British public against Irish nationalists generally and against proposals for Home Rule specifically.[63] Supporters of Charles Stewart Parnell's Land League and Home Rule Party were incessantly represented as savage, ape-like anarchists or as horrible monsters representing 'terrorism, rebellion, lawlessness, sedition' and 'outrage'.[64] As in India, these characterisations were meant to highlight the so-called inherent inferiorities of Irish nationalists, and in so doing to dismiss their claims for self-representation.

The vehemence of racialised and gendered imagery within British and Anglo-Irish sources matched the perceived threat nationalists were believed to represent. And it was frequently concern over military security – although this time at the heart of the Empire – that made these threats appear so menacing. As we know, the Irish contribution to the British Army was marked in the nineteenth century, comprising as much as 42.2 per cent of the total forces at their peak in 1830. While these numbers had dropped by the time of the Fenian crisis in the 1860s, still the Irish proportion of the army remained a significant 30.8 per cent in that decade. Even after a consistent decline in Irish recruits over the next twenty years, Irish soldiers comprised a fifth of the British Army at the height of the Home Rule movement in the 1880s.[65] Because of this, British officers (among them many of Anglo-Irish heritage) consistently feared that Irish Catholic nationalism would 'infect' Irish Catholics serving in the army, thereby compromising the internal efficiency of the army itself.

This fear was immeasurably enhanced by the fact that Ireland was an important garrison for British troops (more than 25,000 men were stationed there yearly between 1875 and 1900), including the traditionally Irish regiments. While British troops were supposed to keep the peace and to dissuade rebellion, officers and authorities feared that politically subversive influences from the Irish Catholic population might work their way into the Irish Catholic portion of the army. At the height of Daniel O'Connell's Repeal movement in the 1840s, for example, officers were directed to use 'dire attention and vigilance' to keep such subversive elements out, which included moving regiments frequently from place to place and monitoring potentially seditious reading material.[66] For this very reason, at times of political or social crisis in Ireland, British Army commanders frequently tried 'where possible to replace Irish troops by English or Scottish regiments'.[67] In situations like these, the contrast between disloyal Irish Celts and loyal Highlanders could be explicit. During the Fenian crisis in the 1860s, then-Commander-in-Chief in Ireland Sir Hugh Rose specifically requested more Scottish soldiers, arguing that this practice had historical precedents during O'Connell's Repeal campaign when especially loyal troops were needed for 'repression of the monster ... meetings'.[68]

The Fenian crisis was in fact a key moment in the polarisation of Irish Catholic and Scottish soldiers. Beginning in 1862, revolutionary Fenians targeted recruiting efforts among the Irish Catholic soldiery in order to gain access to weaponry and ammunition. Although they were only moderately successful, still they managed to recruit several thousand soldiers to the Fenian cause before the planned rebellion was crushed in early 1867. Because of this, many British officers and administrators – especially those who were of Anglo-Irish heredity – came deeply to distrust Irish Catholic soldiers. This was so even though Irish regiments served loyally and without incident from the 1860s until the famous mutiny of the Connaught Rangers in India in 1920.[69] During the Land Wars of the 1870s and the Home Rule crises of the 1880s and 1890s, army officials were continually apprehensive about the possibility of disorder within the Irish regiments, especially when they were serving on Irish soil.[70] The Fenian crisis, then, had seemed to 'prove' that Irish Catholic loyalty could not be trusted and left Irish regiments open to suspicion when political crises arose.

In this, the contrast with Highland soldiers could not have been more stark. Indeed, even though British authorities were aware of the nascent Scottish political movement for Home Rule and of Highland struggles for land reform based on the Irish model, at no time were the political loyalties of Highland soldiers in doubt.[71] Even at the height of the Crofters' War in 1886, when social conflict in the Highlands necessitated that British troops be brought to the region, Highland men in the employ of the British armed forces were considered reliable. One commentator on the Lewis naval reserve provided a summary of such sentiments when he argued that the men's training 'was carried on all through the most critical period of the land agitation [1886]', and that despite what seemed like an imminent conflict and frequent civilian breaches of the law, 'the training went on as usual, without the slightest manifestation of insubordination or breach of discipline amongst the large body of men assembled there'.[72]

Perceptions about the relative loyalty and disloyalty of Highland Scot and Irish Catholic soldiers were, of course, heavily influenced by related perceptions about the potential threat their respective civilian populations posed. In Scotland, despite social disturbances in the Highlands in the 1870s and 1880s, the population had been so depleted by the last century of Clearance that it was no longer plausible to contemplate a Highland insurrection with any seriousness. Moreover, as we will see, Highland soldiers themselves were frequently not from the Highlands at all and thus officials did not regard them as potential revolutionaries for the Highland cause. In Ireland, however, the Catholic civilian population was large, discontented and organised enough to pose a real challenge to the state. Irish Catholic soldiers also came directly out of this discontented civilian population, which, in the eyes of some British and Anglo-Irish contemporaries, increased their potential for disloyalty.

The discourse and imagery associated with Highland soldiers, regardless of their veracity or 'truth', served as a mirror image of the negative qualities Irish Celts were supposed to possess. Though both groups were supposed to be Celts, Highlanders were portrayed as manly and disciplined where Irish Catholics were emotional and uncontrolled. Where Highlanders were represented as tall, handsome and ideally European, Irish Catholics were depicted – especially in times of political crisis – as ape-like, savage and Negroid. Most importantly, in direct contrast to Irish Celts, Highland soldiers had proved their loyalty beyond any doubt. According to popular and official sources, as we have seen, there seemed to be nothing Highland soldiers could not do, and no mission with which they could not be trusted. Where the image of the Irish Celtic soldier was tainted with the stain of disloyalty, the image of the Highland soldier represented both the fighting spirit of the Celt *and* the loyalty required of British soldiers and subjects.

Narratives of martial Highlanders, then, simultaneously countered the racialised and gendered images of the disloyal Irish nationalists with a simple, fiercely loyal image of their own. Instead of Irish nationalists disrupting Parliament and threatening violence over land issues, we see Highlanders imagined in popular fiction taking the Shah Nujeef during the Rebellion, 'the Highland blood throbbing in every vein', 'rolling forward in a great eager wave' to take the fort for the British cause.[73] Highland heroes, too, personified the characteristics desired by the 'good' Celts. In a biography of Hector MacDonald, who commanded the Highland Brigade at the battle of Omdurman in the Sudan campaign of 1897, his heritage is described as a clear benefit to Britain:

> Colonel Macdonald – literally the hero of a hundred fights – is but a typical Highlander, Highland by birth, name, and upbringing, who has risen by the sheer force of his inborn grit from the ranks of the Highland peasantry to the front rank as a soldier in his country. In this he has but followed in the footsteps of many a 'son of the soil' in these Highlands and Islands who have shed lustre on the page of Britain's military glory ... It is ever so with the true Highlander – 'Bold as an eagle and firm as a rock, but meek as a child'. These words are no mere figures of speech in the case of Colonel Hector Archibald Macdonald, as his life-history as a soldier amply testifies.[74]

As such imagery was at pains to prove, these Celtic heroes, 'bold' enough to fight fearlessly for the Empire but 'meek' enough to bend to the will of their superiors, were alive and well in the real world, balancing the pervasive – and deeply threatening – imagery of Irish nationalists, a group believed to harbour an 'old hatred and distrust of the British connection ... always THERE as the background of Irish politics and character'.[75]

Whether the positioning of martial races in opposition to nationalists was self-conscious or implicit, the discursive effect was striking. In place of threatening, critical and demanding nationalists, martial race discourse could be used to posit a loyal image of ideal imperial subjects. In this, characteristics of both race and gender played central roles. Nationalists were depicted as feminine in body or intellect and as racially degenerate, contrasting sharply with strong, brave and true-hearted martial race soldiers. These depictions, though framed in the authoritative voice of racial and gendered 'knowledge', were profoundly political and served to discredit the claims of nationalist criticisms to British rule. In this way, the so-called similarities between Highlanders, Sikhs and Gurkhas were highlighted and employed to the same purpose: to serve as a united discursive front against the disruptive and dangerous challenges posed by Indian and Irish nationalists alike.

The construction of martial races

Although martial race discourse continually asserted the 'natural' racial qualities of its target groups, military authorities were well aware that the 'martial races' were constructions based, at least in part, on military and political needs. In short, officers knowingly manipulated recruiting practices to increase the numbers of martial races in the Indian and British armies, and then proceeded to speak about such groups in terms of inherent racial (and racially gendered) characteristics. However, the various goals of this practice were different in the Indian and British armies. In the Indian Army, the codification of groups according to their status as 'martial' or 'non-martial' was part of a concerted strategy to limit military service to the select few who could be trusted to remain undyingly loyal to the Raj. By contrast, in the British Army the identification of Highlanders as martial races was meant to widen the popular appeal of the army and to challenge both feminist claims of sin and degradation in the army and wider concerns about the racial degeneration of British men.

That is not to say, however, that officers and civilians cynically constructed martial race discourse as though from a preconceived master plan. On the contrary, a strong belief in the 'racial' qualities of all three groups often existed side by side with an awareness that these qualities could be transferred via mechanisms other than biology. This tension highlights the complexity of late Victorian notions of race as well as the ease with which martial race advocates could accept contradictory beliefs according to the situation at hand. Thus, they could apply, and even believe, essentialist rhetoric about race and masculinity when carving out the distinctions between martial races and nationalists, and at other times openly acknowledge the artificial nature of those very martial races and yet use the discourse to achieve military or political goals.

In India, officers in the army expended considerable effort trying to construct a discrete 'race' out of both Sikhs and Gurkhas. Sikhism, as British officers were well aware, denoted a set of religious beliefs based on monotheism, a rejection of caste, and the teachings of the Gurus. It was, moreover, a religion to which conversion was widely accepted, and did not therefore qualify as a biological 'race' even by Victorian standards. Officers also understood that the majority of converts to Sikhism came from the Hindu population of the Punjab, and that in fact the boundary between Sikhism and Hinduism was sometimes ill-defined.[76] The following remarks, taken from a recruiting handbook about Sikhs, demonstrates a lucid awareness that Sikhs could be 'made'. During the 1857 Rebellion, the author argued:

> Sikhs were manufactured just because Sikhs were in demand, and during these years there seemed no limit save our will to the supply ... In a contest with an army composed of high caste Hindus and Mahomedans, it became necessary to create soldiers as little like one or the other as possible, and the sequel justified the selection of the Sikh at that juncture. From that period down to the present time the employment by Government of large bodies of this race, has more than sufficed to preserve it from diminution.[77]

The author's use of words such as 'manufactured' and 'create' denotes a shrewd understanding of Sikhism as a religion open to conversion, and the relationship of Sikh conversions to British demands for soldiers untainted by Hinduism or Islam in the wake of the Rebellion. At the same time, his use of the word 'race' in the last sentence reveals both the ambiguity of the term and the author's willingness to blur the line between 'race' and religion when it came to matters of military strategy.

Others were even more candid about the necessity – and feasibility – of 'creating' Sikhs for the army. One contributor to the Indian Army's *Journal of the United Services Institute of India* proposed a scheme that would change Hindus to Sikhs for the specific purpose of recruitment. To do this, '[t]he Sikh recruiting grounds would be extended and Hindu Jats encouraged to take the pahul [the conversion ritual to martial Sikhism]'. He went on to say that '[t]hese latter might not be as good stuff as that procurable from the present Sikh centres but they would, if of good physique, compare favourably (as regards field service qualifications) with the weedy specimens sometimes enlisted'.[78] In this officer's view, then, the army could 'encourage' Hindus to become Sikhs simply to increase their overall numbers. While these might not be optimal recruits, still these new Sikhs could be expected to become like the fearless Sikh warriors of legend. This was made easier by the fact that, once recruited, newly converted Sikhs were required to follow a 'strict observance of Singh [martial Sikh] customs and ceremonies'.[79] In this way, officers believed the so-called 'martial instincts' of Sikh soldiers could be acquired through the outward observances of Sikhism. The 1896 edition of the Sikh recruiting handbook said precisely that when its author argued:

> Modern Sikhism, in fact, is to a large extent preserved from extinction by the encouragement it receives from the Indian Army, which, by exacting a rigorous observance of the outward signs of the religion from all its Sikh soldiers, keeps the advantages of the faith prominently before the eyes of the recruit-giving classes.[80]

Sikhs, then, were acknowledged to be those who looked and acted the part rather than a 'race' of born fighters, as the discourse of martial races so clearly suggested. Instead they were, at least in part, consciously 'made' for political, strategic and military purposes.

Gurkhas, too, were subject to a similar process of construction. Even the term 'Gurkha', when used to describe soldiers from Nepal, was more a British construction than a reflection of clear ethnic divisions within Nepal. Moreover, the groups the British targeted as 'real' Gurkha recruits shifted over time, and the lines between 'martial' and 'non-martial' groups – supposed to be hard and fixed by British 'knowledge' of the tribes in the region – were in fact quite flexible.[81]

Once in the Indian Army, new 'Gurkha' recruits were subjected to a process of socialisation into the culture of each Gurkha regiment, which reflected British visions about what Gurkha soldiers should be like rather than indigenous customs. Recruits enlisted into the Gurkha regiments of the Indian Army were frequently introduced to a series of dances and traditions that had no meaning in their own cultures, and yet they were expected to adopt them as their own.[82] For example, the annual celebration of Dasai (a harvest festival) within the Gurkha regiments was not actually practised by many Gurkha home communities until soldiers introduced it.[83] In short, the Gurkha 'race', as Britons described it in martial race discourse and institutionalised it in British recruiting practices, was – as Mary des Chene would have it – a 'British invention'.[84]

Soldiers in Scottish Highland regiments were no less constructed than their counterparts in the Indian Army. In fact, perhaps because they were British soldiers and thus more familiar to Britons, both officers and public commentators were more candid about the artificiality of 'Highlandness' within the regiments. By the late nineteenth century, it was common knowledge that the kilted Highland regiments were no longer composed of men born and raised in the 'wilds' of the Scottish Highlands, as they had been in the eighteenth century. Contemporary commentators sometimes joked about the presumed dearth of Scots in the Highland regiments, although Scottish newspapers and regimental magazines railed against such conceptions. A 'camp shave' recorded by a British officer of Hodson's Sikhs is telling:

'Well, my man', said an officer to a strapping Highlander the other day, rigged out in plaid and kilt, etc. 'Well, my man, this is rather a hot country; you'd like to see bonnie Scotland again?' 'Och, your honour, and shure I'd rather see ould Ireland any day.'[85]

The dig, of course, is meant to cast doubt on the essentially 'Scottish' nature of Highland regimental successes.

It was certainly true that there were some Irish and English recruits in nearly all of the Highland regiments. In the case of the 1st Battalion Gordon Highlanders – created from the former 75th and then linked to the Gordons after the reforms of 1881 – the regiment was mainly English and previously had no Highland ties. As 'new' Gordon Highlanders, however, they donned Highland garb and won attention and admiration on campaign as Highland soldiers.

In part, the presence of Irish and English recruits in the Highland regiments was simply a numeric necessity, for over the course of the nineteenth century Scotland contributed fewer and fewer soldiers to the British Army in proportion to its population.[86] By the end of the century, Scotland supplied only 16,000 men to the army, in contrast to England's 162,000 and Ireland's 26,000.[87] As a result, at times the Inspector-General was forced to observe, as he did in 1891, that 'the numbers raised in Scotland have not nearly sufficed for the requirements of the Scottish Regiments, most of which have been necessarily opened to the English districts for the greater part of the year'.[88]

However, the extent of the English and Irish presence in the Highland regiments should not be exaggerated. Returns from throughout the century consistently demonstrate that the nationality of recruits in nearly all of the Highland regiments was predominantly Scottish.[89] For example, in 1878 the 42nd, 71st, 72nd, 78th, 79th, 92nd and 93rd each drew 60 per cent of their men from Scotland.[90] Moreover, the localisation reforms of 1881 helped to ensure this dominance for the rest of the century. As a result of these reforms, the Highland regiments were linked in four two-battalion regiments and one one-battalion regiment, each with its own permanent depot and recruiting district in Scotland.[91] While imperfect in many regards, the system did at least ensure that the supply of Scottish recruits would be exhausted before opening recruitment to the rest of Britain.[92]

That said, the Highland Scottish presence in the Highland regiments should not be exaggerated either. Nineteenth-century statistics on the nationality of soldiers in the Highland regiments did not distinguish on the basis of regional origins, which meant that the term 'Scottish' could refer to either Highland- or Lowland-born Scots. And in the last half of the nineteenth century, the likelihood that 'Scottish' referred to Lowland-born men increased dramatically, for in that period most of Scotland's population became concentrated in the Lowland industrialised region, particularly around Glasgow.[93] Furthermore, Lowland cities – like their English counterparts – were beset with problems of overcrowding and poverty.[94] As a result, recruiters for the Highland regiments often found that they had far better luck in the poor districts of Scottish urban centres, where opportunities were few and far between, than in the increasingly sparsely populated rural areas of the Highlands and Islands.[95] Thus in the late nineteenth century, the men who enlisted in the Highland regiments were increasingly urban and from the lower working classes, in contrast to the rural, clan-based, Highland-born warriors of popular legend. While many were indeed Scottish, most were Lowlanders, and others were not Scottish at all.

Of this, contemporaries – both civilian and military – were well aware. Even so, the fiction was played to its fullest, for even though recruits might not be able to claim Highland blood or ancestry, they could adopt the outward signs of Highlandness to become part of a 'crack corps'. One author, who acknowledged in 1886 that 'true' Highland men were now rare in the regiments, put it like this:

> the composition of the Highland Regiments has changed – and changed, it is alleged, to an extent which threatens to utterly destroy their distinctive character and servicableness in the field. The allegation, coming from men who are equally acquainted with the genuine soldierly qualities of true Highlanders and with the rather different qualities of the Cockney recruits who are sometimes drafted into the Highland Regiments, must, we fear, be accepted with less doubt than is agreeable. Yet there is a mighty strength-giving power in the traditions of a crack regiment, and in the associations which cluster round the old flag, which must never be dishonoured. Sentiment will not alone gain victories; but sentiment will sometimes sustain the faltering heart, and give vigour to the nerveless frame. On every recruit who joins a Highland Regiment is thrown the honour of the corps – a charge so precious that none but the veriest poltroon could prove unfaithful to the duty. As yet no sign of the Highlanders losing their prestige or proving unworthy of their traditions has been exhibited. In their most recent engagements they have behaved with that valour for which they have ever been distinguished.[96]

The lesson here was that even if one was not Highland by birth, by adopting the outward signs of Highlandness 'martial instincts' could be learned. Even without a biological claim to Highland blood, one could 'convert' and still reap the benefits.

This was, in fact, the same lesson that had been applied to the Sikh and Gurkha regiments. Even though officers and contemporaries used the language of race and masculinity to describe supposedly inherent characteristics of Highlanders, Sikhs and Gurkhas, such language was also counterpoised by a frank awareness of their constructed nature. At one moment, then, the language of race and gender in the discourse of martial races might *reflect* wider Victorian beliefs about the 'science' of sex and race. At other moments, however, the same language could become *tools* by which officers and administrators – sometimes collectively, sometimes alone – furthered specific military and political needs.

The uneven impact of martial race discourse

Although we have just seen some of the ways that martial race discourse was employed to the same purpose in colonial and metropolitan arenas, its impact in those arenas was not always similar or uniform. Instead, its effects reflected divergent social, political and military circumstances specific to the army – and society – for which they were intended. In other words, the gendered and biological pretensions of the label 'martial race' were used for different, and even conflicting, purposes in India and in Britain. This reminds us, as Mrinalini Sinha points out, that although the 'metropolitan' and the 'imperial' frequently intersect, it is 'necessary also to demonstrate the essentially uneven and contradictory impact' of those interconnections.[97]

In the Indian Army, as we know, martial race discourse was meant to demonstrate that only select groups of Indians had the 'right' racial (and racially gendered) characteristics for military service. In previous chapters, we have seen how the recruiting base of the Indian Army was fundamentally restructured in the wake of the 1857 Rebellion and then, more recently, in response to the threat of combat with a European army on the northwest frontier. Over the space of a mere four decades, first high-caste Brahmins, then Bengali Hindus generally, then Madrasi and Bombay Hindu sepoys were pushed out of military service. Increasingly, Sikhs (as well as Punjabi Muslims) and Gurkhas took their place. In that period, the exclusion of native groups was justified in terms of inherent racial characteristics: by arguing, for example, that such groups were physically unsuited to warfare because they were 'naturally' too weak or too effeminate. Yet even though these choices were justified by race and gender, the exclusion of certain groups and the inclusion of others for military service was built on a historical memory of loyalty. In other words, race and masculinity were used to disguise a policy that sought to limit armed service to only those Indians who could be trusted with unfailing loyalty.

Indeed, the initial impetus for moving towards a 'martial race' recruiting strategy was, as we have seen, spurred by political and practical considerations during the Rebellion and then strengthened by emotional and political concerns – particularly about the deleterious effects of caste Hinduism in the military – in its aftermath. Sikhs and Gurkhas emerged as preferred recruits due to both their loyalty to the Raj and their perceived distance from caste ritual. To be sure, the criteria upon which 'races' could be judged 'martial' (and manly) were imagined as everything the rebels were not. Where rebels were imagined as high-caste Hindu fanatics, martial races were neither caste conscious nor Hindu. They would, according to British sources, 'eat and drink of everything, after any one, and with any one'.[98] Their distance from Hinduism was further enhanced by the belief that both groups harboured 'contempt, as well as hatred, of the Brahmins of Hindostan'.[99] In a dramatic reversal of pre-1857 military opinion – which viewed high-caste Hindus as ideal recruits because of their purported strength and sturdy physique – post-1857 discourse represented these same soldiers as weak and emasculated due to the debilitating influence of caste ritual. Race and religion became interchangeable, and those who were understood to be high-caste Hindus were increasingly excluded from military service in favour of the more recently defined 'martial' groups. In that turbulent social and political context, 'martial' came to be firmly associated with loyalty and distance from caste Hinduism – epitomised most strongly by Sikhs and Gurkhas.

Later, under different political circumstances, the association between 'martialness', loyalty, and distance from caste Hinduism remained. By the end of the century, with a few important exceptions, Hindu soldiers – though still enlisted in large numbers – were liable to be determined to be weak, effeminate and inherently unfit to take on military duties outside of home defence.[100] By privileging only select groups in the narrative stories that provided the 'proof' of martial race ability, martial race discourse functioned as a reminder that only certain Indians possessed the ability to defend India from outsiders or to fight beside Europeans. One did not hear of Madrasi soldiers victoriously topping well-defended cliffs alongside British soldiers because, as martial race advocates hoped to show, it could not be done. They did not have 'the right stuff' and no amount of training could change it. To be able to fight with the best of the British Army, native troops needed more than training: they needed good blood.

The use of racial language in this context, then, was yet another way in which officers and administrators in the Indian Army sought to marshal scientific theories of race as tools for their own purposes: in this case, to provide authority for their opinions about who was fit for military service on the subcontinent. That, indeed, was the principal message of martial race discourse in the Indian Army, a message at pains to disguise the political functions of selective recruiting. 'Race' in the discourse was the language and the justification for martial race policy, and yet those 'races' had been chosen and constructed on the basis of who could best be trusted with bearing arms in a colony where British rule ultimately depended on force.

In contrast to the Indian Army, in the British Army the Highland element of martial race discourse did not function as an exclusionary ideology. In Britain, as we know, all British men – including the sometimes suspect Catholic Irish – could be targeted as potential recruits, and no ethnic or 'racial' groups were consciously excluded. This practice was based on necessity. As we saw in Chapter 3, the British Army experienced a recruiting crisis throughout the last half of the century, and struggled to raise even the minimal number of troops annually to replace discharges and deaths. As such, a policy that advocated recruiting only from certain groups would hardly have been practical even if it were thought desirable. Moreover, Highlanders would have been an impossible choice, since the population of the Highlands had shrunk drastically over the course of the nineteenth century as a result of Clearance, changes in land ownership and emigration.[101] It is clear, then, that the Highland element of martial race discourse did not function – as it did in India – as the anecdotal foundation for a military policy of selective recruiting. Instead, and in direct opposition to the Indian case, it functioned as a discursive means to *widen*, not to limit, the appeal of the army among Britons and to counteract negative imagery of immorality and dissipation within both the officer corps and the enlisted ranks.

Let us remember that Highlanders were without doubt 'the most feted of all Victorian soldiers'.[102] Scholars have frequently acknowledged the dominance – out of all proportion to their numbers – of Highland soldiers in contemporary art, pictorials, advertising and the reports of war correspondents.[103] On campaign (as soldiers in other regiments often bitterly noted), Highland regiments received the lion's share of media attention at the expense of nearly all other units. While this phenomenon has been dismissed as nothing more than a reflection of Queen Victoria's fascination with the Scottish Highlands or as romantic nostalgia, it was in fact much more than that. It was not serendipitous that the ubiquity of Highland soldiers in the Victorian media reached its zenith in the period between 1885 and 1914 – the same years in which public enthusiasm for the army also reached an unprecedented peak. Not only were these precisely the years in which the British Army felt the sting of the recruiting crisis most deeply; it was also a period of marked anxiety in domestic and international affairs. As we know, Irish and Indian nationalism seemed to threaten the viability of the Empire from within, whereas the threat of war with Russia, France and Germany seemed to threaten it from without. Military commanders worried with increasing intensity that British soldiers did not have the 'right stuff' to face the Empire's myriad domestic and international threats. At the same time, as we shall see, feminist criticisms of the British Army threatened to detract even more from the army's always tenuous prestige. In this overlapping local, imperial and global context, the strong, simple, racialised figure of the Highland soldier served as an icon to inspire Britons and to bolster failing confidence in a period of intense anxiety. In short, the Highland soldier became living shorthand for British racial and masculine prowess, and served as a foundation stone for a positive British military identity in a period of instability and insecurity.

As symbolic figures, Highland soldiers comforted and inspired fellow Britons with their legendary accomplishments in the field. The racially gendered imagery surrounding them – described as 'innate', 'inherent' or 'in the blood' – functioned as the British 'answer' to Indian martial races and to the Continental conscript soldier. Through martial race discourse, Highlanders became the poster boys for the British Army, the 'few good men' that all young British men could aspire to be, the elite corps of an army every bit as fearsome as the savage warrior 'races' of the Indian frontier or the disciplined automatons of the Continental armies. The discourse of martial races, rather than focus on the rather unimpressive figure of the English 'Tommy Atkins', deliberately and continually called up the image of the most popular, most dramatic, most renowned British soldiers in an attempt to inspire admiration, respect and the desire for emulation. Individuals, of course, had their own reasons for playing up the prowess of the Highland regiments, but the cumulative effect was striking. The Highland element of martial race discourse became a fantasy about the martial potential of all British men, and functioned as stylised stories Britons told about themselves to themselves.

This transference between 'Highland' and 'British' worked so well precisely because Britons were aware that the Highland regiments were not, contrary to the discourse about them, 'purely' Highland. English, Irish and Scottish men could, and did, enlist in the Highland regiments. They were, in fact, some of the most sought-after units in the whole army. At the end of the century, for example, the army's largest recruiting centre (at St George's Barracks in Charing Cross, London) reported that the Highland regiments were among the most in demand with new recruits.[104] Britons from any area could claim the Highland regiments as their own and share – vicariously or directly – in the fantasy of taking on the identity of a Highland warrior. Highland soldiers – with their kilts, pipes and associations with a fierce warrior past – were at once exotic and domesticated, part of 'them' but also part of 'us'. This is why the frenzy over the Highland charge at Dargai in 1897 (discussed in Chapter 4) was in no way lessened by the fact that it was carried out by the 1st Battalion Gordon Highlanders, formerly an English regiment (the 75th). 'The Gordons will take it!' summed up not just the legendary capabilities of racialised Highlanders, but also allowed Britons to claim those capabilities as their own.

Used in such a way, the racial and gendered qualities implied by the Highland element of martial race discourse were meant to be inclusive.

They were also, however, defensive. This was true not only in terms of countering the prowess of 'foreign' soldiers, but also as a defence against 'internal' claims about the degraded and sinful nature of the army made by feminist reformers. In other words, the fiercely masculine imagery associated with Highlanders as 'martial races' also came to function as the army's answer to feminist critiques of immorality and dissipation within the ranks.

Feminist criticisms of the army establishment grew especially intense in 1886–87, when reformers under the leadership of Josephine Butler sought to repeal India's system of state-regulated prostitution. The system, in essence, provided licences and lodging to native prostitutes who sought to serve British soldiers in their cantonments. In exchange, these prostitutes were subject to periodic examinations for venereal disease and compulsory retention (until cured) in 'lock' hospitals if they were found to be infected.[105]

Butler and her organisation, the Ladies National Association (LNA), were hardly new to this kind of fight. In 1886 the LNA and its like-minded supporters had just won a seventeen-year battle to repeal Britain's own system of regulation, embodied in the Contagious Diseases Acts of 1864, 1867 and 1869. Over the course of that period, feminists had drawn attention to the ways the system perpetuated the sexual double standard, to its ineffectiveness in curbing the spread of venereal disease, and to its tacit acceptance of prostitution as a necessary 'social evil'. As in India, the British system had been initiated as a means of trying to control the alarming spread of venereal disease in the military.[106] Yet feminists argued that the Contagious Diseases Acts punished only prostitutes and not their clients, and amounted to no less than a state-sanctioned trade in sex. Once repeal was won in Britain, then, Butler lost little time in mobilising the LNA to fight for repeal in India.

Officers and administrators in India received Butler's campaign with hostility. Received wisdom within the government and military establishment there saw the Indian Acts as guarantors of international security rather than as an issue of morality. Venereal disease, they argued, was the leading cause of troop sickness in India and threatened to destroy the fighting ability of soldiers stationed there. In light of the (always looming) possibility of war with Russia on the northwest frontier, this was viewed as a potentially dire situation.[107] British soldiers, therefore, had to be protected from venereal disease, and the system of licensing and lock hospitals was, they reasoned, the most effective way to do so without decreasing the morale of the soldiers themselves. Feminist reformers, according to Indian officials like Viceroy Dufferin, were willing 'to allow disease and death to be propagated wholesale throughout the British Army' because of their moral qualms. They were, in his eyes, no more than a 'raging sisterhood who are troubling our mental purity by their obscene correspondence'.[108]

Some of this apparent hostility may have come from more general anti-feminist antipathy shared by many government and military officials in late century. Women, many believed, had no business in affairs of the state, and their political pressure amounted to an unnatural force that threatened to masculinise them. Yet Indian officers had special reasons to feel threatened by feminists bent on repeal. For one thing, these men may have perceived a dangerous combination of interests developing among feminists and Irish and Indian nationalists. This was not purely illusion. In 1887 Josephine Butler and James Stuart, MP, published a letter in Alfred Dyer's reformist *Sentinel* urging the editors of the Indian press to take up the cause of repeal. The Indian press, let us remember, was considered by military men to be the nemesis of stability and order in India, and the call cannot have been looked upon favourably by them. Butler also maintained connections with prominent Indian social reformers like Behramji Malabari and Dadhabai Naoroji, which further connected the causes of Indian nationalist reform and feminist criticism. Moreover, in 1887 Butler dared to speak out in support of Ireland's right to Home Rule, and suggested that the Irish parliamentary contingent could be useful to the cause of repeal in India.[109] Thus, in a period when the Empire already seemed internally threatened by nationalist politics, feminists appeared to be joining their cause to the same forces of destruction.

Anglo-Indian officers also had another reason to feel threatened by feminists, for they found themselves under direct – and sometimes personal – attack by advocates of the repeal movement. This was particularly true after 1888, when Alfred Dyer published a confidential memorandum on the subject of regulated prostitution signed by none other than Lord Roberts himself, who was now Commander-in-Chief. The memorandum dealt candidly with the subject of venereal disease among the troops, and concluded that 'in the regimental bazaars it is necessary to have a sufficient number of women, to take care that they are sufficiently attractive, [and] to provide them with proper houses'.[110] Prior to the 'infamous memorandum', as it became known, the Indian government had tried to downplay the existence of regulated prostitution among the troops. Once published, of course, this was no longer possible. Instead, the memorandum implicated the highest-placed officials in the system. Because of this, it proved to be a most efficient piece of ammunition for feminist reformers, for on its shocking revelations they spurred parliamentary reformers in the House to push through a resolution – adopted in 1888 – condemning state-regulated prostitution in India.[111] The memo also proved to be personally damaging for Roberts and for the Anglo-Indian military establishment more generally. Increasingly, feminist reformers portrayed

Roberts and his cohort as knowing collaborators in a despicable system of legalised vice, and, in Butler's words, as 'evil tempters of innocent soldiers' virtue'.[112] Nor did the issue go away once the furore over the 'infamous memorandum' wound down. Over the course of the 1890s debate over the issue flared repeatedly.[113] In 1893 Roberts was once again responsible when he back-handedly admitted, through the press, that regulation still was in practice despite the parliamentary resolution against it. Revelations like this helped to fuel feminist portrayals of the Anglo-Indian military establishment as immoral and unchristian precisely at a time when positive images of the army – and its leaders – were considered important to both national and international security.

In this sense, the powerful imagery of chivalrous, moral, healthy, masculine Highlanders may have functioned to draw attention away from charges of sickness and profligacy within the ranks. For every tale of debauchery among the troops, there existed twenty more extolling the bravery, the duty to devotion, and the physical fitness of British – and especially Highland – soldiers. Thus even though two women charged with investigating the truth of regulated prostitution in India discovered in 1891 that the camps of both the Gordon Highlanders and the Argyll and Sutherland Highlanders were pitched right next to the tents of the camp prostitutes, Anglo-Indian officers and press correspondents doggedly publicised the mythical qualities of Highlanders as 'gallant', 'kilted warriors of the North' to great public acclaim.[114]

The racialised and gendered images in martial race discourse were clearly more than just answers to the European military challenge from outside the Empire. They could, as we have seen, also – and simultaneously – be deployed to portray a positive ideal of citizenship in contrast to demonised nationalists, as a body of evidence to exclude men from military service, as popularising narratives to inspire potential recruits, or as devices to distract attention away from the less savoury aspects of military life. While indebted to and connected with the language of late Victorian scientific racism discussed in Chapter 3, then, the architects of martial race discourse also consciously used the symbols, images and terminology of that language – even while understanding its contradictions and constructedness – as a means for conveying a politically charged military agenda. In other words, martial race discourse was more than a reflection of its time. Instead, it was a language through which the very meaning of race and masculinity could be manipulated to serve a variety of ideological purposes. Moreover, once the language of martial races became part of the public domain through newspapers, speeches, despatches and memoirs, it became widely available for public appropriation and interpretation. As a result, even the unintentional juxtaposition of martial race exploits with reports of Irish parliamentary disruption, feminist protest, and the formation of the Indian National Congress made for a striking contrast between images of order, strength and prowess on the one hand, and disorder and chaos on the other. As such, martial race discourse – like all linguistic constructions – easily exceeded its originators' intentions, and thus played a role as an agent of the material world in its own right. In so doing, it literally helped to 'create' contemporary understandings of both race and masculinity.

Notes

1 *Bengalee* (14 Feb. 1880), quoted in Howard Brasted, 'Indian nationalist development and the influence of Irish Home Rule, 1870–1886', *Modern Asian Studies* 14:1 (1980), 61.
2 Quoted in Antoinette Burton, *Burdens of Empire: British Feminists, Indian Women, and Imperial Culture, 1865–1915* (Chapel Hill: University of North Carolina Press, 1994), 147.
3 Complicating notions of 'home' and 'empire' as discrete entities is one of Mrinalini Sinha's goals in *Colonial Masculinity: The 'Manly Englishman' and the 'Effeminate Bengali' in the Late Nineteenth Century* (Manchester: Manchester University Press, 1995). Also, Antoinette Burton's work in *At the Heart of the Empire: Indians and the Colonial Encounter in Late-Victorian Britain* (Berkeley: University of California Press, 1998) has been influential in mapping the interconnectedness of 'metropole' and 'colony'.
4 My understanding of the use of martial race discourse is analogous to Lata Mani's exploration of the colonial debate on sati. She views the debate as a 'ground for a complex and competing set of struggles' that had little to do with its actual subject. Lata Mani, *Contentious Traditions: The Debate on Sati in Colonial India* (Berkeley: University of California Press, 1998), 2.
5 For this notion of unevenness, see Sinha, *Colonial Masculinity*, 10.
6 For this kind of dialogic relationship, see Indira Chowdhury, *The Frail Hero and Virile History: Gender and the Politics of Culture in Colonial Bengal* (Delhi: Oxford University Press, 1998); also John Rosselli, 'The self-image of effeteness: physical education and nationalism in nineteenth-century Bengal', *Past and Present* 86 (1980).
7 For a succinct summary of the connections between Ireland and India, see C. A. Bayly, 'Ireland, India, and the Empire, 1780–1914', *Transactions of the Royal Historical Society* 6:10 (2000).
8 For a good summary of this phenomenon, see T. G. Fraser's 'Ireland and India', in Keith Jeffery (ed.), *An Irish Empire? Aspects of Ireland and the British Empire* (Manchester: Manchester University Press, 1996).
9 Scott Cook, 'The Irish Raj: social origins and careers of Irishmen in the Indian Civil Service, 1885–1914', *Journal of Social History* 21 (Spring 1987), 520.
10 Cook, 'The Irish Raj', 521, 520.
11 Keith Jeffery, 'The Irish military tradition', in Jeffery (ed.), *An Irish Empire?*, 106.
12 Two examples are Sir Hugh Rose (Ireland 1865–70) and Lord Roberts (India 1885–93, Ireland 1895–99).
13 Scott Cook, *Imperial Affinities: Nineteenth Century Analogies and Exchanges Between India and Ireland* (New Delhi: Sage Publications, 1993), 28.
14 Quoted in Cook, *Imperial Affinities*, 30. Indian policies based on Irish precedents included the Bengal Tenancy Act of 1885, the Vernacular Press Act of 1878, and the Indian Criminal Law Act of 1908.
15 O'Connell was president of the Repeal Association, which sought to repeal the 1800 Act of Union between Britain and Ireland. Davis was a prominent member of Young Ireland, a nationalist group that staged a failed uprising in 1848.
16 Quoted in Brasted, 'Indian nationalist development', 47. O'Donnell publicised the

idea in 1878 in the nationalist journals *Nation* and *Freeman's Journal*.

17 Fraser, 'Ireland and India', 85; M. Holmes, 'The Irish and India: imperialism, nationalism, and internationalism', in Andy Bielenberg (ed.), *The Irish Diaspora* (London: Longman, 2001), 243.

18 Fraser, 'Ireland and India', 46; D. George Boyce, *Decolonisation and the British Empire, 1775–1997* (New York: St Martin's Press, 1999), 88. It should be noted that for racial reasons not all Irish nationalists wished to associate themselves with Indian nationalism.

19 'Parnellite convention in Dublin: cheering the Afridis', *Daily Free Press (Aberdeen)* (12 Oct. 1897), 5.

20 Brasted, 'Indian nationalist development', 53, 59.

21 Brasted, 'Indian nationalist development', 44.

22 Fraser, 'Ireland and India', 87.

23 Dufferin to Earl of Kimberly, 21 March 1886, in B. L. Grover, *A Documentary Study of British Policy Towards Indian Nationalism, 1885–1909* (Delhi: National Publications, 1967), 171.

24 Quoted in Stanley Wolpert, *Tilak and Gokhale: Revolution and Reform in the Making of Modern India* (Berkeley: University of California Press, 1961), 122.

25 Letter to the editor by 'An Englishman', *Indian Spectator* (21 Feb. 1886), 154.

26 Boyce, *Decolonisation and the British Empire*, 70.

27 Quoted in Sinha, *Colonial Masculinity*, 15.

28 Sinha, *Colonial Masculinity*, 15–16.

29 Anil Seal, *The Emergence of Indian Nationalism: Competition and Collaboration in the Later Nineteenth Century* (Cambridge: Cambridge University Press, 1970), 145. As it turned out, the Act was repealed upon Lytton's return to Britain in 1881, and few were actually ever punished under its terms.

30 Governor-General Lytton to Caird, 12 Dec. 1879, quoted in Seal, *The Emergence of Indian Nationalism*, 141.

31 Sinha, *Colonial Masculinity*, 41, 44.

32 Lord Roberts was one of the many army officers who made their opinions known to the Viceroy at the time, arguing that if the Bill passed, 'the consequences may be more serious than Your Lordship has hitherto contemplated'. Roberts to Ripon, 8 March 1883, in Brian Robson (ed.), *Roberts in India: The Military Papers of Field Marshal Lord Roberts, 1876–1893* (Phoenix Mill: Alan Sutton, 1993), 276.

33 Sinha, *Colonial Masculinity*, 69, 78.

34 Quoted in Sinha, *Colonial Masculinity*, 80.

35 Memorandum by Lieutenant-General Phayre, 17 June 1885, quoted in Seal, *The Emergence of Indian Nationalism*, 174.

36 Sinha, *Colonial Masculinity*, 69.

37 Jim Masselos, *Indian Nationalism: An History* (New Delhi: Sterling, 1985), 85–86. For more on the Congress, see John McLane, *Indian Nationalism and the Early Congress* (Princeton: Princeton University Press, 1977).

38 India Office Library and Records, London (hereafter OIOL), MSS Eur F 108/28, Sir George White papers, Draft on the Indian Press (1894), 4–5.

39 Quoted in Arnold Kaminsky, *The India Office: 1880–1910* (London: Greenwood, 1986), 170, 169.

40 'The Russian spectre', *India* (July 1896), 196.

41 'Recruiting for India: deterioration in the recruiting material for the Indian Army with suggestions as to causes and remedies', *United Services Magazine* 26 (1898), 330.

42 C. E. Biddulph, 'Army reform in native states in India', *United Services Magazine* 1 (1890), 504.

43 Biddulph, 'Army reform in native states in India', 504. The reference was to a party of 'twenty or thirty Sikhs, Rajputs or Pathans'.

44 Quoted in Chowdhury, *The Frail Hero*, 22.

45 *India* (29 Aug. 1890), 237–238.

46 Chowdhury, *The Frail Hero*, 21–23.

47 C. A. H. Bingley, *Handbooks for the Indian Army: Sikhs* (Simla: Government Central

Printing Office, 1899), 28.

48 'The native army of India', *Blackwood's Magazine* 162 (Aug. 1897), 197.

49 Captain R. W. Falcon, *Handbook on Sikhs For the Use of Regimental Officers* (Allahabad: Pioneer Press, 1896), preface.

50 D. A. Hamer, 'The Irish question and Liberal politics, 1886–1894', in *Reactions to Irish Nationalism (With an Introduction by Alan O'Day)* (London: Hambledon, 1987), 237.

51 R. F. Foster, *Modern Ireland, 1600–1972* (London: Penguin, 1988), 422–423.

52 Jeffrey Richards, in 'Ireland, the Empire, and film', argues that although negative images of the Irish were not necessarily hegemonic in nineteenth-century Britain, they did become more uniformly hostile in the late nineteenth century. In Jeffery (ed.), *An Irish Empire?*, 26.

53 Edward Spiers, 'Army organisation and society in the nineteenth century', in Thomas Bartlett and Keith Jeffery (eds), *A Military History of Ireland* (Cambridge: Cambridge University Press), 336. The numbers of Irish in the army declined after 1850 because of depopulation due to the Famine.

54 Terence Denman, 'The Catholic Irish soldier in the First World War: the "racial environment"', *Irish Historical Studies* 27:108 (1991), 354.

55 National Army Museum, London (hereafter NAM), 7101-23-126-2, F. S. Roberts, On being presented with the freedom of the city of Waterford, 1 Sept. 1893, 47.

56 Quoted in Daniel Dorrity, 'Monkeys in a menagerie: the imagery of Unionist opposition to Home Rule, 1886–1893', *Eire-Ireland* 7 (Autumn 1977), 9.

57 See, for example, Nicholas Canny's 'The ideology of English colonisation: from Ireland to America', *William and Mary Quarterly* 30:4 (1973).

58 Margaret Preston, 'Discourse and hegemony: race and class in the language of charity in nineteenth century Dublin', in Tadhg Foley and Sean Ryder (eds), *Ideology in Ireland in the Nineteenth Century* (Dublin: Four Courts Press, 1998), 101, 102, 104.

59 L. Perry Curtis, Jr., *Apes and Angels: The Irishman in Victorian Caricature*, rev. edn (Washington: Smithsonian Institution Press, 1997), 29, 39.

60 Attributed, respectively, to J. P. Mahaffy (unionist Provost of Trinity College, Dublin), Charles Kingsley and D. H. Lawrence. See Murray Pittock, *Celtic Identity and the British Image* (Manchester: Manchester University Press, 1999), 64, 71, and Luke Gibbons, 'Race against time: racial discourse and Irish history', *Oxford Literary Review* 13 (1991), 96.

61 Liz Curtis, 'Echoes of the present: the Victorian press and Ireland', in Ann Gray and Jim McGuigan (eds), *Studying Culture: An Introductory Reader* (London: Edward Arnold, 1998), 183.

62 Curtis, *Apes and Angels*, 38, 39, 49, 50, 51.

63 Dorrity, 'Monkeys in a menagerie', 6.

64 Quotes from 'The Irish devil-fish', in *Punch* (18 June 1881), in Curtis, *Apes and Angels*, 44. See also 41, 43, 54. Also Curtis, 'Echoes of the present', 182.

65 Spiers, 'Army organisation and society', 337.

66 Spiers, 'Army organisation and society', 342, 346.

67 Virginia Crossman, 'The army and law and order in the nineteenth century', in Bartlett and Jeffery (eds), *A Military History of Ireland*, 360.

68 Quoted in Crossman, 'The army and law and order', 360. See also Spiers, 'Army organisation and society', 347.

69 For the Connaught Rangers mutiny, see Lawrence James, *Mutiny in the British and Commonwealth Forces, 1797–1956* (London: Buchan and Enright, 1987).

70 Denman, 'The Catholic Irish soldier in the First World War', 353; Spiers, 'Army organisation and society', 348.

71 The government collected pamphlets and papers on Home Rule movements in each of the three 'Celtic' regions. The Scottish Home Rule Party was begun in 1886, just after Gladstone lent his support to the Irish Home Rule Party. Public Record Office, Kew (hereafter PRO), 30/69/1826, Home Rule affairs in Scotland, Wales, Ireland.

72 Henry N. Shore, 'The Naval Reserve in the Hebrides', *United Services Magazine* 6 (1892–93), 593.

73 Archibald Forbes, *Colin Campbell, Lord Clyde* (London: Macmillan & Co., 1895), 130.

74 *Hector MacDonald or the Private Who Became a General: A Highland Laddie's Life and Laurels*, 4th edn (London: S. W. Partridge & Co., 1900), 15.

75 PRO, 30/69/1826, Royal Commission on the rebellion in Ireland, Report on Home Rule affairs in Scotland, Wales, Ireland, 5. This was written in 1916 after the Easter Rising, but the words echo sentiments from the period after 1880.

76 Richard Fox, *Lions of the Punjab: Culture in the Making* (Berkeley: University of California Press, 1985), 141–142.

77 Falcon, *Handbook on Sikhs For the Use of Regimental Officers*, 117.

78 Captain A. Johnstone, 'Localisation of recruiting for the infantry of the Indian Army', *United Services Institute of India* 25:123 (1896), 87.

79 Fox, *Lions of the Punjab*, 142.

80 Bingley, *Handbooks for the Indian Army: Sikhs*, 57.

81 Lionel Caplan, *Warrior Gentlemen: 'Gurkhas' in the Western Imagination* (Providence: Berghahn Books, 1995), 52; Michael Hutt, 'A hero or a traitor? The Gurkha soldier in Nepali literature', *South Asia Research* 9:1 (May 1989), 21.

82 Mary des Chene, 'Language and practice in the colonial Indian Army', paper given at the Institute for Global Studies in Culture, Power, and History, Johns Hopkins University, Autumn 1993, 39.

83 Mary des Chene, 'Relics of empire: a cultural history of the Gurkhas, 1815–1987' (Ph.D. dissertation, Stanford University, 1991), 118–119.

84 Des Chene, 'Language and practice in the colonial Indian Army', 39.

85 Lieutenant Macdowell, 19 Jan. 1858, in Captain Coghill, Lieutenant Macdowell and 'Shiny' Williams, *Letters from the Field During the Indian Mutiny* (London: Waterlow & Sons, 1907), 72–73.

86 H. J. Hanham, 'Religion and nationality in the mid-Victorian army', in M. R. D. Foot (ed.), *War and Society* (London: Paul Elek, 1973), 162–163.

87 Lieutenant Colonel John Graham, 'The land forces of the Crown', *Navy and Army Illustrated* 1:4 (1896), 87.

88 House of Commons, 'Annual Report of the Inspector General of Recruiting', *Sessional Papers*, vol. 19, session 1 (1890–91), 7.

89 Diana Henderson, *Highland Soldier: A Social Study of the Highland Regiments, 1820–1920* (Edinburgh: John Donald, 1989), 25.

90 Hanham, 'Religion and nationality in the mid-Victorian army', 165–166.

91 The new regiments were the Seaforth Highlanders (72nd and 78th regiments); Gordon Highlanders (75th and 92nd regiments); Argyll and Sutherland Highlanders (91st and 93rd regiments); Black Watch (42nd and 73rd regiments); and the Queen's Own Cameron Highlanders (79th Regiment).

92 Henderson, *Highland Soldier*, 27.

93 Rosalind Mitchison, *A History of Scotland*, 2nd edn (London: Routledge, 1982), 358.

94 Mitchison, *A History of Scotland*, 361.

95 Henderson, *Highland Soldier*, 43. The dearth of recruits in the rural Highlands is also noted in Edward Spiers, *The Late Victorian Army, 1868–1902* (Manchester: Manchester University Press, 1992), 131.

96 James Cromb, *The Highland Brigade: Its Battles and Its Heroes*, 3rd edn (London: Simkin, Marshall & Co., 1886), 9.

97 Sinha, *Colonial Masculinity*, 10.

98 J. Craufurd, 'India, as connected with a native army', *Journal of the Royal United Services Institute* 2:177 (1858), 184.

99 Craufurd, 'India, as connected with a native army', 184.

100 High-caste Hindu Rajputs were a notable exception.

101 These phenomena will be addressed in the next chapter.

102 Hew Strachan, *The Politics of the British Army* (Oxford: Clarendon, 1997), 204.

103 For example, John MacKenzie asserts that 'the soldier became a popular hero, particularly in his most colourful and striking guise as the Scottish soldier'. MacKenzie, 'Introduction', in John MacKenzie (ed.), *Popular Imperialism and the Military* (Man-

chester: Manchester University Press, 1992), vii. J. W. M. Hichberger also writes that 'the Scottish soldier received more pictorial coverage than any other. The Highland regiments, with their kilt and plaid uniforms, dominate'. In *Images of the Army: The Military in British Art, 1815–1914* (Manchester: Manchester University Press, 1988), 106. Similarly, Roger Stearn argues that 'Correspondents and artists, reinforcing the Victorian cult of the Highlander, featured Highland regiments especially'. In 'War correspondents and colonial war, c. 1870–1900', in MacKenzie (ed.), *Popular Imperialism and the Military*, 148. John Canning contends that 'Highlanders were favourite subjects for heroic military art in the late Victorian period'. In 'The military art of Richard Caton Woodville (I and II)', *Military Illustrated* 11 (Feb./March 1988 and June/July 1988), 39.

104   Lieutenant-Colonel F. C. Turner, 'Recruiting for the army', *Navy and Army Illustrated: A Magazine Descriptive of Everyday Life in the Defensive Services of the British Empire* 1:1 (1895), 11.

105   Burton, *Burdens of History*, 130.

106   In 1864 one out of every three sick cases in the army was because of venereal disease. Judith Walkowitz, *Prostitution and Victorian Society: Women, Class, and the State* (Cambridge: Cambridge University Press, 1980), 75.

107   Philippa Levine, 'Rereading the 1890s: venereal disease as "constitutional crisis" in Britain and British India', *Journal of Asian Studies* 55:3 (Aug. 1996), 591.

108   Quoted in Burton, *Burdens of History*, 133.

109   Burton, *Burdens of History*, 146–148; Levine, 'Rereading the 1890s', 604.

110   Levine, 'Rereading the 1890s', 591.

111   Kenneth Ballhatchet, *Race, Sex, and Class Under the Raj: Imperial Attitudes and Policies and their Critics, 1793–1905* (London: Weidenfeld and Nicolson, 1980), 60.

112   Quoted in Burton, *Burdens of History*, 135.

113   Levine, 'Rereading the 1890s', 586.

114   For the damaging reports about the Gordons and Argyll and Sutherlands, see Ballhatchet, *Race, Sex, and Class*, 71; descriptions of Highlanders are taken from Lord Roberts's speech during a dinner given by the 1st Battalion Gordons and 2nd Battalion Argyll and Sutherland Highlanders. NAM, 7101-23-126-1.

CHAPTER SIX

Representation versus experience: life as a 'martial race' soldier

Most of this book has been concerned with how – and for what reasons – 'martial race' soldiers were portrayed by military officers and by the popular media as icons of an ideal racialised masculinity. Important as such representations were for helping to shape Victorian culture, we must also remember that martial race discourse had material and psychic consequences for the people it was purportedly about. As Diana Henderson reminds us in the case of Scottish Highlanders, 'these were people', and as such they were faced, in varying degrees, with mediating between idealised images of themselves as elite warriors and their own experiences, identities and motivations for serving in 'martial race' regiments.[1]

This chapter charts the dissonances and harmonies between the ideology of martial races and the lives of the people who were supposed to embody it. The point is not simply to argue for the wholesale inaccuracy of 'martial race' representations *vis-à-vis* soldiers' experiences, although the gap between ideal and experience is surely one recurring theme. Rather, I seek to explain, as Kathleen Wilson has done in another context, how to '*account* for the often asymmetrical relationship' between representation and experience.[2] This requires paying as much attention to the silences of martial race discourse as to its inclusions, for martial race discourse was as much about containing unauthorised stories as it was about sanctioning others. Thus, this chapter begins with the untold stories effaced by martial race discourse – stories that chart massive social and economic change and/or poverty in the Highlands, Punjab and Nepal, and that highlight the 'push' factors that led individual men to enlist in 'martial race' regiments. These stories, so well hidden by the power and romance of martial race discourse, allow a better understanding of the choices available to 'martial race' recruits, and what their lives may have been like as soldiers.

Yet even though representations of the 'martial races' often diverged from individual experience, the dissonance between representation and experience is not the whole story. Indeed, fragmented sources that allow us to glimpse how some 'martial race' soldiers saw themselves point toward a conclusion that the men of 'martial race' regiments frequently accepted – and sometimes even relished – the identity of 'martial race' soldier. While the source base for each region varies, it seems that the hyper-masculine, elite group identity self-consciously fostered by 'martial race' regiments did in fact resonate with some recruits. Many found that membership in a privileged military cadre won them social, personal and (in the case of the Indian regiments) economic prestige. However, even while soldiers seem to have accepted martial race identities largely for their own reasons, I argue that they still bought into behaviours and modes of thinking that ultimately benefited the state.

Moreover, martial race discourse had consequences that extended to the larger regional cultures of the Highlands, the Punjab and Nepal, and it is to these that the conclusion to this chapter is devoted. Indeed, the army's use of martial race language reduced all three regions into areas defined primarily by their identification with warrior heroes. As a result, competing regional expressions of cultural identity were marginalised, while the messy processes of regional integration into a global imperial framework were glossed by a fixation on heroic narratives. Even today, the Highlands, the Punjab and Nepal are frequently associated by outsiders with elite soldiers and a warrior past, and the people of each region are still struggling with how to incorporate this historical legacy into a broader, more inclusive cultural identity.

Finally, while this chapter considers Highland, Sikh and Gurkha soldiers together and in light of the same set of problems, none of these groups can be conflated with – or made to stand in for – the others. For one thing, as Doug Peers has pointed out, British and Indian regiments were of two distinct military cultures, and the soldiers in each often came from very different social backgrounds.[3] Also, Highland soldiers – even though frequently portrayed as exotic and racialised figures – nevertheless were able to claim access to Europeanness and all the racial privileges such claims entailed. Sikhs and Gurkhas, in contrast, were always denied this access, and thus experienced the world quite differently from their Highland 'martial race' compatriots. Moreover, even within the Indian Army, Sikh and Gurkha soldiers were of different regional, religious, cultural, linguistic, political and social backgrounds. That said, the many differences between Highlanders, Sikhs and Gurkhas should not distract us from trying to account for the shared problems each group faced: namely, the task of negotiating between their experiences as poor, uneducated men and idealised representations of themselves as fierce, loyal and courageous 'martial race' soldiers.

Marginalised stories

The Gurkha, from the warlike qualities of his forefathers, and the traditions handed down to him of their military prowess as conquerors of the Nepal Valley, is imbued with and cherishes the military spirit. His physique, compact and sturdy build, powerful muscular development, keen sight, acute hearing, and hereditary education as a sportsman, eminently fit him for the duties of a rifleman on the mountain side, while his acquaintance with forest lore makes him almost unrivalled in jungle country ... [T]here is not a single case of a Nepalese chief taking bribes from, or selling himself for money to the British or any other state. This loyalty to themselves is only equalled by their loyalty to us during and ever since the fiery ordeal of the Mutiny ...[4]

[Sikhs] are very hardy, obedient to discipline, faithful and trustworthy, though somewhat given to intrigue among themselves. Considering death on the battlefield a means of salvation, it is part of their creed never to turn their backs on a foe. To relate in detail their services during the Mutiny would be to recount the history of the whole of that great episode, for there were few occasions when fighting took place in which they did not bear their share, vying with British soldiers for the honour of being the first to cross bayonets with the rebels. Here we can only state in general terms that they remained faithful to us during the whole of that trying time, and that theirs was no impassive loyalty, for they were eager to be in the thick of the battle and when there acquitted themselves like men.[5]

In all the Sovereign's wide realms could be found no such chivalrous, true-hearted, brave-souled men [as Highlanders]; nor could they be equalled in those physical qualities which were so much demanded in the harassing system under which war was at the time conducted ... It was in these qualities of limb that the Highlanders excelled. They were strong and muscular, accustomed to violent exercises and fatiguing marches. Their country, with its darksome passes and rugged heights, its treacherous moors and plunging torrents, was to a stranger wild and forbidding. But to them it was a rough training-ground, calculated to bring forth all that was robust and manly in their frame. [There is] as yet no sign of the Highlanders losing their prestige or proving unworthy of their traditions ... In their most recent engagements they have behaved with that valour for which they have ever been distinguished.[6]

In the late nineteenth and early twentieth centuries, passages such as the above were typical in lionising the 'natural' qualities of Gurkha, Sikh and Highland soldiers. Also typical is the explicit link between heredity, geography, temperament and physique. Men from the Highlands, Punjab and Nepal enlisted in the army, so we are led to believe, because they were born to it. In other words, these men were naturally drawn to military service rather than pushed into it.

Such contentions, however, do not bear up well under scrutiny. If we push beyond the romantic rhetoric of martial race discourse, we find instead three regions where poverty and social and economic transformation became critical forces that drove enlistment into the 'martial race' regiments. Thus when we ask what was in it for the men – assuming we would question the idealised, 'official' story – it becomes less a story about natural predilections for military service and much more a story about making a living. Martial race discourse seldom alluded to the regional social and economic conditions of the Highlands, the Punjab and Nepal. As a result, even spectacular regional transformations were masked by a language of myth, racial proclivities and hyper-masculinity.

As conquered regions were brought into relationships with wider imperial markets and political structures, both the Punjab and the Scottish Highlands experienced dramatic social and economic changes in the nineteenth century. These changes, in turn, had a direct impact on military recruiting in both areas, since debt and dislocation pressured thousands of young men to enlist in the army. Nepal, by contrast, was never occupied by Britain, and thus the country maintained more separation from economic and social pressures than areas under formal British rule. Yet conditions in independent Nepal were hardly ideal. Throughout the nineteenth century, life for most ordinary Nepalis involved subsistence farming in extremely harsh conditions, poverty and political repression. Thus, even though Nepal was more isolated from the striking economic and social changes that restructured the Highlands and the Punjab in this period, the people of all three regions were united by the (sometimes desperate) need for wages – a necessity that pushed men into military service.

In the Punjab, annexation in 1849 produced profound and lasting regional changes. As in the Highlands one hundred years earlier, British conquest meant the disarmament not only of Ranjit Singh's army but of Punjabi society more generally, the strict policing of the countryside and the forfeiture of rebel estates. British administrators of the Punjab were particularly concerned with undermining the position of the old aristocracy in order to strengthen peasant ties to the state.[7] As a result, hereditary *jagirs* (estates) held by aristocrats were frequently put up for sale, thereby leaving substantial numbers of peasant proprietors to pay taxes directly to the government. And most importantly for the long term, these revenue assessments were now to be payable only in cash.[8]

The Punjabi area where these new arrangements made the most impact was the central region, which was home to the largest concentration of Sikhs in the Punjab.[9] This fertile and affluent region, with its adequate rainfall and well irrigation, was intensively farmed for wheat and other subsistence crops. It was also dominated – and with British rule came to be more so – by peasant proprietors, who used family labour and family capital in the production of their crops.[10]

Unlike the arid southwest or the dry southeast, the central region proved ideal for British interests to profit handsomely from both the region and its people. This was done by requiring cash payments for land revenues. The need for cash, in turn, encouraged peasants to make their most valuable crop – wheat – consistently available on the market. The result was that available surplus wheat quickly exceeded local demands, which meant that it could be exported to other Indian regions as well as Britain itself. This created a national and international market for Punjabi wheat – a development that had long-term effects for the Punjab, and particularly the central region, for integration into an increasingly global market made the area susceptible to global price fluctuations. Thus, when prices on the international market were low, peasant profits (and the ability to pay cash revenues) were slim. Alternatively, when international wheat prices were high, Punjabi peasants were likely to increase the labour on their farms and to invest in other means of making their farms more productive.[11]

Whether in lean or good years, peasants who had been integrated into the global wheat market discovered that they needed ever more access to cash. Frequently, however, the need for cash did not coincide with the harvest, when cash resources were most available. This problem created substantial opportunities for the traditional Hindu money-lending castes native to the area. In return for cash loans, money-lenders accepted collateral in the borrower's crops or land, or by securing a preemptive right of purchase should the land come up for sale. These loans, commonly fixed at high interest rates, created a cycle of debt that borrowers had difficulty breaking.[12] That, in turn, allowed lenders influence over the crops peasants grew, and made it nearly impossible for peasants to extricate themselves from the 'tyranny of the market'. Moreover, if borrowers were forced to default on their loans, lenders could assume the mortgage and, in essence, turn peasants into tenants on their own land.[13]

By the last quarter of the nineteenth century, alarmed government officials argued that if the Raj failed to protect peasant proprietors in the Punjab from the avaricious grasp of money-lenders, the peasant smallholder in the region would all but disappear. This was the reason behind the passage of the Land Alienation Act of 1900, which forbade the transfer of agricultural land except to other cultivating classes.[14] The government also tried to alleviate some of the land pressure in the central Punjab by encouraging many farmers from the region to migrate to the newly developed canal colonies in the west and southwest Punjab, where wheat could be grown in abundance.[15] These massive irrigation projects, financed by the state, did in fact allow many farmers – including many Sikhs – greater success, but only by making the situation of central Punjabi farmers even more difficult due to increased market competition for their wheat.[16]

Despite the fears of state officials, the system of debt poverty that had developed in the central Punjab did not result in the elimination of peasant proprietors. In fact, given the scale of peasant debt in the region by the turn of the twentieth century, it was remarkable that only 20 per cent of lands were under mortgage, and less than 10 per cent had fallen permanently into the hands of debtors. The reason for this was clear: debt-ridden peasant families supplemented their incomes via military service and, secondarily, by working for wage labour abroad.[17] In other words, young Punjabi men kept the system going by becoming soldiers or labourers and by remitting part of their wages back to their families. For the many Sikhs living in the area, then, enlisting in the army was one of the primary ways by which they could secure the financial solvency of their families. Indeed, contemporaries well understood that the 'most important point' for Sikhs in the army was 'whether he can put by a sufficient sum from his pay'.[18] Others noted that Sikhs in the army had the annoying habit of nearly 'starving themselves for the sake of saving money'.[19]

What this all means is that a majority of Punjabi Sikhs hailed from a region where, because of integration into the global market, peasant families were increasingly subject to a vicious cycle of debt poverty. Since the only way many families remained solvent was to offer their sons as soldiers or wage labourers abroad, it would hardly be accurate to say that the thousands of Sikhs who entered the Indian Army in the late nineteenth century did so because of 'natural' predilections or because of love for the British. Instead, and in direct opposition to the discourse of martial races, it seems that many Sikhs entered military service not because they loved it, but because they had to.

In the Highlands, the situation was both similar and different. In the end, soldiers who enlisted in the Highland regiments tended, like their Sikh counterparts, to do so out of necessity. The reasons, too, stemmed from the painful process of integrating the Highlands into a larger imperial and global economy and polity. However, the specific effects of this integration took their own unique form and chronology.

One hundred years before the annexation of the Punjab, the Highlands of Scotland were forcibly subdued and occupied by the British Army. As in the Punjab, conquest meant the disarmament of Highland society, the forfeiture of rebel estates and the policing of the countryside.[20] As part of these efforts, British troops built a system of roads and forts into the previously inaccessible Highlands to ensure easy access in the event of a future rebellion. The long-term significance of these roads and forts, however, was not military. Rather, they provided the means by which the Highlands were brought into closer contact with the economies and market pressures of the rest of Britain.[21] What followed was more than a century of dramatic social, political and economic transformation.

As part of the pacification programme, Highland landlords were shorn of their traditional leadership and protective responsibilities towards their tenants. Once these ties were sundered, landlords tended to seek to maximise their profits from the land. One way to do this was to convert their properties into sheep farms, the products of which could be profitably sold in the rest of Britain. The problem was that Highland tenants occupied most of the best potential grazing lands in the interior of the region. To solve this problem, Highland landlords raised rents on interior lands to unaffordable levels, and then relocated their tenants to the much more marginal coastal areas, where it was still possible to find work in coastal industries.[22] Between 1760 and 1815, then, most of the once densely populated Highland interior was depopulated, while former residents did their best to eke out a living on the coast or through emigration abroad.

Still more changes followed the close of the Anglo-French wars in 1815. Highland landlords, often indebted through conspicuous consumption in any case, now found themselves bankrupted when the Highland economy collapsed with the war's end.[23] Nearly 60 per cent of them lost their lands over the next four decades. Almost all of these lands fell into the hands of wealthy Scottish Lowlanders or Englishmen, who now found the Highlands a chic and affordable place to maintain an estate. Not surprisingly, these new landowners had new priorities, and most saw the (by now) over-populated and poor coastal villages – as well as their people – as liabilities. New landlords wished to continue the trend of converting inhabited areas into profitable sheep farms or, increasingly, into deer habitats for the recreation of Lowland Scottish and English elites.[24] As a result, these new landlords evicted thousands of the tenants from coastal regions in this period. The villagers, extremely poor and faced with few options for relocation in the region, left the Highlands in droves, moving to the cities of Lowland Scotland and England or out of Britain altogether.[25]

These changes, of course, had important ramifications for military recruiting in the Highlands. Until 1815, recruiting efforts focused on the rural Highland communities so recently relocated to coastal areas, where dismal conditions and overcrowding left few occupational options for many Highland men.[26] After 1815, however, the twin phenomena of Clearance and emigration had so depleted the population of the Highlands that the region was no longer able to supply adequate numbers of recruits to the Highland regiments.[27] For the rest of the nineteenth century, recruiters for the Highland regiments were compelled to find ever more of their men among the urbanised populations of Lowland and English industrial centres – men who had often been pushed into the army through want, legal difficulties or family troubles.[28] Thus, while many may have had family connections to the Highlands, they also, by and large, had not been conditioned by 'darksome passes and rugged heights ... treacherous moors and plunging torrents', nor did they enter military service because fighting was 'in their blood'.[29] Instead, like their Sikh counterparts, soldiers enlisted in the Highland regiments because they had few other choices.

The same was abundantly true for the 'Gurkha' soldiers of Nepal. Ironically, of all the 'martial races' the legend of Gurkhas' love for the British has endured the longest. Books celebrating these so-called 'plucky little hill men' are still produced and still find a ready audience.[30] Not coincidentally, however, of all the regions said to produce 'martial races' Nepal's extreme poverty has also endured the longest. And in the nineteenth century it was this factor above all else that drove – as it still drives – enlistment into the British Army.

Unlike the Punjab and the Highlands, the British in Nepal were of necessity more limited in the pursuit of their political and economic interests. True, the Indian Army had defeated the Nepalese Army in 1816, which resulted in the Nepali durbar (government) ceding 7,000 square miles of territory and agreeing to the establishment of a British Residency at Kathmandu.[31] The durbar of Nepal, however, remained intact, and actively resisted British attempts to interfere with Nepalese social and political life.[32]

This resistance included outright hostility to British efforts to recruit Nepalese hill men to the Indian Army. British residents at Kathmandu originally urged just such a programme because they feared the size and strength of the Nepalese Army, and hoped to stymie future war plans against the Raj. The durbar, for its part, resisted these efforts for the same reasons, for it was suspicious that British recruiting efforts could undermine its own.[33] Until the end of the nineteenth century, then, the durbar expressly forbade enlistment into the Indian Army, threatened to execute any British recruiting agents found within its borders, and sought to punish returning soldiers with arrest and even death. As a result, for much of the century British recruiting efforts in Nepal had to be conducted in secret.[34]

Despite restrictions imposed by the durbar, conditions in the central and eastern hills of Nepal – from whence the British believed the best 'fighting material' hailed – were so poor that enough men were willing to take the necessary risks to fill five Indian Army regiments.[35] As in the Highlands prior to 1815, the reasons were clear: men of these areas had few occupations from which to choose. Remaining in their home villages almost invariably meant facing lives of subsistence farming on marginal lands.[36] Upward mobility was extremely difficult, and educational opportunities were nil.[37] For some, the attractions of regular pay clearly outweighed the risks of defying the durbar.

Difficult as conditions were for the targeted populations of British recruiting, they were not bad enough to turn the trickle of annual recruits into a regular flow. That only occurred after 1885, and was thanks not so much to the desires of individual soldiers as it was to a change of policy by the durbar. In that year, the British Resident convinced Bir Shamsher, the new Nepalese monarch, that the Raj would support his rival's claim to power if open recruiting were not finally allowed.[38] In exchange for the concession of open recruiting, the British promised modern arms and armaments to Shamsher's government – a trade that proved irresistible to succeeding regimes as well.[39]

In fact, increased British pressure to formalise recruiting in Nepal stemmed from Commander-in-Chief Roberts's 1885 sanction of five new Gurkha battalions to combat the Russian threat in the northwest.[40] By agreeing to Britain's demands, Bir Shamsher committed himself not just to a theory of cooperation with British recruiters but to active procurement of Nepali troops to fill the new regiments. Unfortunately for Shamsher, it quickly became apparent that these new demands far exceeded the numbers of men willing to serve. Unable or unwilling to apply to the British for a modification in the demands, Shamsher instead used force to coerce men to enlist. The result was resistance within the hill communities, where whole villages were known to fight against recruiting parties.[41] Moreover, many men who were coerced into enlisting initially resorted to desertion as soon as they arrived at their regimental stations.[42] Even today, oral tradition among Gurung communities portrays nineteenth- and early twentieth-century service with the British as a time when men did not choose service so much as they were forced into it.[43]

Compulsion, however, was never the whole story. Hill men in Nepal continued to enlist in the Indian Army by choice after 1885. As in the Punjab, men otherwise faced with lives of poverty found that remittances from the army could aid in their families' economic survival.[44] Until very recently, in fact, Gurkha soldiers' remittances were the largest source of foreign currency in Nepal.[45] But whether by compulsion or by economic necessity, the point here is that 'Gurkha' motivations for entering into British service were never as simple and as generous as martial race discourse pretended. Instead, like their Sikh and Highland counterparts, Gurkha soldiers enlisted less from choice than from lack of choice.

These stories of hardship, poverty and economic transformation were nearly always marginalised by martial race discourse. The heroes of that discourse – whether they were Sikhs, Highlanders or Gurkhas – were *drawn* to military service, not pushed into it. Yet even the briefest of regional histories demonstrates the significant gap that existed between the romance of the discourse and the material conditions that drove men to enlist in 'martial race' regiments. 'Real' 'martial race' soldiers, it seems, were seldom motivated by an instinct for war or by a love for either the

British or military service more generally. In this respect martial race discourse was never so much a description as it was a fantasy.

Identities and negotiations

Although the lives, experiences and motivations of these men did not necessarily conform to the mythic image of the 'martial races', martial race discourse was nevertheless relevant to their experiences as soldiers. Highland, Sikh and Gurkha regiments were well aware of their status as elite elements in the British imperial forces, and were consistently expected to perform that status both on parade and on active campaign. As a result, these soldiers were consistently faced with negotiating the tensions between their exalted reputation and position in the imperial forces on the one hand, and their individual experiences and motivations on the other. Below, we explore how 'actual' 'martial race' soldiers perceived their roles, as well as how they navigated the (sometimes fine) line between personal and collective identity.

Such a project is, of course, fraught with difficulties. Most important is the dearth of archival sources produced by enlisted Highland, Sikh and Gurkha soldiers. The situation for the Indian Army regiments is by far the most discouraging. Between 1857 and 1914, most Indian Army soldiers hailed from the poor peasantry and were largely illiterate. In the Punjab, only 5 per cent of the peasantry were literate even as late as 1914. To make matters more difficult, literacy rates in rural Punjabi communities – where the British recruited most Sikhs – were even lower.[46] In Nepal, the situation was worse. There, literacy was mainly the preserve of the small urban elite in and around Kathmandu, and thus was a rare feature in the rural mountain villages from whence most 'Gurkha' recruits came.[47] As a result, Sikh and Gurkha soldiers seldom were able to keep written records of their thoughts and experiences, and their voices were rarely directly preserved in the colonial archive.

What this means is that any exploration of Sikh or Gurkha self-perceptions has to be conducted with sources that are far from ideal. In the case of Sikhs, these include a large collection of (mostly dictated) letters that Sikh soldiers sent to their homes during the First World War. Because of the need to censor information leaving from the front, British censors translated, copied and archived several thousand letters from Indian sepoys during the conflict.[48] The use of these letters for the purposes of this study, however, poses some intractable problems. First, these letters cannot be interpreted as private reflections intended for only one reader. Instead, Indian soldiers were well aware that the contents of their letters would be available to scribes (who often wrote for illiterate soldiers), military censors, and their home communities once letters reached their destinations. As such, soldiers may well have found it difficult to convey information they wished to conceal from this wider public.[49] Even more of a problem is the use of letters written at the very end of the period under study here. The First World War can hardly be said to represent typical colonial warfare as it existed in India in the late nineteenth and early twentieth centuries. In fact, the experience of the Great War radically altered many soldiers' perceptions of Europe and colonialism, and therefore it would be dangerous to assume absolute continuity between Sikh sentiments during the war and those of the earlier period.

Extant sources providing insight into Gurkha self-perception are even more elusive. Unlike Sikh letters, Gurkha letters were not well represented in the materials collected and translated by the censor during the Great War. Scholars attempting to explore identity in the late nineteenth and early twentieth centuries, then, have turned instead to oral tradition and interviews of ex-Gurkha soldiers within Nepali communities. Of course, oral tradition poses methodological difficulties of its own, since it is often at quite a remove from the events it describes, and can change over time and with each story-teller. And while interviews can provide fascinating insight into the self-perception of current or recent Gurkha soldiers, there are clear difficulties with assuming too much historical continuity between these men and their predecessors from a century before.

Perhaps not surprisingly, archival sources for exploring soldiers' identities are far more plentiful for the Highland regiments. Literacy rates even among the poorest of Britons were much higher than in either the Punjab or Nepal, which meant that many more ordinary soldiers left diaries, letters and memoirs behind. Even so, only a comparatively small number of these sources still survive in various regimental and national archives. As a result, it is far from clear that the soldiers whose records survive were representative of their peers.

The clear flaws – not to mention the dearth – of sources that give voice to Sikh, Gurkha and Highland soldiers make the project of retrieving their voices difficult, if not ultimately impossible. There are also other problems that go beyond the limited availability of archival and oral sources. Gayatri Spivak has suggested that such a project may not be viable when undertaken by a western intellectual whose privileged academic traditions often claim the ability to speak for the 'downtrodden subaltern'. More problematic still, any attempt to construct some sort of collective identity for any of the 'martial race' groups also carries the danger – Spivak might say the inevitability – of imposing illusory solidarity upon heterogeneous groups.[50] I do not propose here to resolve, or even to argue against, Spivak's uneasiness about the possibility of retrieving subaltern voices. Indeed, this account may suffer from some of the very problems Spivak warns against. At the same time, if we allow British officers and media to have the last word on the qualities and capabilities of the so-called 'martial races', we run the risk of recreating an elitist history that completely leaves out 'the politics of the people', and prevents us from seeing 'martial race' soldiers as important actors in their own right.[51] Instead, faulty and finite as the available sources are, it seems possible that they can at least suggest alternative ways of understanding the various 'martial race' identities than those bequeathed to us from British officers and the British media.

Of course, assessing identity is always, under the best circumstances, a difficult historical challenge. Identity formation is a highly complex process, and is rarely uniform even across cohesive social groups. Individuals might well identify with more than one social group, location or culture, depending on the context. In other words, as Antoinette Burton has suggested, identities can be 'multiple, partial, contradictory, and strategic at different historical moments'.[52] As such, identities are not static or stable. Rather, they are always in flux, always in a state of 'becoming', and are constantly being formed, re-formed and negotiated through daily engagement with social conditions.[53] These negotiations, moreover, often occur in the context of deeply unequal social relations, which frequently means that people – particularly subaltern classes – are never completely free to choose their own identities. Instead, unequal power relations frequently have resulted in groups being 'assigned' particular identities by dominant elements within society because of factors such as poverty, occupation, skin colour, ethnicity or gender.[54] Part of the process of negotiating identity, then, is navigating 'between where one is placed and where one places oneself within social networks, working through what is possible as well as what is forbidden'.[55] This process is of course partly psychic, since identity formation is based on the ability to identify intellectually or emotionally with the experiences of others. But it bears emphasising that the realm of the imaginary is only part of the process. Equally important is the realm of the physical, where symbols, words, dress, actions and interactions literally perform identities in tangible, visible ways.[56]

For the 'martial races', this notion of performance is essential, for every soldier in the Sikh, Gurkha and Highland regiments had no choice but to perform – on a daily basis – an identity more or less chosen for him by his unit. One of the most visible aspects of this performance was in matters of dress. Upon entering a regiment, men with diverse backgrounds and experiences shed their outward differences by donning uniforms that helped instil in them both a corporate identity and a sense of connection with the regimental past. In a theatrical sense, their clothing alone gave them little choice but to 'play the part' of the martial race soldier.

The uniforms of 'martial race' regiments were laden with the symbolic power to conjure memories of past glories and regional distinctiveness.

Highlanders wore the kilt, sporran and bonnet, all of which were meant to recall the romance of a bygone era when wild, ferocious Highlanders fought loyally with their clan leaders. In an exotic contrast, Sikhs carried the *tulwar* and wore their unshorn hair – sign of inclusion in the Khalsa warrior brotherhood – in elaborate turbans. These markers were meant to recall an earlier age when Khalsa Sikhs had formed one of India's most sophisticated and feared armies. Gurkhas dressed in khaki like many British regiments, but visibly carried the dreaded *kukri* – a long, deadly, curved knife that vividly symbolised Gurkhas' bloodthirstiness in battle. Whether on parade, on the march or in battle, through their dress 'martial race' soldiers continuously performed a carefully selected version of regional tradition that required their individual bodily cooperation for its delivery.

This performance was not, however, limited to matters of dress alone. 'Martial race' soldiers were also encouraged to observe rituals, practices and battle anniversaries that served to promote group identity and cohesion. In the Highland regiments, for example, the celebration of St Andrew's Day (Scotland's patron saint) and Hogmanay (New Year's Day) were occasions on which Scottish toasts, piping and feasting gave soldiers ample time to reflect on the Highland character of their unit. Highland dancing and piping were more quotidian practices that served the same function of marking Highland regimental distinctiveness from other British Army units.

While the rituals and practices in Gurkha regiments differed from the Highland regiments, of course, the goals were similar. The annual harvest festival of Dasai, for example, was meant to provide an occasion for Gurkha soldiers to celebrate their unique cultural traditions, which was believed to enhance morale and to encourage group harmony.[57] Religious customs and ceremonies were likewise integrated into both the regimental calendar and standing orders.[58] Gurkha soldiers were expected to perform dances and songs within the regiments that reinforced their cultural cohesiveness, even though these frequently had no meaning in their own varied home cultures in Nepal.[59] Finally, Gurkha recruits, who generally came from a number of linguistic backgrounds, were required to learn and speak Nepali – a language with which few could claim prior familiarity.[60]

Performance was also important in Sikh regiments, where new recruits were required to undergo the initiation ceremony, or *pahul*, to become members of the Sikh Khalsa brotherhood.[61] Khalsa Sikhs swore explicitly to uphold the warrior creed expounded by the Guru Gobind Singh, and were expected to mark their physical appearance with the outward signs of that commitment.[62] Within each Sikh regiment, moreover, daily ritual and prayer meetings based on the Guru Granth Sahib – the Sikh holy book – were intended to keep the faith of the Khalsa strong. In addition, the Granth was given a place of honour in regimental quarters, and was carried at the head of the regiment on the march.[63] As a result, it was virtually impossible for Sikh recruits in the Indian Army not to perform a specific version of martial Sikhism on a daily basis.

Yet while we know that membership in the 'martial race' regiments required the continual performance of a group identity dictated by the units themselves, it is far more difficult to assess the meanings such performances had for the men. Did 'playing the part' of a martial race soldier influence men's identities and self-perceptions? Did men accept martial race constructions of themselves, or did they find ways to resist such constructions? In addition to the costs of performing as martial race soldiers – which could include soldiers' own lives – were there also benefits for the performers?

The answers to these questions – to the extent that we can answer them at all – are extremely complex, and moreover are different not only for each group under study here but also, no doubt, for each individual. With these differences in mind, however, the evidence does seem to indicate one fairly common thread: many 'martial race' soldiers appeared to accept popular constructions of themselves as brave, elite warriors. For some of the men, especially many Gurkhas, this acceptance seems to have been only partial and situational. For others, acceptance appears to have been much more important to their identities as soldiers and men. This pattern, it must be said, does not accord particularly well with the thrust of subaltern studies in academe, which have often assumed that 'subaltern narratives contain trenchant political critiques of the colonial order and its postcolonial effects'.[64] The study of 'martial races', however, indicates that such critiques were not necessarily inevitable. Instead, as Ann Stoler discovered with her memory work among ex-servants in Java, subalterns do not 'always reject outright the roles cast for them in colonialist narratives'.[65] In the case of many 'martial race' soldiers, it would be a mistake to presume they rejected out of hand the identity of a 'martial' soldier.

Diaries written by Highland soldiers provide some suggestive ways of looking at this issue. Even though most of these men rarely wrote introspectively, if we explore writing about the self as a performative act, their choices about what to include offer some revealing evidence about identity formation and negotiation. Writing about the self, indeed, is not a neutral act. It involves inclusion, exclusion, possession, authority and self-fashioning. The very act of writing, in other words, helps constitute the self by linguistically framing – and freezing – experience and perception. It is a performance for the self, a performance, moreover, that can be infinitely re-lived with each re-reading.

Highland soldiers' writings frequently revealed a tendency towards self-fashioning through the borrowed eloquence of speeches, telegrams, general orders and songs praising their regiments. Even the least introspective of writers seemed to share the practice of making meticulous, often word-for-word, copies of such praise. Whether the praise originated in newspapers or with military authorities, soldiers' transcriptions stand out amid their everyday reports of meals, time of reveille, marching and physical discomforts. The journal of Private McIntosh of the Gordon Highlanders is telling in this regard. After his regiment was inspected by a leading general in India, McIntosh copied out the General's speech:

> 92nd Gordon Highlanders (giving us our title) it is 15 years since I had the pleasure of having to command you but I have always had a close connection with you and have found you always good, clever, and nice looking men and I can see you still bear the same appearance as you did then and I hope you always will for the sake of your old colours and ancestors ... you are really the finest regiment that I have had under my command[.] Now 92nd I sincerely hope that you will take good care of yourselfs [sic]. My brave fellows good bye!![66]

The language of this speech covers a wide range of ground, depicting the Gordons as at once handsome, distinguished, elite and brave. McIntosh's commentary accompanying the speech implies no irony or sarcasm in his reaction to the speech, calling it only 'very flattering'.[67] For McIntosh and – if we are to believe his account – his regiment, the speech had a galvanising effect, for afterwards 'during the whole of the day you could hear nothing but the General's speech and wishing we were on the march'.[68] More importantly, by recording the speech McIntosh enlisted the authority of the General's words in his own enterprise of fashioning himself as a legitimate and militarily valuable Highland soldier.

Many other soldiers engaged in similar practices of self-fashioning through the replication of praise. These included William Marr, who recorded Queen Victoria's telegram to his regiment complimenting them 'on the bravery and gallantry of the Battalion in the Charge of Dargai Hill'.[69] Private A. W. McIntosh, a soldier in the Black Watch, copied verbatim Sir Hugh Rose's[70] speech at the presentation of new colours for the regiment in 1861, which began: 'I do not ask you to defend the Colours I have presented to you this day, it would be superfluous, you have defended them for nearly a hundred years with the best blood of Scotland'.[71] David McAusland, another soldier of the Black Watch, recorded H. M. Stanley as saying that the 42nd was a 'model regiment exceedingly disciplined and individually nothing could surpass the standing and gallantry which distinguished each member'.[72] Private E. Finch, as well, recorded his regiment's inspection by Field-Marshal Lord Roberts[73] in South Africa, proudly writing that Roberts 'promises to take us to Pretoria and told us that he depended on us for the relief of Kimberley'.[74]

Far from being merely trivial or random, Highland soldiers' choice in recording such words of praise indicates that the act of writing itself was a part of the continual process by which these men negotiated their identities. Praise, and the act of preserving it indefinitely, provided a marker of positive assessment to which soldiers could frequently return and reabsorb. It is perhaps not difficult to imagine that soldiers in the Highland regiments took pleasure in seeing themselves as brave, strong and gallant, nor that they might have taken pride in believing they were valued by Britain's leadership – surely a distinction few lower-class Scottish men could claim. By 'owning' speeches and telegrams through inclusion in their diaries, Highland soldiers implied their approval of such heroic constructions of themselves. Copying such words also signalled soldiers' identification with the larger regiment, for clearly they believed themselves entitled to claim the glory such praise offered. And, in claiming the glory, Highland soldiers allowed themselves to think of their regiments as elite units, a step above the rest of the British Army.

It is impossible to know what Sikh or Gurkha soldiers would have written about, had more been able to do so in this period. Clearly, the voices of Highland soldiers – as heard through their diaries – cannot be made to speak for either group. That said, the letters and diaries of Highland soldiers at least permit us to explore the possibility that some of the Indian 'martial races' may have similarly accepted British constructions of themselves as 'bravest of the brave'. While we have virtually no evidence of this for Gurkhas, some of the letters written by (or on behalf of) Sikh soldiers seemed also to exhibit eagerness to depict themselves as elite warriors in their homeward letters.[75] Signaller Kartar Singh, for example, bathed himself in the glory of his regiment in a letter home:

> We have been fighting for fourteen months, and the fighting has been very fierce. I have been in every fight and have fought with great valour. Our people have exalted the name of our country. When the order comes that the enemy is advancing in this direction, as a tiger advances on his prey [so we stand to] and with fine spirit knock the senses out of him. Our troops have been accounted the stoutest of all the troops. At this time, they are in such heart that they would stay the tiger unarmed. [Every man] fighting with heroic bravery becomes himself a hero ... I hope we shall renew our Sikh chronicles.[76]

In this passage, Kartar Singh not only identifies himself as a heroic individual, but justifies these claims through membership in the larger Sikh collective which has, according to Singh, been recognised by outsiders as the 'stoutest of all the troops'. In fact, Singh wants his friend to know that the Sikhs in France are so keen to fight that they might even be able to prevail in battle unarmed. Singh hints, indeed, that he and his comrades are so brave that their deeds may be as worthy of legend as the deeds of the original Khalsa warriors depicted in the Sikh chronicles.

Risaldar Jiwan Singh also wrote home about his regiment's great feats in battle. In his account of an attack, he exulted to his correspondent that it 'was made with the utmost bravery and it achieved splendid results ... how could the cowardly Germans stand before the onslaught of the braves of the Khalsa!'[77] By depicting his regiment as invincible warriors, Jiwan Singh may have had several possible goals. Perhaps, as may have been the case with Katar Singh, Jiwan Singh hoped to make himself look good in the eyes of his family and home community. Alternatively, he may have been trying to reassure worried friends or family members that all was well on the front, and that he was safe from German attacks. Or, by taking such a self-confident tone, he may have been trying to convince himself of the same thing. Whatever his personal reasons, however, in this letter Singh actively embraced a construction of Sikh soldiers that his British officers would have instantly recognised and applauded. In fact, he could have been quoting from an Indian Army handbook on Sikhs when he stated, in the same letter, that '[w]e are Sikhs, and the duty of Sikhs is to exalt in battle and show their prowess'.[78]

Other soldiers seemed implicitly to accept such constructions of themselves in their discussion of death. Many soldiers wrote to friends and family advising them not to be sad if they should die in battle, since Khalsa Sikhism viewed such a death as honourable. Jemadar Indar Singh, for example, urged his family not to grieve at his death 'because I shall die arms in hand, wearing the warrior's clothes. This is the most happy death that anyone can die.'[79] Jemadar Ganda Singh likewise encouraged his friend not to pray for his survival, but to pray 'that the enemy may never see my back, but may always be faced by me as a lion ... We must all die some day. It is best that we should die in this great war.'[80] Clearly, Indar and Ganda Singh may have had their own reasons for framing their potential deaths in this way. They may well have hoped to shield their families and friends from some of the inevitable grief that accompanies death by claiming to embrace such a fate. Or, by giving voice to such claims they may have been trying to remind themselves of their religious tenets and to convince themselves that they were prepared for death. In either case, however, both men implied their acceptance of a construction of themselves as heroic, stalwart, fierce and natural soldiers. Like many of their fellow Sikhs who served in the Great War, they provide us with tantalising echoes of Highland soldiers' willingness to accept a 'martial' identity.

Yet while the First World War letters might provide us with some clues about how Sikhs may have hoped to present themselves, they tell us virtually nothing about Gurkhas. If we had more letters from Gurkha soldiers in that conflict, would they have similarly implied an acceptance of British 'martial race' constructions? One way to answer this question is to explore, in a comparative context, the personal and cultural benefits that Highland, Sikh and Gurkha soldiers might have derived from accepting and embracing such a version of themselves. What, in other words, did 'martial race' soldiers get out of being labelled as 'martial'? What was in it for them?

Once again, direct evidence about the potential benefits of 'taking on' a martial race identity is most plentiful for Highland soldiers. For many such men, the idealised representations of 'martial' Highlanders may have seemed very appealing indeed. As increasing numbers of recruits hailed from the lower strata of Scotland's urban centres, these were clearly men who had had few opportunities in life. As civilians, most would have had little public visibility, and their labours would no doubt have passed relatively unnoticed in the bustle of Victorian expansion. Once these ordinary men stepped into full Highland dress as soldiers, however, the world would have regarded them in quite a different light. Suddenly, they would have become a highly visible part of a coveted and admired regiment, lauded by ordinary citizens, high military officials and the Queen alike. In Highland uniform, recruits were able to take on the role of hero whether or not it matched their personality or previous record.[81] They became, through their outer garb, elite fighting men who were believed capable of any and all military feats.

They were encouraged to develop this elitism by both their own and other army officers – a practice sanctioned by Britain's leading military lights. Garnet Wolseley's enormously important and influential *Soldier's Pocket-Book for Field Service*, first published in 1871, spelled out the importance of praise when he advised officers: 'in an army praise is the greatest of all moral levers if administered with discrimination: it is a trump card, costing nothing, that is always at the disposal of the officer, be he commander or captain, which enables him to win if he knows how to use it'.[82] In the Highland regiments, this 'trump card' was used with great consistency and frequency. In addition to speeches of praise included in General Orders, during inspection, and on campaign, praise also filled the pages of regimental histories (increasingly available to the men by the end of the century) and campaign scrapbooks of newspaper cuttings celebrating regimental accomplishments. Regimental journals like the *Highland Light Infantry Chronicle*, the *Thin Red Line*, *Tiger and Sphinx* and the *79th News*, published with increasing frequency at the end of the nineteenth century, included stories, songs and poems that heaped praise on Highland regiments and encouraged nostalgia for the signs and symbols of Highlandism.[83]

Even more effective in encouraging elitism and regimental identification among the men were the reactions of outsiders. Highland soldiers discovered, indeed, that curious onlookers stopped to admire their exotic dress wherever they went, and that their outer garb was associated with heroism and ideal masculinity.[84] In uniform, they found themselves able to command both awe and respect. Some Highland soldiers were well aware of these advantages and – fortunately for us – wrote about them in their letters and diaries. For these men, the theatricality of Highland dress allowed them to assume a role of far greater authority and machismo than they might otherwise have dared. Corporal Patrick of the 78th Highlanders, ruminating on the delights of this advantage, put it plainly in a letter describing his regiment's reception in Montreal in 1867:

> They [the people of Montreal] could not have made a greater fuss about us, if we had only just returned from the Wars. I can assure you, and which I daresay you will suppose, that the 'Rosshire Buffs' were the Lions of the Day, and were praised up to the 'nines', while the other poor soldiers in Montreal, could scarce lift their heads. Whenever I used to go out for a walk in the town, with two or three more Sergeants, we used to swell our chests properly, and put such a swagger on, as if the whole town belonged to us, so that the people used to clear the pavement for us, for we never required to turn to the one side, to get out of the road, for they would never stand in front, and in the way of such fierce looking warriors. I have often felt proud ... to belong to such a noble, distinguished, and splendid dressed regiment. Some people in Montreal had never seen a Highlander before, so when we came here, they stared at us with opened mouth and eyes.[85]

Several things seem to have made Patrick proud to be a Highland soldier in this passage, nearly all of which carried immediate personal rewards. First, he relished the fact that his 'splendid dressed' regiment stole attention away from the other British regiments stationed in Montreal, for he perceived that he was an object of envy by fellow soldiers. Second, he consciously made use of the Highland reputation for his own personal satisfaction when he and his friends visited town in uniform. Adopting a swagger, swelling their chests and imagining themselves as 'fierce looking warriors' provided him with entertainment while it enhanced his own sense of manliness. Finally, he seemed to take pleasure in the exoticism of his regiment, clearly gauged by its effects on Canadians who stared at them 'with opened mouth and eyes'. Clearly, Patrick viewed the attractiveness of his service – at least in part – in terms of personal advantages. As a Highland soldier, he commanded respect, awe and envy. Outside the regiment, he would have been just another man.

Highland soldiers also sometimes found that their uniforms made them objects of sexual attraction. On the matter of dress, Garnet Wolseley's *Pocket-Book for Field Service* had perceptively remarked, 'the better you dress a soldier, the more highly he will be thought of by women, and consequently by himself'.[86] In the case of Highland soldiers, this was particularly true. The reputation of Highland regiments as fighting units had also rendered them in popular imagination the most ferociously masculine of all troops. The wearing of the kilt – with its feminine associations – reinforced rather than detracted from this masculine imagery.[87] Moreover, the common belief that Highland soldiers wore nothing under their kilts drove a whole genre of Victorian jokes and innuendoes suggesting that even respectable women were driven by desire to discover the truth. The kilt, and its suggestion of sexuality, increasingly became associated with the virile sexuality of Highland soldiers. This was certainly acknowledged with envy by soldiers in non-kilted regiments. One officer in India wrote that 'it makes your heart beat to see them march past, the feathers in their bonnets tossing and the graceful kilt giving easy play to their sturdy limbs'.[88] And the regimental magazine of the 71st Highland Light Infantry (the only Highland regiment that wore the trews instead of the kilt) noted: 'we read so much of the kilt ... that we may be pardoned if at times we look on its swinging folds with envy. And we know that the women adore it!'[89]

Corporal Patrick, to whom we have already been introduced, proudly boasted of the attention local women devoted to his regiment on his arrival in Montreal with the 78th Highlanders. When the regiment stepped onto land and paraded through town, Patrick recorded that 'ladies filled every window, who showered down flowers and bouquets, on the heads of the gallant warriors of the North, the "heroes of Lucknow" and "Saviours of India"'.[90] Years later, Fred Bly also noted the considerable advantages and special treatment given to Highland soldiers. Posted on guard in British-occupied Bloemfontein during the South African War, he could not believe his luck. 'The people seem almost to worship us', he mused, 'and are giving us all sorts of eatables and drinkables in fact everything we want.'[91] His attraction as a Highlander was clearly drawing local young women to his side as well, some of whom stayed out very late on his account. After his first night on duty, he wrote, 'I hope this guard lasts for a month', for he had been 'up half the night talking to people' who plied him with whisky, till he 'thought some of the girls would never go home'.[92] In uniform as a Highland soldier, Bly was able to attract women, whisky and good food. As a civilian, the same attentions would have been unavailable to him. Small wonder that he noted the next day, in spite of a rather 'sore head', that he had 'never lived so well' in all his life.[93]

If donning the outer garb of the Highland soldier seems to have encouraged men to accept and identify with the widespread notion that they were elite, masculine warriors, it also seems to have encouraged them to perceive their service in distinctly Scottish terms. In part, this was almost inevitable. All of the Highland regiments were, as we know, dominated by a Scottish majority. The popularity and praise heaped upon the Highland regiments – both in popular and military sources – was phrased in terms of the unique qualities of Scottish Highland recruits, and uniform in the Highland regiments continually recalled the supposed ancient dress of

Highland society. To be a Highland soldier was to be confronted with both real and imaginary Scottishness every day.

At the same time, there is evidence that a more specifically Scottish patriotism motivated some Scottish soldiers.[94] This is not to say their motivations were nationalistic or separatist – indeed, Highland soldiers had little difficulty identifying with Britain's imperial project. Instead, the idea of 'Scotland' seemed to provide a key point of reference and inspiration for some men. William Marr's diary, written during his service with the 92nd Gordon Highlanders on India's northwest frontier in 1895, is particularly revealing in this regard. One of the things he chose to record in his diary was a song called 'The Relief of Chitral', an action in which his regiment had been involved. The tune itself clearly spoke to the specifically Scottish character of the relief:

> Onwards o'er mountain and river
> Facing the heat and the snow
> 'Gay Gordons' and 'Borderers'
> Bravely shoulder to shoulder they go
> What though the road be rough what though the miles be long
> Our Scottish lads are willing and our Scottish lads are strong
> Cheerfully fearlessly onward they march
> In their Tartan arrayed
> Aye fine to the core as in days of yore
> Worthy Sons of the Old Brigade
> Right nobly they've done their duty
> The Malakand Pass will tell
> To future generations how gallant they fought and fell
> Scaling the steepest passes steady and undismayed ...
> Hurrah for the Scottish Brigade.[95]

'The Relief of Chitral' alludes to many of the standard mythic elements of Highland soldiers, this time set in a broader Scottish context. Here, Scottish soldiers of both the Lowland and Highland regiments brave extremes of weather and terrain without complaint or worry. Their martial prowess is evident in their willingness to fight, their lack of fear and their strength. They are recognisable by their tartans, and their performance in this campaign will reflect well on their regiments' glorious histories as well as on their own posterity. These soldiers, while fighting for the British Army, measure their worth by comparison to one another and to their regimental Scottish predecessors. Scotland, here, is the motivating force driving the Brigade to victory. Marr's approval and acceptance of the song, indicated by his choice in recording it, reveals the importance of particularly Scottish inspirations in Highland regimental culture. The same can be said for a copy of a telegram Marr recorded, sent by the Royal Headquarters of the 92nd after the successful battle of Dargai. It read simply, 'Brave Old Comrades, Scotland for Ever'.[96]

Private George Greig of the 93rd Highlanders also wrote in specifically Scottish terms about his experience as a soldier in the British Army. An amateur poet and song-writer, Greig penned a number of original verses that looked to Scotland as his inspiration for enlisting and fighting in the 93rd, and praised Scottish troops for their valour and courage above all others. In particular, 'When the Author Left his Native Land' describes his motivation for fighting in terms of his ancestry as a Lochiel:

> When the sound of the cannon did rattle
> And the cry of Lochiel reached my ear
> I was eager to be in the battle
> With a courage that never knew fear[97]

Here, Greig links himself to his Highland past. He seeks to create an image in which the clan cry resonates within him as it did his ancestors, and which spurs him to fight with courage in battle.

For Highland soldiers, then, the benefits of living up to the 'martial' ideal – especially in terms of status, popularity, and a strong sense of group, cultural or regional identity – could be ample indeed. In the context of British popular and military culture, both of which valued the figure of the Highland soldier for its symbolic and historic appeal, 'playing the part' of a Highland warrior to the fullest brought tangible rewards. Thus, as much as the military sought to inculcate a certain martial identity within the Highland regiments, the success of such an endeavour was hardly due to those efforts alone. Instead, Highland soldiers elected to take on aspects of that identity because it made sense for them to do so.

Like Highland soldiers, Sikh soldiers also seem to have derived substantial rewards from embracing a 'martial' identity within the Indian Army. Perhaps not surprisingly, some of these rewards were remarkably similar to those enjoyed by Highland soldiers. At the same time, however, such similarities should not obscure the differing social, historical and cultural contexts separating the two groups. For one thing, Sikh soldiers were unlike their Highland counterparts in that they did not hail from the lowest classes of society. In fact, military service in India was generally regarded as a more honourable career than it was in Britain, and thus enlistment carried little of the social stigma that it did at the Empire's centre.[98] Indeed, certain groups viewed military service as an important part of their historical and cultural tradition, and hence as a worthy career for many classes of men. This was certainly true of the Jat peasants who came to dominate the ranks of the Sikhs.[99] Moreover, Sikhs who followed the teachings of Guru Gobind Singh – founder of the militant Khalsa in 1699 – believed that martial traditions were crucial to their faith and way of life.

Khalsa Sikhs (also known as Kesdhari Sikhs) placed great importance on the fight for freedom, and thus men of the Khalsa were supposed to be brave, bold and skilled fighters.[100] In fact, the Sikh prayer (Ardas), recited at the end of most rituals, conspicuously calls to mind the martial traditions of the Khalsa as well as the bloody sacrifices that have been made in its name.[101] Because of these traditions, Khalsa Sikhs were accustomed to thinking about military service in terms of individual and collective honour (izzat).[102] According to the teachings of Guru Gobind Singh, extreme courage and/or death in the heat of battle was said to bring honour to the whole community. Conversely, cowardice in battle was considered unacceptable and unmasculine, and those who demonstrated it were likely to face the contempt of family or of entire villages.[103]

Given the cultural resonance that a 'warrior spirit' already carried in Khalsa Sikh communities, some Sikh soldiers may have derived substantial social rewards from embracing the army's particular version of 'martial race' identity. Certainly, some evidence exists that Sikh soldiers were under pressure from their home communities to perform well in the service. Jemadar Jai Singh could hardly have failed to get the message in a letter he received from home in 1916. The writer, an Inspector of Police, told Singh:

> I shall be very pleased to hear of your valorous deeds. You are a brave soldier. Now is the time to display your manhood. Now is the time for loyalty. You are a true Sikh. By the Guru's order you must remember the promise of the Almighty, who said:
> Recognise the hero in him who fights for his faith;
> Though cut to pieces he will not quit his ground.[104]

In a few short lines, Jai Singh's correspondent reminded him that his home community would be on the lookout for news of brave deeds, and that his duty to home and religion required him to fight – and perhaps die – as a hero.

That some soldiers were less than happy to be on the receiving end of such pressure is suggested by one Sikh soldier who retorted to his correspondent: 'What you say in your letter about not being disloyal to the Emperor, and it being the religion of Sikhs to die facing the foe – all that you say is true. But if only you yourself could be here and see for yourself! … You tell me to fight face to the foe. Die we must – but alas, not facing the foe!'[105] While this letter obviously indicates the unique circumstances and frustrations of the First World War, it also hints that Sikh soldiers were expected by their home communities to live up to the ideal of the Khalsa soldier. Balwant Singh promised that it was not just his own honour that would be enhanced by this. When he wrote home from the front in 1917, he assured his correspondent that '[w]e believe that the Guru will soon give victory to our King, and that you will receive great izzat [honour]'.[106]

It seems probable, then, that some Sikh soldiers may have embraced the army's vision of 'martial race-ness' as a means of obtaining the reward of enhanced reputations, status and honour with friends and family at home. That such rewards may have been expected by soldiers is suggested by their many letters that emphasised the valour and importance of their own actions. Sham Singh is a case in point. Writing to a friend in the Punjab, Singh claimed that '[w]e are now in the trenches and fighting with great courage ... We do not wish the war to stop yet; we want it to continue ... You will understand [our worth] when we return with rows of medals on our breasts.'[107] Bakhlawar Singh expressed similar sentiments to a friend, assuring him that '[w]e are full of fight and ready to do our bit as long as the war lasts. We are fortunate men to have been able to join in this great war. We will do our best to uphold the family traditions and the reputation of our tribe.'[108] Other soldiers, like Lance Dafadar Chattar Singh, hoped to impress upon family members the social value of military service. In a letter home, Singh reminded his correspondent that '[f]ortunate indeed are those parents whose sons have come to this war and are taking part in it. It is fitting that such sons should be born to their parents, otherwise they are useless.'[109]

Soldiers also displayed a strong awareness that death in battle was a means of gaining *izzat* in their home communities, both for themselves and for their families. Writing to a fellow soldier serving in the Punjab, Dafadar Nathan Singh maintained that 'He who dies on the field of battle / His name never dies, but lives in history'.[110] Ressaldar Jowan Singh, writing to console the family of a fallen soldier, advised: 'Do not be dismayed. Your son is a hero who has given his life for his King. He is not dead; he lives forever.'[111] And Jemadar Ganda Singh demonstrated his understanding of the benefits of a soldier's death when he wrote to a friend that '[t]his is the time when he who desires to do so may illuminate his name and [that of] his clan by sacrificing himself'.[112] As most of these soldiers knew, however, death was not a necessary prerequisite for achieving heroic status. Rather, it was only the most dramatic result of behaviours that might bring honour and local fame to a soldier and his family. And such honour, in turn, may well have been an important factor in encouraging at least some Sikhs to attempt to live up to the ideal of themselves as 'martial races'.

Attention and respect from their home communities was only one of the potential rewards of embracing a 'martial' identity within the British Army. Another, perhaps equally important, was the benefit of receiving favoured treatment from the Raj. Indeed, 'martial race' status could be quite lucrative. As we already know, groups able to claim such status were able to supplement family incomes to stave off bankruptcy and extreme poverty. In fact, in some areas whole groups converted to Sikhism in order to gain this advantage for themselves and their families.[113] Even higher-caste Hindus, such as Khatris and Aroras, began joining the dominant – but lower-caste – Jats as Sikhs in the late nineteenth century: a phenomenon that demonstrates a clear awareness of the advantages of British favour.[114] Consequently, Sikh numbers rose significantly in the late nineteenth and early twentieth centuries – from two million in 1881 to four million in 1931.[115] Indeed, one of the results of British favour was that even middle-class reform groups not normally associated with the military began to privilege Khalsa Sikhism as the only true expression of the Sikh religion.[116]

But there was more to it than just money. By embracing the version of Khalsa Sikhism nurtured by the army, soldiers reaped the rewards of special praise, attention and an enhanced sense of group identity. One Sikh, who had gone to London to receive two medals during the war, was deeply impressed that he received a hero's welcome – with all of the accompanying media flurry – in Britain. Writing home, he remarked that 'they treat me with very great respect in London'.[117] Sikhs also found that their special status as a 'martial race' meant that they were accorded special honours and rewards. In 1898, for example, an influential British committee set up an unprecedented fund to honour Sikh soldiers who had died in the frontier warfare of 1897–98 with a special memorial. Moreover, and even more unusually, the committee raised money for the families of these fallen soldiers as a testament to British gratefulness for such loyal service.[118] In 1911 the favoured status of Sikhs was reconfirmed once again when Sikh soldiers were selected for George V's guard of honour at his coronation durbar.[119]

British favour, in combination with the army's explicit use of Sikh ritual, doctrine and visual symbols, made it easy for soldiers to perceive their service in distinctly Sikh terms. Sikh letters displayed a marked lack of identification with 'India', and instead framed their motives for fighting by evoking explicitly Sikh cultural and religious references.[120] Many men, indeed, saw their service as the fulfilment of the teachings of the Gurus, especially in terms of Guru Gobind Singh's Khalsa brotherhood. As Risaldar Jiwan Singh put it after describing a successful Sikh attack: 'This credit is not due to us, but to the Guru, through whose favour we speared many of the routed enemy on our lances, and brought back many prisoners'.[121] For this soldier, the men in his unit were bound together through an identity based not just on common service, but on a common faith too.

Some soldiers' letters made it clear that they understood the army's critical role in nurturing this enhanced Sikh identity. Kishan Singh, writing to his son in France, reminded his son that the Raj deserved special loyalty from the Sikhs, for in contrast to Mughal rulers who 'desired to root out our race root and branch', '[t]oday our King, ruler over the seven

Kingdoms, is the protection of our race'.[122] Eshar Singh, writing to Jai Singh at the front, agreed. For him, British rule had been a blessing for the Sikhs, and 'was established in India only for the protection and help of us Sikhs'. Moreover, he continued, '[i]t was on the voice of the Guru that the Eternal sent the English here. The blessings which this rule has brought to India are not concealed from you. The rise of the Sikhs is due solely to this power.'[123] In other words, according to these men, Sikhs owed their very religious and cultural survival to the British.

Thus, many soldiers' identities seemed to be intricately bound up with a sense of loyalty to the British Empire – most especially in the form of the British sovereign.[124] As one wounded Sikh put it in a letter to his brother at home, 'our father the King-Emperor needs us and any of us who refuses to help him in his need should be counted among the most polluted sinners. It is our first duty to show our loyal gratitude to Government.'[125] Another declared that 'loyalty to the King compels me to serve him and be true to my salt'.[126] For many men, this sense of loyalty seems to have been quite unaffected and tinged with affection. In 1917, when the King sent pictures of himself to the Indian troops serving in Europe, Sikh soldiers seemed genuinely touched. One man even advised his wife to hang the picture in their home and to worship it. Balwant Singh, however, was more typical when he wrote: 'May God grant long life to the generous-hearted sovereign who has deigned to think of his humblest soldiers'.[127] For these Sikhs, special treatment in the Indian Army allowed them to think of themselves as uniquely distinct units who owed that distinction to the favour and protection of the British monarch.

For Sikhs, then, the advantages of accepting the 'martial' ideal might have included renown and honour at home, attention and rewards from the British Raj, and an enhanced sense of cultural and religious identity. Certainly, it seems plausible enough that Sikh soldiers would have been able to gauge these advantages for themselves, and to seek to take every opportunity to make them work to their own advantage. Thus, rather than seeing these men as either brainwashed victims of British propaganda or as passively accepting, we might instead see them as active agents in seeking to improve their own – and their families' – lives.

In contrast to Highland and Sikh soldiers, for whom the advantages of taking on the role of 'martial race' soldiers may have carried substantial benefits, the case for Gurkhas seems much more problematic. Indeed, the ultra-masculine, warlike and violent 'martial race' ideal did not seem to resonate strongly among Nepal's hill communities from whence the British drew their 'Gurkha' recruits. Certainly, some Nepalese hill men had served in the military even before the British raised the first 'Gurkha' battalions, but this occupation does not seem to have been widespread. Nor, in contrast to the discourse surrounding the 'natural' military qualities of

Gurkha soldiers, does military service seem to have been regarded as a particularly honourable career.[128] In fact, anthropological field work has demonstrated that even among the Gurungs – one of the most sought-after 'martial' groups in Nepal – the values of martial race ideology represented both a break with and a simplification of indigenous practices and understandings.[129] Unlike Sikh culture, with its history of armed resistance against Mughal domination, Gurung culture does not celebrate violence. Moreover, the qualities that the British thought made these 'Gurkhas' such natural soldiers – such as a love of fighting and an aggressive sense of masculinity – were markedly absent in Gurung culture.[130] As a result, soldiers who went away to fight for the British were not typically viewed as particularly honourable or heroic in their home communities, and could expect little in the way of cultural rewards for behaviours commonly associated with the 'martial races'.[131]

One indicator of this less-than-heroic status was the name by which so-called 'Gurkha' soldiers were called in their own language. Rather than 'Gurkhas' or even soldiers, these men were known simply as *lahures*: men who contributed to their families and villages by exchanging labour for wages outside the community. Originally taken from the name Lahore, the city where men would travel to sell their labour, in time it came to represent all such work performed outside the home community. What must be emphasised is that the main function of a *lahure* was always economic, to aid in the survival of the home. While present-day *lahures* do enjoy special status in their home communities, this is largely because men who are selected for service within the British Army can expect to make about a hundred times more than the average income.[132] Prior to Indian independence, however, the social status of *lahure* soldiers was little better than other Nepalis who sold their labour in markets far from home.[133]

The isolated and largely illiterate nature of Nepalese hill societies would have made it difficult for 'Gurkha' soldiers to be rewarded for 'martial' behaviours in their home communities in any case. *Lahures* typically spent very long periods of time away from their home communities, and because of low literacy were often unable to communicate with friends and family in their absence.[134] Before 1885 especially – when the Nepalese government forbade enlistment in the Indian Army – soldiers could expect to be separated from family for years. Even after recruiting was allowed, however, the isolation of many rural villages, not to mention their distance from garrisons where *lahures* might be stationed in India, made visits infrequent. As a result, in contrast to Sikh soldiers (who typically were able to return home with some frequency), it would have been far more difficult for 'Gurkha' soldiers to sing their own praises at home. Furthermore, those villages targeted for 'Gurkha' recruitment had precious little opportunity to discover how much the British valued the so-called 'martial' traits of their young men, since illiteracy and isolation prohibited exposure to media, to printed recruiting materials, or even to Britons who held high opinions of 'Gurkha' soldiers.

Even in the recent past, field research has suggested that many 'Gurkha' soldiers do not identify with the warrior identity that martial race ideology has assigned them. When confronted with both old and new anecdotes about the ferocity, masculinity and prowess of Gurkhas in battle, Mary des Chene discovered that 'Lahores simply did not recognise themselves'.[135] For these men, military service was not a natural extension of an inherent predilection for war. Instead, they saw military service as a necessary sacrifice, during which they resigned themselves to living and working in a separate society and operating under wholly different expectations.[136]

Although *lahures* could expect few rewards from their home communities for adopting 'martial' identities, they were clearly willing to at least perform such identities for the purposes of active service. Why? Like Sikhs and Highlanders, 'Gurkhas' may well have understood that British favour carried certain advantages. Gurkha soldiers were frequently the targets of special praise – by both officers and the reigning monarch – for their prowess in battle. Gurkhas were also treated as a 'class apart' from most other native soldiers, and were in fact the only Indian Army soldiers allowed into the messes of British soldiers.[137] And while we have no evidence that serving in Gurkha regiments afforded men an enhanced sense of group identity, we do at least have fragmentary evidence that some Gurkhas, like their Sikh counterparts, felt they owed the Empire a debt of loyalty. As one Gurkha soldier put it in a letter to a fellow soldier in France, 'Brother this is the opportunity to show your worth. To give help to your family and render aid to Government, fight well, kill your enemy and do not let him attain his object.'[138] Despite this sense of loyalty, however, it all came back to money, duty and family.[139] In interviews with ex-soldiers, Lionel Caplan noted that the men 'made it abundantly clear that obedience, along with the acceptance of hardship and danger, are explicable in terms of obligations toward kin and family: the compelling need to provide support for the household. Ultimately, these are the paramount values for which they are willing, albeit reluctantly, to sacrifice everything.'[140] It seems ironic, then, that the group with the most enduring 'martial race' label may have secured the fewest overall benefits – with the exception of income – of all the 'martial' groups.

Consequences

While Highlanders, Sikhs and Gurkhas were willing to accept 'martial' identities – or at least, in the case of Gurkhas, to perform them – it seems clear that the ultimate effects were profoundly conservative.[141] At the very least, acceptance of a 'martial race' ideal may have helped mitigate – or at least mute – soldiers' frustrations with the frequently dismal and highly unglamorous conditions of military service in the nineteenth century. Not surprisingly, regimental life seldom bore much resemblance to the tales of daring and adventure which featured so prominently in nineteenth-century popular media. Highland soldiers' own writings, in fact, frequently depict long, brutal marches,[142] disease,[143] overcrowding,[144] extreme cold or heat,[145] and lack of adequate food and water.[146] And although we know that in many respects Highland soldiers' experiences were not representative of either Sikhs' or Gurkhas', in this respect we can be sure that the Indian 'martial races' fared no better. However, if soldiers within the 'martial race' regiments were willing to perform to British expectations about their toughness and their ability to endure even the most severe conditions, their ability to orchestrate vocal and effectual protest of such conditions may have been compromised.

More importantly, when soldiers accepted constructions of themselves as fearless warriors, they effectively bought into a regimental and institutional culture that supported and strengthened the British Empire. Regardless of whether they were inspired by regional or cultural loyalties (as in the cases of Sikhs and Highlanders) these soldiers nevertheless helped, as one poem put it, 'Great Britain's greatness to increase'.[147] Such loyalties, reified by the conscious use of cultural symbols, were safely channelled into regimental competition. Moreover, identification with or acceptance of idealised constructions of themselves – however partial – also may have encouraged individual soldiers to attempt to live up to the past glories of their regiments. Indeed, if the records of late nineteenth- and early twentieth-century colonial warfare are anything to go by, it seems clear that Highland, Sikh and Gurkha regiments all managed to live up to their reputation as 'crack corps'. If this is so, martial race ideology may have been at least partly responsible for shaping soldiers' behaviours in ways that benefited the British state.

In addition to shaping the identities of 'martial race' soldiers, martial race ideology also had an enduring impact on the regional cultures of the Highlands, the Punjab and Nepal. The romanticisation of the Highland soldier, for example, helped to freeze the region of the Highlands in British popular culture as the mythic stage upon which heroes were born.[148] In the nineteenth century and even today, the Highlands came to be so closely associated with the image of the Highland warrior that all other associations – subversive or not – have been obscured. In the Punjab, the British effort to inculcate a Sikh warrior identity within the army helped to encourage a sense of ethnic, religious and cultural difference in the Sikh community as a whole that, ultimately, fanned the flame of communalism in the region.[149] And in Nepal, martial race ideology has encouraged desperately poor families to pin all their hopes on having a son who can succeed – amid the now-fierce competition – in winning a place in the British Army. Moreover, as in the Highlands, the image of the Gurkha soldier is so closely associated with Nepal that all other representations – except, in recent years, that of the Sherpa – have been effectively marginalised. In all three regions, then, the language of martial races overshadowed diverse cultural expressions and obscured massive regional changes brought about by incorporation into the Empire's global reach. Instead, martial race discourse produced a masculinised, stylised vision of these regions and their people that has been extraordinarily difficult to resist both by outsiders and, as we have seen, sometimes even by insiders.

Notes

1 Diana Henderson, 'The Scottish soldier abroad: the sociology of acclimatisation', in Grant G. Simpson (ed.), *The Scottish Soldier Abroad, 1247–1967* (Edinburgh: John Donald, 1992), 123.
2 Kathleen Wilson, *The Island Race: Englishness, Empire, and Gender in the Eighteenth Century* (London: Routledge, 2003), 93. Emphasis mine.
3 Douglas Peers, 'Sepoys, soldiers and the lash: race, caste and army discipline in India, 1820–1850', *Journal of Imperial and Commonwealth History* 23:2 (1995), 213.
4 Major C. J. Morris, *The Gurkhas: An Ethnology* (Delhi: B. R. Publishing Company, 1936), 52.
5 British Library, London (hereafter BL), B.S. 21/21, Alexander G. Stuart, *The Indian Empire: A Short Review and Some Hints for the Use of Soldiers Proceeding to India* (1912), 59.
6 James Cromb, *The Highland Brigade: Its Battles and Its Heroes*, 3rd edn (London: Simkin, Marshall & Co., 1886), 9.
7 For these policies, see Kripal Chandra Yadav, 'British policy towards the Sikhs, 1849–1857', in Gerald Barrier and Ganda Singh (eds), *Punjab Past and Present: Essays in Honour of Dr Ganda Singh* (Patiala: Punjabi University, 1976); also Khushwant Singh, *History of the Sikhs: Volume 2, 1839–1964* (Princeton: Princeton University Press, 1966), esp. ch. 5.
8 Richard Fox, *Lions of the Punjab: Culture in the Making* (Berkeley: University of California Press, 1985), 32.
9 This region included Ferozepore, Ludhiana, Gurdaspur, Amritsar, Jullundur and Hoshiarpur districts. Fox, *Lions of the Punjab*, 31. This region was also inhabited by a large number of Hindu agriculturalists.
10 Fox, *Lions of the Punjab*, 31–32.
11 For a detailed discussion of this process, see Fox, *Lions of the Punjab*, 38–43.
12 J. S. Grewal, *The Sikhs of the Punjab* (Cambridge: Cambridge University Press, 1994), 130–1.
13 Fox, *Lions of the Punjab*, 39, 40. The phrase 'tyranny of the market' is Fox's.
14 For details on land transfers from farmers to money-lenders, as well as government alarm, see John Cell, *Hailey: A Study in British Imperialism, 1872–1969* (Cambridge: Cambridge University Press, 1992).
15 For a thorough history of the canal colonies, and their effect on Punjab society and economy, see Imran Ali, *The Punjab Under Imperialism, 1885–1947* (Princeton: Princeton University Press, 1988).
16 Fox, *Lions of the Punjab*, 62.
17 Fox, *Lions of the Punjab*, 43–44.

18   C. R. W. Falcon, *Handbook on Sikhs For the Use of Regimental Officers* (Allahabad: Pioneer Press, 1896), 105.

19   H. C. P. Rice, 'Notes on the Sikhs as soldiers for our army', *United Services Institution India* 2:57 (1896), 68.

20   For the measures taken to pacify the Highlands, see Alexander Murdoch, *The People Above: Politics and Administration in Mid-Eighteenth Century Scotland* (Edinburgh: John Donald, 1980), 35–38; John Stuart Shaw, *The Management of Scottish Society, 1707–1764* (Edinburgh: John Donald, 1983), 169–179; Rosalind Mitchison, 'The government and the Highlands, 1707–1745', in N. T. Phillipson and Rosalind Mitchison (eds), *Scotland in the Age of Improvement* (Edinburgh: Edinburgh University Press, 1970), 44–45.

21   T. M. Devine, *Clanship to Crofters' War: The Social Transformation of the Scottish Highlands* (Manchester: Manchester University Press, 1994), 31.

22   The most lucrative industries were fishing and kelp harvesting. Devine, *Clanship to Crofters' War*, 37; Diana Henderson, *Highland Soldier: A Social Study of the Highland Regiments, 1820–1920* (Edinburgh: John Donald, 1989), 17.

23   One of the chief reasons for this was the fact that with the re-opening of French markets, kelp (used to make soap) from the Highlands was no longer needed.

24   T. M. Devine, 'The emergence of the new Highland elite in the Western Highlands and Islands, 1800–1860', in Devine (ed.), *Improvement and Enlightenment* (Edinburgh: John Donald, 1989); Eric Richards, *A History of the Highland Clearances, Volume 2: Emigration, Protest, Reasons* (London: Croom Helm, 1985).

25   On emigration to North America, see Eric Richards, 'Scotland and the uses of the Atlantic Empire', in Bernard Bailyn and Philip Morgan (eds), *Strangers Within the Realm: Cultural Margins of the First British Empire* (Chapel Hill: University of North Carolina Press, 1991); on migration to the Lowlands, see Charles Withers, 'Highland clubs and Gaelic chapels: Glasgow's Gaelic community in the eighteenth century', *Scottish Geographical Magazine* 100 (1984).

26   T. M. Devine, 'The transformation of Gaeldom', in *Clanship to Crofters' War*, 37; Henderson, *Highland Soldier*, 17.

27   Henderson, *Highland Soldier*, 18.

28   This is a point of some controversy. Diana Henderson suggests that the men who enlisted in Highland regiments tended to be of a better class than recruits who enlisted in English regiments, and there is some evidence to support this claim. On the other hand, Alan Skelley and Edward Spiers believe that Scottish recruiting was far more similar to English recruiting in terms of class base. My own research tends to support the latter claim. Random sampling from the Gordon Highlander discharge papers (1855–72) suggests that the majority of recruits were young (under twenty-one) labourers when they enlisted, with a significant number claiming no occupation at all. See Public Record Office, Kew (hereafter PRO), WO 97/1658. Diaries from other soldiers suggest that difficulty drove them into service.

29   Cromb, *The Highland Brigade*, 9; 'The heroes of Perthshire', *Blackwood's Magazine* 184 (Nov. 1908), 647.

30   One example of many is E. D. Smith's *Johnny Gurkha: Friends in the Hills* (London: Leo Cooper, 1985).

31   Lionel Caplan, *Warrior Gentlemen: 'Gurkhas' in the Western Imagination* (Providence: Berghahn Books, 1995), 17, 19.

32   For a summary of the Nepali government's evolving perceptions of itself as a nation vis-à-vis British India, see Richard Burghart, 'The concept of nation-state in Nepal', *Journal of Asian Studies* 44:1 (Nov. 1984), 114–116.

33   Caplan, *Warrior Gentlemen*, 20.

34   Purushottam Banksota, *The Gurkha Connection: A History of the Gurkha Recruitment in the British Army* (Jaipur: Nirala Books, 1994), 30.

35   Banksota, *The Gurkha Connection*, 27, 61.

36   Michael Hutt, 'A hero or a traitor? The Gurkha soldier in Nepali literature', *South Asia Research* 9:1 (May 1989), 22. J. P. Cross and Buddhiman Gurung stress the same thing for the present in *Gurkhas at War: In their Own Words* (London: Greenhill,

2002), 16.
37 As late as 1989 literacy in Nepal was still below 30 per cent. Hutt, 'A hero or a traitor', 23.
38 Banksota, *The Gurkha Connection*, 30.
39 Caplan, *Warrior Gentlemen*, 21.
40 Brian Robson (ed.), *Roberts in India: The Military Papers of Field Marshal Lord Roberts, 1876–1893* (Phoenix Mill: Alan Sutton, 1993), 370.
41 Banksota, *The Gurkha Connection*, 101–102; Nanda Shrestha, *Landlessness and Migration in Nepal* (Boulder: Westview Press, 1990), 84.
42 This was especially true just after Shamsher resorted to these tactics in 1886. Banksota, *The Gurkha Connection*, 94.
43 Mary des Chene, 'Relics of empire: a cultural history of the Gurkhas, 1815–1987' (Ph.D. dissertation, Stanford University, 1991), 247.
44 Shrestha, *Landlessness and Migration in Nepal*, 184.
45 Caplan, *Warrior Gentlemen*, 6.
46 David Omissi (ed.), *Indian Voices of the Great War: Soldiers' Letters, 1914–18* (London: Macmillan, 1999), 1, 2, 4.
47 Hutt, 'A hero or a traitor?', 23.
48 Thanks to David Omissi, many of these letters are available in published form, in his *Indian Voices of the Great War*.
49 Omissi (ed.), *Indian Voices*, 5.
50 See Gayatri Spivak, 'Can the subaltern speak?', in Cary Nelson and Lawrence Grossberg (eds), *Marxism and the Interpretation of Culture* (Urbana: University of Illinois Press, 1988).
51 The goal of understanding subaltern classes as 'principal actors' was set out in the very first volume of *Subaltern Studies*. See Ranajit Guha, 'On some aspects of the historiography of colonial India', *Subaltern Studies I: Writings on South Asian History and Society* (Delhi: Oxford University Press, 1982), 4.
52 Antoinette Burton, *At the Heart of the Empire: Indians and the Colonial Encounter in Late-Victorian Britain* (Berkeley: University of California Press, 1998), 18.
53 Burton, *At the Heart of the Empire*, 15, 20; also Wilson, *The Island Race*, 3.
54 For an excellent example of the way these unequal relations played out in the United States, see Matthew Guterl, *The Color of Race in America: 1900–1940* (Cambridge: Harvard University Press, 2002).
55 Wilson, *The Island Race*, 3.
56 Wilson's chapter on T. C. Phillips is particularly evocative in this regard. See ch. 4, 'The black widow: gender, race and performance in England and Jamaica', in *The Island Race*.
57 Des Chene, 'Relics of empire', 118–119.
58 David Omissi, *The Sepoy and the Raj: The Indian Army, 1860–1940* (London: Macmillan, 1994), 100.
59 Mary des Chene, 'Language and practice in the colonial Indian Army', paper given at the Institute for Global Studies in Culture, Power, and History, Johns Hopkins University, Autumn 1993, 39; Caplan, *Warrior Gentlemen*, 276.
60 Tod Ragsdale, *Once a Hermit Kingdom: Ethnicity, Education and National Integration in Nepal* (New Delhi: Manohar, 1989), 50.
61 Fox, *Lions of the Punjab*, 141.
62 J. S. Grewal, *The Sikhs of the Punjab: The New Cambridge History of India, Volume II.3*, rev. edn (Cambridge: Cambridge University Press, 1999), 77; W. H. McLeod, *The Sikhs: History, Religion, and Society* (New York: Columbia University Press, 1989), 4.
63 Fox, *Lions of the Punjab*, 142; Omissi, *The Sepoy and the Raj*, 96.
64 Ann Laura Stoler, *Carnal Knowledge and Imperial Power: Race and the Intimate in Colonial Rule* (Berkeley: University of California Press, 2002), 170. Here, Stoler is summing up subaltern studies, not agreeing with it.
65 Stoler, *Carnal Knowledge and Imperial Power*, 183.
66 National Army Museum, London (hereafter NAM), 7703-26, Private McIntosh, 92nd Highlanders, Journal of service in India (1876–77), 5 Jan. 1877.

67 McIntosh, Journal of service in India, 5 Jan. 1877.
68 McIntosh, Journal of service in India, 5 Jan. 1877.
69 Gordon Highlander Museum, Aberdeen (hereafter GHM), PB 180, William Marr, Diary in Chitral and Tirah campaigns, loose paper in frontispiece (1895–97).
70 Commander-in-Chief in India at the time.
71 Black Watch Museum, Perth (hereafter BWM), Accession #421, Private Archibald W. McIntosh, Diary in India (1858–68), 1 Jan. 1861. Private Alexander Robb also copied out this speech in his *Reminiscences of a Veteran: Being the Experiences of a Private Soldier in the Crimea, and During the Indian Mutiny* (1888), BWM, O/NO795, Accession #6161, 124–125.
72 BWM, Accession #0214, David McAusland, Diary while in the 42nd (1848–60), 54.
73 Commander-in-Chief of South African forces, formerly CIC in India (1885–93), and soon to be CIC Britain (1901–4).
74 BWM, Accession #648, Private E. Finch, 42nd Black Watch Highlanders, Diary kept during the Boer War, 10 Feb. 1900. Private Fred Bly also recorded Lord Roberts's words to his regiment, the Seaforth Highlanders (72nd), when they were reviewed on 10 Jan. 1900. See his Diary in Boer War (1899–1900), NAM, 7310-85.
75 This was by no means true of all Sikh letter-writers, however. Some, instead, expressed their deep dissatisfaction with the carnage of the war, and tried to discourage friends and family from enlisting. For examples, see the letters in Omissi (ed), *Indian Voices*, 37, 102, 147, 251, 271, 305.
76 Kartar Singh to Punjab, 22 Jan. 1916, in Omissi (ed.), *Indian Voices*, 142–143.
77 Ressaldar Jewan Singh to Punjab, 4 March, 1917, in Omissi (ed.), *Indian Voices*, 280.
78 Jewan Singh, in Omissi (ed.) *Indian Voices*, 280.
79 Jemadar Indar Singh to Punjab, 15 Sept. 1916, in Omissi (ed.), *Indian Voices*, 234–235.
80 Jemadar Ganda Singh to Punjab, 5 May 1916, in Omissi (ed.) *Indian Voices*, 181–182.
81 G. Urquhart notes a similar willingness to take on a 'Highland' identity among recruits to the Highland regiments during the First World War. See his 'Negotiations for war: Highland identity under fire', in B. Taithe and T. Thornton (eds), *War: Identities in Conflict, 1300–2000* (Gloucestershire: Sutton Publishing, 1998), 168–169.
82 General Viscount Wolseley, *The Soldier's Pocket-Book for Field Service*, 2nd and 5th edns (London: Macmillan & Co., 1871 and 1886), 1.
83 These journals represented the 71st, 92nd Gordons, 93rd Highlanders, and 79th Cameron Highlanders, respectively. All of them began publication in the 1890s.
84 Robert Giddings, 'Delusive seduction: pride, pomp, circumstance and military music', in John MacKenzie (ed.), *Popular Imperialism and the Military* (Manchester: Manchester University Press, 1992).
85 NAM, 7107, 23-1 and 23-2, Corporal George Patrick, Manuscripts on service with the 78th Regiment (1865–67).
86 Wolseley, *The Soldier's Pocket-Book for Field Service*, 4.
87 Urquhart, 'Negotiations for war', 160.
88 Lieutenant MacDowell, 19 Jan. 1858, in Captain Coghill, Lieutenant Macdowell and 'Shiny' Williams, *Letters from the Field During the Indian Mutiny* (London: Waterlow & Sons, 1907), 72.
89 Truth, 'The honour of the trews', *Highland Light Infantry Chronicle* 1:1 (Jan. 1893), 32.
90 NAM, Corporal George Patrick, Manuscripts on service with the 78th Regiment.
91 NAM, 7310-85, Private Fred Bly, 72nd Seaforth Highlanders, Diary in Boer War, 16 March 1900.
92 Fred Bly, 16 March 1900.
93 Fred Bly, 17 March 1900.
94 On Scotland and Empire, see John MacKenzie, 'Empire and national identities: the case of Scotland', *Transactions of the Royal Historical Society* 4:6 (1998), and his 'Essay and reflection: on Scotland and the Empire', *International History Review* 15:4 (1993).
95 GHM, PB 180, William Marr, Diary in Chitral and Tirah campaigns, no date, 1895.

96   Marr, Diary in Chitral and Tirah campaigns, loose paper in frontispiece, 1897.
97   These include 'A Scottish Ballad', 'Ballad for a Friend in the 93rd' and 'When the Author Left His Native Land'. Argyll and Sutherland Highlander Museum, Stirling (hereafter ASHM), N-C93 GRE, Diary of Private George Grieg, 93rd Highlanders.
98   Omissi, *The Sepoy and the Raj*, 78.
99   W. H. McLeod, *Exploring Sikhism: Aspects of Sikh Identity, Culture, and Thought* (New Delhi: Oxford University Press, 2000), 60.
100 Gurbachan Singh Talib, 'Some fundamental doctrines of Sikhism', in Wazir Singh (ed.), *Sikhism and Punjab's Heritage* (Patiala: Punjabi University Publication Bureau, 1990), 64; McLeod, *Exploring Sikhism*, 81. Not all Sikhs were Keshdharis. Others, called Sahajdharis, followed the teachings of the first nine Gurus and did not wear their hair long. However, by the late nineteenth century Sikh identity was coming to be much more firmly identified with Khalsas, while Sahajdharis were increasingly associated with Hinduism. See Surinder S. Jodkha, 'The Sikh identity in historical perspective', in M. Ramakrishnayya (ed.) *Historical Memories and Nation Building in India* (Hyderabad: Hum Sab Hindustani Trust and Booklinks Corp, 2001), 149.
101 McLeod, *Exploring Sikhism*, 74.
102 Omissi, *The Sepoy and the Raj*, 82.
103 Omissi, *The Sepoy and the Raj*, 81, 83.
104 Inspector of Police Eshar Singh to Jemadar Jai Singh, 19 Jan. 1916, in Omissi (ed.), *Indian Voices*, 140–141.
105 Sikh soldier to Mahant Partab Das, in Omissi (ed.), *Indian Voices*, 110.
106 Balwant Singh (Sikh) to Jammeja Singh in Punjab, 25 Feb. 1917, in Omissi (ed.), *Indian Voices*, 279.
107 Sham Singh to friend in Punjab, 30 July 1916, in Omissi (ed.), *Indian Voices*, 212–213.
108 Bakhlawar Singh to friend in Punjab, 23 Aug. 1916, in Omissi (ed.), *Indian Voices*, 227.
109 Lance Dafadar Chattar Singh to Punjab, 15 Oct. 1917, in Omissi (ed.), *Indian Voices*, 325.
110 Dafadar Nathan Singh to soldier in Punjab, 18 April 1916, in Omissi (ed.), *Indian Voices*, 177.
111 Ressaldar Jowan Singh to Punjab, 10 Dec. 1917, in Omissi (ed.), *Indian Voices*, 340.
112 Jemadar Ganda Singh to friend in Punjab, 5 May 1916, in Omissi (ed.), *Indian Voices*, 181–182.
113 Omissi, *The Sepoy and the Raj*, 89, 96.
114 Ethne Marenco, *The Transformation of Sikh Society* (Portland: HaPi Press, 1974), 141.
115 Grewal, *The Sikhs of the Punjab*, 137, 138.
116 Jodkha, 'The Sikh identity in historical perspective', 152.
117 Subedar-Major Sundar Singh Bahadur, in Omissi (ed.), *Indian Voices*, 111.
118 Significantly, this fund was also supposed to benefit Gurkha soldiers. Some of the members of the committee included Lord Roberts himself and Rudyard Kipling. See India Office Library and Records, London (hereafter OIOL), L/MIL/7/15901, Papers on the 'Indian Heroes Fund' and 'Sikh Memorial Fund' for the benefit of native soldiers and families after the N.W. frontier operations (1897–98).
119 Highlanders also served as the King's guard of honour.
120 Omissi notes that most Indian soldiers – regardless of religion or origin – did not express themselves in terms of the Indian nation. Omissi (ed.), *Indian Voices*, 19.
121 Risalder Jiwan Singh to Punjab, 10 Dec. 1917, in Omissi (ed.), *Indian Voices*, 339.
122 Kishan Singh to son, 2 Nov. 1917, in Omissi (ed.), *Indian Voices*, 330.
123 Inspector of Police Eshar Singh to Jemadar Jai Singh, 19 Jan. 1916, in Omissi (ed.), *Indian Voices*, 141.
124 This phenomenon was not limited to Sikhs. Omissi (ed.), *Indian Voices*, 20.
125 Wounded Sikh to brother in Punjab, 15 Jan. 1915, in Omissi (ed.), *Indian Voices*, 28.
126 Risaldar Dayal Singh to Punjab, 14 July 1917, in Omissi (ed.), *Indian Voices*, 302–303.

127 Balwant Singh to Punjab, 21 Jan. 1917, in Omissi (ed.), *Indian Voices*, 271. For the letter about worshipping the picture, see 275.
128 Caplan, *Warrior Gentlemen*, 34.
129 Ragsdale, *Once a Hermit Kingdom*, 48. While Gurungs were only one of the four groups targeted by the British (the others were Magars, Limbus and Rais), Alan MacFarlane argues that they 'overlap in origins and culture with many of the neighbouring tribes' in *Resources and Population: A Study of the Gurungs of Nepal* (Cambridge: Cambridge University Press, 1976), 12.
130 MacFarlane, *Resources and Population*, 21; Des Chene, 'Relics of empire', 70, 333, 229.
131 Des Chene, 'Relics of empire', 240.
132 Caplan, *Warrior Gentlemen*, 37.
133 Des Chene, 'Relics of empire', 246, 247.
134 This is a continuing problem. Caplan notes studies that show from a third to a half of soldiers who survive their terms of service never return to Nepal. Caplan, *Warrior Gentlemen*, 43.
135 Des Chene, 'Relics of empire', 333, quote on 330.
136 Des Chene, 'Relics of empire', 311; Caplan, *Warrior Gentlemen*, 138.
137 Caplan, *Warrior Gentlemen*, 146.
138 Gurkha soldier to Gurkha soldier in France, 7 Feb. 1915, in Omissi (ed.), *Indian Voices*, 35. Note that the soldier still mentioned help to family as the first priority.
139 Ernestine McHugh emphasises the primacy of kin relationships and responsibilities among the Gurungs in 'Concepts of the person among Gurungs of Nepal', *American Ethnologist* 16:1 (Febrary 1989), 78.
140 Caplan, *Gentlemen Warriors*, 138.
141 David McCrone, *Understanding Scotland: The Sociology of a Stateless Nation* (London: Routledge, 1992), 186.
142 GHM, PB 157, Robert Bruce McEwen, Diary during Mutiny, 12 Sept. 1858; GHM, PB 180, William Marr, Diary in Chitral and Tirah campaigns, 1 and 18 Oct. 1897.
143 Robb, *Reminiscences of a Veteran*, 89–90.
144 NAM, 7107, Corporal George Patrick, Manuscripts on service with the 78th Regiment.
145 GHM, PB 2476, Captain John Lewis Randolph Gordon, Diary during Tirah campaign, 7 Oct. 1897; GHM, PB 173, Private Peter McRae, Letters during Sudan campaign, 1 June 1884.
146 NAM, 7310-85, Private Fred Bly, Diary in Boer War, 18 Jan. 1900; ASHM, N-B93-DUG 16205, William Duguid, Diary.
147 J. Gilchrist, 'A soldier's farewell to his native home', *Tiger and Sphinx* 1 (15 Jan. 15), 7.
148 Charles Withers, 'The historical creation of the Highlands', in Ian Donnachie and Christopher Whatley (eds), *The Manufacture of Scottish History* (Edinburgh: Polygon, 1992), 143.
149 Jodkha, 'The Sikh identity in historical perspective', 151–152.

CONCLUSION

This project has taken as its focus the strenuous efforts of key figures within the British and Indian armies to shape the recruiting base of both forces in the wake of the 1857 Rebellion through the discourse of martial races. Yet just how successful were these endeavours? In the end, did these military figures realise their goals?

The answer seems to be both yes and no. Clearly, as Susan Thorne has noted, 'social imperial policies rarely produced the results their makers intended',[1] and this case is no exception. In India, as we have seen, advocates of martial race policy were able to shift profoundly and dramatically the recruiting base of the army to the populations of the north and north-west in the last quarter of the nineteenth century. By 1914, a stunning three-quarters of the Indian Army hailed from populations believed to produce 'martial races'.[2] And despite the political and strategic motivations of this shift, through the use of the language of scientific racism such people also played an important role in shaping the structure of racial discourse on the subcontinent.

Yet in spite of such success, martial race discourse remained fractured and vulnerable to the very anxieties which had produced it in the first place. Indeed, for all its confidence and bluster, the discourse surrounding martial race ideology – like the 'new imperial' jingoism itself – was as much about anxieties of performance and persuasion as it was about conviction.[3] Worries over whether the 'martial races' would themselves some day degenerate, or whether these 'races' would in fact really be able to stand up to a European enemy, crept into military writings as quickly as martial race discourse attempted to ease them with its seamless narratives of confidence. One officer, writing in 1890, anxiously fretted over the emasculating effects British 'civilisation' might bring to even the most martial of races. Looking into the near future, he argued:

> We must now look for the flower of our native army among peoples who have more recently come under our rule, and whom the blessings of the 'Pax Britannica' have not yet enervated as well as tranquilised ... Nor can we hope that even those races whom we now rely upon to provide us with sturdy warriors can escape the influences to which their predecessors have succumbed.[4]

Peace, in this man's estimate, was no boon to an empire that needed to maintain the fiercest of warriors.

Others agreed, adding the nagging fear that in addition to the degeneration of martial abilities over time, it was possible that no Indian troops – not even the martial races – would be able to stand the pressures of a European war:

> There are not wanting men of discernment who hold the view that no natives of India would stand the fire of modern arms under the conditions of modern battle. The Sikhs, however, proved their worth on the battlefields of the Punjab sixty years ago, whilst the Gurkhas offered a stout resistance to our arms in 1813. But the numbers of these brave and warlike soldiers are limited, and we already recruit them probably to their utmost capacity. Moreover, the Sikhs are diminishing in numbers and probably losing their warlike attributes. Under the beneficent operation of a long period of peace, it is at least questionable whether their quality is what they proved it to be on the battlefield of Chillianwala [during the Second Sikh War in 1848].[5]

Despite their supposed martial abilities, this writer suggested, Sikhs and Gurkhas had only ever been tested against Europeans once each, sixty and ninety years earlier. How they would conduct themselves in the present, he argued, was a matter open to question and genuine concern.

Even Lord Roberts, martial race enthusiast and advocate *par excellence*, found himself anxiously pondering the possibility that the Punjab Frontier Force – that haven of manly warriors – was falling subject to degeneration. In a letter to General Lockhart, he asked: 'Do you think [the] physique of the men in the Punjab Frontier Force regiments is as good as formerly, and are the corps as efficient? I may be mistaken, but, with the exception of the 5th Gurkhas and the 3rd Sikhs, I thought I could detect a falling off.'[6] No sooner, in fact, did martial race discourse and policy win hegemony in India than it began to succumb to the anxieties of race against which it pitted itself. Once, Bengali Brahmins had been considered martial, and now Bengal produced not soldiers but some of the most virulent critics of British imperial rule. Could the same thing some day happen to Sikhs and Gurkhas?

In Britain, the successes of martial race discourse and military intervention in popular culture were even more ambiguous. As we know, despite the best efforts of some officers, the military in Britain was unable to improve substantially the number and quality of recruits entering the service annually. Perhaps the single most important factor in this failure was the inability of the military administration to secure adequate pay for its men. As a result, at the turn of the century the Army Medical Service's report bewailed the 'disturbing and disquieting' fact that 'a very large proportion of the men who offer themselves for enlistment in the Army are found to be physically unfit for military service'.[7] In light of the hostile climate between Britain and Europe this was a serious problem indeed, for the report solemnly declared that 'no nation was ever yet for any long time great and free, when the army it put into the field no longer represented its own virility and manhood'.[8]

Yet while it cannot be said that the military achieved its goals for recruiting, in many ways the efforts of the military and its most conspicuous figures did contribute to the rehabilitation of the popular image of both soldiers and war. To be sure, the three decades preceding the outbreak of the First World War were marked by popular approval for soldiers, the military, and the prospect of a European conflict. Invasion literature, military parades and pageantry, the Boy Scout movement, and widespread popular participation in the Volunteer movement were undeniably visible features of this era.[9]

Surely, military efforts to popularise the army played a role in helping to create this more militaristic popular culture. Through propaganda like martial race discourse, references to the gritty realities of military service in the Empire were patently written out of military despatches and popular stories alike. The prospects of disease, physical hardship and death gave way to promises of glory and adventure in exotic places. Soldiers (especially in their most popular guise as Highlanders) increasingly symbolised the ideal qualities of imperial masculinity – loyalty, hardiness, gallantry and bravery. At the outbreak of the First World War, such deliberate use of the popular media to increase its recruiting efforts finally seemed richly rewarded by the throngs of recruits from all classes and backgrounds who rushed to the colours, hoping to 'fight the good fight' and to taste glory and adventure. That Highland soldiers still featured strongly in this imagination of glory and adventure was borne out by the propaganda posters of the day, one of which depicted a kilted Highland soldier dressed in a khaki jacket, war-worn but proudly carrying a large British flag. The caption urged Britons to support the war financially, declaring: 'He carried the flag to Victory. Share his Glory by buying National War Bonds.'[10]

Finally, what of the groups who had been targeted as 'martial races'? In the context of the late Victorian British Empire, Highlanders, Sikhs and Gurkhas were identified so strongly with the attributes and values of martialness that alternative constructions of their identities and realities all but disappeared from public discourse. They became, in effect, the alter ego of British men – the colonised, simple, violence-prone imperial subjects who would fight Britain's battles without question. As a result, both the military and the British public found it increasingly easy to ignore the social realities behind Highland, Sikh and Gurkha enlistment in the military, which included, most importantly, economic hardship and lack of viable alternatives. Surely we must be compelled to admit this phenomenon as one of the successes – however insidious – of martial race ideology. Even now, a century after the zenith of martial race ideology's influence, all three regions and their peoples are still widely and most popularly known for their connections to a warrior past and an exotic imperial pageantry.

Notes

1 Susan Thorne, *Protestant Ethics and the Spirit of Imperialism: Congregational Missions and the Making of an Imperial Culture in Nineteenth-Century England* (Stanford: Stanford University Press, 1999), 54. Here, she is paraphrasing Geoff Eley.
2 David Omissi, *The Sepoy and the Raj: The Indian Army, 1860–1914* (London: Macmillan, 1994), 19.
3 Sara Suleri has argued that the confident narratives of British imperial rule in fact masked deep fears and anxieties about the precariousness of that rule. Sara Suleri, *The Rhetoric of English India* (Chicago: University of Chicago Press, 1992).
4 C. F. Lance, 'Recruiting for the native army', *United Services Institution of India* 19 (1890), 386.
5 Punjabi, 'The Indian Army as it is', *United Services Magazine* 31 (1905), 374.
6 India Office Library and Records, London, L/MIL/17/5/1615/12, F. S. Roberts, Correspondence and minutes while in India (1877–93), Roberts to Major. Gen. Sir William Lockhart, Dec. 1891.
7 House of Commons, 'Memorandum by the Director-General, Army Medical Service, on the physical unfitness of men offering themselves for enlistment in the army', *Sessional Papers* 1903, vol. XXXVIII [cd. 1501], 921.
8 'Memorandum by the Director-General, Army Medical Service, on the physical unfitness of men offering themselves for enlistment in the army', 921.
9 See Cecil Eby, *The Road to Armageddon: The Martial Spirit in English Popular Literature, 1870–1914* (Durham: Duke University Press, 1987); Michael C. C. Adams, *The Great Adventure: Male Desire and the Coming of World War I* (Bloomington: Indiana University Press, 1990).
10 United Services Museum, Ref. # 1990.27, Recruiting poster for the First World War.

SELECT BIBLIOGRAPHY

The material for this book has been drawn from a wide variety of primary and secondary sources. This list contains only a sample of some of the most important or repeatedly cited material. For a complete list of all sources used, for references to Parliamentary Papers, and for articles and items from newspapers, journals and regimental magazines, readers should consult the notes for each chapter.

Primary sources

Argyll and Sutherland Highlander Museum, Stirling
William Duguid papers. N-B93-DUG 16205.
Nationality returns, 91st Highlanders. R-D1.SCE.05065a.
George Greig papers. N-C93 GRE.

Black Watch Museum, Perth
Private E. Finch diary. Accession #648.
David McAusland diary while in the 42nd. Accession #0214.
Private A. W. McIntosh diary. Accession #421.
Alexander Robb reminiscences. Catalog #O/NO795, Accession #6161.

British Library, London
Stuart, Alexander G. *The Indian Empire: A Short Review and Some Hints for the Use of Soldiers Proceeding to India* (1912). B.S. 21/21.
War Office. Regulations for recruiting the regular army (1900).
War Office. Regulations for recruiting the regular army (1907).

Gordon Highlanders Museum, Aberdeen
Charles William Booker letters. PB 2006/1/2.
Captain John Lewis Randolph Gordon diary. PB 2476.
William Marr diary. PB 180.
Robert Bruce McEwen diary. PB 157.
Private Peter McRae letters. PB 173.

India Office Library, London
Classes of men of the native army who have best withstood the hardships of the Afghan campaign (1881). L/MIL/7/7018.
Despatches re. organization of army and strength of forces for India (1861). L/MIL/5/525.
Eden Commission report (1879). L/MIL/17/5/1687.
General Orders by the Commander in Chief (1858). L/MIL/17/2/307.

General Orders India. General Orders for the military for 1857. L/MIL/17/2/306.

General Orders India. Order of merit proceedings (1893). L/MIL/7/5343, 5349, 5356.

General Orders India. Summary of measures considered or carried out in the military department of the Government of India (1899). L/MIL/17/5/1616.

General Orders Punjab. Report on the size of the Punjab force (1860). MSS Eur F 90.

Frederick Haines. Memorandum on the report of the special army commission (1880). L/MIL/17/5/1698.

H. Hudson. Recruiting in India before and during the war of 1914–18 (1919). L/MIL/17/5/2152.

'Indian heroes fund' and 'Sikh memorial fund' for the benefit of native soldiers and families after the N.W. Frontier operations (1897–98). L/MIL/7/15901.

John Lawrence. Correspondence. MSS Eur C 203/1.

Memorandum of important affairs carried out or considered by the Government of India in the Military Department (1891–92). L/MIL/17/5/1614.

Charles Napier. Report following the conquest of the Punjab (1849). MSS Eur C 0123.

F. S. Roberts. Correspondence and minutes while in India (1877–93). L/MIL/17/5/1615/6.

F. S. Roberts. On the desirability of clearly defining the principles on which the administration of the army in India should be based (1893). L/MIL/7/7056.

F. S. Roberts printed papers. MSS Eur D 734.

L. O. Smith journal during the Mutiny (1857). MSS Eur C 718.

Telegrams to Lord Clyde during Mutiny (1857). MSS Eur C 124/19.

Vote of thanks from the House of Commons for the campaign in Afghanistan (1881). L/MIL/5/689.

Sir George White papers (1879–1905). MSS Eur F 108.

National Army Museum, London

John Blockley. 'Jessie's dream: or the relief of Lucknow. A descriptive fantasia'. Sheet Music, 8310-74.

Private Fred Bly diary in Boer War (1899–1900). 7310-85.

J. Fairweather. Through the Mutiny with the 4th Punjab Infantry, Punjab Irregular Force. Memoir, date unknown. 7305-9.

R. H. Gall letters in the Sikh War and the Mutiny (1848–58). 92 GAL.

Private McIntosh, 92nd Highlanders, journal of service in India (1876–77). 7703-26.

Corporal George Patrick. Manuscripts on service with the 78th Regiment (1865–67). 7107, 23-1 and 23-2.

Brevet-Major R. Poore letters in Indian Mutiny (1854–58). 9504-22.

Frederick Roberts letters while commanding in Afghanistan (1878–81). 7101-23-101-1.

Frederick Roberts speeches and printed works. 7101-23-126-1.

Frederick Roberts scrapbooks. 7101-23-139-10.

Sir Alexander Taylor letters. 7605-21.

National Library of Scotland, Edinburgh

Bertie, 4th Earl of Minto. Letters to family during the Second Afghan War under Lord Roberts (1879). MSS 12536–40.

Observations about the improvements and reformation of the West Highlands made in the year 1754: remarks on the improvement of the land &C (1754). MSS 17504, fos 56–74.

William Blackwood papers. MS 30687 C, 4352, 4340, 4618, 4519, 4575.

Public Record Office, Kew

British Army, half-yearly inspection returns (1857). WO 27:468.

Discharge papers, Gordon Highlanders (1855–72). WO 97:1658.

Fees to pensioners for bringing in recruits (1857). WO 32:6879.

John Robert Godley. Memorandum on the means of recruiting the army, and on an army reserve (Confidential) (1859). WO 33:7 #29.

Home rule affairs in Scotland, Wales, Ireland. 30/69/1826.

India and her future military organization, in a series of letters addressed to Sir Joshua Walmsley (Confidential) (1858). WO 33:6A #101.

Methods, advertising in press and post office and rewards (1881–82). WO 32:6886.

On recruiting (1874). WO 33:26 #569.

Reports from the inspecting officers of recruiting districts (1871). WO 33:22.

Report of the committee on recruiting (1875). WO 33:27 #585.

Lord Roberts. Four papers recently prepared or referred to by General Lord Roberts with reference to subjects connected with the report on terms and conditions of service in the army (1892). WO 33:52 #244.

Lieutenant-Colonel Frederick Roberts. Memorandum on the employment of soldiers in the several government offices, state railways, &c, &c, with a view to the formation of an efficient reserve. WO 105/41.

Lord Wantage. Terms and conditions of service in the army (recruiting) (1892). WO 33:52 #226.

Rare Book, Manuscript and Special Collections, Duke University

Sir Reginald Pole-Carew papers.

Frederick Roberts papers.

James George Smith Neill papers.

Evelyn Wood papers.

Secondary sources

Contemporary

Bingley, C. A. H. *Handbooks for the Indian Army: Sikhs*. Simla: Government Central Printing Office, 1899.

Coghill, Captain, Lieutenant Macdowell and 'Shiny' Williams. *Letters from the Field During the Indian Mutiny*. London: Waterlow & Sons, 1907.

Falcon, Captain R. W. *Handbook on Sikhs For the Use of Regimental Officers*. Allahabad: Pioneer Press, 1896.

Goodenough, W. H. and J. C. Dalton. *The Army Book for the British Empire: A*

Record of the Development and Present Composition of the Military Forces and Their Duties in Peace and War. London: Harrison & Sons, 1893.

Hensman, Howard. *The Afghan War of 1879-80*. London: H. Allen & Co., 1881.

Roberts, Frederick. *Letters Written During the Indian Mutiny*. New Delhi: Lal Publishers, reprinted 1979.

—— *Forty-One Years in India: From Subaltern to Commander-in-Chief*. London: Macmillian & Co., 1921 (first published in 1897 by Richard Bentley & Son).

Wolseley, Garnet. *The Soldier's Pocket-Book for Field Service*, 2nd and 5th edns. London: Macmillan & Co., 1871 and 1886.

Unpublished

Des Chene, Mary. 'Relics of empire: a cultural history of the Gurkhas, 1815-1987'. Unpublished Ph.D. Dissertation, Stanford University, 1991.

—— 'Language and practice in the colonial Indian Army'. Paper presented at the Institute for Global Studies in Culture, Power and History, Johns Hopkins University, 1993.

Published

Adams, R. J. Q. 'Field Marshal Earl Roberts: army and empire'. In J. A. Thompson and Arthur Mejia (eds), *Edwardian Conservatism: Five Studies in Adaptation*. London: Croom Helm, 1988.

Ali, Imran. *The Punjab Under Imperialism, 1885–1947*. Princeton: Princeton University Press, 1988.

Ballhatchet, Kenneth. *Race, Sex, and Class Under the Raj: Imperial Attitudes and Policies and their Critics, 1793–1905*. London: Weidenfeld and Nicolson, 1980.

Banksota, Purushottam. *The Gurkha Connection: A History of the Gurkha Recruitment in the British Army*. Jaipur: Nirala, 1994.

Bartlett, C. J. *Defence and Diplomacy: Britain and the Great Powers, 1815–1914*. Manchester: Manchester University Press, 1993.

Barua, Pradeep. 'Inventing race: the British and India's martial races'. *The Historian* 58:1 (Autumn 1995).

Brasted, Howard. 'Indian nationalist development and the influence of Irish Home Rule, 1870–1886'. *Modern Asian Studies* 14:1 (1980).

Brown, Lucy. *Victorian News and Newspapers*. Oxford: Clarendon, 1985.

Burton, Antoinette. *Burdens of Empire: British Feminists, Indian Women, and Imperial Culture, 1865–1915*. Chapel Hill: University of North Carolina Press, 1994.

—— *At the Heart of the Empire: Indians and the Colonial Encounter in Late-Victorian Britain*. Berkeley: University of California Press, 1998.

Caplan, Lionel. 'Martial Gurkhas: the persistence of a British military discourse on "race"'. In Peter Robb (ed.), *The Concept of Race in South Asia*. New Delhi: Oxford University Press, 1995.

—— *Warrior Gentlemen: 'Gurkhas' in the Western Imagination*. Providence: Berghahn Books, 1995.

Chamberlain, Muriel. *Pax Britannica? British Foreign Policy, 1789–1914*. London: Longman, 1988.

Chowdhury, Indira. *The Frail Hero and Virile History: Gender and the Politics of*

Culture in Colonial Bengal. Delhi: Oxford University Press, 1998.

Clyde, Robert. *From Rebel to Hero: The Image of the Highlander, 1745–1830*. East Linton: Tuckwell Press, 1995.

Cook, Scott. 'The Irish Raj: social origins and careers of Irishmen in the Indian Civil Service, 1885–1914'. *Journal of Social History* 21 (Spring 1987).

—— *Imperial Affinities: Nineteenth Century Analogies and Exchanges Between India and Ireland*. New Delhi: Sage Publications, 1993.

Curtis, L. Perry Jr. *Apes and Angels: The Irishman in Victorian Caricature*, rev. edn. Washington: Smithsonian Institution Press, 1997.

Dawson, Graham. *Soldier Heroes: British Adventure, Empire and the Imagining of Masculinities*. London: Routledge, 1994.

Devine, T. M. *Clanship to Crofters' War: The Social Transformation of the Scottish Highlands*. Manchester: Manchester University Press, 1994.

Enloe, Cynthia. *Ethnic Soldiers: State Security in Divided Societies*. Athens: University of Georgia Press, 1980.

Fox, Richard. *Lions of the Punjab: Culture in the Making*. Berkeley: University of California Press, 1985.

Fraser, T. G. 'Ireland and India'. In Keith Jeffery (ed.), *An Irish Empire? Aspects of Ireland and the British Empire*. Manchester: Manchester University Press, 1996.

Gillard, David. *The Struggle for Asia, 1828–1914: A Study in British and Russian Imperialism*. London: Methuen, 1977.

Girouard, Mark. *Return to Camelot: Chivalry and the English Gentlemen*. New Haven: Yale University Press, 1981.

Gold, John and Margaret Gold. *Imagining Scotland: Tradition, Representation and Promotion in Scottish Tourism Since 1750*. Aldershot: Scolar Press, 1995.

Grewal, J. S. *The Sikhs of the Punjab: The New Cambridge History of India, Volume II.3*, rev. edn. Cambridge: Cambridge University Press, 1999.

Guha, Ranajit. *Elementary Aspects of Peasant Insurgency in Colonial India*. Delhi: Oxford University Press, 1983.

Hanham, H. J. 'Religion and nationality in the mid-Victorian army'. In M. R. D. Foot (ed.), *War and Society*. London: Paul Elek, 1973.

Harries-Jenkins, Gwyn. *The Army in Victorian Society*. London: Routledge & Kegan Paul, 1977.

Heathcote, T. A. *The Indian Army: The Garrison of British Imperial India, 1822–1922*. London: Hippocrene, 1974.

—— *The Military in British India: The Development of British Land Forces in South Asia, 1600–1947*. Manchester: Manchester University Press, 1995.

Henderson, Diana. *Highland Soldier: A Social Study of the Highland Regiments, 1820–1920*. Edinburgh: John Donald, 1989.

Hichberger, J. W. M. *Images of the Army: The Military in British Art, 1815–1914*. Manchester: Manchester University Press, 1988.

Holmes, Michael. 'The Irish and India: imperialism, nationalism, and internationalism'. In Andy Bielenberg (ed.), *The Irish Diaspora*. London: Longman, 2001.

Ingram, Edward. *The Beginning of the Great Game in Asia, 1828–1834*. Oxford: Clarendon, 1979.

Kaminsky, Arnold. *The India Office: 1880–1910*. London: Greenwood, 1986.

Khanduri, Chandra. *A Re-discovered History of Gorkhas*. Delhi: Gyan Sagar, 1997.

Koss, Stephen. *The Rise and Fall of the Political Press in Britain: The Nineteenth Century*. Chapel Hill: University of North Carolina Press, 1981.

Lee, Alan. *The Origins of the Popular Press, 1855–1914*. London: Croom Helm, 1976.

Levine, Philippa. 'Rereading the 1890s: venereal disease as "constitutional crisis" in Britain and British India'. *Journal of Asian Studies* 55:3 (August 1996).

MacFarlane, Alan. *Resources and Population: A Study of the Gurungs of Nepal*. Cambridge: Cambridge University Press, 1976.

MacKenzie, John. *Propaganda and Empire: The Manipulation of British Public Opinion, 1880–1960*. Manchester: Manchester University Press, 1984.

—— (ed.). *Imperialism and Popular Culture*. Manchester: Manchester University Press, 1986.

—— (ed.). *Popular Imperialism and the Military*. Manchester: Manchester University Press, 1992.

MacMunn, Sir George. *The Martial Races of India*. London: Low, Marston & Co., 1933.

Mangan, J. A. and James Walvin (eds). *Manliness and Morality: Middle-Class Masculinity in Britain and America, 1800–1940*. New York: St Martin's Press, 1987.

Mani, Lata. *Contentious Traditions: The Debate on Sati in Colonial India*. Berkeley: University of California Press, 1998.

Marenco, Ethne. *The Transformation of Sikh Society*. Portland: HaPi Press, 1974.

McLeod, W. H. *The Sikhs: History, Religion, and Society*. New York: Columbia University Press, 1989.

—— *Exploring Sikhism: Aspects of Sikh Identity, Culture, and Thought*. New Delhi: Oxford University Press, 2000.

Metcalf, Thomas. *Ideologies of the Raj: The New Cambridge History of India, Volume III:4*. Cambridge: Cambridge University Press, 1994.

Moreman, Tim. *The Army in India and the Development of Frontier Warfare, 1849–1947*. London: Macmillan, 1998.

Morris, A. J. A. *The Scaremongers: The Advocacy of War and Rearmament, 1896–1914*. London: Routledge & Kegan Paul, 1984.

Mukherjee, Rudrangshu. *Awadh in Revolt, 1857–58: A Study of Popular Resistance*. Delhi: Oxford University Press, 1984.

—— *Spectre of Violence: The 1857 Kanpur Massacres*. Delhi: Viking, 1998.

Omissi, David. *The Sepoy and the Raj: The Indian Army, 1860–1940*. London: Macmillan, 1994.

—— (ed.). *Indian Voices of the Great War: Soldiers' Letters, 1914–18*. London: Macmillan, 1999.

Peers, Douglas. *Between Mars and Mammon: Colonial Armies and the Garrison State in India, 1819–1835*. London: I. B. Tauris, 1995.

—— '"Those noble exemplars of the true military tradition": constructions of the Indian Army in the mid-Victorian press'. *Modern Asian Studies* 31:1 (1997).

Robson, Brian. *The Road to Kabul: The Second Afghan War, 1878–1881*. London: Arms and Armour Press, 1986.

—— (ed.). *Roberts in India: The Military Papers of Field Marshal Lord Roberts, 1876–1893*. Phoenix Mill: Alan Sutton, 1993.

Roper, Michael and John Tosh (eds). *Manful Assertions: Masculinities in Britain Since 1800.* London: Routledge, 1991.

Seal, Anil. *The Emergence of Indian Nationalism: Competition and Collaboration in the Later Nineteenth Century.* Cambridge: Cambridge University Press, 1970.

Sen, Surendra Nath. *Eighteen Fifty-Seven.* Delhi: Publications Division, 1957.

Singh, Amandeep and Parmjit Singh. *Warrior Saints: Three Centuries of the Sikh Military Tradition.* London: I. B. Tauris, 1999.

Singh, Khushwant. *History of the Sikhs: Volume 2, 1839–1964.* Princeton: Princeton University Press, 1966.

Sinha, Mrinalini. *Colonial Masculinity: The 'Manly Englishman' and the 'Effeminate Bengali' in the Late Nineteenth Century.* Manchester: Manchester University Press, 1995.

Skelley, Alan Ramsay. *The Victorian Army at Home: The Recruitment and Terms and Conditions of the British Regular, 1859–1899.* London: Croom Helm, 1977.

Spiers, Edward. *The Army and Society, 1815–1914.* London: Longman, 1980.

—— *The Late Victorian Army, 1868–1902.* Manchester: Manchester University Press, 1992.

Spivak, Gayatri. 'Can the subaltern speak?' In Cary Nelson and Lawrence Grossberg (eds), *Marxism and the Interpretation of Culture.* Urbana: University of Illinois Press, 1988.

Stanley, Peter. *White Mutiny: British Military Culture in India.* New York: New York University Press, 1998.

Stearn, Roger T. 'War and the media in the 19th century: Victorian military artists and the image of war, 1870–1914'. *Journal of the Royal United Services Institute for Defence* 131:3 (1986).

—— 'War correspondents and colonial war, c. 1870–1900'. In John MacKenzie (ed.), *Popular Imperialism and the Military.* Manchester: Manchester University Press, 1992.

Stepan, Nancy. *The Idea of Race in Science: Great Britain, 1800–1960.* Hamden, Conn.: Archon Books, 1982.

Stokes, Eric. *The Peasant Armed: The Indian Revolt of 1857.* Oxford: Clarendon, 1986.

Stoler, Ann Laura. *Carnal Knowledge and Imperial Power: Race and the Intimate in Colonial Rule.* Berkeley: University of California Press, 2002.

Strachan, Hew. *The Politics of the British Army.* Oxford: Clarendon, 1997.

Trautmann, Thomas. *Aryans and British India.* Berkeley: University of California Press, 1997.

Trousdale, William (ed.). *War in Afghanistan, 1879–80.* Detroit: Wayne State University Press, 1985.

Withers, Charles. 'The historical creation of the Highlands'. In Ian Donnachie and Christopher Whatley (eds), *The Manufacture of Scottish History.* Edinburgh: Polygon, 1992.

Womack, Peter. *Improvement and Romance: Constructing the Myth of the Highlands.* London: Macmillan, 1989.

INDEX